BK 973.91 R432P 1967
PROGRESSIVES
/RESEK, CAR
1967 .00 FP
3000 154214 20034
St. Louis Community College

973.91 R432p 1967 c.3
RESEK
THE PROGRESSIVES 3.75
EP

INVENTORY 98

1-30-75

JUNIOR COLLEGE DISTRICT
of St. Louis-St. Louis County
LIBRARY
7508 Forsyth Bl
St. Louis, Missouri

INVENTORY 1985

The Progressives

THE AMERICAN HERITAGE SERIES

THE

American Heritage

Series

UNDER THE GENERAL EDITORSHIP OF

LEONARD W. LEVY AND ALFRED YOUNG

The Progressives

EDITED BY

CARL RESEK

Sarah Lawrence College

THE BOBBS-MERRILL COMPANY, INC.

Indianapolis *and* New York

Copyright © 1967 by the Bobbs-Merrill Company, Inc.
Printed in the United States of America
Library of Congress Catalog Card Number 66-16754
Designed by Stefan Salter Associates

First Printing

Foreword

The generation of articulate, self-conscious, middle-class men and women who threw themselves into the crusades for reforms from the late nineteenth century to World War I produced a remarkable body of literature which describes conditions, catches the excitement of their movement, and at the same time sums up their ideals. It therefore seems particularly appropriate that a volume on the progressives should assemble selections from their autobiographies, memoirs, and reminiscences.

Professor Resek, an accomplished writer of intellectual biography, has assembled excerpts from the writings of a score of representative progressive figures. Some of the works have acquired a reputation as minor classics in American literature—Jane Addams' *Twenty Years at Hull House,* W.E.B. Du Bois' *Dusk of Dawn,* and Jacob Riis's *The Making of an American.* Others—the writings of Margaret Sanger, Mary Simkhovitch, and Ida Tarbell, for example—deserve a wider audience for recapturing the flavor and passion of their crusades. Two, taken from the Oral History project of Columbia University—the taped recollections of politician William Prendergast, and civil libertarian Roger Baldwin—are published here for the first time.

In his Introduction Professor Resek explores the origins of progessivism, giving more stress to objective conditions and intellectual sources than have some recent commentators. He also makes clear, as do his selections, that there was often a wide range of approaches among progressives, from W.E.B. Du Bois' attack on the color line to Josephus Daniels' defense of it, from Jacob Riis's chauvinism in World War I to Roger Baldwin's conscientious objection. Contemporary readers may find some progressive crusades warmly "modern," for example, their war against poverty. They may also find serious limitations to their analyses and solutions. This volume provides the materials for both an appreciation and a realistic analysis of a group that shaped twentieth-century America.

This book is one of a series whose aim is to provide the essential primary sources of the American experience, especially of American thought. The series, when completed, will constitute a documentary library of American history, filling a need long felt among scholars, students, libraries, and general readers for authoritative collections of original materials. Some volumes will illuminate the thought of significant individuals, such as James Madison or Louis Brandeis; some will deal with movements, such as the Antifederalists or the Populists; others will be organized around special themes, such as Puritan political thought, or American Catholic thought on social questions. Many volumes will take up the large number of subjects traditionally studied in American history for which, surprisingly, there are no documentary anthologies; others will pioneer in introducing new subjects of increasing importance to scholars and to the contemporary world. The series aspires to maintain the high standards demanded of contemporary editing, providing authentic texts, intelligently and unobtrusively edited. It will also have the distinction of presenting pieces of substantial length which give the full character and flavor of the original. The series will be the most comprehensive and authoritative of its kind.

Alfred Young
Leonard W. Levy

Contents

Part Three

IN THE PATH OF BIG BUSINESS

Part Four

IN BATTLES FOR DEMOCRACY

Part Five

IN WARTIME

Introduction

In the two decades preceding United States entry into World War I a great reform spirit shook American society. Crusades that had started haltingly in the last years of the nineteenth century drew ever more public support. In 1912 nearly three-fourths of the electorate voted for presidential candidates who urged vigorous uplifting of the national life. The impulse to reform spread into all classes, sections, and political parties. It brought to leadership a Southern-born college professor. It raised to eminence a Nebraska farm boy and a former fish-peddler from New York's lower east side. The movement stirred the religious communities, Catholic and Jewish as well as Protestant. It included white supremacists, and Negro spokesmen, men who loved war and those who despised it. And the movement opened to substantial numbers of women the traditionally male province of public affairs. With the possible exception of Theodore Roosevelt, Jane Addams most fully symbolized the spirit of the age.

This wide variety of individuals and groups held in common an attitude usually called "progressive." Though they might agree on little else, progressives shared the view that the social order could and must be improved and that such change must not await God's will, natural laws, including the laws of the marketplace, or any other beneficent force. Through most of their history Americans had believed in social progress; now progressives meant to speed it up. They attacked poverty, class war, wasteful competition, and graft, evils that an earlier generation had accepted as the results of an overpopulated, capitalistic, or immoral society from which there seemed no appeal until a distant judgment day. In 1914 a progressive theorist clearly summarized the new attitude: "We can no longer treat life as something that has trickled down to us," wrote Walter Lippmann. "We have to deal with it deliberately, devise its social organization, alter its tools, formulate its method, educate and control it."[1] Lippmann's language indicated the determined, practical temper of progressivism. It meant to face squarely the social problems left in the wake of the industrial revolution and to solve them with the inventiveness characteristic of industrial society.

I

The generation that produced the progressive movement grew up in the aftermath of the Civil War. The war seemed to open, as well as close, an era of violence. It formed the first public intrusion into the childhood of many progressives, and for some it provided a symbol of the permanent disorder of society. In particular, the assassination of Lincoln seemed to mark the end of a kind of innocence, as it did to the young Ida Tarbell, who suddenly realized that mystery and tragedy awaited her beyond the circle of Allegheny hills that bounded her childhood. For the four-year-old Jane Addams, the murder of "the greatest man in the world," as her sorrowing father described him, came as an "initiation by baptism, as it were, into the thrilling and solemn interests of the world lying quite outside."[2] And Lincoln's was only the first of three assassinations of presidents that the progressive generation witnessed before the inauguration of Theodore Roosevelt.

The Civil War and reconstruction did not end the violence slavery had infused into the national life. In the closing decades of the nineteenth century an awesome conflict broke out be-

---

[1] Walter Lippman, *Drift and Mastery: An Attempt to Diagnose the Current Unrest* (New York: Mitchell Kennerley, 1914), p. 267.

[2] Jane Addams, *Twenty Years at Hull House* (New York: The Macmillan Company, 1916), p. 23.

tween the races. Amidst hatred and disorder, Southern states scrapped the fourteenth and fifteenth amendments, driving freedmen from any assumption of their equality. In the 1890's there were nearly two hundred lynchings a year, almost all of Negroes. That lynchings were not simply the crimes of desperadoes was evident from the habit of Southern statesmen and newspapers of excusing "unparalleled punishments for unparalleled crimes."[3] In cities across the country, but especially in the South, race riots, often lasting for days at a time, were fomented by newspapers. In many Southern communities one could have witnessed hundreds of armed, red-shirted men celebrating "white supremacy jubilees."

Although racial wars caused more suffering than any other conflicts within American society, most white progressives remained unaffected by the plight of the Negro. A few eventually joined in founding the National Association for the Advancement of Colored People. But most shielded themselves from this area of controversy by adopting prevalent racist ideas. One of the very few muckraking works on the problem, Ray Stannard Baker's *Following the Color Line,* assumed that "dislike of a different people is more or less instinctive in all men"; the book was typical in its readiness to accept the Southern view of "the millions of inert, largely helpless Negros who, imbued with a sharp sense of their rights, are attaining only slowly a corresponding appreciation of their duties and responsibilities."[4] Especially in the South, progressivism, as C. Vann Woodward has written, "generally was progressivism for white men only."[5] Accommodationist Negro leaders and white progressives agreed to a color line that defined the Negro's subordinate

---

3 Rayford W. Logan, *The Negro in American Life and Thought: The Nadir, 1877–1901* (New York: Dial Press, 1954), p. 23.

4 Ray Stannard Baker, *Following the Color Line: American Negro Citizenship in the Progressive Era* (Doubleday, Page and Co., 1908; reprinted, New York: Harper Torchbook Edition, 1964), pp. 294, 298.

5 C. Vann Woodward, *Origins of the New South, 1877–1913* (Baton Rouge: Louisiana State University Press, 1951), p. 373.

status. Although closely guarded, it remained an ill-kept armistice. (See this volume, Document 13.)

From the point of view of the progressive generation, the Civil War not only freed the slaves; it also freed the full force of the industrial revolution and brought on mounting conflict between owning and working classes. Of this history, too, the progressives in their formative years lived through the worst chapters. From the terroristic coal miners organized as the Molly Maguires, ten of whom were hanged in 1876, to the bombing of the Los Angeles *Times* Building in 1910, there stretched, it seemed, an era of dynamite. In the railroad strike of 1877 a dozen cities were rocked by clashes between troops and workers. In Pittsburgh alone twenty-five persons were killed and the city's railroad station destroyed along with 125 cars. This first nationwide strike was followed in the next year by the founding of the National Assembly of the Knights of Labor, which within a few years claimed a class-conscious membership of 700,000. In 1886, when the Haymarket bomb exploded, most of the nation's newspapers declared that the country was in danger of an anarchist uprising. And still class war raged on into the nineties and into the next century. In the reminiscences of progressives, the names of Homestead, Coeur d'Alene, Paterson, and Lawrence, all scenes of industrial violence, recur in the guise of skirmishes of an averted revolution.

Shaken by these rents in the social structure, many Americans condemned both capital and labor for violating the nation's tranquillity. In a mood of melancholy some blamed the city, the machine, the usurer, or the immigrant laborer for disrupting the traditional civilization of small property and personal initiative. Progressivism itself often emerged from this outlook to transcend it. Many a progressive reformer was born in a prosperous rural home. He would look back, sometimes longingly, to an idyllic youth; to a boyhood spent on horseback along the valleys of central California; to high-school banquets followed by sleigh rides through snowy Indiana nights; to annual coming-out parties in fashionable Chestnut Hill. He would aspire in college to surpass provincial origins, and often he would go on to law or graduate school. A surprising number of progressives studied in universities in England and specially in Germany, where sooner or later all seemed to have tramped along the Rhine. From the vantage point of this secure social footing the agitation of the "underprivileged classes" might be increasingly understood, but it always seemed at least faintly dangerous.

At times, as in the convulsive year 1886, it frightened the best-intentioned of men. Addressing workingmen in the aftermath of the Haymarket Riot, the Reverend Washington Gladden voiced such concern, declaring that "the present state of the industrial world is a state of war." He willingly granted labor "belligerent rights"—that is, the right to organize so that it might better carry its side of the conflict. But the conflict itself appeared to Gladden as a "senseless, brutal, barbarous business" that could win no just victory. Either the classes must bridge their differences or all Americans would probably lose their liberties. Gladden thought matters might well come to that.[6] So did Theodore Roosevelt, who, on his Dakota ranch in the same year, wanted to round up his cowboys, arm them, and lead them to Chicago to teach the anarchists a lesson. Henry George, whose work shaped the minds of numerous reformers, sanctioned the imprisonment and execution of the men accused of the Haymarket bombing even before he examined the case against them.

The dominant ideas of the day held out almost no prospect of meliorating industrial strife. In this respect orthodox socialists and advocates of *laissez faire* reached similar conclusions: Capitalist economics excluded humane considerations. Dur-

---

[6] Washington Gladden, *Recollections* (Boston and New York: Houghton Mifflin Co., 1909), p. 301.

ing a debate at Hull House in the nineties a radical claimed that slum children could not have healthy teeth until capitalism was destroyed and replaced by a more considerate system. Such prevalent "calendar socialism," as an English critic called it, had little to offer except the hope of falling into a Rip Van Winkle-like sleep and waking up a few generations later, as did the hero of Edward Bellamy's *Looking Backward,* to find society providentially reorganized. It was a view that sanctioned inaction in the face of distress as much as William Graham Sumner's argument that most hardships were irrevocably a part of the struggle for existence. "We cannot blame our fellow man for our share of these," Sumner held, adding that hardship could be met only by "manly effort and energy."[7] Most economists of the day agreed with him, regarding poverty as the consequence of resources inadequate to the growth of population. This Malthusian outlook in turn enshrined the "wage-fund theory," which held that only a limited part of an employer's wealth could be paid out in wages. And since employers naturally picked and promoted the most efficient workers, those who remained at the bottom of the scale could blame no one but themselves. "No man in this land suffers from poverty," the Reverend Henry Ward Beecher believed, "unless it be more than his fault—unless it be his *sin.*" A professor at Union Theological Seminary drew the only logical conclusion from this premise: "at bottom it is an immorality to fight against the inequality of condition, which simply corresponds with inequality of endowment."[8]

The progressives anxiously witnessed still another social upsurge of the late nineteenth century, the "uncontrollable

---

[7] William Graham Sumner, *What the Social Classes Owe to Each Other* (Caldwell, Idaho: The Caxton Press, Ltd., 1954), p. 17 (first published, New York: Harper and Bros., 1883).

[8] Quoted in Sidney Fine, *Laissez Faire and the General Welfare State: A Study of Conflict in American Thought, 1865–1901* (Ann Arbor: University of Michigan Press, 1956), pp. 119–120.

prairie fire of populism," as Senator George Norris called it in retrospect. In typical fashion Norris contended that a few honest men could be counted among leaders of the farm revolt but that most were "unscrupulous, insincere, bent upon exploiting to the fullest a most natural and distressing discontent."[9] Similarly, Ray Stannard Baker, assigned to report the progress of Coxey's Army of unemployed veterans marching on Washington in 1894, suspected that most of the army were malcontents looking for a handout. In Topeka, Kansas, another newspaperman spoke for many of the progressive generation. "That's the stuff!" roared William Allen White editorially at the populists:

> Give the prosperous man the dickens! Legislate the thriftless man into ease, whack the stuffing out of the creditors and tell the debtor . . . that the contraction of the currency gives him a right to repudiate.
>
> Whoop it up for the ragged trousers! put the lazy, greasy fizzle, who can't pay his debts, on the altar, and bow down and worship him. Let the state ideal be high. What we need is not the respect of our fellow men, but the chance to get something for nothing.

White was just twenty-eight years old. Within a few months he met Theodore Roosevelt, who instantaneously, as White later recalled, "sounded in my heart the first trumpet call of the new time that was to be."[10]

II

A variety of forces helped to dissolve the conservative attitudes on which the progressive generation had been reared, giving numerous Americans, along with Roosevelt and White,

---

[9] *Fighting Liberal: The Autobiography of George W. Norris* (New York: The Macmillan Company, 1946), p. 60.

[10] *The Autobiography of William Allen White* (New York: The Macmillan Company, 1946), pp. 282, 297.

a sense of the "new time that was to be." At the end of the century few would have been able to define the promise of the new age. But they felt the slipping away of the past. Untrammeled individualism, whether of the romantic frontier brand or of the kind prescribed by classical liberals, revealed itself as an anachronism.

For one thing, it became emotionally insupportable. Although aspiring men and women could be repelled by class upheavals, they found difficulty in withholding sympathy once the conditions of the lower classes stood fully revealed. Perhaps the most brilliant analyst of the progressive movement, Professor Edward A. Ross, suggested that a creative force in the evolution of social control lay in the "sympathetic functioning of the sense of injustice." Examining the relationship between middle class reform and working class disorder, Ross wrote:

> Sympathy alone makes for *helpfulness*. The sense of injury makes for *retaliation*. But their *interaction* yields that "moral indignation" which leads a community to interfere in quarrels or aggressions that in no way harm it. To this force is due, in a measure, that gradual encroachment of society on private action which is registered in the progressive transformation of wrongs or torts into crimes.[11]

The progressive movement, then, may be seen as an interaction of helpfulness and retaliation. The former sentiment often grew among the middle classes from a direct, emotional confrontation with some especially dreadful part of the record of the industrial revolution. The muckrakers, like their predecessors in the newspapers of William Randolph Hearst and Joseph Pulitzer, grew expert at searing the emotions of readers. The conditions of work in factories and mines supplied the

---

[11] Edgar F. Borgatta and Henry J. Meyer, eds., *Social Control and the Foundations of Sociology: Pioneer Contributions of Edward A. Ross to the Study of Society* (Boston: Beacon Press, 1959), p. 27.

most frequent measure of industrial misery, conditions so dangerous that the Reverend Walter Rauschenbusch doubted whether anyone could ever really compile or believe the statistics of industrial accidents. The tales of horror in Chicago's packing houses, in the canneries of the Northwest, and in the sweatshops of New York's needle trades were a part of the literature of the day. Explosions in mines and oil fields occurred with apalling frequency. "What a chain of catastrophes it took to teach the men and women who were developing the new industry, the constant risk they ran in handling crude and refined oil," Ida Tarbell recalled. Her own childhood nightmares contained visions of charred bodies left in the wake of fires raging through the oil region where she grew up.[12] But the worst statistics came from the railroad yards. In the last decade of the century, a quarter of a million railroad workers were injured on the job, and more than twenty-five thousand were killed.[13] That automatic, but expensive, coupling systems capable of reducing this record by fifty per cent were only slowly introduced won back for railroad workers much of the public support they lost during strikes. The Triangle factory fire in New York in 1911, in which 146 seamstresses were burned to death because of inadequate safety precautions, produced a small army of reformers.

The misery of tenement life, of child labor and the effect on children of their mother's employment generated much fellow feeling in the middle classes. Who could fail to respond when children in Chicago were discovered to suffer from complex curvature of the spine because of long hours spent attending heavy sewing machines? In every city children lived alone, sometimes locked in rooms, even tied to bedposts, while parents worked. Lillian Wald of New York's Henry Street Settle-

---

12 Ida Tarbell, *All in the Day's Work: An Autobiography* (New York: The Macmillan Company, 1939), p. 11.

13 U.S. Department of Commerce, *Historical Statistics of the United States* (Washington: U.S. Government Printing Office, 1961), p. 427.

ment testified that no one who ever sat in Children's Court could forget the experience. These confrontations with working-class life sometimes seized observers with such ferocity, a social worker recalled, that life itself became impossible without a commitment to social action. So too, Richard Ely, descending the gang plank of the ship that brought him back to the United States in 1880, took unbelieving sight of the tenements in the dock area and wondered whether he could any longer live in America. In 1912 Margaret Sanger, a visiting nurse, stood in the dark of an immigrant flat on the lower east side of Manhattan and watched a young mother dying of a self-inflicted abortion. In the agony of the moment, Mrs. Sanger recalls, "the Revolution came—but not as it has been pictured, nor as history relates that revolutions have come. It came in my own life."[14]

Within this emotional context few reformers tolerated the deterministic and utopian ideology of the previous era. No true progressive kept vigil for a golden age. The hallmarks of the movement were its sense of immediacy, its insistence on direct action, its refusal to temporize. At Hull House, Miss Addams even deprived the poor of the comfort of blaming their troubles on their poverty. (See Document 4.) Progressives rejected the sermons of churchmen directed to awaiting the moral regeneration of man. "It is true," Walter Rauschenbusch thundered, "that any regeneration of society can come only through the act of God and the presence of Christ, but God is now acting, and Christ is now here."[15]

Fresh intellectual currents also worked to dissolve the individualism of an earlier era. Perhaps the strongest influences emanated from Henry George's *Progress and Poverty,* which was published in 1879 and quickly became one of the most

---

[14] Margaret Sanger, *My Fight for Birth Control* (New York: Farrar and Rinehart, Inc., 1931), p. 55. (See this volume, Document 5.)

[15] Walter Rauschenbusch, *Christianity and the Social Crisis* (New York: Harper Torchbook Edition, 1964), p. 346.

widely read books in America. Judging by the autobiographies of progressives, George was a kind of Luther to the movement, a critic whose challenge to orthodoxy opened the gateway to numerous conversions to the reform movement. His influence also reached overseas, the distinctive prose of *Progress and Poverty* affecting even the literary style of the age, including that of George Bernard Shaw.

Writing in the midst of the depression of the seventies, with its widespread unemployment, George pondered the anomalies of the industrial revolution: "It *is* a strange and unnatural thing that men who wish to labor, in order to satisfy their wants, cannot find the opportunity." It seemed even more unnatural that as "we add knowledge to knowledge, and utilize invention after invention . . . it becomes no easier for the masses of our people to make a living. On the contrary it is becoming harder."[16] Europeans too had noted this paradox, and Karl Marx stated it as the irredeemable condition of capitalist production. For his part, George found the origin of modern poverty in the tendency to monopoly in land ownership, and he offered as antidote a single tax on unearned increments in land values. But this specific panacea, attractive as it was to many of his readers, was actually less important to future progressivism than George's thorough criticism of broad, theoretical explanations of inequality. Against Malthus he mustered powerful arguments to show that nature did not begrudge man universal prosperity and happiness; nor did the capitalist process seem to reach any preordained limits determining the distribution of wealth. In his most passionate prose, George seared the social Darwinists who sought to find in race or in individual biological inheritance the sources of social inequality. None of these factors limited the human condition. But the "garments of laws, customs and political

---

[16] Henry George, *Progress and Poverty* (50th Anniversary Edition; New York: Robert Schalkenbach Foundation, 1929), p. 270.

institutions which each society weaves for itself, are constantly tending to become too tight as the society develops."[17] Progress as a social process, rather than a mere advance of science or a fulfillment of individual fortunes, involved meliorative adjustments, not of the whole society but in its behalf. In a fine metaphor that struck the keynote of progressive thought, George suggested that men in a community, like sailors adrift in a lifeboat, must pull together to conserve their energies and together chart their course.

George's work led off a mounting attack on the theory of *laissez faire*. The opposition rested on the traditional American assumption that government must perform the functions which the people cannot carry out themselves and, in particular, that matters of general public interest must be taken out of the hands of private parties. New in the progressive outlook was the broad definition of matters of general public interest.

In this respect many progressives were influenced by German thought and practice. The cradle of the nineteenth-century welfare state, Germany had seen professors and theologians draw together in the 1870's to study and discuss what they usually called the "social question." They had pressed statesmen for legislation in behalf of the depressed classes, emphasizing especially the government's responsibility in matters that employers shunned. Thus, by 1884, when unemployed or injured workers in the United States could turn only to private charities for aid, Germany had a government-administered insurance system for sickness and industrial accidents. In 1890 the Reichstag established old-age pensions. By the end of the century stringent federal codes regulated conditions of labor and prohibited the employment of children. In 1916, when Frederic Howe established the first experimental federal employment bureau in New York City, most German states had had such institutions for a decade and a half. Howe had carefully studied the German experience; in 1914 he pub-

---

[17] *Ibid.*, p. 514.

lished a work entitled *Socialized Germany.* Three years later he was unhappy about a war against a nation that had pioneered so much legislation. So were many others who in Germany had found precedents for welfare government. (See Documents 2 and 3.)

Whether they drew their ideas from George, from Germany or elsewhere, American progressives soon produced an impressive body of theory and data on which to base specific reforms. Muckrakers in search of the "hidden cesspool . . . fouling American life," to use Vernon Parrington's imagery, quickly discovered "not one cesspool but many, under every city hall and beneath every state capitol." They found that *laissez faire* in fact meant that business controlled government. The muckrakers became such experts on this phenomenon that both statesmen and university professors called on them for information. (See Document 9.) Among scholars the attack on classical liberalism generated an immense ferment in every field of learning. The social sciences in particular were now virtually reborn under the influence of such pioneers as Lester Ward, Edward A. Ross, Charles Beard, William James, John Dewey, and Thorstein Veblen. An entire generation of teachers seemed to turn from the traditional moral indoctrination of their pupils to examining the practical affairs of state. Many served on commissions investigating corporative malpractices, employment conditions, urban housing, and education, helping legislatures to reach solutions to such problems. Stimulated by this concrete application of their skills, professors passed the excitement of learning on to their students. In the privacy of their studies many produced great works of scholarship. It was a school, Parrington wrote, in which "the mind opened of its own will." (See Document 1.)

III

The central force to destroy the individualistic ideals of the previous era was the rise of corporative monopoly. Progressivism and corporative monopoly matured alongside one another. In the year in which Henry George published *Progress and Poverty* (1879), the Standard Oil corporation, pioneer of industrial consolidation, controlled eighty per cent of the nation's refined oil production, and J. P. Morgan achieved his first success in railroad financing. During the next decades, as the reform impulse grew, so did the organization of trusts in the sugar industry, in mining, tobacco, meat packing, and other fields. In 1901, the year in which Theodore Roosevelt assumed the presidency, Morgan created his masterpiece, the United States Steel corporation, the world's first billion-dollar enterprise. During Roosevelt's administrations, the railroads, first symbols of the industrial revolution in the lives of the progressive generation, came under the control of six combines of investors, two of which threatened to merge and dominate the rest. Nor was the thrust to monopoly confined to industry. As progressive fervor approached its height in 1912, a congressional committee reported with alarm the existence of a "money trust" which it described as "an established and well defined identity and community of interest between a few leaders of finance . . . created and . . . held together through stock holdings, interlocking directorates and other forms of domination over banks, trust companies, railroads, public service and industrial corporations." In New York City the committee discovered that four allied investment groups controlled 341 directorships in 112 corporations whose total resources amounted to over twenty-two billion dollars.[18]

To this new business threat, as to the problems of the laboring classes, progressivism responded in complex and sometimes contradictory ways. Like most Americans, progressives abhorred the early tactics of concentration. Exposés of these tactics long antedated the heyday of muckraking. In 1871, when Ida Tarbell was a child, Henry and Brooks Adams had

---

[18] Quoted in Harold U. Faulkner, *The Decline of Laissez Faire, 1897–1917* (New York: Rinehart & Co., 1951), p. 43.

already described the villainy of New York's railroad wars. The Standard Oil Company was infamous from its inception. Henry Demarest Lloyd's narration of its ruthless methods, published in 1894, fanned popular hatred; by 1907 Standard Oil and its subsidiaries faced nearly a thousand legal indictments throughout the nation. In the South and in the prairies, the residue of populism added fuel to sentiments against the trust, a hated symbol of Eastern financial control. When Washington Gladden refused an endowment for the Protestant Board of Missions from John D. Rockefeller, his action, while not widely imitated, came as no surprise. (See Document 8.)

Equally disturbing was the relationship of big business to the political process. For some time after the Civil War most Americans seemed not to know, or care, about the control that business leaders exercised over local communities, state houses, political parties, and national legislation. While they saw themselves as part of an open, competitive economy whose benefits accrued to the industrious, Americans assumed that business interests and national interests were identical. Social control appeared secondary to the ethic of free enterprise. But where competition declined and the controls of supply and demand disappeared, where special privilege became entrenched and economic opportunity was shut off, there reformers drew support in behalf of using the police powers of government. Restraining the businessman's political influence became an important part of the reform program. The progressive mayors, Samuel "Golden Rule" Jones and Brand Whitlock in Toledo, Tom Johnson in Cleveland, and Hazen Pingree in Detroit, provided a background of experience in ridding politics of special interests. In turn Governor Robert La Follette in Wisconsin, Albert Cummins in Iowa, and Hiram Johnson in California, among many others, devised methods of curbing corporations that dominated entire states. (See Document 14.) Eventually, in Congress, many of these same men led the insurgents against the Old Guard of the Republican Party, to free government for the task of dealing with big business at the national level.

Often progressives did not oppose corporate concentration as such. The distinction between Henry D. Lloyd's more nearly populist attack on the Standard Oil Company and Ida Tarbell's muckraking lay in Lloyd's view that monopoly was "business at the end of its journey," while Miss Tarbell, as she later explained, had "no quarrel with corporate business, so long as it played fair." She had nothing against the new lords of wealth, and indeed became their ardent biographer, if in back of their fortunes "they could show performance . . . untainted by privilege."[19] To many progressives the hope of going back to an economy of small producers—Woodrow Wilson's "New Freedom"—appeared a false, impractical ideal. It could be thought of as the Arminian heresy of the movement. "I submit," wrote Walter Lippmann, "that the intelligent men of my generation can find a better outlet for their energies than making themselves masters of little businesses."[20] Industrial mergers that wiped out wasteful competition—practical rather than mere money-making combinations—would increase the nation's productive wealth, to the benefit of all. And not a few progressives pointed out that such growth in industry increased the nation's power among other nations. With the coming of World War I, even Wilson, who in 1912 had championed the antitrust side of the reform movement, had to give up any idea of breaking up the corporations so efficiently backing up the war effort.

The greatly overpublicized "trust busting" of the progressive era, especially that of Theodore Roosevelt's administrations, involved more indictments, often halfhearted, than it did convictions. Roosevelt held firmly that little could be gained from punishing corporations merely for their size. He would indict trusts that took illicit advantage of their power, although he

---

[19] Tarbell, *All in the Day's Work,* p. 296.
[20] Lippmann, *Drift and Mastery,* p. 141.

left undefined the principles that separated the "bad" from the "good" trusts, as he called them. (See Document 10.) In the courts too, the "rule of reason" that sought to distinguish between "reasonable" and "unreasonable" trusts was never clearly formulated. And from 1911, when *U.S.* v. *Standard Oil Co.* announced the rule, to 1920, when even the United States Steel Company was held reasonable, the concept went far to destroy the power of the Sherman Anti-Trust Act. Thus, the ground for the great mergers of the 1920's was prepared in the progressive era.

More effective and lasting than their trust busting was the progressives' creation or strengthening of regulatory agencies and the passage of pioneering laws safeguarding consumers and labor from the excesses of the profit motive. State legislatures restricted the use of child and women's labor, passed factory safety acts, and began the long and tedious task of controlling urban housing conditions. At the federal level Roosevelt's Pure Food and Drug Act of 1906 was followed in Wilson's first administration by laws easing the conditions of farmers, federal employees, railroad workers, and seamen in the merchant marine. Among the agencies charged with the regulation of various sectors of the economy, the most important were the strengthened Interstate Commerce Commission, the Federal Trade Commission, the Federal Reserve Board, the Forestry Service, and the Inland Waterways Commission. Such incursions on their freedom of enterprise were by no means resisted by all business leaders. Many were pleased to have uniform codes established that stabilized their relations with competitors and with government. Wilson's Federal Trade Commission, for example, was welcomed by some magnates as an agency to which they could submit plans for future mergers and thus avert possible antitrust prosecutions. And not a few businessmen fully expected to control the new agencies.

In another respect, too, progressivism and big business found common ground. Beginning with Andrew Carnegie's avowal in 1889 that the millionaire must be a trustee for the poor, "intrusted for a season with a great part of the increased wealth of the community, but administering it for the community far better than it could or would have done for itself,"[21] the new owners of corporate wealth appeared to realize the potential of their fortunes for accomplishing good works. At the turn of the century they gave vast sums to charities or as endowments for general funds to be used in behalf of the community. The Rockefeller, Guggenheim, and Russell Sage foundations provided apparently unlimited financial sources to which welfare workers could turn for aid. Nor was corporate giving limited to social-welfare projects. Progressive political crusades also received financial support from big business whenever their objectives appeared consonant. Thus in the life of every reformer, from Washington Gladden to Theodore Roosevelt, there seemed sooner or later to arise the problem of accepting "tainted money." Most followed George Bernard Shaw's dictum, expressed in 1905 in *Major Barbara*, that reformers and business leaders "could no more escape one another than they can escape the air they breathe."[22] Like Shaw's heroine, urgently needing to act effectively in the world as it was, rather than as it might be, reformers could not usually afford to turn down aid or to ignore power. And like one captain of industry who testified before a federal commission that foundation giving prevented social upheavals, business leaders often appreciated the meliorative effects of progressive reform. In that light, the startling mixture of businessmen and reformers who came together at the Progressive Party convention in Chicago in 1912 did not seem so unnatural. Although the al-

---

[21] Carnegie's numerous assertions of this point may be found in *The Gospel of Wealth and Other Timely Essays* (New York: The Century Company, 1900), and in his *Problems of Today: Wealth, Socialism and Labor* (New York: Doubleday, Page and Co., 1909). He dedicated the latter book to Theodore Roosevelt.

[22] Shaw, "Preface," *Major Barbara* (Baltimore: Penguin Edition, 1964), p. 27.

liance was often under strain, even differences over military programs failed to break it. Like Major Barbara, who inherited a munitions factory, Jane Addams reluctantly found herself, in 1912, alongside George Perkins, lately of the House of Morgan, approving a party plank that called for a big navy. (See Document 17.)

IV

But if progressives facilitated the growth of big business, and turned to it for aid, they never thought themselves its servants or the political representatives of any special group. On the contrary, the progressive political tradition rested on the assumption that public officials should divest themselves of all connections with private interests, a view that for decades found expression in the civil service ideal as the ultimate program. Convinced that graft formed the original sin of the political process, reformers fought it at every level of government. They disliked populist politicians for serving the selfish ends of farmers and stood aghast at the immigrant wards of big cities, ruled by bosses like feudal baronies. The machine's custom of buying votes on a winter's day with a scuttle of coal appeared to threaten the foundations of democracy. So did the immigrants' habit of voting for their own kind. Practical Irish politicians in New York, Frederic Howe confessed, were men "whose every act my code condemned."

The continuous string of defeats they suffered as mere civil-service reformers in the 1880's and 1890's taught future progressives that honesty in politics did not suffice as a platform in the urban industrial age. To an unemployed breadwinner's family the politician's gift of coal was not the price of a vote, but a means of keeping warm. Whatever his motives, the ward heeler sometimes acted like a human being and therefore deserved support. The Irish immigrants, Howe discovered, "warmed the state into a human being, made frank demands on it for things they could not get themselves." (See Document 12.) In a similar way Robert La Follette learned to defeat the machine that long ruled Wisconsin; he built a larger and more efficient one. But instead of granting favors selectively, progressive politicians won constituencies by aiding the public at large.

In its mature state, the progressive political ideal rested on a balance of power between contending interests. Alongside the great organizations of capital were to be arrayed organizations of farmers, laborers, consumers, professionals, and all other interest groups of society. The National Association of Manufacturers, the Farmers' League, the Consumers' League, the American Federation of Labor, and the American Association of University Professors represented interests in a commonwealth of factions. Over these groups government would rule, protecting each against the others, often aiding them in inverse proportion to their strength. This political balance, as Charles Beard and Herbert Croly reminded the progressive generation, resembled the vision of the Founding Fathers, whose system of constitutional checks and balances was also intended to institutionalize stability in the midst of factional conflict. Progressives invented or imported from abroad new methods of redressing imbalances, such as the mediation of labor disputes, strong regulatory commissions, conservation laws, and the inspection of consumer products. The Progressive Party platform of 1912, which called for government aid to agriculture, minimum-wage and maximum-hour laws, and the protection of women and children in industry, aimed at healing the rifts of the day. Capital, secure enough at home, was to receive aid in establishing its interests abroad, against obstacles that could be overcome by stronger diplomacy and a larger navy.

As the ideal of a strong administrative government evolved, more young men of good family who had once considered politics a lower-class sport suddenly discovered they were not above a career in government. Just as it did for the once despised machine boss, politics opened to them a profession, one that was especially favored if it provided an escape from the alternative of employment in a corporation. Such men distinguished themselves in public office by their education or by what Lincoln Steffens termed their political vision, the ability to sacrifice the petty, immediate rewards of office for the greater good of general social progress. This rare quality Steffens believed to be the prerequisite of true leadership and, in the greatest men, akin to Christian regeneration. For a time he idolized some progressive leaders, as did many of his contemporaries, who were attracted by a trait that the German sociologist, Max Weber, called "charisma." According to Weber, charisma was a quality of personal leadership so extraordinary that men submit to it even though they may not rationally comprehend it.

Of all the progressive leaders, Theodore Roosevelt best fitted Weber's description. Roosevelt had won his heroic image in any number of arenas: as cowboy, as an assistant Secretary of the Navy dispatching Admiral Dewey to Manila, as a Roughrider leading the charge up San Juan Hill, as a big-game hunter and trust buster. "I am going to ask you to be very quiet and please excuse me from making a long speech. I'll do the best I can. But there is a bullet in my body. It is nothing," he told an audience in the campaign of 1912 after a fanatic had shot him.[23] Max Weber could not have wanted a better example. To hundreds of Americans for whom life had gone stale, Roosevelt sounded a trumpet blast: The greatest victories were yet to be won. In 1912, in Chicago, his hosts stood at Armageddon, ready to battle for the Lord. Had he not split the Republican forces, and had not an equally charismatic leader, Woodrow Wilson, opposed him, Roosevelt surely would have led the nation to new battles. As it turned out, charismatic politics reached ever greater heights during and after World War I.

---

[23] Quoted in Henry F. Pringle, *Theodore Roosevelt: A Biography* (New York: Harcourt Brace, 1931), p. 399.

The sense of identity between voters and progressive leaders was furthered by the electoral reforms that progressives everywhere took up from populists and pushed through. Unlike the populist, who considered direct primaries, the secret ballot, the initiative, recall, and the direct election of U. S. Senators as a means of enhancing control of government by the disinherited classes, progressives hoped these measures would make government responsive to all groups. They also favored the extension of suffrage to women, who were so important in their own ranks. "In all my campaigns in Wisconsin," Robert La Follette recalled, "I had been much impressed with the fact that women were as keenly interested as men in the questions of railroad taxation, reasonable transportation charges, direct primaries and indeed in the whole progressive program."[24] After their services in the war effort, exemplified by Mrs. Mary Simkhovitch's work at Greenwich House, it was difficult to exclude women from the democracy. (See Document 20.)

Paradoxically, as democracy was extended the latent paternalism of progressives grew more apparent. Progressive leaders pictured themselves as spokesmen of the popular will, exhibiting a testy impatience with their critics. Few distinguished themselves in dialogue. Often colorful, the progressive leader also seemed temperamental, narrow in his concept of a loyal opposition, frequently intolerant of the darker races at home and abroad, of revolutionaries, and, in times of war, of pacifists like Roger Baldwin. (See Document 21.) None of these limitations were peculiar to progressive leaders, or universal among them. But they were pronounced in some of the best-known figures, including Roosevelt, La Follette, Wilson, and Hiram Johnson. And in an era in which progressives themselves had strengthened the authority of government, limitations like these were all the more dangerous. Not a few reformers who had

---

[24] *La Follette's Autobiography* (Madison, Wisconsin: The University of Wisconsin Press, 1960), p. 43.

resurrected the spirit of Alexander Hamilton to support the growth of governmental authority were eventually haunted by the ghost of Thomas Jefferson, when such authority was used, during and after World War I, to limit the freedom of aliens and radical dissenters.

V

The following anthology consists of autobiographical selections because the autobiography formed the most characteristic literature of the progressive movement. Reformers acted in concert in professional societies, associations, and political conventions, where they traded ideas and presented programs. But however much they joined together, they seemed much less aware of the total scope of progressivism than of their own immediate crusades. The movement that interested them most was that which came into their own lives as a result of a commitment to improve society. In autobiographies they were less concerned with communicating their ideals, which they took for granted, than with describing the spirit permeating their careers and their associations as reformers. To all of them reform became a way of life to which the autobiography extended a general invitation.

CARL RESEK

Leonia, New Jersey
August 1965

Selected Bibliography

Differing in emphasis, five general works on the progressive movement provide a superb history of the subject: Harold U. Faulkner, *The Quest for Social Justice* (New York: The Macmillan Company, 1931), is still the fullest treatment of the many reform crusades; Eric F. Goldman, *Rendezvous With Destiny* (New York: Alfred A. Knopf, Inc., 1956), communicates the spirit and intellectual sweep of the movement; Richard Hofstadter, *The Age of Reform* (New York: Alfred A. Knopf, Inc., 1955), illuminates the limits and the subjective impulses of reformers; George E. Mowry, *The Era of Theodore Roosevelt, 1900–1912,* (New York: Harper & Bros., 1958), and Arthur S. Link, *Woodrow Wilson and the Progressive Era, 1910–1917* (New York: Harper & Bros., 1954), define the institutional and political history of the time.

The international scope of the progressive response to industrialism may be sensed in Edward H. Carr, *The New Society* (London: Macmillan & Co., Ltd., 1951); in Helen M. Lynd, *England in the Eighteen-Eighties* (New York: Oxford University Press, Inc., 1945); and in Koppel S. Pinson, *Modern Germany* (New York: The Macmillan Company, 1954).

Among the many studies of the movement on the local level, the most valuable are: Ray Ginger, *Altgeld's America, 1892–1905* (New York: Funk & Wagnalls Co., Inc., 1958), a picture of Chicago; Arthur Mann, *Yankee Reformers in the Urban Age* (Cambridge, Mass.: Belknap Press of Harvard University, 1954), an analysis of Boston; George E. Mowry, *The California Progressives* (Berkeley: The University of California Press, 1951); Russel B. Nye, *Midwestern Progressive Politics* (East Lansing: Michigan State University Press, 1951); and C. Vann Woodward, *Origins of the New South, 1877–1913* (Baton Rouge: Louisiana State University Press, 1951).

Among intellectual histories of progressivism, Daniel Aaron, *Men of Good Hope* (New York: Oxford University Press, Inc., 1951), is valuable for its treatment of nineteenth-century predecessors; Charles Forcey, *The Crossroads of Liberalism* (New York: Oxford University Press, Inc., 1961), is the definitive study of Croly, Weyl, and Lippmann; Henry May, *The End of American Innocence* (New York: Alfred A. Knopf, Inc., 1959), puts progressive thought in the context of other intellectual currents; H. Stuart Hughes, *Consciousness and Society* (New York: Alfred A. Knopf, Inc., 1958), is a revealing study of the European revolt against formalism.

Important books treating special phases of the subject are: Robert H. Bremner, *From the Depth: The Discovery of Poverty in the United States* (New York: New York University Press, 1956); Lawrence A. Cremin, *The Transformation of the School: Progressivism in American Education, 1876–1957* (New York: Alfred A. Knopf, Inc., 1961); Samuel P. Hays, *Conservation and the Gospel of Efficiency: The Progressive Conservation Movement, 1890–1920* (Cambridge, Mass.: Harvard University Press, 1959); and Robert H. Wiebe, *Businessmen and Reform: A Study of the Progressive Movement* (Cambridge, Mass.: Harvard University Press, 1962).

The real Vernon Parrington emerges in James L. Colwell, "The Populist Image of Vernon Parrington," *Mississippi Valley Historical Review,* XVIX (1962), 52–66. Joseph Dorfman, *The Economic Mind in American Civilization* (New York: The Viking Press, 1949), Vol. III, is the best treatment of the rise of the new economics. The best study of Du Bois is Francis L. Broderick, *W. E. B. Du Bois: Negro Leader in a Time of Crisis* (Stanford: Stanford University Press, 1959).

An excellent picture of Jane Addams is by Jill Conway, "Jane Addams: An American Heroine," *Daedalus,* XCIII (Spring 1964), 761–780. In Margaret Sanger, *An Autobiography* (New York: Farrar & Rinehart, 1938), the author continues her narrative of the crusade for birth control. Moses Rischin, *The Promised City: New York's Jews, 1870–1914* (Cambridge, Mass.: Harvard University Press, 1962), is a masterly treatment of poverty and progress in the Jewish community. Francis L. Broderick portrays the *Right Reverend New Dealer, John A. Ryan* (New York: The Macmillan Company, 1963); Robert Cross, *The Emergence of Liberal Catholicism in America* (Cambridge, Mass.: Harvard University Press, 1958), sets the context for Ryan's work.

Henry F. May, *Protestant Churches and Industrial America* (New York: Harper & Bros., 1949), provides the context of Gladden's social thought; Peter Lyon, *Success Story: The Life and Times of S. S. McClure* (New York: Charles Scribner's Sons, 1963) explains the muckrakers; in his relation to the trusts, as in other aspects of his career, Roosevelt is carefully depicted in William H. Harbaugh, *Power and Responsibility* (New York: Farrar, Straus & Co., Inc., 1958).

The many impacts of the immigrants on politics and progressivism are treated in John Higham, *Strangers in the Land: Patterns of American Nativism, 1860–1925* (New Brunswick: Rutgers University Press, 1955); Helen G. Edmonds, *The Negro and Fusion Politics in North Carolina, 1894–1901* (Chapel Hill: University of North Carolina Press, 1951), explains the setting of the Bassett affair. Charles C. McCarthy, *The Wisconsin Idea* (New York: The Macmillan Company, 1912), complements La Follette's autobiography. Richard Lowitt, *George W. Norris: The Making of A Progressive, 1861–1912* (Syracuse, N.Y.: Syracuse University Press, 1963), is definitive. George E. Mowry, *Theodore Roosevelt and the Progressive Movement* (Madison: The University of Wisconsin Press, 1947), treats insurgency and the events related by Prendergast; Allen F. Davis, "The Social Workers and the Progressive Party, 1912–1916," *The American Historical Review*, LXIX (1964), 671–688, is the last word on the subject.

William E. Leuchtenburg, "Progressivism and Imperialism: The Progressive Movement and American Foreign Policy, 1898–1916," *The Mississippi Valley Historical Review*, XXXIX (1952), 483–504, treats the progressives as warriors; an alternate side of the movement is portrayed in Mercedes M. Randall, *Improper Bostonian: Emily Greene Balch* (New York: Twayne Publishers, Inc., 1964). The beginnings of the civil liberties problem are depicted in William Preston, *Aliens and Dissenters: Federal Suppression of Radicals, 1903–1933* (Cambridge, Mass.: Harvard University Press, 1963).

Editor's Note

The excerpts from the autobiographies and reminiscences in this volume have been reprinted exactly as they were in the original editions. Omitted passages are indicated by an ellipsis (. . .). Individuals mentioned in the narrative are identified where such identification is necessary for an understanding of the author's meaning.

PART ONE

In the Universities

1.

Vernon Louis Parrington Recalls the Spirit of an Age

As a young man Vernon Parrington lived in the eye of the storm of populism. Born in 1871, he grew up in Emporia, Kansas, the son of a prosperous lawyer and judge. Except for two years spent at Harvard College he lived among Kansas farmers in the time of their worst distress. He heard Mary "Yellin" Lease and other populist leaders roar their cause. But the evidence shows that he had little sympathy for it.

Nor did Parrington participate in the crusades of the progressive era. In 1908 he was appointed professor of literature at the University of Oklahoma and subsequently, from 1912 until his death in 1929, he taught at the University of Washington. He spent his life in the study and in the classroom. Thus, for him the reform years were an intellectual experience, a time of gradual, deeply felt intellectual transformation, climaxed in 1913 by his reading of Charles Beard's *An Economic Interpretation of the Constitution.* On this book he reflected for five years. Then, in the twilight of reform, he began his own study of American liberalism, the monumental *Main Currents of American Thought,* two volumes of which were completed when he died.

A third, posthumously published volume of fragments included an essay on the intellectual development of progressives, a piece that was at once a personal memoir and the history of a generation. In it may be seen the impact on Parrington's mind, "still clinging to the ideals of an older, simpler America," of muckraking, economic determinism, and socialism.

Liberals whose hair is growing thin and the lines of whose figures are no longer what they were, are likely to find themselves today in the unhappy predicament of being treated as mourners at their own funerals. When they pluck up heart to assert that they are not yet authentic corpses, but living men with brains in their heads, they are pretty certain to be gently chided and led back to the comfortable armchair that befits senility. Their counsel is smiled at as the chatter of a belated post-Victorian generation that knew not Freud, and if they must go abroad they are bidden take the air in the garden where other old-fashioned plants—mostly of the family *Democratici*—are still preserved. It is not pleasant for them. It is hard to be dispossessed by one's own heirs, and especially hard when those heirs, in the cheerful ignorance of youth, forget to acknowledge any obligations to a hard-working generation that laid by a very substantial body of intellectual wealth, the income from which the heirs are spending without even a "Thank you." If therefore the middle-aged liberal occasionally grows irritable and indulges in caustic comment on the wisdom of talkative young men it may be set down as the prerogative of the armchair age and lightly forgiven.

Yet in sober fact there are the solidest reasons for such irritation. The younger liberals who love to tweak the nose of democ-

---

From Vernon Louis Parrington, *The Beginnings of Critical Realism in America,* Vol. III of *Main Currents of American Thought* (New York: Harcourt, Brace & Co., 1927), "A Chapter in American Liberalism," Addenda, pp. 401–413. Copyright, 1927, 1930, by Harcourt, Brace & World, Inc.; renewed, 1955, by Vernon L. Parrington, Jr., Louise P. Tucker, and Elisabeth P. Thomas. Reprinted by permission of the publishers.

racy are too much enamored of what they find in their own mirrors. They are indisputably clever, they are spouting geysers of smart and cynical talk, they have far outrun their fathers in the free handling of ancient tribal totems—but they are afflicted with the short perspective of youth that finds a vanishing-point at the end of its own nose. There is no past for them beyond yesterday. They are having so good a time playing with ideas that it does not occur to them to question the validity of their intellectual processes or to inquire into the origins of the ideas they have adopted so blithely. Gaily engaged in smashing *bourgeois* idols, the young intellectuals are too busy to realize that it was the older generation that provided them with a hammer and pointed out the idols to be smashed. It is the way of youth.

Middle-aged liberals—let it be said by way of defense—at least know their history. They were brought up in a great age of liberalism—an age worthy to stand beside the golden forties of last century—and they went to school to excellent teachers. Darwin, Spencer, Mill, Karl Marx, Haeckel, Taine, William James, Henry George, were masters of which no school in any age need feel ashamed; nor were such tutors and undermasters as Ruskin, William Morris, Matthew Arnold, Lester Ward, Walt Whitman, Henry Adams, to be dismissed as incompetent. To the solution of the vexing problems entailed by industrialism—in America as well as in Europe—was brought all the knowledge that had been accumulating for a century. It was a time of reëvaluations when much substantial thinking was done; when the flood of light that came with the doctrine of biological evolution lay brilliant on the intellectual landscape and the dullest mind caught some of the reflection. Few of the young scholars attended the lectures of Friedrich Nietzsche, and behavioristic psychology had not yet got into the curriculum; but Ladd and James were inquiring curiously into the mechanism of the brain, and animal psychology was preparing the way for the later Freudians. It was the end of an age perhaps, the rich afterglow of the Enlightenment, but the going down of the sun was marked by sunset skies that gave promise of other and greater dawns.

To have spent one's youth in such a school was a liberal education. The mind opened of its own will. Intellectual horizons were daily widening and the new perspectives ran out into cosmic spaces. The cold from those outer spaces had not yet chilled the enthusiasms that were a heritage from the Enlightenment, and the social idealism begotten by the democratic nature school still looked confidently to the future. They were ardent democrats—the young liberals of the nineties—and none doubted the finality or sufficiency of the democratic principle, any more than Mill or Spencer had doubted it. All their history and all their biology justified it, and the business of the times was to make it prevail in the sphere of economics as it prevailed in the realm of the political. The cure for the evils of democracy was held to be more democracy, and when industrialism had been brought under its sway—when America had become an economic democracy—a just and humane civilization would be on the threshold of possibility. To the achievement of that great purpose the young liberals devoted themselves and the accomplishments of the next score of years were the work of their hands. Certain intellectuals had been democrats—Paine and Jefferson and Emerson and Thoreau and Whitman and Melville—but they were few in comparison with the skeptical Whigs who professed democracy only to bind its hands. The Republican party had not been democratic since former days—and as Henry Adams said in 1880, it was accounted foolishness to believe in it in 1880. Autocracy was a toy to distract the voting man from the business of money-getting.

It was from such a school—richer in intellectual content, one might argue, than any the younger liberals have frequented—that the ferment of twenty years ago issued; a school dedicated to the ideals of the Enlightenment and bent on carrying through the unfulfilled program of democracy. Democratic aspirations had been thwarted hitherto by the uncontrolled play of the acquisitive instinct; the immediate problem of democracy was the control of that instinct in the common interest. Economics had controlled the political state to its narrow and selfish advantage; it was for the political state to resume its sovereignty and extend its control over economics. So in the spirit of the Enlightenment the current liberalism dedicated itself to history and sociology, accepting as its immediate and particular business a reëxamination of the American past in order to forecast an ampler democratic future. It must trace the rise of political power in America in order to understand how that power had fallen into the unsocial hands of economics. The problem was difficult. American political history had been grossly distorted by partisan interpretation and political theory had been dissipated by an arid constitutionalism. The speculative thinker had long been dispossessed by the eulogist and the lawyer, both of whom had subsisted on a thin gruel of patriotic myths. Even the social historians, though dealing in materials rich in suggestion, had been diffident in the matter of interpretation, without which history is no more than the dry bones of chronicle. Inheriting no adequate philosophy of historical evolution, the young school of historians must first provide themselves with one, in the light of which the American past should take on meaning, and the partisan struggles, hitherto meaningless, should fall into comprehensible patterns.

That necessary work was to engage them for years, but in the meanwhile, as critical realists, their immediate business was with facts and the interpretation of facts. John Fiske a few years before had essayed to interpret the rise of democracy in America by analogy from biological evolution, tracing the source of American democracy to the New England town meeting, which he explained as a resurgence of ancient Teutonic folk-ways. The theory was tenuous and it was not till Professor Turner drew attention to the creative influence of the frontier on American life that the historians were provided with a suggestive working hypothesis. Before that hypothesis could be adequately explored, however, and brought into just relations to a comprehensive philosophy of history, the rise of liberalism was well under way, marked by a rich ferment of thought that made the early years of the new century singularly stimulating. That ferment resulted from pouring into the vial of native experience the reagent of European theory—examining the ways of American industrialism in the light of continental socialism; and the result was an awakening of popular interest in social control of economics, a widespread desire to bring an expanding industrialism into subjection to a rational democratic program, that was to provide abundant fuel to the social unrest that had burst forth in sporadic flames for a generation. The great movement of liberalism that took possession of the American mind after the turn of the century—a movement not unworthy to be compared with the ferment of the eighteen forties—was the spontaneous reaction of an America still only half urbanized, still clinging to ideals and ways of an older simpler America, to an industrialism that was driving its plowshare through the length and breadth of the familiar scene, turning under the rude furrows what before had been growing familiarly there. It was the first reaction of America to the revolutionary change that followed upon the exhaustion of the frontier—an attempt to secure through the political state the freedoms that before had come from unpre-empted opportunity.

For a quarter of a century following the great westward expansion of the late sixties America had been drifting heedlessly towards a different social order. The shambling frontier democracy that had sufficed an earlier time was visibly breaking down in presence of the imperious power of a centralizing capitalism. The railways were a dramatic embodiment of the new machine civilization that was running head on into a primitive social organism fashioned by the old domestic economy, and the disruptions and confusions were a warning that the country was in for vast changes. New masters, new ways. The rule of the captain of industry had come. The farmers had long been in ugly mood, but their great rebellion was put down in 1896, and never again could they hope to wrest sovereignty from capitalism. The formal adoption of the gold standard in 1900 served notice to the world that America had put away its democratic agrarianism, that a shambling Jacksonian individualism had had its day, and that henceforth the destiny of the country lay in the hands of its business men. Capitalism was master of the country and though for the present it was content to use the political machinery of democracy it was driving towards an objective that was the negation of democracy.

The immediate reaction to so broad a shift in the course of manifest destiny was a growing uneasiness amongst the middle class—small business and professional men—who looked with fear upon the program of the captains of industry. Industrialization brought its jars and upsets. The little fish did not enjoy being swallowed by the big, and as they watched the movement of economic centralization encroaching on the field of competition they saw the doors of opportunity closing to them. It was to this great body of *petite bourgeoisie* that members of the lesser intellectuals—journalists, sociologists, reformers—were to make appeal. The work was begun dramatically with the spectacularly advertised *Frenzied Finance,* written by Thomas W. Lawson, and appearing as a series in *McClure's Magazine* in 1903.[1] The immense popular success of the venture proved that the fire was ready for the fat, and at once a host of volunteer writers fell to feeding the flames. The new ten-cent magazines provided the necessary vehicle of publicity, and enterprising editors were soon increasing their circulations with every issue. As it became evident how popular was the

---

[1] *McClure's* actually began this phase of the movement in the previous year with the publication of Lincoln Steffens' article, "Tweed Days in St. Louis" [ED.].

chord that had been struck, more competent workmen joined themselves to the group of journalists: novelists—a growing army of them—essayists, historians, political scientists, philosophers, a host of heavy-armed troops that moved forward in a frontal attack on the strongholds of the new plutocracy. Few writers in the years between 1903 and 1917 escaped being drawn into the movement—an incorrigible romantic perhaps, like the young James Branch Cabell, or a cool patrician like Edith Wharton; and with such popular novelists as Winston Churchill, Robert Herrick, Ernest Poole, David Graham Phillips, Upton Sinclair, and Jack London embellishing the rising liberalism with dramatic heroes and villains, and dressing their salads with the wickedness of Big Business; with such political leaders as Bob La Follette and Theodore Roosevelt and Woodrow Wilson beating up the remotest villages for recruits; with such scholars as Thorstein Veblen, Charles A. Beard, and John Dewey, and such lawyers as Louis Brandeis, Frank P. Walsh, and Samuel Untermyer, the movement gathered such momentum and quickened such a ferment as had not been known before in the lands since the days of the Abolition controversy. The mind and conscience of America were stirred to their lowest sluggish stratum, and a democratic renaissance was all aglow on the eastern horizon.

At the core it was a critical realistic movement that spread quietly amongst intellectuals, but the nebulous tail of the comet blazed across the sky for all to wonder at: and it was the tail rather than the core that aroused the greatest immediate interest. Lincoln Steffens, Charles Edward Russell, Ida Tarbell, Gustavus Myers, and Upton Sinclair were read eagerly because they dealt with themes that many were interested in—the political machine, watered stock, Standard Oil, the making of great fortunes, and the like—and they invested their exposures with the dramatic interest of a detective story. Up to 1910 it was largely a muckraking movement—to borrow President Roosevelt's picturesque phrase; a time of brisk housecleaning that searched out old cobwebs and disturbed the dust that lay thick on the antiquated furniture. The Gilded Age had been slovenly and such a housecleaning was long overdue. There was a vast amount of nosing about to discover bad smells, and to sensitive noses the bad smells seemed to be everywhere. Evidently some hidden cesspool was fouling American life, and as the inquisitive plumbers tested the household drains they came upon the source of infection—not one cesspool but many, under every city hall and beneath every state capitol—dug secretly by politicians in the pay of respectable business men. It was these cesspools that were poisoning the national household, and there would be no health in America till they were filled in and no others dug.

It was a dramatic discovery and when the corruption of American politics was laid on the threshold of business—like a bastard on the doorsteps of the father—a tremendous disturbance resulted. There was a great fluttering and clamor amongst the bats and owls, an ominous creaking of the machine as the wrenches were thrown into the well-oiled wheels, and a fierce sullen anger at the hue and cry set up. To many honest Americans the years between 1903 and 1910 were abusive and scurrilous beyond decency, years when no man and no business, however honorable, was safe from the pillory; when wholesale exposure had grown profitable to sensation-mongers, and great reputations were lynched by vigilantes and reputable corporations laid under indictment at the bar of public opinion. Respectable citizens did not like to have their goodly city held up to the world as "corrupt and contented"; they did not like to have their municipal housekeeping brought into public disrepute no matter how sluttish it might be. It was not pleasant for members of great families to read a cynical history of the origins of their fortunes, or for railway presidents seeking political favors to find on the newsstand a realistic account of the bad scandals that had smirched their roads. It was worse than unpleasant, it was hurtful to business. And so quietly, and as speedily as could be done decently, the movement was brought to a stop by pressure put on the magazines that lent themselves to such harmful disclosures. Then followed a campaign of education. Responding to judicious instruction, conducted in the columns of the most respectable newspapers, the American public was soon brought to understand that it was not the muck that was harmful, but the indiscretion of those who commented in print on the bad smells. It was reckoned a notable triumph for sober and patriotic good sense.

So after a few years of amazing activity the muckraking movement came to a stop. But not before it had done its work; not before the American middle class had been indoctrinated in the elementary principles of political realism and had rediscovered the social conscience lost since the days of the Civil War. Many a totem had been thrown down by the irreverent hands of the muckrakers, and many a fetish held up to ridicule, and plutocracy in America would not recover its peace of mind until at great cost the totems should be set up again and the fetishes reanointed with the oil of sanctity. The substantial result of the movement was the instruction it afforded in the close kinship between business and politics—a lesson greatly needed by a people long fed on romantic unrealities. It did not crystallize for the popular mind in the broad principle of economic determinism; that remained for certain of the intellectuals to apply to American experience. But with its sordid object—service—it punished the flabby optimism of the Gilded Age, with its object-lessons in business politics; it revealed the hidden hand that was pulling the strings of the political puppets; it tarnished the gilding that had been carefully laid on our callous exploitation, and it brought under common suspicion the captain of industry who had risen as a national hero from the muck of individualism. It was a sharp guerrilla attack on the sacred American System, but behind the thin skirmish-line lay a volunteer army that was making ready to deploy for a general engagement with plutocracy.

With the flood of light thrown upon the fundamental law by the historians, the movement of liberalism passed quickly through successive phases of thought. After the first startled surprise it set about the necessary business of acquainting the American people with its findings in the confident belief that a democratic electorate would speedily democratize the instrument. Of this first stage the late Professor J. Allen Smith's *The Spirit of American Government* (1907) was the most adequate expression, a work that greatly influenced the program of the rising Progressive Party. But changes came swiftly and within half a dozen years the movement had passed from political programs to economic, concerned not so greatly with political democracy as with economic democracy. Of this second phase Professor Beard's notable study, *An Economic Interpretation of the Constitution* (1913), was the greatest intellectual achievement. Underlying this significant work was a philosophy of politics that set it sharply apart from preceding studies—a philosophy that unsympathetic readers were quick to attribute to Karl Marx, but that in reality derived from sources far earlier and for Americans at least far more respectable. The current conception of the political state as determined in its form and activities by economic groups is no modern Marxian perversion of political theory; it goes back to Aristotle, it underlay the thinking of Harrington and Locke and the seventeenth-century English school, it shaped the conclusions of Madison and Hamilton and John Adams, it ran through all the discussions of the Constitutional Convention, and it reappeared in the arguments of Webster and Calhoun. It was the main-traveled road of political thought until a new highway was laid out by French engineers, who, disliking the bog of economics, surveyed another route by way of romantic equalitarianism. The logic of the engineers was excellent, but the drift of politics is little influenced by logic, and abstract equalitarianism proved to be poor material for highway construction. In divorcing political theory from contact with sobering reality it gave it over to a treacherous romanticism. In seeking to avoid the bog of economics it ran into an arid desert.

To get back once more on the main-traveled road, to put away all profitless romanticisms and turn realist, taking up again the method of economic interpretation unused in America since the days of Webster and Calhoun, became therefore the business of the second phase of liberalism to which Professor Beard applied himself. The earlier group of liberals were ill equipped to wage successful war against plutocracy. Immersed in the traditional equalitarian philosophy, they underestimated the strength of the enemies of democracy. They did not realize what legions of Swiss Guards property can summon to its defense. They were still romantic idealists tilting at windmills, and it was to bring them to a sobering sense of reality that *The Economic Interpretation of the Constitution* was written. If property is the master force in every society one cannot understand American institutional development until one has come to understand the part property played in shaping the fundamental law. Interpreted thus the myths that had gathered about the Constitution fell away of themselves and the document was revealed as English rather than French, the judicious expression of substantial eighteenth-century realism that accepted the property basis of political action, was skeptical of romantic idealisms, and was more careful to protect title-deeds to legal holdings than to claim unsurveyed principalities in Utopia. If therefore liberalism were to accomplish any substantial results it must approach its problems in the same realistic spirit, recognizing the masterful ambitions of property, recruiting democratic forces to overmaster the Swiss Guards, leveling the strongholds that property had erected within the organic law, and taking care that no new strongholds should rise. The problem confronting liberalism was the problem of the subjection of property to social justice.

Yet interesting as was the muckraking tail of the comet, far more significant was the core—the substantial body of knowledge gathered by the scholars and flung into the scale of public opinion. The realities of the American past had been covered deep with layers of patriotic myths, provided in simpler days when the young Republic, suffering from a natural inferiority complex, was building up a defense against the acrid criticism of Tory Europe. Those myths had long since served their purpose and had become a convenient refuge for the bats and owls of the night; it was time to strip them away and apply to the past objective standards of scholarship, and to interpret it in the light of an adequate philosophy of history. To this work, so essential to any intelligent understanding of the American experiment, a group of historians and political scientists turned with competent skills, and the solid results of their labor remained after the popular ferment subsided, as a foundation for later liberals to build on.

The journalistic muckrakers had demonstrated that America was not in fact the equalitarian democracy it professed to be, and the scholars supplemented their work by tracing to its historical source the weakness of the democratic principle in governmental practice. America had never been a democracy for the sufficient reason that too many handicaps had been imposed upon the majority will. The democratic principle had been bound with withes like Samson and had become a plaything for the Philistines. From the beginning—the scholars discovered—democracy and property had been at bitter odds; the struggle invaded the Constitutional Convention, it gave form to the party alignment between Hamilton and Jefferson, Jackson and Clay, and then during the slavery struggle, sinking underground like a lost river, it nevertheless had determined party conflicts down to the present. In this ceaseless conflict between the man and the dollar, between democracy and property, the reasons for persistent triumph of property were sought in the provisions of the organic law, and from a critical study of the Constitution came a discovery that struck home like a submarine torpedo—the discovery that the drift toward plutocracy was not a drift away from the spirit of the Constitution, but an inevitable unfolding from its premises; that instead of having been conceived by the fathers as a democratic instrument, it had been conceived in a spirit designedly hostile to democracy; that it was, in fact, a carefully formulated expression of eighteenth-century property consciousness, erected as a defense against the democratic spirit that had got out of hand during the Revolution, and that the much-praised system of checks and balances was designed and intended for no other end than a check on the political power of the majority—a power acutely feared by the property consciousness of the times.

It was a startling discovery that profoundly stirred the liberal mind of the early years of the century; yet the really surprising thing is that it should have come as a surprise. It is not easy to understand today why since Civil War days intelligent Americans should so strangely have confused the Declaration of Independence and the Constitution, and have come to accept them as complementary statements of the democratic purpose of America. Their unlikeness is unmistakable: the one a classical statement of French humanitarian democracy, the other an organic law designed to safeguard the minority under republican rule. The confusion must be charged in part to the lawyers who had taken over the custodianship of the Constitution, and in part to the florid romantic temper of the middle nineteenth century. When the fierce slavery struggle fell into the past, whatever honest realism had risen from the passions of the times was buried with the dead issue. The militant attacks on the Constitution so common in Abolitionist circles after 1835, and the criticism of the Declaration that was a part of the southern argument, were both forgotten, and with the Union re-established by force of arms, the idealistic cult of the fundamental law entered on a second youth. In the blowsy Gilded Age the old myths walked the land again, wrapped in battle-torn flags and appealing to the blood shed on southern battlefields. It was not till the advent of a generation unblinded by the passions of civil war that the Constitution again was examined critically, and the earlier charge of the Abolitionists that it was designed to serve property rather than men, was heard once more. But this time with far greater weight of evidence behind it. As the historians dug amongst the contemporary records they came upon a mass of fact the Abolitionists had been unaware of. The evidence was written so plainly, in such explicit and incontrovertible words—not only in *Elliott's Debates,* but in the minutes of the several State Conventions, in contemporary letters and memoirs, in newspapers and pamphlets and polite literature—that it seemed incredible that honest men could have erred so greatly in confusing the Constitution with the Declaration.

With the clarification of its philosophy the inflowing waters of liberalism reached flood-tide; the movement would either recede or pass over into radicalism. On the whole it followed the latter course, and the years immediately preceding 1917 were years when American intellectuals were immersing themselves in European collectivistic philosophies—in Marxianism, Fabianism, Syndicalism, Guild Socialism. New leaders were rising, philosophical analysts like Thorstein Veblen who were mordant critics of American economics. The influence of socialism was fast sweeping away the last shreds of political and social romanticism that so long had confused American thinking. The doctrine of economic determinism was spreading widely, and in the light of that doctrine the deep significance of the industrial revolution was revealing itself for the first time to thoughtful Americans. In its reaction to industrialism America had reached the point Chartist England had reached in the eighteen-forties and Marxian Germany in the eighteen-seventies. That was before a mechanistic science had laid its heavy discouragements on the drafters of democratic programs. Accepting the principle of economic determinism, liberalism still clung to its older democratic teleology, convinced that somehow economic determinism would turn out to be a fairy godmother to the proletariat and that from the imperious drift of industrial expansion must eventually issue social justice. Armed with this faith liberalism threw itself into the work of cleaning the Augean stables, and its reward came in the achievements of President Wilson's first administration.

Then the war intervened and the green fields shriveled in an afternoon. With the cynicism that came with post-war days the democratic liberalism of 1917 was thrown away like an empty whiskey-flask. Clever young men began to make merry over democracy. It was preposterous, they said, to concern oneself about social justice; nobody wants social justice. The first want of every man, as John Adams remarked a hundred years ago, is his dinner, and the second his girl. Out of the muck of the war had come a great discovery—so it was reported—the discovery that psychology as well as economics has its word to say on politics. From the army intelligence tests the moron emerged as a singular commentary on our American democracy, and with the discovery of the moron the democratic principle was in for a slashing attack. Almost overnight an army of enemies was marshaled against it. The eugenist with his isolated germ theory flouted the perfectional psychology of John Locke, with its emphasis on environment as the determining factor in social evolution—a psychology on which the whole idealistic interpretation was founded; the beardless philosopher discovered Nietzsche and in his pages found the fit master of the moron—the biological aristocrat who is the flower that every civilization struggles to produce; the satirist discovered the flatulent reality that is middle-class America and was eager to thrust his jibes at the complacent denizens of the Valley of Democracy. Only the behaviorist, with his insistence on the plasticity of the new-born child, offers some shreds of comfort to the democrat; but he quickly takes them away again with his simplification of conduct to imperious drives that stamp men as primitive animals. If the mass—the raw materials of democracy—never rises much above sex appeals and belly needs, surely it is poor stuff to try to work up into an excellent civilization, and the dreams of the social idealist who forecasts a glorious democratic future are about as substantial as moonshine. It is a discouraging essay. Yet it is perhaps conceivable that our current philosophy—the brilliant coruscations of our younger intelligentsia—may indeed not prove to be the last word in social philosophy. Perhaps—is this *lèse-majesté*—when our youngest liberals have themselves come to the armchair age they will be smiled at in turn by sons who are still cleverer and who will find their wisdom as foolish as the wisdom of 1917 seems to them today. But that lies on the knees of the gods.

2.

Richard Ely Inaugurates the New Economics

In contrast to Parrington, Richard T. Ely became a reformer early in life and early in the history of the agitation that grew into the progressive movement. His books and his teaching, first at the Johns Hopkins University and after 1892 at the University of Wisconsin, had formative influences on numerous progressives. As an expert on the regulation of trusts and public resources he left a deep mark on laws governing corporations.

Ely was born in 1854 and brought up on a farm in Fredonia, New York, in the family of a civil engineer who knew little about agriculture but believed a farm was the only place to raise children. Ely recalled his father as a hard taskmaster, a stern Presbyterian, and a crusader. To emphasize his belief that the church must receive all classes equally, Mr. Ely, to everyone's distress, arrived in church one Sunday in farmer's overalls.

Young Ely attended Dartmouth and finished his college education at Columbia. In 1877 he sailed for Germany to continue his studies in philosophy. But at Halle he met a group of young Americans, including Simon Patten and Edmund James, who had discovered German political economy. Under their influence he gave up his quest "to find the absolute truth" and took up economics, which would, he thought, allow him room for speculation but would also "keep his feet on the ground."

Returning to America, he was shocked by the industrial conflicts then raging, and he followed in his father's footsteps in lecturing the churches on their duty to the social order. In 1889 he published *Social Aspects of Christianity*, which became a widely read classic.

Before that he led in the founding of the American Economic Association, a chapter of his career whose profound effects he recalls in the following selection.

We, who had tasted the new and living economics which was taught in the German universities, were depressed with the sterility of the old economics which was being taught in the American colleges. We became weary of the controversies, the wordy conflicts over free trade and protection, and the endless harangues over paper money which seemed to us to savor more of political partisanship than of scientific inquiry. We had little patience with a press which preached conceptions of orthodoxy, and we were prepared to fight these conceptions as not belonging to the realm of science. There was a pugnacious element in our attitude, for we were young and had the pugnacity of youth. We felt that men, who thought as we did, were denied the right to exist scientifically, and this denial we believed to proceed from certain older men able to exercise a very large influence over thought, particularly thought in university circles. Therefore we felt called upon to fight those who we believed stood in the way of intellectual expansion and of social growth. We were determined to inject new life into American economics.

Two aspects of the early history of the American Economic Association should be stressed: First, it represented a protest against the system of laissez faire, as expounded by writers

---

From Richard T. Ely, *Ground Under Our Feet* (New York: The Macmillan Company, 1938), pp. 132–159.

of the older school of "orthodox" American economics. Several of the founders of our association, particularly Simon N. Patten,[1] wished to register their protest against this aspect of orthodox economic theory. The second aspect, and the one on which we were all in complete agreement, was the necessity of uniting in order to secure complete freedom of discussion; a freedom untrammeled by any restrictions whatsoever. It was this second point that came, in final analysis and after much debate, to be accepted as the foundation stone of our association.

But the protest against the "laissez faire" philosophy must not be underemphasized in the history of the foundation of the American Economic Association. In this connection, an attempt was made to organize an association which was to have been known as the Society for the Study of National Economy. The idea of this society, sponsored particularly by Simon N. Patten and Edmund J. James,[2] was that we young economists should organize in order to advocate a definite program and a definite platform, as well as to encourage objective, scientific research. The Society for the Study of National Economy was to have resembled the German *Verein für Sozialpolitik* (Society for Social Policy), which had been organized in Germany during the years 1872–73. The *Verein für Sozialpolitik* included a group of German economists who had broken loose from the "laissez faire" economic philosophy characteristic of the English classical school, which they described rather contemptuously as "Manchesterthum." "Manchesterthum" represented, in their eyes, the advocacy of unrestricted individual freedom from any form of governmental intervention in matters of industry and trade. . . .

---

[1] Patten was then Professor of Economics at the University of Pennsylvania [ED.].

[2] James, who was then teaching at the Wharton School of Finance and Commerce, also took part, later, in the founding of the American Academy of Political and Social Science [ED.].

As an indication of the thoughts stirring in the minds of young Americans, the draft of the constitution of the proposed Society for the Study of National Economy has had great significance in the history of economic thought. We soon found, however, that the proposed constitution rested on too narrow a basis to enlist the sympathy of a sufficiently large group of American economists. The attempts at the formation of this society were, in a sense, preparatory; they indicated a stirring of the soil, and they exerted an influence on me in my efforts to draft a satisfactory statement of principles for the American Economic Association. However, my effort was not a rival one. I had already intended to form an association of American economists before the efforts of Dr. James and Dr. Patten took any definite shape. That sort of thing was in the air at the Johns Hopkins and was encouraged by the authorities. When the society sent out a draft of its constitution I held back until it became absolutely certain that success could not be achieved along that line.

When it became evident that the "Society for the Study of National Economy" could not be established, I undertook to draw up a project for the formation of a society to be called "The American Economic Association," which should be broad enough to appeal to all the younger economists who, irrespective of their personal views, felt the stirring of the new life in economics and who wished to unite in order to secure complete liberty of thought and discussion, even if their thought led them to "unorthodox" conclusions. In the statement of our "objects" and "declaration of principles" I retained the central idea of the authors of the constitution of the "Society for the Study of National Economy," namely, that the dogma of "laissez faire" should be abandoned by our leaders. My program was a much simpler one and differed from theirs in two important particulars. In the first place, it emphasized historical and statistical study rather than deductive speculation, and, in the second place, it laid less stress on government intervention and, on the whole, was "toned down" in the direction of conservatism. It was designed to attract as many members as possible. The prospectus sent out read as follows:

AMERICAN ECONOMIC ASSOCIATION

Objects of This Association

I. The encouragement of economic research.
II. The publication of economic monographs.
III. The encouragement of perfect freedom in all economic discussion.
IV. The establishment of a bureau of information designed to aid all members with friendly counsels in their economic studies.

Platform

1. We regard the state as an educational and ethical agency whose positive aid is an indispensable condition of human progress. While we recognize the necessity of individual initiative in industrial life, we hold that the doctrine of laissez faire is unsafe in politics and unsound in morals; and that it suggests an inadequate explanation of the relations between the state and the citizens.

2. We do not accept the final statements which characterized the political economy of a past generation; for we believe that political economy is still in the first stages of its scientific development, and we look not so much to speculation as to an impartial study of actual conditions of economic life for the satisfactory accomplishment of that development. We seek the aid of statistics in the present, and of history in the past.

3. We hold that the conflict of labor and capital has brought to the front a vast number of social problems whose solution is impossible without the united efforts of church, state, and science.

4. In the study of the policy of government, especially with respect to restrictions on trade and to protection of domestic manufactures, we take no partisan attitude. We are convinced

that one of the chief reasons why greater harmony has not been attained is because economists have been too ready to assert themselves as advocates. We believe in a progressive development of economic conditions which must be met by corresponding changes of policy.

In drawing up this prospectus I was especially assisted by my colleague, Professor H. B. Adams,[3] who the year before had been chiefly instrumental in organizing the American Historical Association. Adams had a genius for organization, and was probably never happier than when bringing an institution into existence. Dr. E. J. James also co-operated most generously and effectively, never expressing the slightest concern for any egoistic ends, but striving to promote the common aim. No one was more energetic and loyal in co-operation than Dr. E. R. A. Seligman.[4] This is all the more to Dr. Seligman's credit because he held the view that economics had not yet "attained that certainty in results which would authorize us to invoke increased governmental action as a check to various abuses of free competition."

The emphasis I laid on inductive studies was not altogether to the liking of S. N. Patten, who represented the deductive school among our group. He also felt that the fourth article of our platform was too much "toned down." At the time he said this:

"It seems to me that the very object of our association should be to deny the right of individuals to do as they please, and that of course is restricting trade. . . . I believe that our platform should state explicitly what we intend to do . . . we should give in some specific form our attitude on all the lead-

---

[3] Herbert Baxter Adams, Professor of History and Political Science at the Johns Hopkins University, was perhaps the most influential teacher of graduate students in his day [ED.].

[4] E. R. A. Seligman had just received his Ph.D. in economics at Columbia University where, in 1891, he became Professor of Political Economy, a post he retained for forty years [ED.].

ing economic questions where state intervention is needed."

Even in its modified and more conservative form, our platform met with a certain amount of friendly criticism. A mimeographed circular was distributed among all the economists who might be supposed to be in sympathy with the general ideas expressed in the new constitution; and it was proposed to gather at Saratoga in September, 1885, in connection with the American Historical Association, to which nearly all the economists belonged. The response to the invitation was general. On September 8, 1885, a call signed by H. C. Adams, J. B. Clark, and R. T. Ely was read at a public meeting of the Historical Association. All those interested were invited to meet at the Bethesda Parish Building at 4 P.M. on that same day to take into consideration plans for the formation of an American Economic Association. Among those present at this first meeting, besides the original sponsors of the project (E. J. James and H. C. Adams, and I), were John B. Clark, Edwin R. A. Seligman, Davis R. Dewey, Andrew D. White, C. K. Adams, Katherine Coman, and E. Benjamin Andrews, to mention only a few.

I recall clearly that first meeting we held at Saratoga and I can see, as if it were yesterday, Professor Seligman tramping through the rain with me to the office of the Associated Press to see that we had such publicity as we both felt we deserved. Professor Seligman, then, as always, put his shoulder to the wheel when that was necessary, and always exhibited courage when that was required. At our modest beginning in that first meeting at Saratoga there were less than fifty people—a small room held us all, even counting those who were there because of curiosity. For many years any one of our large universities had auditoriums quite ample for all those who attended. Now, when we hold our meetings, we raise the question when some particular city is proposed for our next annual meeting whether or not the city's accommodations are adequate for our general meetings and for our many conferences. Now we debate questions concerning the investment of amounts like five thousand or ten thousand dollars. In the early days the problem was how to get money for the next step in our activities or for the publication of a monograph. Perhaps if I can claim credit for any virtue it is that of persistence. I was almost ready to go out on the street corner and pass the hat. While I never did quite that, once when our finances were in a bad state, I recall writing to a distinguished New Yorker, Abram S. Hewitt,[5] and asking him to help us out with a life membership. This he generously did and mildly reproved me because I had not written to him earlier. Need I say that the gentleman holds a warm place in my heart?

Since I was elected "temporary secretary," it was my duty to state the aims of the newly formed association, as I saw them. One of the main points I made on this occasion was that the doctrine of "laissez faire" implied that the laws of economic life were "natural laws" like those of physics and chemistry, and that this life must be left to the free play of natural forces. The scientific attitude towards this question was, however, I said, one of inquiry, and, necessarily, one of modesty. I spoke as I felt when I said that:

"Our attitude is a modest one, and must, I think, appeal to the best intelligence of the country. We acknowledge our ignorance, and if we claim superiority to others it is largely on the very humble ground that we know better what we do not know. We confess our ignorance; but are determined to do our best to remedy it, and we call upon those who are willing to go to work in this spirit to come forward and help us."

---

[5] Iron manufacturer, philanthropist, and long a power in New York City politics, Hewitt, in the year following, defeated Henry George and Theodore Roosevelt for the mayoralty of New York [ED.].

Professor Henry C. Adams said that, admitting that the philosophy of "laissez faire," which regarded the state as nothing more than a necessary evil, was untenable, our problem was still unsolved. The doctrine which presented the state as the "final analysis of human relations" was, he maintained, as untenable as the doctrine of "laissez faire" itself. And he concluded that, "The great problem of the present day is properly to correlate public and private activity so as to preserve harmony and proportion between the various parts of organic society."

Much the same idea was expressed by E. J. James, who said that he wished to make it clear that there was "a legitimate sphere of state activity" and that the question of government intervention ought to be judged, in every case, on its own merits.

John Bates Clark pointed out that, in a society such as the American Economic Association, it was hardly fitting to adopt any one platform, upon which all the members could scarcely be expected to agree. He claimed that: "The point upon which individuals will be unable to unite is, especially, the strong condemnation of the 'laissez-faire' doctrine."

In the end, it was decided to refer our platform to a committee of five, consisting of H. C. Adams, the Reverend Washington Gladden, Professor Alexander Johnston, and Professor J. B. Clark and me. The committee decided that it was desirable to make it plain that the founders of the American Economic Association did not intend to formulate any creed which should restrict freedom of inquiry or independence of thought. With this end in view, the following note was appended to the "statement of principles" which was finally adopted:

"This statement was proposed and accepted as the general indication of the views and the purposes of those who founded the American Economic Association, but it is not to be regarded as binding upon individual members."

The statement of principles read as follows:

1. We regard the state as an agency whose positive assistance is one of the indispensable conditions of human progress.
2. We believe that political economy as a science is still in an early stage of its development. While we appreciate the work of former economists, we look, not so much to speculation as to the historical and statistical study of actual conditions of economic life for the satisfactory accomplishment of that development.
3. We hold that the conflict of labor and capital has brought into prominence a vast number of social problems, whose solution requires the united efforts, each in its own sphere, of the church, of the state, and of science.
4. In the study of the industrial and commercial policy of governments we take no partisan attitude. We believe in a progressive development of economic conditions, which must be met by a corresponding development of legislative policy.

It should be noticed that our statement of principles was never regarded as a creed. In the report of the secretary on the organization of the American Economic Association, I find the following words: "This platform, it must be distinctly asserted, was never meant as a hard and fast creed, which should be imposed on all members, and least of all was it intended to restrict the freest investigation." If anyone ever signed the statement of principles, it must have come to my notice, as I held the position of secretary for the first seven years, and I feel safe in saying that absolutely no one ever signed it, and that no officer of the association ever asked anyone to sign it. It was not intended to be signed, and this reply was made by the secretary when once or twice a willingness to sign was expressed. The "note" printed with the constitution precisely expressed the situation.

This statement of principles, it will be observed, was a compromise on behalf of catholicity. First we have the detailed declarations of E. J. James and of S. N. Patten, then the broader and more general "platform" drawn up by myself, and finally the "statement" adopted; each modification representing what has been called a "toning down" process. The changes made were in deference to the fact that various views were represented in the membership of our newly formed association and still more in the membership we hoped to get. We were anxious to win the great body of economists. While not all the original members may have held precisely the views expressed in the "statement of principles," all certainly felt at home and comfortable in the association; and it was hoped and expected that the statement would oppose no barrier among students who held less pronounced views. We all considered ourselves scientific investigators and not propagandists.

What was its purpose then? Let us be perfectly frank. It had an inclusive as well as an exclusive aim. Like the earlier statement in the proposed Society for the Study of National Economy, it aimed to gather together like-minded men, congenial men who it was supposed could profitably work together. Not every economist was at first asked to join, although no economist who expressed a desire to join was refused enrollment. Our statement had doubtless puzzled and perplexed many because, looking upon it as a creed, they asked themselves, "How could this creed proceed from those animated by scientific ideals of freedom?" It was, however, simply a statement showing conclusions which up to that time those of us who were most instrumental in founding the association held. . . .

Certainly a practical purpose was dominant among those who were in control at the time. There was a striving for righteousness and perhaps here and there might have been one who felt a certain kinship with the old Hebrew prophets. Another element perhaps laid more emphasis upon correct thought, holding that so long as men think correctly we need not concern ourselves with their action. Certainly everyone was animated by the love of truth for its own sake. Undoubtedly a dominant note was to do things practically and scientifically and bring to pass results.

Rightly or wrongly to many, the statement of principles seemed like a proclamation of emancipation. At this time the enthusiasm with which we were greeted may appear a little difficult to comprehend. . . .

Why this jubilation? Why this feeling of emancipation? It was felt by many that political economy was opposed to the recognition of any ethical element in our economic life, that it opposed all social reforms for social uplift as futile, that it exalted into a principle of economic righteousness the individual and unrestrained pursuit of self-interest, that it almost deified a monstrosity known as the economic man, that it looked upon laissez faire as a law of beneficent providence, and held that free trade must be received as an ethical dogma, being a practical application of the command, "Thou shalt not steal," for here inconsistently an ethical principle was admitted as all-controlling. Now let it be said that no support, or at any rate very little support, for such views could be found in the writings of the great economists of England or any other country; but a false and undue emphasis of certain teachings of the masters had led to this misapprehension; and for this one-sided development, popularization and the exigencies of practical politics were largely responsible. Hence when the recognition of evils was proclaimed as in harmony with science, when it was proposed to examine the actual situation of the wage-earner and to reason on the basis of observation, when it made known that a body of economists was prepared to examine free trade and protection scientifically and not dogmatically, and that economics embraced the whole of the economic life; the simple message, which now no one would think it necessary to proclaim, produced an impression and aroused an enthusiasm which can be understood only by those who by the aid of the scientific imagination work their way back to the situation of 1885.

It has been said by some that the founders of the American Economic Association had absorbed German ideas and attempted to transplant them into American soil, and that this was an alien soil. This is undoubtedly erroneous, for our association was essentially American in its origin and ideas. German influences were felt and we are all thankful for German science, but, as Professor Farnam pointed out, these ideas of the founders, and in particular the opposition to laissez faire and the expressions in favor of an active policy of government, ascribed to a German influence are not un-American. Professor Farnam was quite right in this view that laissez faire is not a peculiar American product. It is worthy of special note that we must look to the prairies of Illinois, swept by the free air of the Mississippi Valley, for the authorship of the constitution of the proposed Society for the Study of National Economy, in which still more emphatically than in our own statement of principle we find proclaimed opposition to non-interference in economic affairs and the advocacy of very large and broad functions of government. What Germany did for us was, in the sense in which Socrates used the term, to serve as midwife, helping to birth the ideas which had been conceived under American conditions. We were impressed in the German universities by a certain largeness and freedom of thought which was novel but very refreshing and delightful. Speaking for myself—and I believe for most of us—I may say that the idea of relativity as opposed to absolutism and the insistence upon exact and positive knowledge produced a profound influence upon my thought. I must not fail to mention the impression produced upon my thought (and again I believe I may speak for most of my associates) by the ethical view of economics taught by Conrad, by Wagner, and above all by Knies, under whom I took my degree.[6] These economists had a sufficiently clear perception of the difference between ethics and economics. They had a feeling, however, that ethical influences should be brought to bear on our economic life, and

---

[6] Johannes Conrad, Karl Knies, and Adolf Wagner were Ely's teachers at Halle, Heidelberg, and Berlin, respectively.

they believed also that those ethical influences which were actually at work shaping economic life to a greater or less extent should be examined carefully as existing forces. And, finally, it is doubtless safe to say that the warm humanitarianism of the German theorists moved the Americans of my day deeply. But we remained Americans whose intellectual life had been quickened by our own life in the atmosphere of the German universities.

The American Economic Association took a stand at its organization for entire freedom of discussion. We were thoroughly devoted to the ideal of the German university—*Lehrfreiheit und Lernfreiheit;* and we have not hesitated to enter the lists vigorously in favor of freedom when we have considered it endangered. Here there has been no apparent difference. Whatever opinions otherwise may have separated our members, we have stood shoulder to shoulder as one man for free discussion. But was this ever necessary? Rightly or wrongly, we did feel at first that it required a struggle to find a place in our academic life for free expression of our views.

For the first seven years my office as secretary was a part of my general office at the Johns Hopkins University and served as the secretarial office, editorial office, publishing office, and I don't know what else besides. There was no appropriation for secretarial assistance and at first not even a typewriter. I took care of the printing, rushing down to the printing office and sometimes exploding with youthful wrath on account of the delay in getting out a monograph. I made all the contacts and contracts with book dealers; if there is no one else who can be designated by the name of advertising manager, I claim that title.

Women have always been welcomed into our ranks, but in our early days there were few of them. When we held our first annual meeting in Philadelphia there were perhaps fifteen or twenty women present, including such distinguished women as Florence Kelley and President M. Carey Thomas, of Bryn

Mawr College. Dr. Stuart Wood [of Haverford College] planned a reception in his beautiful home but he had evidently overlooked the fact that women were members of our association, and according to the inflexible social code of Philadelphia, he did not see how he could receive women and men both in his home. So it fell to me unhappily to tell our women members that they were not expected at Stuart Wood's reception. In an eleventh hour attempt to smooth over an embarrassing situation, Dr. Wood's sister offered them a reception in her home and extended to them all a most cordial invitation to attend. The good ladies boycotted this reception and while the men enjoyed Dr. Wood's hospitality, his sister's parlors, all brilliantly lighted in anticipation of the ladies' arrival, were empty. How times have changed since then, perhaps even in Philadelphia!

The secretary's office also acted as a bureau of information for the members. For a number of years the bureau performed a very useful function in aiding members scattered throughout the country in the selection of works on topics in which they were interested, in giving information about leading thinkers on various sides of controverted questions, and in answering all sorts of questions in relation to economics. It supplied a real need at a time when there were comparatively few economists in the country, and compared with recent years, a very meager American literature.

It was the opinion of some of our founders that detailed reports and recommendations should be made by committees, and that these would be debated and have a direct influence on public opinion and legislation. The original idea was that each member of the association should belong to a committee, and that the work of the association would be essentially a work of standing committees. This idea was soon abandoned because our members were generally too busy with other duties to develop the work of the standing committees. We were building up departments in our universities, schools and institutions (such as the National Consumers League, the Child Labor Committee, and the American Association for Labor Legislation) to make scientific work easier for those who would follow us. Soon the theory of standing committees was modified. A plan for special committees was drawn up by Professor Charles H. Hull in his report to the council at the thirteenth annual meeting, December, 1900. "The theory of these special committees, as the secretary understands it, is that the association makes no attempt to impose the work of a committeeman upon any member, but, wherever a sufficient and well-balanced group of members desires to take up some subject of investigation which promises results, the council is inclined to give them its blessing, and the publication committee is likely to look with favor upon the proposal to print their report." It will be seen that this was a considerable departure from the original theory of the standing committees.

Another line of activity was the effort to encourage popular interest in economic questions by offers of prizes for essays on various economic questions of the day. These prizes performed an extremely useful purpose in their day, in awakening an intelligent appreciation of economics, in helping start at least a few young people in useful careers, and in attracting support to our association at a time when the struggle for existence was keenly felt by those who assumed the burden of our affairs.

Although its formation was greeted with enthusiasm by a few, there was a strange failure, on the part of others, to comprehend that it really inaugurated a new era in the history of American economics. Even now, it is sometimes forgotten how much the foundation of the association meant to American economists. At the close of the nineteenth century, it was especially the older group of economists, with comparatively few exceptions, who really did not know what it was all about. . . .

Some have thought, and perhaps still think, that we were chiefly concerned about differences in method, or what the

Germans called *Methodenstreit.* Certainly, most of us emphasized the inductive method of inquiry and, following the German economists who had trained us, we frequently spoke about the historical method. Sometimes we may have used the expressions statistical method and comparative method. All the talk about method, however, concerned things that were merely on the surface, and did not at all get down to those things which were really fundamental, and about which we were seriously concerned.

It has been said, and said wisely, that when a discussion takes place, apparently about words and forms of words, there are always things lying back of words which do have a real and vital meaning. In the Christian church there was at one time a very active discussion moving men profoundly which turned merely upon the spelling of a word. Those versed in theology know that what was called an iota subscript, which was simply a mark under a letter, played a large role in the history of theology. It seems perfectly ridiculous to the ordinary man that people should have got excited about a little mark. Those who know the history of theology understand that there was something real and vital at the bottom of this controversy concerning a little mark called the iota subscript.

What we young fellows were concerned about was life itself, and the controversy in regard to methodology was simply a surface indication of forces operating more deeply. We believed that economics had, in itself, the potency of life. In the vast field of research which lay before us, and through research, the opening up of fields which had been cultivated only to a limited extent, we felt that we had opportunities for service of many kinds. We had found among our teachers in Germany a warm humanitarianism, and that inspired us. Looking about us with open eyes we saw a real labor question, whereas some of the older school talked about a "so-called labor question." We saw a good deal of poverty on the one hand and a concentration of wealth on the other hand; and we did not feel that all was well with our country. We felt that something should be done to bring about better conditions. We had had a glimpse into the fundamental institutions of our economic life, and discovered that these were in a state of flux. We had learned the idea of evolution and never ceasing change as a condition of life. We thought that by getting down into this life and studying it carefully, we would be able to do something toward directing the great forces shaping our life, and directing them in such a way as to bring improvement.

The most fundamental things in our minds were, on the one hand, the idea of evolution, and on the other hand, the idea of relativity. These two ideas meant far more than the debate about methodology. A new world was coming into existence, and if this world was to be a better world, we knew that we must have a new economics to go along with it.

But why did we talk about inductive method? It was because this was the way of breaking down the old barriers in the path of progress and preparing the ground for something new and constructive. Surely no one of us and no one of our teachers in Germany objected to the use of deduction in its proper place; certainly it had its place, but deduction as it was then used, was inadequate. It did not explain the world as it was. We thought that we could get new premises and new generalizations by opening our eyes and looking at the world as it was. When we began to use the "look and see" method, we found a failure in the conclusions reached by the older economists to harmonize with the life that was unfolding about us. We found also that, as a matter of fact, the conclusions of the other economists, as they existed in the popular mind, and as they existed in the minds of leaders of thought and action, especially, stood in the way of real progress. The way to get out of such closed circles was to study life itself. We believed in gathering together facts, in order that they might tell the story of life. Of course if we had common sense and any intellectual acumen at all, we did not think that the mere accumulation of facts could give us scientific light or practical guidance. We did not need to be told that one could gather facts for a century and not be any wiser. The facts had to be gathered in accordance with some hypothesis and arranged in such a way that they might give us new knowledge. Hypotheses, observation—such procedure was fundamental to us.

We did have a new economics. The apathy and indifference with respect to the old economics were replaced by an enthusiasm which has continued from 1885 down to the present time. We had a message and this kindled enthusiasm. Our message was hailed by the best minds in the rising generation with a joy begotten of hope. All of this explains what our "statement of principles" really signified. The crust that had been formed on economics was broken, and real economic inquiry expanded and grew and has kept on growing until this very day.

An English writer who exercised some considerable influence on the "new economics" of 1885 was John Stuart Mill. Mill stands, in a way, between the new and the old in economic theory. He is Janus-faced; and I say this without intending any reproach whatever. The Germans say of John Stuart Mill that he lacked system, using the term *systemlos*. In his early youth he had been rigorously trained in the Ricardian system of economics by his father, James Mill, who was a close friend of Ricardo himself. In his autobiography he tells us how difficult it was for him, during the time of his father, to break away from the old economics. When he did so, he was hard put to it to replace a system that he had come to feel was inadequate and obsolete. John Stuart Mill says that his "eyes were opened to the very limited and temporary value of the old political economy" partly through the early writings of Auguste Comte (at a time when that author still called himself a pupil of the French socialist, Saint Simon) and, to an even greater extent, through the Saint Simonians themselves. From Auguste Comte he learned how great an error it is to mistake the "moral and intellectual characteristics" of one era for "the normal attributes of humanity." From the Saint Simonians he learned to distrust some of the assumptions on which the old political economy was based, and especially the assumption of believing in freedom of production and exchange as the *dernier mot* of social improvement.

Under these influences, John Stuart Mill says that he came gradually to change his earlier and taught opinions:

"I found the fabric of my old and taught opinion giving way in many fresh places, and I never allowed it to fall to pieces, but was incessantly occupied in weaving it anew."

A captious critic might say that he patched the holes rather than wove a new fabric, and Mill himself might have admitted that there was some truth in this statement. . . . What he did was to state the old propositions and then to modify them so radically as almost to destroy them. His influence upon us economists of the younger generation was undoubtedly very great. Many of us were particularly impressed by a passage in which he said that, when discussing how much or how little should be done by the government, or how far the government should go in restricting what the older economists called "natural liberty," it was impossible to draw any rigid line or to say "thus far and no further." Let me quote this passage:

"Enough has been said to show that the admitted functions of government embrace a much wider field than can easily be included within the ring-fence of any restrictive definition, and that it is hardly possible to find any ground of justification common to them all, except the comprehensive one of general expediency; nor to limit the interference of government by any universal rule, save the simple and vague one that it should never be admitted but when the case of expediency is strong." This passage expressed the way most of us felt.

For several years after I began to work in the Johns Hopkins University I used John Stuart Mill's *Political Economy* as a text; and other contemporaries of mine did so for a number of years. We found that, in spite of Mill's half-hearted defense of the "let alone" system, he really justified pretty much of everything that those of the younger group stood for. We, also, all liked his warm humanitarianism and especially his sympathy with the wage-earning classes, and the frank way in which he renounced his earlier wage-fund theory, having the courage to say, "I was mistaken." In the course of a review of Thornton's *Labour* published by Mill in the *Fortnightly Review* for May, 1869, the English economist admits:

"The doctrine hitherto taught by all or most economists (including myself), which denied it to be possible that trade combinations can raise wages, or which limited their operations in that respect to the somewhat earlier attainment of a rise which the competition of the market would have produced without them—this doctrine is deprived of its scientific foundation, and must be thrown aside. The right and wrong of the proceedings of trade unions becomes a common question of prudence and social duty, not one which is peremptorily decided by unbending necessities of political economy."

The men who founded the American Economic Association look upon its foundation as the great event in American economics; but they were only the medium through which deep currents of life found expression. We may regard the history of economic thought before this event as leading up to it, and the events of importance since its foundation may be regarded in the main as flowing from it. Eighteen hundred and eighty-five may be designated as our hegira. The American Economic Association is not to be looked upon as the sole creator of the thought forces within our field, but it is one of the thought causes. It is beyond question that had the Economic Association not come into existence we should have had a development of economic thought in this country; but it is certainly true that our association has gathered together the thought forces and has given expression to them. It has served as a stimulus to young and old. It has rewarded youth by recognition.

Our association has stimulated improvement in economic and statistical work. All who have followed our history will recall our critical treatment of the census office and the active part that we took in favoring the establishment of a permanent census bureau. We may fairly claim an appreciable influence in the improvement which is going on in the census work of the country. In 1905, a special committee was appointed to consider the scope and method of the twelfth census. This committee consisted of Richard Mayo-Smith, Walter Wilcox, Carroll D. Wright, Roland Falkner, and Davis R. Dewey. The resultant volume on *The Scope and Method of the Twelfth Census—Critical discussion by over Twenty Statistical Experts* exercised a great and beneficent influence on succeeding censuses. The world of railway reform is associated with our history. Railway problems have been discussed faithfully by men representing different points of view, and members of our association are now engaged in bringing about improvements of value both to the railways and the general public. Our association has been one of the forces in favor of sound money, helping the country to weather storms and avert threatened evils. The trust problem has received fruitful discussion in our meetings, and our members have been among those who have thrown light on the scientific and practical aspects of industrial combinations. The good roads movement received an impetus in an able monograph contributed by one of our presidents. Social reform has been guided and stimulated by our efforts. . . .

Another interesting event in our internal history was the position taken towards endowments. The council at our Detroit meeting in 1900 virtually rejected the offer of an endowment, it being feared by some that an endowment might come from sources that would prove embarrassing and would hamper our free development. The feeling was even expressed that we should from year to year be dependent upon our friends. It is possibly of some significance that the movement for an endowment came first of all from one connected with a state university and that the opposition sprang almost altogether from men associated with privately endowed universities. Now we have reached a period in our life when we make use of the funds which endowments furnish and do so without danger, conscious or unconscious, to our scientific integrity.

3.

W. E. B. Du Bois Proposes a Science of Equality

The autobiography of W. E. Burghardt Du Bois begins with an apology: "My life had its significance and its only deep significance because it was part of a Problem; but that problem was, as I continue to think, the central problem of the greatest of the world's democracies and so the Problem of the future world." Most reformers of the progressive era did not regard the conflict between the races in this way, although its violence and its cost in lives far exceeded that of industrial or rural disorder. Virtually alone, Du Bois extended the central tenets of progressivism to include the American Negro.

He was born in 1868 in Great Barrington, Massachusetts, a town with so strong an abolitionist heritage that Du Bois was not subjected to discrimination there. But when, at the age of seventeen, he was sent to Fisk University in Nashville, he suffered insults "of which I never dreamed." Negro students carried firearms for protection. Of the recurrent lynchings during his college days he wrote "each death was like a scar upon my soul."

In 1888 he was admitted to Harvard, where he was to receive three degrees. He studied under William James, George Santayana, and Albert Bushnell Hart, among others. His doctoral dissertation on the suppression of the slave trade was published as the first volume of the Harvard Historical Studies. The first of numerous pioneering works of scholarship, it was followed by his masterful sociological study of the Philadelphia Negro, described below, and in later years by studies in Negro history that prepared the way for realistic interpretations of the subject.

As Vernon Parrington arrived at Harvard, Du Bois left it to travel and study in Europe. In Berlin he studied under the historian Heinrich Treitschke and under Max Weber and Gustav Schmoller. But despite the opportunity to work with these titans of German scholarship, Europe's most important impact on Du Bois was that in the absence of race consciousness he could, at times, "sit still." Then, as he recalled, "something of the possible beauty and elegance of life permeated my soul." Perhaps this experience, as much as any, led to his successful challenge to Booker T. Washington's hold on the Negro movement shortly after the return to America which Du Bois describes below.

From the fall of 1894 to the spring of 1910, for sixteen years, I was a teacher. For two years I remained at Wilberforce; for something over a year, at the University of Pennsylvania; and for thirteen years at Atlanta University in Georgia. I sought in these years to teach youth the meaning and way of the world. What did I know about the world and how could I teach my knowledge?

The main result of my schooling had been to emphasize science and the scientific attitude. I got some insight into the laws of the physical world at Fisk and in the chemical laboratory and class in geology at Harvard. I was interested in evolution, geology, and the new psychology. I began to conceive of the world as a continuing growth rather than a finished product. In Germany I turned still further from religious

---

From W. E. B. Du Bois, *Dusk of Dawn* (New York: Harcourt, Brace & Co., 1940), chap. 4, "Science and Politics," pp. 50–70. Copyright 1940 by Harcourt Brace & Co. Reprinted by permission of the publishers.

dogma and began to grasp the idea of a world of human beings whose actions, like those of the physical world, were subject to law. The triumphs of the scientific world thrilled me: the X-ray and radium came during my teaching term, the airplane and the wireless. The machine increased in technical efficiency and the North and South Poles were invaded.

On the other hand the difficulties of applying scientific law and discovering cause and effect in the social world were still great. Social thinkers were engaged in vague statements and were seeking to lay down the methods by which, in some not too distant future, social law analogous to physical law would be discovered. Herbert Spencer finished his ten volumes of Synthetic Philosophy in 1896. The biological analogy, the vast generalizations, were striking, but actual scientific accomplishment lagged. For me an opportunity seemed to present itself. I could not lull my mind to hypnosis by regarding a phrase like "consciousness of kind" as a scientific law. But turning my gaze from fruitless word-twisting and facing the facts of my own social situation and racial world, I determined to put science into sociology through a study of the condition and problems of my own group.

I was going to study the facts, any and all facts, concerning the American Negro and his plight, and by measurement and comparison and research, work up to any valid generalization which I could. I entered this primarily with the utilitarian object of reform and uplift; but nevertheless, I wanted to do the work with scientific accuracy. Thus, in my own sociology, because of firm belief in a changing racial group, I easily grasped the idea of a changing developing society rather than a fixed social structure.

The decade and a half in which I taught, was riotous with happenings in the world of social development; with economic expansion, with political control, with racial difficulties. Above all, it was the era of empire and while I had some equipment to deal with a scientific approach to social studies, I did not have any clear conception or grasp of the meaning of that industrial imperialism which was beginning to grip the world. My only approach to meanings and helpful study there again was through my interest in race contact.

That interest began to clear my vision and interpret the whirl of events which swept the world on. Japan was rising to national status and through the Chinese War and the Russian War, despite rivalry with Germany, Russia and Great Britain, she achieved a new and nearly equal status in the world, which only the United States refused to recognize. But all this, I began to realize, was but a result of the expansion of Europe into Africa where a fierce fight was precipitated for the labor, gold, and diamonds of South Africa; for domination of the Nile Valley; for the gold, cocoa, raw materials, and labor of West Africa; and for the exploitation of the Belgian Congo. Europe was determined to dominate China and all but succeeded in dividing it between the chief white nations, when Japan stopped the process. After sixteen years, stirred by the triumph of the Abyssinians at Adowa, and pushing forward of the French in North Africa, England returned to the Egyptian Sudan.

The Queen's Jubilee then, I knew, was not merely a sentimental outburst; it was a triumph of English economic aggression around the world and it aroused the cupidity and fear of Germany who proceeded to double her navy, expand into Asia, and consolidate her European position. Germany challenged France and England at Algeciras, prelude to the World War. Imperialism, despite Cleveland's opposition, spread to America, and the Hawaiian sugar fields were annexed. The Spanish war brought Cuban sugar under control and annexed Puerto Rico and the Philippines. The Panama Canal brought the Pacific nearer the Atlantic and we protected capital investment in San Domingo and South America.

All this might have been interpreted as history and politics. Mainly I did so interpret it; but continually I was forced to consider the economic aspects of world movements as they were developing at the time. Chiefly this was because the group in which I was interested were workers, earners of wages, owners of small bits of land, servants. The labor strikes interested and puzzled me. They were for the most part strikes of workers led by organizations to which Negroes were not admitted. There was the great steel strike; the railway strikes, actual and threatened; the teamsters' strike in Chicago; the long strike in Leadville, Colorado. Only in the coal strike were Negroes involved. But there was a difference. During my school days, strikes were regarded as futile and ill-advised struggles against economic laws; and when the government intervened, it was to cow the strikers as law-breakers. But during my teaching period, the plight of the worker began to sift through into the consciousness of the average citizen. Public opinion not only allowed but forced Theodore Roosevelt to intervention in the coal strike, and the steel strikers had widespread sympathy.

Then there were the tariff agitations, the continual raising and shifting and manipulation of tariff rates, always in the end for the purpose of subsidizing the manufacturer and making the consumer pay. The political power of the great organizations of capital in coal, oil and sugar, the extraordinary immunities of the corporations, made the President openly attack the trusts as a kind of super-government and we began to see more and more clearly the outlines of economic battle. The Supreme Court stood staunchly behind capital. It outlawed the labor boycott, it denied the right of the states to make railway rates. It declared the income tax unconstitutional.

With all that, and the memory of the Panic of 1873 not forgotten, came the Panic of 1893 and the financial upheaval of 1907. Into this economic turmoil, politics had to intrude. The older role of free, individual enterprise, with little or no government interference, had to be surrendered and the whole political agitation during these days took on a distinct economic tinge and object. The impassioned plea of Bryan in 1896 that labor be not "crucified upon a cross of gold" could not be wholly ridiculed to silence. The Populist Movement which swept over the West and South, I began now to believe, was a third party movement of deep significance and it was kept from political power on the one hand by the established election frauds of the South of which I knew, and by the fabulous election fund which made McKinley President of the United States. With this went the diversion of the Spanish war with its sordid scandals of rotten beef, cheating and stealing, fever and death from neglect. Politics and economics thus in those days of my teaching became but two aspects of a united body of action and effort.

I tried to isolate myself in the ivory tower of race. I wanted to explain the difficulties of race and the ways in which these difficulties caused political and economic troubles. It was this concentration of thought and action and effort that really, in the end, saved my scientific accuracy and search for truth. But first came a period of three years when I was casting about to find a way of applying science to the race problem. In these years I was torn with excitement of quick-moving events. Lynching, for instance, was still a continuing horror in the United States at the time of my entrance upon a teaching career. It reached a climax in 1892, when 235 persons were publicly murdered, and in the sixteen years of my teaching nearly two thousand persons were publicly killed by mobs, and not a single one of the murderers punished. The partition, domination and exploitation of Africa gradually centered my thought as part of my problem of race. I saw in Asia and the West Indies the results of race discrimination while right here in America came the wild foray of the exasperated Negro soldiers at Brownsville and the political-economic riot at Atlanta.

One happening in America linked in my mind the race problem with the general economic development and that was the speech of Booker T. Washington in Atlanta in 1895.[1] When many colored papers condemned the proposition of compromise with the white South, which Washington proposed, I wrote to the *New York Age* suggesting that here might be the basis of a real settlement between whites and blacks in the South, if the South opened to the Negroes the doors of economic opportunity and the Negroes co-operated with the white South in political sympathy. But this offer was frustrated by the fact that between 1895 and 1909 the whole South disfranchised its Negro voters by unfair and illegal restrictions and passed a series of "Jim Crow" laws which made the Negro citizen a subordinate caste.

As a possible offset to this came the endowment of the General Education Board and the Sage Foundation;[2] but they did not to my mind plan clearly to attack the Negro problem; the Sage Foundation ignored us, and the General Education Board in its first years gave its main attention to the education of whites and to black industrial schools. Finally the riot and lynching at Springfield, the birthplace of Abraham Lincoln, one hundred years after his birth, sounded a knell which in the end stopped my teaching career.[3] This, then, was the general setting when I returned to America for work.

Wilberforce was a small colored denominational college, married to a state normal school. The church was too poor to

---

[1] Director of Tuskegee Institute and the most powerful Negro leader of the day, Washington assured Southerners at the Atlanta Cotton States and International Exposition that Negroes would prefer economic opportunities and vocational training to political and social equality. The speech was to become known as "The Atlanta Compromise" [ED.].

[2] Between 1902 and 1909 John D. Rockefeller contributed $53,000,000 to a fund for the furtherance of education. The General Education Board, which administered the fund, aided institutions preparing teachers for Negro schools in the South. Similar provisions were made by the Russell Sage Foundation [ED.].

[3] In the summer of 1908 a race riot raged for two days in Springfield. Two Negroes were lynched and scores of Negro homes and shops were burned to the ground [ED.].

run the college; the State tolerated the normal school so as to keep Negroes out of other state schools. Consequently, there were enormous difficulties in both church and state politics. Into this situation I landed with the cane and gloves of my German student days; with my rather inflated ideas of what a "university" ought to be and with a terrible plainness of speech that was continually getting me into difficulty; when, for instance, the student leader of a prayer meeting into which I had wandered casually to look local religion over, suddenly and without warning announced that "Professor Du Bois would lead us in prayer," I simply answered, "No, he won't," and as a result nearly lost my job. It took a great deal of explaining to the board of bishops why a professor in Wilberforce should not be able at all times and sundry to address God in extemporaneous prayer. I was saved only by the fact that my coming to Wilberforce had been widely advertised and I was so willing to do endless work when the work seemed to me worth doing.

My program for the day at Wilberforce looked almost as long as a week's program now. I taught Latin, Greek, German, and English, and wanted to add sociology. I had charge of some of the most unpleasant duties of discipline and had outside work in investigation. But I met and made many friends: Charles Young,[4] not long graduated from West Point, was one; Charles Burroughs, a gifted reader, was a student in my classes; Paul Laurence Dunbar came over from Dayton and read to us. I had known his work but was astonished to find that he was a Negro. And not least, I met the slender, quiet, and dark-eyed girl who became Mrs. Du Bois in 1896. Her father was chef in the leading hotel of Cedar Rapids, Iowa, and her dead mother a native of Alsace.

We younger teachers had a hard team fight, and after a two years' struggle I knew I was whipped and that it was impossi-

---

[4] In 1917 Colonel Charles Young was the highest ranking Negro officer in the U.S. Army [ED.].

ble to stay at Wilberforce. It had a fine tradition, a strategic position, and a large constituency; but its religion was narrow dogma; its finances cramped; its policies too intertwined with intrigue and worse; and its future in grave doubt. When, therefore, a temporary appointment came from the University of Pennsylvania for one year as "assistant instructor" at $600, I accepted forthwith in the fall of 1896; that year Abyssinia overthrew Italy and England, suddenly seeing two black nations threatening her Cape to Cairo plans, threw her army back into the Sudan and re-captured Khartoum. The next year, the free silver controversy of Bryan and McKinley flamed.

The two years at Wilberforce was my uneasy apprenticeship, and with my advent into the University of Pennsylvania, I began a more clearly planned career which had an unusual measure of success, but was in the end pushed aside by forces which, if not entirely beyond my control, were yet of great weight.

The opportunity opened at the University of Pennsylvania seemed just what I wanted. I had offered to teach social science at Wilberforce outside of my overloaded program, but I was not allowed. My vision was becoming clearer. The Negro problem was in my mind a matter of systematic investigation and intelligent understanding. The world was thinking wrong about race, because it did not know. The ultimate evil was stupidity. The cure for it was knowledge based on scientific investigation. At the University of Pennsylvania I ignored the pitiful stipend. It made no difference to me that I was put down as an "assistant instructor" and even at that, that my name never actually got into the catalogue; it goes without saying that I did no instructing save once to pilot a pack of idiots through the Negro slums.

The fact was that the city of Philadelphia at that time had a theory; and that theory was that this great, rich, and famous municipality was going to the dogs because of the crime and venality of its Negro citizens, who lived largely centered in the slum at the lower end of the seventh ward. Philadelphia wanted to prove this by figures and I was the man to do it. Of this theory back of the plan, I neither knew nor cared. I saw only here a chance to study an historical group of black folk and to show exactly what their place was in the community.

I did it despite extraordinary difficulties both within and without the group. Whites said, Why study the obvious? Blacks said, Are we animals to be dissected and by an unknown Negro at that? Yet, I made a study of the Philadelphia Negro so thorough that it has withstood the criticism of forty years. It was as complete a scientific study and answer as could have then been given, with defective facts and statistics, one lone worker and little money. It revealed the Negro group as a symptom, not a cause; as a striving, palpitating group, and not an inert, sick body of crime; as a long historic development and not a transient occurrence.[5]

Of the methods of my research, I wrote:

"The best available methods of sociological research are at present so liable to inaccuracies that the careful student discloses the results of individual research with diffidence; he knows that they are liable to error from the seemingly ineradicable faults of the statistical method; to even greater error from the methods of general observation; and, above all, he must ever tremble lest some personal bias, some moral conviction or some unconscious trend of thought due to previous training, has to a degree distorted the picture in his view. Convictions on all great matters of human interest one must have to a greater or less degree, and they will enter to some extent into the most cold-blooded scientific research as a disturbing factor.

"Nevertheless, here are some social problems before us demanding careful study, questions awaiting satisfactory answers. We must study, we must investigate, we must attempt to solve;

---

[5] *The Philadelphia Negro* (Philadelphia: Publications of the University of Pennsylvania, 1899) [ED.].

and the utmost that the world can demand is, not lack of human interest and moral conviction, but rather the heart-quality of fairness, and an earnest desire for the truth despite its possible unpleasantness."

At the end of that study, I announced with a certain pride my plan of studying the complete Negro problem in the United States. I spoke at the forty-second meeting of the American Academy of Political and Social Sciences in Philadelphia, November 19, 1897, and my subject was "The Study of the Negro Problems." I began by asserting that in the development of sociological study there was at least one positive answer which years of research and speculation had been able to return, and that was: "The phenomena of society are worth the most careful and systematic study, and whether or not this study may eventually lead to a systematic body of knowledge deserving the name of science, it cannot in any case fail to give the world a mass of truth worth the knowing." I then defined and tried to follow the development of the Negro problem not as one problem, but "rather a plexus of social problems, some new, some old, some simple, some complex; and these problems have their one bond of unity in the fact that they group themselves about those Africans whom two centuries of slave-trading brought into the land."

I insisted on the necessity of carefully studying these problems and said: "The American Negro deserves study for the great end of advancing the cause of science in general. No such opportunity to watch and measure the history and development of a great race of men ever presented itself to the scholars of a modern nation. If they miss this opportunity—if they do the work in a slip-shod, unsystematic manner—if they dally with the truth to humor the whims of the day, they do far more than hurt the good name of the American people; they hurt the cause of scientific truth the world over, they voluntarily decrease human knowledge of a universe of which we are ignorant enough, and they degrade the high end of truth-seeking in a day when they need more and more to dwell upon its sanctity."

Finally I tried to lay down a plan for the study, postulating only: that the Negro "is a member of the human race, and as one who, in the light of history and experience, is capable to a degree of improvement and culture, is entitled to have his interests considered according to his numbers in all conclusions as to the common weal."

Dividing the prospective scientific study of the Negro into two parts: the social group and his peculiar social environment, I proposed to study the social group by historical investigation, statistical measurement, anthropological measurement and sociological interpretation. Particularly with regard to anthropology I said:

"That there are differences between the white and black races is certain, but just what those differences are is known to none with an approach to accuracy. Yet here in America is the most remarkable opportunity ever offered of studying these differences, of noting influences of climate and physical environment, and particularly of studying the effect of amalgamating two of the most diverse races in the world—another subject which rests under a cloud of ignorance."

In concluding, I said:

"It is to the credit of the University of Pennsylvania that she has been the first to recognize her duty in this respect and in so far as restricted means and opportunity allowed, has attempted to study the Negro problems in a single definite locality. This work needs to be extended to other groups, and carried out with larger system; and here it would seem is the opportunity of the Southern Negro college. We hear much of higher Negro education, and yet all candid people know there does not exist today in the center of Negro population a single first-class fully equipped institution, devoted to the higher education of Negroes; not more than three Negro institutions in the South deserve the name of 'college' at all; and yet what is a Negro college but a vast college settlement for the study of a particular set of peculiarly baffling problems? What more effective or suitable agency could be found in which to focus the scientific efforts of the great universities of the North and East, than an institution situated in the very heart of these social problems, and made the center of careful historical and statistical research? Without doubt the first effective step toward the solving of the Negro question will be the endowment of a Negro college which is not merely a teaching body, but a center of sociological research, in close connection and co-operation with Harvard, Columbia, Johns Hopkins, and the University of Pennsylvania.

"Finally the necessity must again be emphasized of keeping clearly before students the object of all science, amid the turmoil and intense feeling that clouds the discussion of a burning social question. We live in a day when in spite of the brilliant accomplishments of a remarkable century, there is current much flippant criticism of scientific work; when the truth-seeker is too often pictured as devoid of human sympathy, and careless of human ideals. We are still prone in spite of all our culture to sneer at the heroism of the laboratory while we cheer the swagger of the street broil. At such times true lovers of humanity can only hold higher the pure ideals of science, and continue to insist that if we would solve a problem we must study it, and there is but one coward on earth, and that is the coward that dare not know."

I had, at this time, already been approached by President Horace Bumstead of Atlanta University and asked to come there and take charge of the work in sociology, and of the new conferences which they were inaugurating on the Negro problem. With this program in mind, I eagerly accepted the invitation, although at the last moment there came a curious reminiscence of Wilberforce in a little hitch based on that old matter of extemporaneous public prayer. Dr. Bumstead and I compromised on my promise to use the Episcopal prayer book;

later I used to add certain prayers of my own composing. I am not sure that they were orthodox or reached heaven, but they certainly reached my audience.

Without thought or consultation I rather peremptorily changed the plans of the first two Atlanta Conferences.[6] They had been conceived as conferences limited to city problems, contrasting with the increasingly popular conferences on rural problems held at Tuskegee. But I was not thinking of mere conferences. I was thinking of a comprehensive plan for studying a human group and if I could have carried it out as completely as I conceived it, the American Negro would have contributed to the development of social science in this country an unforgettable body of work.

Annually our reports carried this statement of aims: "This study is a further carrying out of a plan of social study by means of recurring decennial inquiries into the same general set of human problems. The object of these studies is primarily scientific—a careful search for truth conducted as thoroughly, broadly, and honestly as the material resources and mental equipment at command will allow; but this is not our sole object; we wish not only to make the Truth clear but to present it in such shape as will encourage and help social reform. Our financial resources are unfortunately meager: Atlanta University is primarily a school and most of its funds and energy go to teaching. It is, however, also a seat of learning and as such it has endeavored to advance knowledge, particularly in matters of racial contact and development which seemed obviously its nearest field. In this work it has received unusual encouragement from the scientific world, and the published results of these studies are used in America, Europe, Asia, and Africa."

Social scientists were then still thinking in terms of theory

---

[6] Du Bois was the leading spirit behind the Atlanta University Conference on Negro Problems which met annually between 1896 and 1914. Its bulky reports were among the first sociological treatises on Southern life [ED.].

and vast and eternal laws, but I had a concrete group of living beings artificially set off by themselves and capable of almost laboratory experiment. I laid down an ambitious program for a hundred years of study. I proposed to take up annually in each decade the main aspects of the group life of Negroes with as thorough study and measurement as possible, and repeat the same program in the succeeding decade with additions, changes and better methods. In this way, I proposed gradually to broaden and intensify the study, sharpen the tools of investigation and perfect our methods of work, so that we would have an increasing body of scientifically ascertained fact, instead of the vague mass of the so-called Negro problems. And through this laboratory experiment I hoped to make the laws of social living clearer, surer, and more definite.

Some of this was accomplished, but of course only an approximation of the idea. For thirteen years we poured forth a series of studies; limited, incomplete, only partially conclusive, and yet so much better done than any other attempt of the sort in the nation that they gained attention throughout the world. We studied during the first decade Negro mortality, urbanization, the effort of Negroes for their own social betterment, Negroes in business, college-bred Negroes, the Negro common school, the Negro artisan, the Negro church, and Negro crime. We ended the decade by a general review of the methods and results of this ten year study and a bibliography of the Negro. Taking new breath in 1906 I planned a more logical division of subjects but was not able to carry it out quite as I wished, because of lack of funds. We took up health and physique of American Negroes, economic co-operation and the Negro American family. We made a second study of the efforts for social betterment, the college-bred Negro, the Negro common school, the Negro artisan, and added a study of morals and manners among Negroes instead of further study of the church. In all we published a total of 2,172 pages which formed a current encyclopaedia on the American Negro problems.

These studies with all their imperfections were widely distributed in the libraries of the world and used by scholars. It may be said without undue boasting that between 1896 and 1920 there was no study of the race problem in America made which did not depend in some degree upon the investigations made at Atlanta University; often they were widely quoted and commended.

It must be remembered that the significance of these studies lay not so much in what they were actually able to accomplish, as in the fact that at the time of their publication Atlanta University was the only institution in the world carrying on a systematic study of the Negro and his development, and putting the result in a form available for the scholars of the world.

In addition to the publications, we did something toward bringing together annually at Atlanta University persons and authorities interested in the problems of the South. Among these were Booker T. Washington, Frank Sanborn, Franz Boaz, Jane Addams and Walter Wilcox. We were asked from time to time to co-operate in current studies. I wrote a number of studies for the Bureau of Labor in Washington. I co-operated in the taking of the Twelfth Census and wrote one of the monographs. I not only published the Atlanta Conference reports, but wrote magazine articles in the *World's Work* and in the *Atlantic Monthly* where I joined in a symposium and one of my fellow contributors was Woodrow Wilson. At the same time I joined with the Negro leaders of Georgia in efforts to better local conditions; to stop discrimination in the distribution of school funds; to keep the legislature from making further discriminations in railway travel. I prepared an exhibit showing the condition of the Negro for the Paris Exposition which gained a Grand Prize. I became a member of the American Association for the Advancement of Science in 1900 and was made a fellow in 1904.

I testified before Congressional Commissions in Washington and appeared on the lecture platform with Walter Page, afterwards war ambassador to England; I did a considerable amount of lecturing throughout the United States. I had wide correspondence with men of prominence in America and Europe: Lyman Abbott of the *Outlook;* E. D. Morel, the English expert on Africa; Max Weber of Heidelberg; Professor Wilcox of Cornell; Bliss Perry of the *Atlantic Monthly;* Horace Traubel, the great protagonist for Walt Whitman; Charles Eliot Norton and Talcott Williams. I began to be regarded by many groups and audiences as having definite information on the Negro to which they might listen with profit.

At the very time when my studies were most successful, there cut across this plan which I had as a scientist, a red ray which could not be ignored. I remember when it first, as it were, startled me to my feet: a poor Negro in central Georgia, Sam Hose, had killed his landlord's wife. I wrote out a careful and reasoned statement concerning the evident facts and started down to the Atlanta *Constitution* office, carrying in my pocket a letter of introduction to Joel Chandler Harris. I did not get there. On the way news met me: Sam Hose had been lynched, and they said that his knuckles were on exhibition at a grocery store farther down on Mitchell Street, along which I was walking. I turned back to the University. I began to turn aside from my work. I did not meet Joel Chandler Harris[7] nor the editor of the *Constitution.*

Two considerations thereafter broke in upon my work and eventually disrupted it: first, one could not be a calm, cool, and detached scientist while Negroes were lynched, murdered and starved; and secondly, there was no such definite demand for scientific work of the sort that I was doing, as I had confidently assumed would be easily forthcoming. I regarded it as axiomatic that the world wanted to learn the truth and if the truth was sought with even approximate accuracy and painstaking

---

[7] Harris, the author of the widely read Uncle Remus stories, was then on the staff of the *Atlanta Constitution* [ED.].

devotion, the world would gladly support the effort. This was, of course, but a young man's idealism, not by any means false, but also never universally true. The work of the conference for thirteen years including my own salary and small office force did not average five thousand dollars a year. Probably with some effort and sacrifice Atlanta University might have continued to raise this amount if it had not been for the controversy with Booker T. Washington that arose in 1903 and increased in virulence until 1908.

There were, of course, other considerations which made Atlanta University vulnerable to attack at this time. The university from the beginning had taken a strong and unbending attitude toward Negro prejudice and discrimination; white teachers and black students ate together in the same dining room and lived in the same dormitories. The charter of the institution opened the doors of Atlanta University to any student who applied, of any race or color; and when the state in 1887 objected to the presence of a few white students, all children of teachers and professors, the institution gave up the small appropriation from the State rather than repudiate its principles. In fact, this appropriation represented not State funds, but the Negroes' share of the sum received from the Federal government for education. When later there came an attempt on the part of the Southern Education Board and afterwards of the General Education Board to form a working program between educated Negroes and forward-looking whites in the South, it gradually became an understood principle of action that colored teachers should be encouraged in colored schools; that the races in the schools should be separated socially; that colored schools should be chiefly industrial; and that every effort should be made to conciliate Southern white public opinion. Schools which were successfully carrying out this program could look for further help from organized philanthropy. Other schools, and this included Atlanta University, could not.

Even this would not necessarily have excluded Atlanta University from consideration at the hands of the philanthropists. The university had done and was doing excellent and thorough work. Even industrial training in the South was often in the hands of Atlanta graduates. Tuskegee had always been largely manned by graduates of Atlanta and some of the best school systems of the South were directed by persons trained at Atlanta University. The college department was recognized as perhaps the largest and best in the South at the time. But unfortunately, at this time, there came a controversy between myself and Booker Washington, which became more personal and bitter than I had ever dreamed and which necessarily dragged in the University.

It was no controversy of my seeking; quite the contrary. I was in my imagination a scientist, and neither a leader nor an agitator; I had nothing but the greatest admiration for Mr. Washington and Tuskegee, and I had applied at both Tuskegee and Hampton for work. If Mr. Washington's telegram had reached me before the Wilberforce bid, I should have doubtless gone to Tuskegee. Certainly I knew no less about mathematics than I did about Latin and Greek.

Since the controversy between myself and Mr. Washington has become historic, it deserves more careful statement than it has had hitherto, both as to the matters and the motives involved. There was first of all the ideological controversy. I believed in the higher education of a Talented Tenth who through their knowledge of modern culture could guide the American Negro into a higher civilization. I knew that without this the Negro would have to accept white leadership, and that such leadership could not always be trusted to guide this group into self-realization and to its highest cultural possibilities. Mr. Washington, on the other hand, believed that the Negro as an efficient worker could gain wealth and that eventually through his ownership of capital he would be able to achieve a recognized place in American culture and could then educate his childern as he might wish and develop his possibilities. For this reason he proposed to put the emphasis at present upon training in the skilled trades and encouragement in industry and common labor.

These two theories of Negro progress were not absolutely contradictory. I recognized the importance of the Negro gaining a foothold in trades and his encouragement in industry and common labor. Mr. Washington was not absolutely opposed to college training, and sent his own children to college. But he did minimize its importance, and discouraged the philanthropic support of higher education; while I openly and repeatedly criticized what seemed to me the poor work and small accomplishment of the Negro industrial school. Moreover, it was characteristic of the Washington statesmanship that whatever he or anybody believed or wanted must be subordinated to dominant public opinion and that opinion deferred to and cajoled until it allowed a deviation toward better ways. This is no new thing in the world, but it is always dangerous.

PART TWO

In the First War on Poverty

4.

Jane Addams Weighs the Burdens of the Poor

Progressives, especially social workers among them, resolved to ameliorate the conditions of the urban poor. Some patronized the inhabitants of the tenement districts, but others, managing to cross the traditional barriers of class and nationality, discovered that the poor had a culture and dignity of their own. In the following passage of her autobiography, Jane Addams describes the face of poverty as she grew to know it at her settlement house in Chicago.

But for her frail health, Jane Addams appears to have spent an idyllic youth in Cedarville, Illinois, where she was born in 1860. Her father, a prosperous miller, a friend of Lincoln, and, like him, a homespun philosopher, appears to have spent much time instructing his daughter. Walking through Cedarville's forests, they discussed such matters as inequality and predestination.

After graduating from Rockford Seminary, Jane Addams took two trips to Europe; during the second she visited London's Toynbee Hall, the first social settlement, where groups of university students lived and aided working people. On her return to Chicago, together with an old classmate, Ellen Gates Starr, she searched the city's tenement districts to find a suitable place for a settlement. In the former home of Charles J. Hull on South Halsted Street, she established a day nursery, a kindergarten, an employment bureau, and a discussion club. And there, in the winter of 1889, she opened her doors to the poor.

That neglected and forlorn old age is daily brought to the attention of a Settlement which undertakes to bear its share of the neighborhood burden imposed by poverty was pathetically clear to us during our first months of residence at Hull-House. One day a boy of ten led a tottering old lady into the House, saying that she had slept for six weeks in their kitchen on a bed made up next to the stove; that she had come when her son died, although none of them had ever seen her before; but because her son had "once worked in the same shop with Pa she thought of him when she had nowhere to go." The little fellow concluded by saying that our house was so much bigger than theirs that he thought we would have more room for beds. The old woman herself said absolutely nothing, but looking on with that gripping fear of the poorhouse in her eyes, she was a living embodiment of that dread which is so heartbreaking that the occupants of the County Infirmary themselves seem scarcely less wretched than those who are making their last stand against it.

This look was almost more than I could bear for only a few days before some frightened women had bidden me to come quickly to the house of an old German woman, whom two men from the county agent's office were attempting to remove to the County Infirmary. The poor old creature had thrown herself bodily upon a small and battered chest of drawers and clung there, clutching it so firmly that it would have been impossible to remove her without also taking the piece of furniture. She did not weep nor moan nor indeed make any human

---

From Jane Addams, *Twenty Years at Hull House* (New York: The Macmillan Company, 1910), chap. 8, "Problems of Poverty," pp. 118–132. Copyright 1910 by The Macmillan Company, 1938 by James W. Linn. Reprinted by permission of the publishers.

sound, but between her broken gasps for breath she squealed shrilly like a frightened animal caught in a trap. The little group of women and children gathered at her door stood aghast at this realization of the black dread which always clouds the lives of the very poor when work is slack, but which constantly grows more imminent and threatening as old age approaches. The neighborhood women and I hastened to make all sorts of promises as to the support of the old woman and the county officials, only too glad to be rid of their unhappy duty, left her to our ministrations. This dread of the poorhouse, the result of centuries of deterrent Poor Law administration, seemed to me not without some justification one summer when I found myself perpetually distressed by the unnecessary idleness and forlornness of the old women in the Cook County Infirmary, many of whom I had known in the years when activity was still a necessity, and when they felt bustlingly important. To take away from an old woman whose life has been spent in household cares all the foolish little belongings to which her affections cling and to which her very fingers have become accustomed is to take away her last incentive to activity, almost to life itself. To give an old woman only a chair and a bed, to leave her no cupboard in which her treasures may be stowed, not only that she may take them out when she desires occupation, but that her mind may dwell upon them in moments of revery, is to reduce living almost beyond the limit of human endurance.

The poor creature who clung so desperately to her chest of drawers was really clinging to the last remnant of normal living—a symbol of all she was asked to renounce. For several years after this summer I invited five or six old women to take a two weeks' vacation from the poorhouse which they eagerly and even gaily accepted. Almost all the old men in the County Infirmary wander away each summer taking their chances for finding food or shelter and return much refreshed by the little "tramp," but the old women cannot do this unless they have some help from the outside, and yet the expenditure of a very little money secures for them the coveted vacation. I found that a few pennies paid their carfare into town, a dollar a week procured lodging with an old acquaintance; assured of two good meals a day in the Hull-House coffeehouse they could count upon numerous cups of tea among old friends to whom they would airily state that they had "come out for a little change" and hadn't yet made up their minds about "going in again for the winter." They thus enjoyed a two weeks' vacation to the top of their bent and returned with wondrous tales of their adventures, with which they regaled the other paupers during the long winter.

The reminiscences of these old women, their shrewd comments upon life, their sense of having reached a point where they may at last speak freely with nothing to lose because of their frankness, makes them often the most delightful of companions. I recall one of my guests, the mother of many scattered children, whose one bright spot through all the dreary years had been the wedding feast of her son Mike—a feast which had become transformed through long meditation into the nectar and ambrosia of the very gods. As a farewell fling before she went "in" again, we dined together upon chicken pie, but it did not taste like "the chicken pie at Mike's wedding" and she was disappointed after all.

Even death itself sometimes fails to bring the dignity and serenity which one would fain associate with old age. I recall the dying hour of one old Scotchwoman whose long struggle to "keep respectable" had so embittered her that her last words were gibes and taunts for those who were trying to minister to her. "So you came in yourself this morning, did you? You only sent things yesterday. I guess you knew when the doctor was coming. Don't try to warm my feet with anything but that old jacket that I've got there; it belonged to my boy who was drowned at sea nigh thirty years ago, but it's warmer yet with human feelings than any of your damned charity hot-water bottles." Suddenly the harsh gasping voice was stilled in death and I awaited the doctor's coming shaken and horrified.

The lack of municipal regulation already referred to was, in the early days of Hull-House, paralleled by the inadequacy of the charitable efforts of the city and an unfounded optimism that there was no real poverty among us. Twenty years ago there was no Charity Organization Society in Chicago and the Visiting Nurse Association had not yet begun its beneficent work, while the relief societies, although conscientiously administered, were inadequate in extent and antiquated in method.

As social reformers gave themselves over to discussion of general principles, so the poor invariably accused poverty itself of their destruction. I recall a certain Mrs. Moran, who was returning one rainy day from the office of the county agent with her arms full of paper bags containing beans and flour which alone lay between her children and starvation. Although she had no money she boarded a street car in order to save her booty from complete destruction by the rain, and as the burst bags dropped "flour on the ladies' dresses" and "beans all over the place," she was sharply reprimanded by the conductor, who was further exasperated when he discovered she had no fare. He put her off, as she had hoped he would, almost in front of Hull-House. She related to us her state of mind as she stepped off the car and saw the last of her wares disappearing; she admitted she forgot the proprieties and "cursed a little," but, curiously enough, she pronounced her malediction, not against the rain nor the conductor, nor yet against the worthless husband who had been sent up to the city prison, but, true to the Chicago spirit of the moment, went to the root of the matter and roundly "cursed poverty."

This spirit of generalization and lack of organization among the charitable forces of the city was painfully revealed in that terrible winter after the World's Fair, when the general financial depression throughout the country was much intensified in

Chicago by the numbers of unemployed stranded at the close of the exposition. When the first cold weather came the police stations and the very corridors of the city hall were crowded by men who could afford no other lodging. They made huge demonstrations on the lake front, reminding one of the London gatherings in Trafalgar Square.

It was the winter in which Mr. Stead wrote his indictment of Chicago.[1] I can vividly recall his visits to Hull-House, some of them between eleven and twelve o'clock at night, when he would come in wet and hungry from an investigation of the levee district, and, while he was drinking hot chocolate before an open fire, would relate in one of his curious monologues, his experience as an out-of-doors laborer standing in line without an overcoat for two hours in the sleet, that he might have a chance to sweep the streets; or his adventures with a crook, who mistook him for one of his own kind and offered him a place as an agent for a gambling house, which he promptly accepted. Mr. Stead was much impressed with the mixed goodness in Chicago, the lack of rectitude in many high places, the simple kindness of the most wretched to each other. Before he published *If Christ Came to Chicago* he made his attempt to rally the diverse moral forces of the city in a huge mass meeting, which resulted in a temporary organization, later developing into the Civic Federation. I was a member of the committee of five appointed to carry out the suggestions made in this remarkable meeting, and our first concern was to appoint a committee to deal with the unemployed. But when has a committee ever dealt satisfactorily with the unemployed? Relief stations were opened in various parts of the city, temporary lodging houses were established. Hull-House undertaking to lodge the homeless women who could be received nowhere else; employment stations were opened giving sewing to the

---

[1] In the winter of 1893 William Thomas Stead, the English journalist and reformer, visited Chicago and rallied trade unions, churches, and philanthropists to combat the city's degradation [ED.].

women, and street sweeping for the men was organized. It was in connection with the latter that the perplexing question of the danger of permanently lowering wages at such a crisis, in the praiseworthy effort to bring speedy relief, was brought home to me. I insisted that it was better to have the men work half a day for seventy-five cents than a whole day for a dollar, better that they should earn three dollars in two days than in three days. I resigned from the street-cleaning committee in despair of making the rest of the committee understand that, as our real object was not street cleaning but the help of the unemployed, we must treat the situation in such wise that the men would not be worse off when they returned to their normal occupations. The discussion opened up situations new to me and carried me far afield in perhaps the most serious economic reading I have ever done.

A beginning also was then made toward a Bureau of Organized Charities, the main office being put in charge of a young man recently come from Boston, who lived at Hull-House. But to employ scientific methods for the first time at such a moment involved difficulties, and the most painful episode of the winter came for me from an attempt on my part to conform to carefully received instructions. A shipping clerk whom I had known for a long time had lost his place, as so many people had that year, and came to the relief station established at Hull-House four or five times to secure help for his family. I told him one day of the opportunity for work on the drainage canal and intimated that if any employment were obtainable, he ought to exhaust that possibility before asking for help. The man replied that he had always worked indoors and that he could not endure outside work in winter. I am grateful to remember that I was too uncertain to be severe, although I held to my instructions. He did not come again for relief, but worked for two days digging on the canal, where he contracted pneumonia and died a week later. I have never lost trace of the two little children he left behind him, although I cannot see them without a bitter consciousness that it was at their expense I learned that life cannot be administered by definite rules and regulations; that wisdom to deal with a man's difficulties comes only through some knowledge of his life and habits as a whole; and that to treat an isolated episode is almost sure to invite blundering.

It was also during this winter that I became permanently impressed with the kindness of the poor to each other; the woman who lives upstairs will willingly share her breakfast with the family below because she knows they "are hard up"; the man who boarded with them last winter will give a month's rent because he knows the father of the family is out of work; the baker across the street who is fast being pushed to the wall by his downtown competitors, will send across three loaves of stale bread because he has seen the children looking longingly into his window and suspects they are hungry. There are also the families who, during times of business depression, are obliged to seek help from the county or some benevolent society, but who are themselves most anxious not to be confounded with the pauper class, with whom indeed they do not in the least belong. Charles Booth,[2] in his brilliant chapter on the unemployed, expresses regret that the problems of the working class are so often confounded with the problems of the inefficient and the idle, that although working people live in the same street with those in need of charity, to thus confound two problems is to render the solution of both impossible.

I remember one family in which the father had been out of work for this same winter, most of the furniture had been pawned, and as the worn-out shoes could not be replaced the children could not go to school. The mother was ill and barely able to come for the supplies and medicines. Two years later she invited me to supper one Sunday evening in the little home which had been completely restored, and she gave as a reason

---

[2] Booth, pioneer English social investigator, wrote many volumes on the conditions of the poor in London [ED.].

for the invitation that she couldn't bear to have me remember them as they had been during that one winter, which she insisted, had been unique in her twelve years of married life. She said that it was as she had met me, not as I am ordinarily, but as I should appear misshapen with rheumatism or with a face distorted by neuralgic pain; that it was not fair to judge poor people that way. She perhaps unconsciously illustrated the difference between the relief-station relation to the poor and the Settlement relation to its neighbors, the latter wishing to know them through all the varying conditions of life, to stand by when they are in distress, but by no means to drop intercourse with them when normal prosperity has returned, enabling the relation to become more social and free from economic disturbance.

Possibly something of the same effort has to be made within the Settlement itself to keep its own sense of proportion in regard to the relation of the crowded city quarter to the rest of the country. It was in the spring following this terrible winter, during a journey to meet lecture engagements in California, that I found myself amazed at the large stretches of open country and prosperous towns through which we passed day by day, whose existence I had quite forgotten.

In the latter part of the summer of 1895, I served as a member on a commission appointed by the mayor of Chicago to investigate conditions in the county poorhouse, public attention having become centered on it through one of those distressing stories, which exaggerates the wrong in a public institution while at the same time it reveals conditions which need to be rectified. However necessary publicity is for securing reformed administration, however useful such exposures may be for political purposes, the whole is attended by such a waste of the most precious human emotions, by such a tearing of living tissue, that it can scarcely be endured. Everytime I entered Hull-House during the days of the investigation, I would find waiting for me from twenty to thirty people whose friends and relatives were in the suspected institution, all in such acute distress of mind that to see them was to look upon the victims of deliberate torture. In most cases my visitor would state that it seemed impossible to put their invalids in any other place, but if these stories were true, something must be done. Many of the patients were taken out only to be returned after a few days or weeks to meet the sullen hostility of their attendants and with their own attitude changed from confidence to timidity and alarm.

This piteous dependence of the poor upon the good will of public officials was made clear to us in an early experience with a peasant woman straight from the fields of Germany, whom we met during our first six months at Hull-House. Her four years in America had been spent in patiently carrying water up and down two flights of stairs, and in washing the heavy flannel suits of iron foundry workers. For this her pay had averaged thirty-five cents a day. Three of her daughters had fallen victims to the vice of the city. The mother was bewildered and distressed, but understood nothing. We were able to induce the betrayer of one daughter to marry her; the second, after a tedious lawsuit, supported his child; with the third we were able to do nothing. This woman is now living with her family in a little house seventeen miles from the city. She has made two payments on her land and is a lesson to all beholders as she pastures her cow up and down the railroad tracks and makes money from her ten acres. She did not need charity for she had an immense capacity for hard work, but she sadly needed the service of the State's attorney office, enforcing the laws designed for the protection of such girls as her daughters.

We early found ourselves spending many hours in efforts to secure support for deserted women, insurance for bewildered widows, damages for injured operators, furniture from the clutches of the installment store. The Settlement is valuable as an information and interpretation bureau. It constantly acts between the various institutions of the city and the people for whose benefit these institutions were erected. The hospitals, the county agencies, and State asylums are often but vague rumors to the people who need them most. Another function of the Settlement to its neighborhood resembles that of the big brother whose mere presence on the playground protects the little one from bullies.

We early learned to know the children of hard-driven mothers who went out to work all day, sometimes leaving the little things in the casual care of a neighbor, but often locking them into their tenement rooms. The first three crippled children we encountered in the neighborhood had all been injured while their mothers were at work: one had fallen out of a third-story window, another had been burned, and the third had a curved spine due to the fact that for three years he had been tied all day long to the leg of the kitchen table, only released at noon by his older brother who hastily ran in from a neighboring factory to share his lunch with him. When the hot weather came the restless children could not brook the confinement of the stuffy rooms, and, as it was not considered safe to leave the doors open because of sneak thieves, many of the children were locked out. During our first summer an increasing number of these poor little mites would wander into the cool hallway of Hull-House. We kept them there and fed them at noon, in return for which we were sometimes offered a hot penny which had been held in a tight little fist "ever since mother left this morning, to buy something to eat with." Out of kindergarten hours our little guests noisily enjoyed the hospitality of our bedrooms under the so-called care of any resident who volunteered to keep an eye on them, but later they were moved into a neighboring apartment under more systematic supervision.

Hull-House was thus committed to a day nursery which we sustained for sixteen years first in a little cottage on a side street and then in a building designed for its use called the Children's House. It is now carried on by the United Charities of Chicago in a finely equipped building on our block, where the immigrant mothers are cared for as well as the children, and where they are taught the things which will make life in America more possible. Our early day nursery brought us into natural relations with the poorest women of the neighborhood, many of whom were bearing the burden of dissolute and incompetent husbands in addition to the support of their children. Some of them presented an impressive manifestation of that miracle of affection which outlives abuse, neglect, and crime,—the affection which cannot be plucked from the heart where it has lived, although it may serve only to torture and torment. "Has your husband come back?" you inquire of Mrs. S., whom you have known for eight years as an overworked woman bringing her three delicate children every morning to the nursery; she is bent under the double burden of earning the money which supports them and giving them the tender care which alone keeps them alive. The oldest two children have at last gone to work, and Mrs. S. has allowed herself the luxury of staying at home two days a week. And now the worthless husband is back again—the "gentlemanly gambler" type who, through all vicissitudes, manages to present a white shirtfront and a gold watch to the world, but who is dissolute, idle and extravagant. You dread to think how much his presence will increase the drain upon the family exchequer, and you know that he stayed away until he was certain that the children were old enough to earn money for his luxuries. Mrs. S. does not pretend to take his return lightly, but she replies in all seriousness and simplicity, "You know my feeling for him has never changed. You may think me foolish, but I was always proud of his good looks and educated appearance. I was lonely and homesick during those eight years when the children were little and needed so much doctoring, but I could never bring myself to feel hard toward him, and I used to pray the good Lord to keep him from harm and bring him back to us; so, of course, I'm thankful now." She passes on with a dignity which gives one a new sense of the security of affection.

I recall a similar case of a woman who had supported her three children for five years, during which time her dissolute husband constantly demanded money for drink and kept her perpetually worried and intimidated. One Saturday, before the "blessed Easter," he came back from a long debauch, ragged and filthy, but in a state of lachrymose repentance. The poor wife received him as a returned prodigal, believed that his remorse would prove lasting, and felt sure that if she and the children went to church with him on Easter Sunday and he could be induced to take the pledge before the priest, all their troubles would be ended. After hours of vigorous effort and the expenditure of all her savings, he finally sat on the front doorstep the morning of Easter Sunday, bathed, shaved and arrayed in a fine new suit of clothes. She left him sitting there in the reluctant spring sunshine while she finished washing and dressing the children. When she finally opened the front door with the three shining children that they might all set forth together, the returned prodigal had disappeared, and was not seen again until midnight, when he came back in a glorious state of intoxication from the proceeds of his pawned clothes and clad once more in the dingiest attire. She took him in without comment, only to begin again the wretched cycle. There were of course instances of the criminal husband as well as of the merely vicious. I recall one woman who, during seven years, never missed a visiting day at the penitentiary when she might see her husband, and whose little children in the nursery proudly reported the messages from father with no notion that he was in disgrace, so absolutely did they reflect the gallant spirit of their mother.

While one was filled with admiration for these heroic women, something was also to be said for some of the husbands, for the sorry men who, for one reason or another, had failed in the struggle of life. Sometimes this failure was purely economic and the men were competent to give the children, whom they were not able to support, the care and guidance and even education which were of the highest value. Only a few months ago I met upon the street one of the early nursery mothers who for five years had been living in another part of the city, and in response to my query as to the welfare of her five children, she bitterly replied, "All of them except Mary have been arrested at one time or another, thank you." In reply to my remark that I thought her husband had always had such admirable control over them, she burst out, "That has been the whole trouble. I got tired taking care of him and didn't believe that his laziness was all due to his health, as he said, so I left him and said that I would support the children, but not him. From that minute the trouble with the four boys began. I never knew what they were doing, and after every sort of a scrape I finally put Jack and the twins into institutions where I pay for them. Joe has gone to work at last, but with a disgraceful record behind him. I tell you I ain't so sure that because a woman can make big money that she can be both father and mother to her children."

As I walked on, I could but wonder in which particular we are most stupid to judge a man's worth so solely by his wage-earning capacity that a good wife feels justified in leaving him, or in holding fast to that wretched delusion that a woman can both support and nurture her children.

One of the most piteous revelations of the futility of the latter attempt came to me through the mother of "Goosie," as the children for years called a little boy who, because he was brought to the nursery wrapped up in his mother's shawl, always had his hair filled with the down and small feathers from the feather brush factory where she worked. One March morning, Goosie's mother was hanging out the washing on a shed roof before she left for the factory. Five-year-old Goosie was trotting at her heels handing her clothespins, when he was suddenly blown off the roof by the high wind into the alley below. His neck was broken by the fall, and as he lay piteous and limp on a pile of frozen refuse, his mother cheerily called him to "climb up again," so confident do overworked mothers become that their children cannot get hurt. After the funeral, as the poor mother sat in the nursery postponing the moment when she must go back to her empty rooms, I asked her, in a futile effort to be of comfort, if there was anything more we could do for her. The overworked, sorrow-stricken woman looked up and replied, "If you could give me my wages for tomorrow, I would not go to work in the factory at all. I would like to stay at home all day and hold the baby. Goosie was always asking me to take him and I never had any time." This statement revealed the condition of many nursery mothers who are obliged to forego the joys and solaces which belong to even the most poverty-stricken. The long hours of factory labor necessary for earning the support of a child leave no time for the tender care and caressing which may enrich the life of the most piteous baby.

With all of the efforts made by modern society to nurture and educate the young, how stupid it is to permit the mothers of young children to spend themselves in the coarser work of the world! It is curiously inconsistent that with the emphasis which this generation has placed upon the mother and upon the prolongation of infancy, we constantly allow the waste of this most precious material. I cannot recall without indignation a recent experience. I was detained late one evening in an office building by a prolonged committee meeting of the Board of Education. As I came out at eleven o'clock, I met in the corridor of the fourteenth floor a woman whom I knew, on her knees scrubbing the marble tiling. As she straightened up to greet me, she seemed so wet from her feet up to her chin, that I hastily inquired the cause. Her reply was that she left home at five o'clock every night and had no opportunity for six hours to nurse her baby. Her mother's milk mingled with the very water with which she scrubbed the floors until she should return at midnight, heated and exhausted, to feed her screaming child with what remained within her breasts.

These are only a few of the problems connected with the lives of the poorest people with whom the residents in a Settlement are constantly brought in contact.

I cannot close this chapter without a reference to that gallant company of men and women among whom my acquaintance is so large, who are fairly indifferent to starvation itself because of their preoccupation with higher ends. Among them are visionaries and enthusiasts, unsuccessful artists, writers, and reformers. For many years at Hull-House, we knew a well-bred German woman who was completely absorbed in the experiment of expressing musical phrases and melodies by means of colors. Because she was small and deformed, she stowed herself into her trunk every night, where she slept on a canvas stretched hammock-wise from the four corners and her food was of the meagerest; nevertheless if a visitor left an offering upon her table, it was largely spent for apparatus or delicately colored silk floss, with which to pursue the fascinating experiment. Another sadly crippled old woman, the widow of a sea captain, although living almost exclusively upon malted milk tablets as affording a cheap form of prepared food, was always eager to talk of the beautiful illuminated manuscripts she had sought out in her travels and to show specimens of her own work as an illuminator. Still another of these impressive old women was an inveterate inventor. Although she had seen prosperous days in England, when we knew her, she subsisted largely upon the samples given away at the demonstration counters of the department stores, and on bits of food which she cooked on a coal shovel in the furnace of the apartment house whose basement back room she occupied. Although her inventions were not practicable, various experts to whom they were submitted always pronounced them suggestive and ingenious. I once saw her receive this complimentary verdict—"this ribbon to stick in her coat"—with such dignity and gravity that the words of condolence for her financial disappointment died upon my lips.

These indomitable souls are but three out of many whom I might instance to prove that those who are handicapped in the race for life's goods sometimes play a magnificent trick upon the jade, life herself, by ceasing to know whether or not they possess any of her tawdry goods and chattels.

5.

Margaret Sanger Takes Up the Fight for Birth Control

Margaret Sanger's father, Michael Hennessey Higgins, left Ireland to settle in Corning, New York, where, his daughter wrote, "he made his living chiseling angels and saints out of huge blocks of white marble or grey granite, for tombstones." In his spare time he was a philosopher and a rebel, an advocate of Henry George's theories and the first Socialist in his community.

Margaret attended local schools, trained as a nurse, and married William Sanger, an architect. Together they moved to New York City, where she was a visiting nurse and where their apartment became a gathering place for reformers of every kind. Her own custom was to take the opposite side of any debate, "right in a left crowd, and vice versa."

In the following passage she recalls how she came on her life's mission, teaching methods of birth control. This first practical assault both on a special agony of the tenement districts and on the theories of Malthus provided a singular chapter in the history of the reform years.

The passage ends with Mrs. Sanger's departure for Europe to study birth-control problems with Havelock Ellis and to visit contraceptive clinics on the Continent. On her return, in 1915, she was indicted for sending birth-control information through the mails, and in the following year she was arrested for conducting a contraceptive clinic in Brooklyn. Eventually she won support from the courts. In 1921 she organized the first American birth-control conference. In its wake her work and influence extended around the globe.

Early in the year 1912 I came to a sudden realization that my work as a nurse and my activities in social service were entirely palliative and consequently futile and useless to relieve the misery I saw all about me.

For several years I had had the good fortune to have the children's paternal grandmother living with us and sharing in their care, thereby releasing more of my time and renewed energy for the many activities and professional work of the nursing field. I had longed for this opportunity, and it now enabled me to share in the financial responsibility of the home, which, owing to the heavy expenditures caused by my illness, I felt was the only self-respecting thing to do. I eventually took special obstetrical and surgical cases assigned to me from time to time, and had glimpses into the lives of rich and poor alike.

When I look back upon that period it seems only a short time ago; yet in the brief interval conditions have changed enormously. At that time it was not the usual thing for a poor woman to go to a hospital to give birth to her baby. She preferred to stay at home. She was afraid of hospitals when any serious ailment was involved. That is not the case today. Women of all classes are more likely to have their babies in lying-in hospitals or in private sanatoriums than at home; but in those days a woman's own bedroom, no matter how inconveniently arranged, was the usual place for con-

---

From Margaret Sanger, *My Fight for Birth Control* (New York: Holt, Rinehart and Winston, Inc., 1931), chap. 3, "Awakening and Revolt," pp. 46–61. Copyright 1931 by Holt, Rinehart and Winston, Inc. Reprinted by permission of the author.

finement. That was the day of home nursing, and it gave a trained nurse splendid opportunities to learn social conditions through actual contact with them.

Were it possible for me to depict the revolting conditions existing in the homes of some of the women I attended in that one year, one would find it hard to believe. There was at that time, and doubtless is still today, a sub-stratum of men and women whose lives are absolutely untouched by social agencies.

The way they live is almost beyond belief. They hate and fear any prying into their homes or into their lives. They resent being talked to. The women slink in and out of their homes on their way to market like rats from their holes. The men beat their wives sometimes black and blue, but no one interferes. The children are cuffed, kicked and chased about, but woe to the child who dares to tell tales out of the home! Crime or drink is often the source of this secret aloofness; usually there is something to hide, a skeleton in the closet somewhere. The men are sullen, unskilled workers, picking up odd jobs now and then, unemployed usually, sauntering in and out of the house at all hours of the day and night.

The women keep apart from other women in the neighborhood. Often they are suspected of picking a pocket or "lifting" an article when occasion arises. Pregnancy is an almost chronic condition amongst them. I knew one woman who had given birth to eight children with no professional care whatever. The last one was born in the kitchen, witnessed by a son of ten years who, under his mother's direction, cleaned the bed, wrapped the placenta and soiled articles in paper, and threw them out of the window into the court below.

They reject help of any kind and want you to "mind your own business." Birth and death they consider their own affairs. They survive as best they can, suspicious of everyone, deathly afraid of police and officials of every kind.

They are the submerged, untouched classes which no labor

union, no church nor organization of a highly expensive, organized city ever reaches and rarely tries to reach. They are beyond the scope of organized charity or religion; not even the Salvation Army touches them. It was a sad consolation to hear other women in the stratum just slightly above breathe contented sighs and thank God that they had not sunk so low as that.

It is among the mothers here that the most difficult problems arise—the outcasts of society with theft, filth, perjury, cruelty, brutality, oozing from beneath.

Ignorance and neglect go on day by day; children born to breathe but a few hours and pass out of life; pregnant women toiling early and late to give food to four or five children, always hungry; boarders taken into homes where there is not sufficient room for the family; little girls eight and ten years of age sleeping in the same room with dirty, foul smelling, loathsome men; women whose weary, pregnant, shapeless bodies refuse to accommodate themselves to the husbands' desires find husbands looking with lustful eyes upon other women, sometimes upon their own little daughters, six and seven years of age.

In this atmosphere abortions and birth become the main theme of conversation. On Saturday nights I have seen groups of fifty to one hundred women going into questionable offices well known in the community for cheap abortions. I asked several women what took place there, and they all gave the same reply: a quick examination, a probe inserted into the uterus and turned a few times to disturb the fertilized ovum, and then the woman was sent home. Usually the flow began the next day and often continued four or five weeks. Sometimes an ambulance carried the victim to the hospital for a curetage, and if she returned home at all she was looked upon as a lucky woman.

This state of things became a nightmare with me. There seemed no sense to it all, no reason for such waste of mother life, no right to exhaust women's vitality and to throw them on the scrap-heap before the age of thirty-five.

Everywhere I looked, misery and fear stalked—men fearful of losing their jobs, women fearful that even worse conditions might come upon them. The menace of another pregnancy hung like a sword over the head of every poor woman I came in contact with that year. The question which met me was always the same: What can I do to keep from it? or, What can I do to get out of this? Sometimes they talked among themselves bitterly.

"It's the rich that know the tricks," they'd say, "while we have all the kids." Then, if the women were Roman Catholics, they talked about "Yankee tricks," and asked me if I knew what the Protestants did to keep their families down. When I said that I didn't believe that the rich knew much more than they did I was laughed at and suspected of holding back information for money. They would nudge each other and say something about paying me before I left the case if I would reveal the "secret."

It all sickened me. It was heartbreaking to witness the rapt, anxious, eager expression on their pale, worried faces as I told them necessary details concerning cleanliness and hygiene of their sex organs. It was appalling how little they knew of the terms I was using, yet how familiar they were with those organs and their functions and how unafraid to try anything, no matter what the results.

I heard over and over again of their desperate efforts at bringing themselves "around"—drinking various herb-teas, taking drops of turpentine on sugar, steaming over a chamber of boiling coffee or of turpentine water, rolling down stairs, and finally inserting slippery-elm sticks, or knitting needles, or shoe hooks into the uterus. I used to shudder with horror as I heard the details and, worse yet, learned of the conditions *behind the reason* for such desperate actions. Day after day these stories were poured into my ears. I knew hundreds of these women personally, and knew much of their hopeless, barren, dreary lives.

What relief I had came when I shifted my work for a few weeks to the then fashionable Riverside Drive or to the upper western section of New York City, but inevitably I was called back into the lower East or West Side as if magnetically attracted by its misery.

The contrast in conditions seemed only to intensify the horrors of those poverty-stricken homes, and each time I returned it was to hear that Mrs. Cohen had been carried to a hospital but had never come back, that Mrs. Kelly had sent the children to a neighbor's and had put her head into the gas oven to end her misery. Many of the women had consulted midwives, social workers and doctors at the dispensary and asked a way to limit their families, but they were denied this help, sometimes indignantly or gruffly, sometimes jokingly; but always knowledge was denied them. Life for them had but one choice: either to abandon themselves to incessant childbearing, or to terminate their pregnancies through abortions. Is it any wonder they resigned themselves hopelessly, as the Jewish and Italian mothers, or fell into drunkenness, as the Irish and Scotch? The latter were often beaten by husbands, as well as by their sons and daughters. They were driven and cowed, and only as beasts of burden were allowed to exist. Life for them was full of fear.

Words fail to express the impressions these lives made on my sensitive nature. My own happy love life became a reproach. These other lives began to clutch at all I held dear. The intimate knowledge of these misshapen, hapless, desperate women seemed to separate me from the right of happiness.

They claimed my thoughts night and day. One by one these women, with their worried, sad, pensive and ageing faces would marshal themselves before me in my dreams, sometimes appealingly, sometimes accusingly. I could not escape from the facts of their misery, neither was I able to see the way out of their problems and their troubles. Like one walking in a sleep, I kept on.

Finally the thing began to shape itself, to become accumulative during the three weeks I spent in the home of a desperately sick woman living on Grand Street, a lower section of New York's East Side.

Mrs. Sacks was only twenty-eight years old; her husband, an unskilled worker, thirty-two. Three children, aged five, three and one, were none too strong nor sturdy, and it took all the earnings of the father and the ingenuity of the mother to keep them clean, provide them with air and proper food, and give them a chance to grow into decent manhood and womanhood.

Both parents were devoted to these children and to each other. The woman had become pregnant and had taken various drugs and purgatives, as advised by her neighbors. Then, in desperation, she had used some instrument lent to her by a friend. She was found prostrate on the floor amidst the crying children when her husband returned from work. Neighbors advised against the ambulance, and a friendly doctor was called. The husband would not hear of her going to a hospital, and as a little money had been saved in the bank a nurse was called and the battle for that precious life began.

It was in the middle of July. The three-room apartment was turned into a hospital for the dying patient. Never had I worked so fast, never so concentratedly as I did to keep alive that little mother. Neighbor women came and went during the day doing the odds and ends necessary for our comfort. The children were sent to friends and relatives and the doctor and I settled ourselves to outdo the force and power of an outraged nature.

Never had I known such conditions could exist. July's sultry days and nights were melted into a torpid inferno. Day after day, night after night, I slept only in brief snatches, ever too anxious about the condition of that feeble heart bravely carrying on, to stay long from the bedside of the patient. With but one toilet for the building and that on the floor below, everything had to be carried down for disposal, while ice, food and other necessities had to be carried three flights up. It was one of those old airshaft buildings of which there were several thousands then standing in New York City.

At the end of two weeks recovery was in sight, and at the end of three weeks I was preparing to leave the fragile patient to take up the ordinary duties of her life, including those of wifehood and motherhood. Everyone was congratulating her on her recovery. All the kindness of sympathetic and understanding neighbors poured in upon her in the shape of convalescent dishes, soups, custards, and drinks. Still she appeared to be despondent and worried. She seemed to sit apart in her thoughts as if she had no part in these congratulatory messages and endearing welcomes. I thought at first that she still retained some of her unconscious memories and dwelt upon them in her silences.

But as the hour for my departure came nearer, her anxiety increased, and finally with trembling voice she said: "Another baby will finish me, I suppose."

"It's too early to talk about that," I said, and resolved that I would turn the question over to the doctor for his advice. When he came I said: "Mrs. Sacks is worried about having another baby."

"She well might be," replied the doctor, and then he stood before her and said: "Any more such capers, young woman, and there will be no need to call me."

"Yes, yes—I know, Doctor," said the patient with trembling voice, "but," and she hesitated as if it took all of her courage to say it, "*what* can I do to prevent getting that way again?"

"Oh ho!" laughed the doctor good naturedly, "You want your cake while you eat it too, do you? Well, it can't be done." Then, familiarly slapping her on the back and picking up his hat and bag to depart, he said: "I'll tell you the only sure thing to do. Tell Jake to sleep on the roof!"

With those words he closed the door and went down the stairs, leaving us both petrified and stunned.

Tears sprang to my eyes, and a lump came in my throat as I looked at that face before me. It was stamped with sheer horror. I thought for a moment she might have gone insane, but she conquered her feelings, whatever they may have been, and turning to me in desperation said: "He can't understand, can he?—he's a man after all—but you do, don't you? You're a woman and you'll tell me the secret and I'll never tell it to a soul."

She clasped her hands as if in prayer, she leaned over and looked straight into my eyes and beseechingly implored me to tell her something—something *I really did not know*. It was like being on a rack and tortured for a crime one had not committed. To plead guilty would stop the agony; otherwise the rack kept turning.

I had to turn away from that imploring face. I could not answer her then. I quieted her as best I could. She saw that I was moved by the tears in my eyes. I promised that I would come back in a few days and tell her what she wanted to know. The few simple means of limiting the family like *coitus interruptus* or the condom were laughed at by the neighboring women when told these were the means used by men in the well-to-do families. That was not believed, and I knew such an answer would be swept aside as useless were I to tell her this at such a time.

A little later when she slept I left the house, and made up my mind that I'd keep away from those cases in the future. I felt helpless to do anything at all. I seemed chained hand and foot, and longed for an earthquake or a volcano to shake the world out of its lethargy into facing these monstrous atrocities.

The intelligent reasoning of the young mother—how to *prevent* getting that way again—how sensible, how just she had been—yes, I promised myself I'd go back and have a long talk with her and tell her more, and perhaps she would not laugh but would believe that those methods were all that were really known.

But time flew past, and weeks rolled into months. That wistful, appealing face haunted me day and night. I could not banish from my mind memories of that trembling voice begging so humbly for knowledge she had a right to have. I was about to retire one night three months later when the telephone rang and an agitated man's voice begged me to come at once to help his wife who was sick again. It was the husband of Mrs. Sacks, and I intuitively knew before I left the telephone that it was almost useless to go.

I dreaded to face that woman. I was tempted to send someone else in my place. I longed for an accident on the subway, or on the street—anything to prevent my going into that home. But on I went just the same. I arrived a few minutes after the doctor, the same one who had given her such noble advice. The woman was dying. She was unconscious. She died within ten minutes after my arrival. It was the same result, the same story told a thousand times before—death from abortion. She had become pregnant, had used drugs, had then consulted a five-dollar professional abortionist, and death followed.

The doctor shook his head as he rose from listening for the heart beat. I knew she had already passed on; without a groan, a sigh or recognition of our belated presence she had gone into the Great Beyond as thousands of mothers go every year. I looked at that drawn face now stilled in death. I placed her thin hands across her breast and recalled how hard they had pleaded with me on that last memorable occasion of parting. The gentle woman, the devoted mother, the loving wife had passed on leaving behind her a frantic husband, helpless in his loneliness, bewildered in his helplessness as he paced up and down the room, hands clenching his head, moaning "My God! My God! My God!"

The Revolution came—but not as it has been pictured nor as history relates that revolutions have come. It came in my own life. It began in my very being as I walked home that night after I had closed the eyes and covered with a sheet the body of that little helpless mother whose life had been sacrificed to ignorance.

After I left that desolate house I walked and walked and walked; for hours and hours I kept on, bag in hand, thinking, regretting, dreading to stop; fearful of my conscience; dreading to face my own accusing soul. At three in the morning I arrived home still clutching a heavy load the weight of which I was quite unconscious.

I entered the house quietly, as was my custom, and looked out of the window down upon the dimly lighted, sleeping city. As I stood at the window and looked out, the miseries and problems of that sleeping city arose before me in a clear vision like a panorama; crowded homes, too many children; babies dying in infancy; mothers overworked; baby nurseries; children neglected and hungry—mothers so nervously wrought they could not give the little things the comfort nor care they needed; mothers half sick most of their lives—"always ailing, never failing"; women made into drudges; children working in cellars; children aged six and seven pushed into the labor market to help earn a living; another baby on the way; still another; yet another; a baby born dead—great relief, an older child dies—sorrow; but nevertheless relief—insurance helps; a mother's death—children scattered into institutions; the father, desperate, drunken; he slinks away to become an outcast in a society which has trapped him.

Another picture of the young couple full of hope with faith in themselves. They start life fresh. They are brave and courageous. The first baby is welcome; parents and relatives come from near and far to witness this mystery. The next year the second baby arrives; all agree it's a little early, but husband receives congratulations. The third child arrives, and yet a fourth. Within five years four children are born. The mother, racked and worn, decides this can't go on, and attempts to interrupt the next pregnancy. The siren of the ambulance—death of the mother—orphan children—poverty, misery, slums, child labor, unhappiness, ignorance, destitution!

One after another these pictures unreeled themselves before me. For hours I stood, motionless and tense, expecting something to happen. I watched the lights go out, I saw the darkness gradually give way to the first shimmer of dawn, and then a colorful sky heralded the rise of the sun. I knew a new day had come for me and a new world as well.

It was like an illumination. I could now see clearly the various social strata of our life; all its mass problems seemed to be centered around uncontrolled breeding. There was only one thing to be done: call out, start the alarm, set the heather on fire! Awaken the womanhood of America to free the motherhood of the world! I released from my almost paralyzed hand the nursing bag which unconsciously I had clutched, threw it across the room, tore the uniform from my body, flung it into a corner, and renounced all palliative work forever.

I would never go back again to nurse women's ailing bodies while their miseries were as vast as the stars. I was now finished with superficial cures, with doctors and nurses and social workers who were brought face to face with this overwhelming truth of women's needs and yet turned to pass on the other side. They must be made to see these facts. I resolved that women should have knowledge of contraception. They have every right to know about their own bodies. I would strike out—I would scream from the housetops. I would tell the world what was going on in the lives of these poor women. I *would* be heard. No matter what it should cost. *I would be heard.*

I went to bed and slept.

That decision gave me the first undisturbed sleep I had had in over a year. I slept soundly and free from dreams, free from haunting faces.

I announced to my family the following day that I had finished nursing, that I would never go on another case—and I never have.

I asked doctors what one could do and was told I'd better keep off that subject or Anthony Comstock[1] would get me. I was told that there were laws against that sort of thing. This was the reply from every medical man and woman I approached.

Then I consulted the "up and doing" progressive women who then called themselves Feminists. Most of them were shocked at the mention of abortion, while others were scarcely able to keep from laughing at the idea of my making a public campaign around the idea of too many children. "It can't be done," they said. "You are too sympathetic. You can't do a thing about it until we get the vote. Go home to your children and let things alone."

When I review the situation and see myself in the eyes of those who gave me such circumspect advice, I can see what they felt. I was considered a conservative person, bourgeoise from the radical point of view. I was not trained in the arts of the propagandist, I had no money with which to start a rousing campaign. I was not a trained writer nor speaker, never having lifted my voice in public above the throng. I had no social position. I had no influential friends. I was digging deep into an illegal subject, alone and unaided. It seemed to them that I was scheduled for Blackwell's Island or the penitentiary, and it looked as if I was determined to get there.

I spent my time reading in the vain hope that I would get

---

[1] Comstock, the founder (in 1873) of the New York Society for the Suppression of Vice, crusaded for the suppression of literature considered obscene [ED.].

the "secret" women were asking for. I read Havelock Ellis' then forbidden volumes of *Psychology of Sex* in one gulp, and had psychic indigestion for several months afterwards.

The following spring found me still seeking and more determined than ever to find out something about contraception and its mysteries. Why was it so difficult to obtain information on this subject? Where was it hidden? Why would no one discuss it? It was like the missing link in the evolution of medical science. It was like the lost trail in the journey toward freedom. Seek it I would. If it was in existence it should be found. I would never give up until I had obtained it, nor stop until the working women of my generation in the country of my birth were acquainted with its substance. I was so settled in this determination that I ceased to worry further about the details of how this should be brought about. I approached this problem in a manner characteristic of my makeup. I settled the principle first and left the details to work themselves out. In other words, I put some of the burden of this great task into the hands of the gods.

The effect of this conviction, however, began to have a tremendous bearing upon my personal life. My three lovely, healthy children were full of life, vigor and happiness. They were glorious examples of wanted children, mentally and physically. Gradually, however, there came over me the feeling and dread that the road to my goal was to separate me from their lives, from their development, growth and happiness. The feeling grew stronger and stronger within me, and this, together with my temporary psychic indigestion, led me to gather the three of them onto a Fall River boat one late afternoon in June and sail off to Provincetown, Massachusetts.

I tried to run away from life, from its turmoil and perplexities. I wanted the quiet of the sea, the loneliness of the dunes, to be alone with myself forever. I wanted to have the children solely to myself, too. I wanted to drive away that descending, foreboding barrier of separation by closer contact with them. I wanted to feed, to bathe, to clothe them myself. I wanted to bind them to me and allow nothing to force us apart. I clutched at them like a drowning woman in a raging current, as if to save myself from its swiftness.

In Provincetown I rented a small cottage on the beach far on the outskirts of the picturesque Cape Cod village, toward Truro. In 1913 Provincetown was not the busy resort of artists and art students it has become these summers, now that policemen are needed to control the incessant motor traffic.

We found ourselves among a congenial group of social rebels and writers: Mary Heaton Vorse, the social leader of this group, and her husband, Joseph O'Brien; Hutchins Hapgood and his charming wife, the novelist Neith Boyce; Charles Hawthorne, who had discovered Provincetown for his fellow artists and conducted a summer school there. It was not until 1914 that the hegira to Provincetown began; not until 1916 that the Provincetown Players were organized and gave the first production of a play by Eugene O'Neill on a dilapidated wharf belonging to Mary Heaton Vorse.

Our own cottage verandah faced the bay, and when the tide was high the children would sit on the steps and dip their toes into the water. When the tide was out we had two miles of beach for our front yard on which they skipped and ran. These days were filled with the joy of playing and romping with the children, away from the turmoil and from the ever pulling desire to be into the fight and battle of life. It was a wonderful place in which to forget the woes of the world.

The late William D. Haywood—"Big Bill," as he was affectionately called—was in Provincetown that summer.[2] He had been East advising the workers in Paterson who had been on

---

[2] Haywood, leader of the Western Federation of Miners and one of the organizers (1905) of the Industrial Workers of the World, was indicted in 1906 as an accessory to the murder of former Governor Steunenberg of Idaho. He was tried and acquitted in Boise, Idaho, not, as Mrs. Sanger recalls, in Butte, Montana [ED.].

strike in the silk mills. His health was failing, and the strain of work had put him on the verge of a nervous breakdown. Jessie Ashley, that aristocratic rebel gentlewoman, had carried "Bill" off for a much needed rest by the sea.

This picturesque hero of the Western Federation of Miners reminded me of the giant Polyphemus I had read about in the Odyssey as a child. One of his eyes had been destroyed in some violent mine explosion. This gave him the habit of turning his head slightly when he looked at you. He gave the impression of a bull ready to attack an adversary. In reality "Big Bill" was as gentle as a child. His frame was enormous; he was like a giant in stature. He had emerged from the celebrated Haywood-Moyer-Pettibone case in Butte, Montana, an intransigent rebel against the then existing conditions of the workers. Like his young friend, John Reed, poor Bill was destined years later to die the death of an exile in Soviet Russia.

But that summer in Provincetown our outlook was sanguine, and there was no shadow of disillusion on the horizon of our sky-blue hopes.

Bill came to see me often. We talked and read together day after day. He was a keen student of human nature, though like many American men he knew nothing of the finer sensibilities of woman's being. Still, I remember a remark of his one day as we walked along the beach. "Say girl," he said, "you're getting ready to kick over the traces!"

Then, taking my hand and pointing to the children, he added: "Don't do anything to spoil their happiness—will you?"

Despite the joy of those days I knew that I was only delaying the inevitable. It was no use. I could not forget the mothers bringing to birth children in poverty and misery. Even the fishermen's wives in Provincetown had the same dread, the same problems and fear of pregnancy as the workingmen's wives in the slums of New York. They were like a great army of untouchables. Their voices were never raised, their agonies were unrevealed, their hopelessness ignored by church and society. This, the greatest of problems, as untouched as if it did not exist.

I went back and forth to Boston during these months to study in the medical library, ever seeking the information which was to relieve women of the burden of unlimited childbearing.

At the end of six months I was convinced that there was no practical medical information on contraception available in America. I had visited the Library of Congress in Washington, I had pored over books in the library of the New York Academy of Medicine and in the Boston Public Library, to find only the information no more reliable than that already obtainable from "back fence gossip" in any small town. It was discouraging to contemplate, but I refused to accept defeat.

Since childhood I had always been interested in social and political questions and had looked thoroughly into Free Trade, Socialism of its various kinds and schools, Syndicalism, as well as the theories of the Industrial Workers of the World. While I had heard of Malthus and knew there was a Malthusian doctrine, I had associated it in my mind with overpopulation and economic pressure, and not with knowledge of contraception or any artificial means of family limitation.

I had previously cast my lot with the women of the Socialist movement. I listened intently to all debates, arguments and theories of this great school of liberal thought. Their ardent and passionate faith in legislation, however, I could never share. Their answer to the misery of women and the ignorance of contraceptive knowledge was like that of the Feminists: "Wait until we get the vote to put *us* in power!"

Wherever I turned, from every one I approached I met the same answer: "Wait!" "Wait until women get the vote." "Wait until the Socialists are in power." "Wait for the Social Revolution." "Wait for the Industrial Revolution." Thus I lost my faith in the social schemes and organizations of that day.

Only the boys of the I.W.W. seemed to grasp the economic

significance of this great social question. At once they visualized its importance, and instead of saying "Wait" they gave me names of organizers in the silk, woolen and copper industries, and offered their assistance to get any facts on family limitation I secured direct to the workingmen and their wives.

Again "Big Bill" Haywood came to my aid with that cheering encouragement of which I was so sorely in need. He never wasted words in advising me to "wait." I owe him a debt of gratitude which I am proud to acknowledge. It was he who suggested that I go to France and see for myself the conditions resulting from generations of family limitation. This idea, together with my interest in the social experiment then going on in Glasgow, convinced me that I was to find new ways to solve old problems in Europe. I decided to go and see.

6.

Rabbi Stephen Wise Sides with Labor

Stephen Wise was born in Budapest, Hungary, in 1874, the son and grandson of rabbis. In the next year his father migrated to New York, where, on East Fifth Street, Stephen grew up. He attended public schools, City College, and Columbia University, then returned to Vienna to be ordained.

Wise served as rabbi in New York City from 1893 to 1900, when he accepted a call to a congregation in Portland, Oregon. He had already won a reputation as a reformer, including among his enemies Tammany Hall's Boss Croker. In Portland he crusaded against gambling dens, Chinese restriction, and child labor. He helped to write Oregon's child-labor law, one of the first in the nation.

In 1905 he refused a call to Temple Emanuel in New York because in the course of his interview with the temple's trustees he was told that they controlled its pulpit. But he returned to New York in the following year and, holding services in the Hudson Theater, he announced his plans for a free synagogue. The Free Synagogue was established in 1906 and attached to it was a social service division. It remained Stephen Wise's rabbinate until his death in 1949.

Wise was an ardent Republican until 1912, when he supported Woodrow Wilson. He became Wilson's close friend and advisor on

Jewish affairs. A leader of American Zionism, Wise went to Versailles in 1919 to press for the establishment of a Jewish state.

In the following selection he describes the evolution of one of the central concerns of his life, the rights of labor to collective bargaining. In the strength of his convictions on this subject he was almost unique among progressives.

My first contact with labor conditions and labor problems came as early as 1895. A street-car strike took place in Brooklyn, and some strikers were killed. The strike arose over questions of wages and hours. The following Sabbath morning in the course of my sermon I spoke on the evil of shooting down strikers who sought nothing more than the right to live decently and humanly. After the service I noticed a little group of officers of the congregation in excited conversation. The treasurer of the synagogue, a member of a banking and investment firm, approached me asking, "What do you know about conditions in that street-car strike in Brooklyn?" I answered that I had informed myself as well as I could with regard to living conditions of the strikers. "They are grievously overworked and underpaid." He grumbled and muttered inarticulately, and I seized on a moment's pause to say, "I shall continue to speak for the workers whenever I come to feel that they have a real grievance and a just cause."

I had no formal contacts with labor organizations in those days. But a little later in Oregon I was one of a small group, including Dr. Thomas L. Eliot, Thomas N. Strong, and Millie Trumbull, which, knowing of child-labor conditions in the fish canneries of Astoria and the Columbia River fisheries, brought about the introduction and ultimately the legislative

---

From Stephen S. Wise, *The Challenging Years* (New York: G. P. Putnam and Sons, 1949), chap. 4, "A Rabbi Sides with Labor," pp. 56–74. Copyright 1949 by G. P. Putnam and Sons. Reprinted by permission of the publishers.

adoption of a child-labor law. This created a State Child Labor Commission of which I became a member by gubernatorial appointment, serving on it until 1906 when I returned to New York.

What we struggled to achieve for children in those days now seems so pitiable that one can only wonder at the anger and opposition we met. Even after we secured the law and the State Child Labor Commission was appointed by the Governor, enforcement was extremely difficult. But the methods used to defeat enforcement were not altogether different from some of the methods now used to defeat the purposes of such new legislation as our state laws against discrimination in employment.

One intervention of mine in a strike difficulty proved to be serious and availing. The Los Angeles *Times-Herald* had long been a "hot spot" in the field of industrial relations. The *Times-Herald* building was wrecked in a dynamite explosion. Feeling ran very high in 1911–1912 against organized labor, on whom the burden of the violence of the McNamaras was placed.[1] It was easy to whip up hysteria not only against the men involved in the dynamiting, but also against the labor movement and against those few friends who sought to explain why such violence was the inevitable result of the social conditions of that time and the treatment of workers who insisted on their right to organize and to be heard. In an address at Carnegie Hall at that time, I pointed out:

> As long as labor organizations are denied a hearing save just before election seasons; as long as they are treated with scorn and contumely; as long as they are cast out and denied, it is not to be wondered at that the leaders, finding themselves and their

---

[1] J. J. McNamara, secretary-treasurer of the International Association of Bridge and Structural Workers (AFL), and his brother, J. B. McNamara, confessed to the dynamiting [ED.].

organizations outlawed, should in turn be guilty of outlawry; that being cast out, they should resort to the weapon of the outcast; that being denied a hearing after the manner of orderly and reasoning friends, they should make themselves heard after the manner of destructive and unreasoning foes.

At about the same time, John Haynes Holmes[2] delivered an address in which he said:

> I would rather be in the McNamara cell than in the office of the President of the Steel Trust. . . . I say that there is more peril to America in the criminal corporation, than in the criminal laborer, and I say this also, that if I had to make my choice between being leader of the corporations or being sent to the dungeons of San Quentin, I would choose the latter.

Because of these addresses, Holmes and I were described as "the McNamaras of the pulpit" by *American Industries*. This journal of the manufacturers also published a delightful cartoon in which Dr. Holmes and I were depicted as the Dr. Jekyll and Mr. Hyde of organized labor. I was so outraged by this designation, which described Holmes and myself as two men guilty of violence and murder, or inciting to it, that I even questioned whether I should not bring a libel action and consulted my good friend, Benjamin Cardozo, who was then practicing law in New York City. He wrote in answer to my question:

> I think that the heading of the article, 'McNamaras of the Pulpit,' is a libel. I think that the statement that you have condoned or defended violence or assassination is also a libel.

His further advice was that

> Civil actions [in libel matters] are not expedient where the subject of the libel is criticism of the public utterance of a man

---

[2] Holmes, minister of the Unitarian Community Church in New York, was a founder of the National Association for the Advancement of Colored People and of the American Civil Liberties Union [ED.].

> occupying a public or quasi-public position, except in those cases where resort to the law becomes a real duty in order to vindicate a deep and not merely nominal injury to one's character and reputation. Here . . . the wrong consisted not in imputing a disgraceful act, but in an unjust—a cruel and unjust—interpretation of the meaning of your words, which, however, were quoted so that the injustice was manifest to anyone who took the trouble to read the article through.

I followed this advice not only at that time but always thereafter, feeling that my own actions and my own words must at all times speak for themselves. In this decision Holmes joined me in characteristic fashion:

> I had been filled more with amazement and disgust than anything approaching anger. I fear that I have become so used to being called names during the past few weeks that I have become callous to assaults of this nature.

It occurred to me that this labor war, as evidenced in the McNamara case, called for an impartial federal investigation. I discussed the matter with the editor of *The Survey*, Paul U. Kellogg, and subsequently with Florence Kelley, Lillian Wald, and Samuel McCune Lindsay. We called a meeting of a group, including those named and Jane Addams, and we resolved to unite in a request to the President to name a Commission on Industrial Relations. After some months of united effort to secure the appointment of such a commission under the chairmanship of Samuel McCune Lindsay[3] and with special public-relations assistance from that uniquely valuable organ of the common welfare, *The Survey*, President Taft agreed to name a commission.

Although we had high hopes, we learned to our dismay that President Taft submitted to the Senate for approval a group of names who, in the words of one of our committee members,

---

[3] Lindsay, Professor of Sociology at Columbia University, was an authority on labor law [ED.].

"consisted of appointees largely unknown; commission lacks weight; money wasted; better none." We, therefore, had to undertake a vigorous protest to the Senate to defeat the confirmation of the commission as proposed. We urged that a commission be appointed which could, in the eyes of the public, command such respect as would meet the needs stated by President Taft himself in recommending the creation of the commission. He had said: "The time is ripe for searching inquiry into the subject of industrial relations, which shall be official, authoritative, balanced and well-rounded."

In the light of this need and this promise, we could not accept a commission that included no well-known economist or social workers or adequate representatives of the public. Happily, after President Wilson took office, the work of the commission was strengthened by the appointment of Frank Walsh[4] of Kansas City as chairman, in September, 1913. The commission studied the problem over a period of months and under the excellent and resourceful leadership of Walsh made a constructive and significant report to the President. In a sense it was the first formal attempt of the government to concern itself with facts and threats in the field of industrial relations.

In 1911 I was invited to speak—for the first and last time—at the annual banquet of the New York Chamber of Commerce. I welcomed the invitation because it gave me the opportunity to face some of America's greatest captains of industry and finance. Present that night among others were Andrew Carnegie, James J. Hill, J. P. Morgan, Charles Schwab, George Baker.

I knew that this was a critical occasion, not for the Chamber of Commerce but for me. I could ingratiate myself with this

---

[4] A trial lawyer by profession, Walsh had gained a national reputation as the scourge of Kansas City's political bosses [ED.].

august assembly and lose my soul; I could displease them and keep it. Suffice it to say that when I sat down the only comfortable man in the room was Admiral Peary—seasoned to subarctic temperatures!

> Mr. President and Gentlemen of the Chamber of Commerce—I must say to you tonight that which I have said about you upon many other occasions—flattering you with that frank truth-speaking than which I could offer you no sincerer tribute.
>
> When I have read from time to time of religious noonday meetings held in shops and factories for the wage-earners, I have ventured to observe that the important thing is not so much to bring religious ministration to the daily toilers,—the soldiers of the common good,—as to bring it to the captains of industry and commerce, which you are. For the conscience of the nation, after all, will be that which you make it,—yours is the high and solemn duty not only of registering, but in large part of determining the character of the conscience of the nation. . . .
>
> Not only ought the barter or trade side of business be completely moralized, but we need to ethicize what might be called the processes of creating and production, of distribution and consumption. No business order is just nor can it long endure if it be bound up with the evil of unemployment on the one hand and over-employment on the other, the evil of a man's underwage and a child's toil, and all those social maladjustments incidental to our order which we lump together under the name of poverty. Let us not imagine that we can shift to the shoulders of over-worked charity the burdens that can be borne only by the strength of underworked justice. Yes, the stricken ask not the occasional tonic of charity, but the daily meat and substance of justice. We are never to forget that ours is a democracy, that a democracy, in the words of a high servant of the commonwealth means "the use of all the resources of nature by all the faculties of man for the good of all the people. . ."
>
> The conscience of the nation is not real unless the nation safeguard the workingman, safeguard him from the peril of overwork, as well as from the occasional accidents of industry. The conscience of the nation is not vital unless we protect women and

children in industry, and protect them with half the thoroughness and generosity with which, for many decades, we have protected infant industries. We have not the right to speak of the importance of conserving the opportunity for initiative on the part of the individual as long as masses of individuals are suffered to perish without the opportunity of real life. The aim of democracy is not to be the production of efficient, machine-like men in industry. The first business of democracy is to be the industry of turning out completely effective, because completely free and self-determining, citizens.

It was about this same time or a few months earlier that the terrible fire, commonly known as the Triangle Fire, occurred in a factory in New York City. Many girls were burned to death because the doors had been locked so that no goods would be removed by any of the employees, and when the fire broke out they were unable to escape. The hideous tragedy led a few of us to seek to arouse the community to face the necessity of demanding that there be legislation to protect workers against such catastrophes. We therefore called a citizens' committee meeting at the Metropolitan Opera House on Sunday, April 22, 1911, at which I said:

This ought to be a fast day of the citizens of New York, our day of guilt and humiliation. Let it not become a day of unavailing regret, but let it be a day of availing contriteness and redeeming penitence.

It is not the action of God, but the inaction of man that is responsible. I see in this disaster not the deed of God, but the greed of man. For law is divine, and this disaster was brought about by lawlessness and inhumanity. Certain calamities man can do no more than vainly deplore—such calamities as the San Francisco earthquake and the destruction by volcano of Martinique. But this was not an inevitable disaster which man could neither foresee nor control. We might have foreseen it, and some of us did; we might have controlled it, but we chose not to do so. The things that are inevitable we can do no more than vainly regret, but the things that are avoidable we can effectively forestall and prevent.

It is not a question of enforcement of law nor of inadequacy of law. We have the wrong kind of laws and the wrong kind of enforcement. Before insisting upon inspection and enforcement, let us lift up the industrial standards so as to make conditions worth inspecting, and, if inspected, certain to afford security to the workers. Instead of unanimity in the shirking of responsibility, we demand that departments shall cooperate in planning ahead and working for the future, with some measure of prevision and wisdom. And when we go before the Legislature of the State, and demand increased appropriations in order to ensure the possibility of a sufficient number of inspectors, we will not forever be put off with the answer: We have no money.

This meeting is not summoned in order to appeal for charity on behalf of the families of the slain. What is needed is the redress of justice and the remedy of prevention. The families of the victims ought to be beyond the reach of the need of charity. Having denied them the justice of physical security, we ought at least be willing to give their survivors the justice of economic redress. They need justice, not charity. It is we who need charity, for dare we face inexorable justice? . . .

We know that we cannot and should not take away property without due process of law. Neither may we take away life with or without due process of law. Alas, for another one of a multitude of proofs that we regard property as sacred, and are ready to suffer a violation of the rights of life as if these were not sacred but violable, and violable with impunity.

This consuming fire will have been nothing more than a flash in the pan if other evils are suffered to go unchecked and uncorrected—evils not less terrible because less swift and less sudden. It is just as necessary to protect women workers from the industrial and occupational diseases as it is to protect them from industrial accidents. We need to provide not only for security from accidents but security from the incidents of the industrial regime. I would have women workers safeguarded in every way, —safeguarded from the economically, physically, morally and spiritually disastrous consequences of over-work and under-pay and under-nourishment and insanitary housing, which seem to be the inevitable accompaniments of things as they are today. . . .

If the church and the synagogue were forces of righteousness in the world instead of being the farces of respectability and convention, this thing need not have been. If it be the shame and humiliation of the whole community, it is doubly the humiliation of the synagogue and of the church which have suffered it to come to pass. We may not be ready to prescribe a legislative program nor devise an industrial panacea, but we must demand and demand unceasingly an ever-increasing measure of social equity and social justice.

The hour has come for industrial peace. It must be peace with honor,—say some. But it must be more than peace with honor. It must be peace with security as well. We would have no peace with honor for some, and, at the same time, deny security to all. The issue at stake is not the open shop but the closed door, which shuts out the toilers from safety and justice.

The lesson of the hour is that while property is good, life is better, that while possessions are valuable, life is priceless. The meaning of the hour is that the life of the lowliest worker in the nation is sacred and inviolable, and, if that sacred human right be violated, we shall stand adjudged and condemned before the tribunal of God and of history.

As a result of the response of the community and the very hard work of some young citizens who were deeply moved by this disaster, including Abram I. Elkus, Belle Moskowitz, Frances Perkins, and a young man later to become known as "Al" Smith, we organized a permanent group and began the battle for adequate safety legislation for factory workers.

In 1912, I found myself engaged in what was a new kind of work for me, which helped me to understand more intimately the conditions of workers at that time. As a result of a lockout in some textile mills in Pennsylvania, it was agreed by the employer and employees that I should hear both sides and seek to mediate the dispute. As I go over the notes of my first mediation case in 1912, I find the following list of salaries:

winders	$4.75
doublers	4.75
reelers	4.25
lacers	4.25
1st-time spinners	4.75
2nd-time spinners	6.00
bobbin boys	4.50
openers	4.75
shakers	4.75
learners	3.00 to start

They were not daily but *weekly* wages. It was through this experience that I became intimately aware of the conditions in our textile mills. I found that a large proportion of the employees were children, that the actual wages were averaging two and three dollars a week, and that the forelady was receiving six dollars a week for fifty-eight hours of work. Serious complaints were submitted by the workers that the superintendent cursed and even struck some of the women and children. At that time the situation of one child was brought before me, which I shall never forget. This boy at first attempted to work in the mines, where he had earned $1.10 a day, but had been forced to leave because of the legislation against children working in the mines, only to be forced to work in a textile factory for many hours for fifteen cents a day. The strike had been brought to a head, and the employees had demanded one dollar a day. At this point, the employer told them to pack up and leave. Even my most earnest effort to secure the most limited improvement of these conditions failed, because the employer would concede practically nothing, and it was only after a strike that certain concessions were forced upon him.

Throughout this experience, I was struck by the degrading conditions of the workers, including small children, their inability to win even the most modest wages, which were not sufficient to buy the merest necessities of life. I was also deeply challenged by a letter that had been addressed to the employer from a board of trade in a neighboring community, which suggested the employer move to its town so as to avoid labor troubles. That letter stated, and I quote:

> We have made a canvass of the town and find there are ninety girls over fourteen years of age who would be willing to work in a properly conducted silk mill and they are of a class above the ordinary, in which the spirit of labor unions do not prevail.

It had become increasingly clear to me from my work on behalf of children in Oregon, from the conditions that preceded the acts of violence of the McNamara brothers, from my intimate contact with the workers in the silk mills, and from the attitude of employers and boards of trade that no basic change could be made in the life of workers until they had won the right to organize and bargain collectively. I had seen during the years the development of the corporate control of industry, with its substitution of directors representing scattered, absentee shareholders for the personal employer of bygone days. I had come to realize fully that confronted with an organization on the side of the employer, like the then billion-dollar steel trust, the individual worker was indeed helpless. I had seen that legislation forbidding employers to discharge employees on the ground of their membership in labor unions had been repeatedly held unconstitutional by the courts and that, unless America expressed itself through support of labor's struggle to organize, we would have increasing violence as well as the continuation of intolerable industrial conditions.

It was, therefore, inevitable that in October, 1919, I felt impelled to face the obligation to speak out concerning the smear campaign then developing in our country against workers who sought the right to organize. The chief objective of the assault by the employers was the organization of the workers. The employers by and large felt that if these could be broken down "inordinate claims" would no longer be made by the workers. Their share in war profits seemed incredibly irksome to many masters of industry. Nowhere was this more true than in the steel industry, where, as I recall it, more than half of the employees of the United States Steel Corporation were still working twelve hours a day and where the employers had resorted to the use of the black list and the labor spy as weapons in their industrial war upon their own workers. Not satisfied with this, they had also employed secret-service agencies to instigate civil war among workers. One circular at that time, addressed by an agency to one of its operatives, reveals these methods:

> We want you to stir up as much bad faith as you possibly can between the Serbians and the Italians. Spread data among the Serbians that the Italians are going back to work. Call up every question you can in reference to racial hatred between these two nationalities.

I came to see that as between Judge Gary and Samuel Gompers there had arisen an ethical, social issue of deepest concern to the whole American people. At that time, too, there were heard the first, shall we say, grumblings or mumblings about the endangering Bolsheviki. I felt the absurdity of lightly and naïvely using the word Bolsheviks as a term of reproach and scorn for anything or any person unapproved. If there were groups in American life guilty of repression and suppression, it was such a group as the United States Steel Corporation under the leadership of Judge Gary. It was not the workers demanding their right through organization to share in the American way of life but the heads of the United States Steel Corporation who, through rejection of unionism among the workers, sought permanently to deny them that basic and inalienable right.

On June 18, 1919, I therefore wrote to Samuel Gompers and told him that I learned with great pleasure that the American Federation of Labor, under his direction, would attempt to organize the steel workers, and that I wanted him to know that if I could be of any help, I was at his command. I was naïve enough to add in that letter:

> Surely the heads of the steel industry will not be idiotic enough to attempt to withstand the organization of their workers. I cannot believe, despite their record, that they will be so Bourbonish.

I was wrong and in the following strike months every form of violence and economic pressure was used by the steel industry against the workers who were on strike. As I followed the strike during the summer months—the violence practiced against women and children, the denial of the right to meet, the corruption of local public officials, and the indifference for the most part of Church and press alike—I felt that I must speak out. I therefore announced that the subject of my first sermon before the Free Synagogue, at Carnegie Hall, after the High Holy Days, would be: "Who Are the Bolshevists at Home and Abroad—How Shall We Know Them?"

Before going to Carnegie Hall that Sunday morning, I said to my wife, "My sermon of this morning will light a million-dollar blaze." As she smiled incredulously, I explained that the synagogue building, for which we had gathered large sums and which was to cost more than a million dollars, would not be built because of the cancellation of large gifts sure to follow upon my sermon. It all happened as I predicted—only more so!

In opening my address, I reminded my congregation that I knew that some of the members might refuse to lend their help in the building of the synagogue home as a result of what I was about to say but also again made clear that, while it might not be necessary for them to build a synagogue, it was necessary for me to speak the truth as I saw the truth on great issues. I then turned to the subject of the steel workers in America.

The war ends, the war was ended and it was won just as much by the workers in the steel-mills of Pennsylvania and Ohio as by the American soldiers in France. And now immediately after the war, partially because of the feeling of reaction that follows upon the moral stimulus of a great undertaking such as the war, the heads of industry—and I think it is true of the heads of a great number of industries in America—have set out to reverse Government sanctioned, in any event, Government recognized standards and to undo the work of the war as far as the gains to the workers are concerned.

The men in the iron and steel industry are striving for a fundamental right of industry, at least so I conceive it;—the right to organize and to deal organizedly with their employers. I don't like the term, "collective bargaining," because it is misunderstood. I use simpler English, the right of the workers to organize and organizedly and unitedly to deal with their employers.

Now, to urge, as it is urged and all the time urged, that Unionism makes for abuses is to state the veriest commonplace. But has it ever occurred to you that terrorism and outlawry do not breed nice manners?

For fifteen years the men in the steel industry worked twelve hours in the day, seven days in the week, and I would ask someone among you to be good enough to point to anything that Judge Gary and his gallant associate defenders of the liberty of the workers said during those fifteen years with regard to the freedom of men during all that time. Things would still be as they were up to five years ago in the steel industry if Judge Gary and his associates could have averted the pressure of public judgment, of public wrath and of public contempt. The Steel Corporation granted nothing voluntarily nor will it ever.

As for the so-called freedom of the workers, which Judge Gary considers so sacred a theme that he would not discuss it with the United States Senate, how can the judgment and the will of the workers be ascertained? They have never been free to organize. Mr. Gary and his associates,—in profound and American solicitude for the rights of the majority, tell us that a minority controls a majority. Well, the fact is that a minority always leads, precedes, and liberates a majority. Moreover, some fifteen or twenty-one men, who meet in Hoboken annually, talk about maintaining the freedom of the majority, and at the same time that they are fooling you and deluding the nation, refuse to meet in conference with the representatives of a great number of workers.

I charge Mr. Gary with having made it impossible for me as an American citizen to know what the thought and what the will of the workers in the steel industry is. They never have been free to utter themselves. They are not free today.

I charge the United States Steel Corporation with resorting to every manner of coercion and even of violence. If I am stating that which is untrue, if I am libelling the heads of the Steel Corporation, they have the power of redress. I am a responsible person and can be found at any time. I charge Judge Gary and the men associated with him with resorting to every manner of coercion, intimidation, and violence . . . in order to avoid the organization of the workers.

The press reported the address rather fully. Letters of approval from men whom I deeply respected, and letters of violent disapproval came together. I was advised that a previous invitation to Pittsburgh would not be cancelled, but that I should know that in view of my remarks on the steel strike, the rabbi felt that I should be made aware "that the Gentiles are putting us in a bad light as a result of Dr. Wise's talk and that it will hurt the Jewish cause in this section." I advised the gentleman that I regarded the invitation as withdrawn. A Mid-Western rabbi, Dr. Silver, sanctimoniously advised his congregation that a minister was justified in attacking evil but not evildoers. A so-called minister of religion in New York preached a vituperative sermon in which he charged that I was playing politics in the pulpit and prostituting the pulpit for "personal notoriety and sensationalism."

Within twenty-four hours resignations had begun to pour in. I immediately answered each member who resigned, advising him that owing to comment in agreement and disagreement with the address, I had resolved to give a second address on the same theme the following Sunday, under the title: "How

Ought the Pulpit Deal with the Industrial Situation?" and that I should be glad if he could be present and hear the address, adding that the letter of resignation would be acted upon by the membership committee, unless after the following Sunday the member wished to rescind such decision.

Incidentally, I might observe that one special type of piety I uniformly evoked from the membership of the Free Synagogue—the piety of resignation! At the risk of punning, I must admit that time and time again a sermon on any theme of current interest was followed by one or more resignations. One of the foremost Jewish financiers of the country led the procession by resigning from the synagogue's Executive Council, also a large employer of labor whose industrial plant, after thirty-five years, is still nonunion. The synagogue's first treasurer resigned. This time the resignations came in such large numbers that for the first and only time I felt the matter should be put to the test of a congregational decision.

I did the thing which I have always believed a minister or rabbi should do. When a congregation seems ready in goodly numbers to dissent from or protest against the word or deed of its minister, he must offer his resignation and the congregation must be left free to accept or reject such resignation. The Executive Council met under the temporary chairmanship of an old and honored friend, Oscar Straus, the first member of the Jewish community to attain Cabinet rank as secretary of commerce. My resignation was presented to the Executive Council and was refused in friendliest terms with the dictum that the principle of the Free Synagogue stands—the pulpit is free, but the rabbi speaks not *for* but *to* the congregation. It was the only time in the history of the Free Synagogue, now in its forty-second year, that the ideal of pulpit freedom was put to the test—and the ideal was sustained. But the building was lost.

The central and basic principle of the Free Synagogue, however, has enduringly been maintained, throughout my lifetime in any event, and will be continued throughout the lifetime of my successors if they choose, as they will choose, to be equal to the test, beginning with my disciple and comrade, friend and successor, Rabbi Edward E. Klein.

I cannot close my reference to the steel strike without speaking of the Inter-Church World Movement. Shortly after the founding of the Inter-Church World Movement in October, 1919, when I made my address, a committee on the steel strike was appointed to investigate the facts. This committee consisted of the Bishop of the Methodist Church, the Bishop of the Episcopal Church, one of the secretaries of the Presbyterian Church, and a number of other earnest, thoughtful, conservative people. The first thing they did was to offer to mediate between Judge Gary and the men on strike. The men accepted; Mr. Gary at once refused the tender. The strike went on for a while and then was lost, and the men returned to work. In the meantime these men representing their churches went on with their investigation. In April, 1920, they submitted a typed report. Every effort was made to suppress that report because the findings were against the United States Steel Corporation, although temperate in spirit and couched in conservative fashion. After a delay, a handful of men demanded the right to publish the report and it was printed. From that moment on the Inter-Church World Movement was dead.

One might ask who killed the Inter-Church World Movement? At the time someone wittily suggested to me that "a steel splinter got into its eye." The fact remains that the publication of the investigation report killed the movement of the Protestant Churches in America that was created and designed to bring about the union of the religious and church forces in America.

We were still in a period when men not only believed but admitted that the public utterances of ministers should be supervised and restricted by church officers. I remember the comment of various ministers concerning the struggle of a

Christian minister with his congregation regarding his right to speak on any subject which he believed his congregation should know about. Some ministers supported him while others held that a pastor's domain was the Bible and biblical subjects and that when a minister interfered with current politics he was exceeding his ecclesiastical authority.

During this controversy, some ministers still took the position that if the minister were tactful he would not get into trouble, others that the minister should preach only the gospel, and still others that "the pastor should be governed by the officers of his church, and the officers should be the governing body to decide on all public utterances of the pastor." One minister even went so far as to say of himself in answer to the question on this subject: "I am employed by a community of people who pay me my salary. They give me their pulpit and their following. If I have the gift of free speech so much that I can say what I please regardless of who or what is involved, I am dishonoring my position." Although I have frequently been attacked for speaking the truth on many issues, I was never attacked more viciously than for speaking out in regard to the rights of workers and making my attack specific against the exploitation of steel workers and the denial of their right to organize.

The word sensationalism was used over and over again to discredit me, and more important to discredit what I had said. I said that Judge Gary had Cossackized the steel industry. The term may have sounded sensational but it was nonetheless true because graphic and vivid. The later Inter-Church Steel Report proved that Judge Gary used the spy system and that there had been a system of terrorism within the industry for years. This is Cossackism. As I look back, I recall a man in the Jewish pulpit who called me a sensation monger at the time. He dealt with the steel strike shortly after I did and justified Judge Gary. I was sensational only in that I dared to speak the truth as I saw it, and he was unsensational in that he did not see the truth or, if he saw it, he did not have the manliness and the decency to speak out in a place dedicated above all things to truth-speaking.

If a man wishes to avoid the appearance of sensationalism, the only thing he need do is what most men in the pulpit do—tap social wrongdoers on the wrists without, of course, mentioning their names. The fact is that my business as a teacher of religion and moralism is not to call attention to wrongdoing in such fashion that people shall not really know what I say, but to make it clear that certain wrongs are being done by certain people. In arguing this point I was once reminded that Nathan, the Prophet, did not hold a meeting when he wished to speak to David but went quietly into his chamber and said, "Thou art the man." The implication of much of the criticism leveled against me at that time was that public speaking against the wrongdoer, as well as for the wronged, was not in keeping with biblical tradition. I still wonder whether some of the gentlemen who thought of this excuse for not speaking out with courage, and who claim to believe in Nathan's method of influencing others while refraining as they do from pulpit utterance touching the man who does wrong, find and avail themselves of opportunities to go to that man's banking office or counting house or shop or factory and say to him "Thou art the man."

There are things that are absurd and sensational and vulgar in the pulpit, but that is no reason for confusing the vulgarian in the pulpit with the man who makes people think and feel aright. I for my part have found that the term sensationalist or sensation monger is oftenest applied to the men in the pulpit by those of their colleagues who have a peculiar genius for leaving their congregations undisturbed in their weekly church or synagogue slumber.

Startling is another name for or an interchangeable term with sensational. Do not men need to startle? Are there not times men require to be aroused, when they must be awakened out of the depths of their slumber? It was said of Tolstoy that he stabbed men awake. There are times when men need to be dynamited into wakefulness.

I have never felt the need of defending myself against the charge of sensationalism for I have known my own motives. In a world of shame, the truth bravely uttered is bound to sound sensational. I have sought the truth and aimed to further the sovereignty of righteousness among men. Within my limited powers, I have purposed to magnify the ideal of justice, and I have spoken and speak for the sake of these things and only for them. . . .

7.

Monsignor John Ryan Calls for a Living Wage

The Roman Catholic Church in the United States, its roots deep among Irish and Italian immigrants, was long familiar with urban poverty. A few of its clergy gave it urgent attention. But not until 1891, when in his encyclical, *Rerum Novarum*, Pope Leo XIII arraigned capitalism, did concern with the problem become widespread.

Among those deeply stirred by the encyclical was John Ryan, a Minnesota farm boy attending St. Paul's Seminary. His interest in urban problems had been aroused by *Irish World*, a newspaper published in New York. He agreed with much in Henry George's *Progress and Poverty*, and he was influenced by the writings of Richard Ely. The defeat of populism in 1892 Ryan took as a sign that the masses were easily duped.

Ryan was ordained in 1898 and then began graduate study at the Catholic University of America in Washington, D.C. He concentrated on economics and wrote a doctoral dissertation on *A Living Wage: Its Ethical and Economic Aspects*, in which he argued the necessity of guaranteeing each man a proper share of the social product. The work was published with an introduction by Richard Ely. From 1902 to 1915 Ryan taught at St. Paul's Seminary. Then he received an appointment at Catholic University, where he remained until he retired in 1939.

Often alone in his views and usually a spokesman of the minority among the clergy, Ryan nonetheless saw his views integrated by the progressive movement and written into the Progressive Party platform in 1912. Many of his ideas were permanently enacted in the labor legislation of the New Deal.

In the following selection, he recalls his activities among social welfare workers and estimates his influence on them.

Soon after *A Living Wage*[1] was published, I began to take considerable interest in charitable activities and particularly in the theory and practice of organized charity. This interest grew naturally out of my concern with living wages and with industrial reform generally. A minimum just wage, the alleviation of poverty, and relief for needy individuals, are interrelated concepts; the actions and policies which they involve all aim at the uplifting of ill-fed, ill-clothed, and ill-housed men, women, and children to a level of existence worthy of creatures made in the image and likeness of God. The motive of charity does, indeed, differ from that of justice: in the former case, it is brotherly love; in the latter it is personal dignity, equality, and independence. Charity contemplates the human needs as those of a brother, while justice regards them as affecting an independent person endowed with rights; but the needs in both situations are or can be identical.

To be sure, charity is not an adequate substitute for justice.

From John A. Ryan, *Social Doctrine in Action* (New York: Harper & Brothers, 1941), chaps. 6, 7, pp. 86–115. Copyright 1941 by Harper & Brothers. Reprinted by permission of Harper & Row, Publishers, Inc.

---

[1] New York: The Macmillan Company, 1906 [ED.].

In his encyclical *Quadragesimo Anno,* Pius XI declares: "Charity cannot take the place of justice unfairly withheld."[2] On an earlier page of the same document, Pope Pius had written:

> Towards the close of the nineteenth century the new economic methods and the new development of industry had sprung into being in almost all civilized nations, and had made such headway that human society appeared more and more divided into two classes. The first, small in numbers, enjoyed practically all the comforts so plentifully supplied by modern invention. The second class, comprising the immense multitude of workingmen, was made up of those who, oppressed by dire poverty, struggled in vain to escape from the straits which encompassed them.
>
> This state of things was quite satisfactory to the wealthy, who looked upon it as the consequence of inevitable and natural economic laws, and who, therefore, were content to abandon to charity alone the full care of relieving the unfortunate, as though it were the task of charity to make amends for the open violation of justice, a violation not merely tolerated, but sanctioned at times by legislators.

The assumption that the "full care of relieving the unfortunate" belongs to charity and charitable agencies alone, was for a long time "tolerated" and "sanctioned" not only by legislators but by the leaders of organized charity. Both in Great Britain and in the United States, these men ignored or were ignorant of the relation between social distress and economic injustice. They endeavored to remove the causes, as they saw them, of individual dependency and individual distress, but they gave very little attention to the social and economic causes. They regarded the indigence which they sought to relieve as due mainly to individual fault and individual misfortune. By 1906, however, this attitude had undergone a considerable change. Many of the ablest leaders in

---

[2] The encyclical was issued in 1931 in celebration of the fortieth anniversary of *Rerum Novarum* [ED.].

the field of charity or social work had come to recognize the inadequateness, indeed, the essential falsity of the traditional assumptions about the causes of poverty. Discussing English conditions and attitudes in 1908, a historian of English philanthropy, B. Kirkman Gray, mentioned the formerly prevailing "notion that poverty and the diseases now known to be consequent on poverty, were usually the result of personal misdemeanor on the part of the sufferer." Continuing, he noted:

> It is now generally recognized that in addition to such want as results to the ill-doer from his own ill-doing there is a vast amount of suffering which comes from general social causes; and for which the sufferer is responsible either remotely or not at all.

In the United States, the most striking expression of the new attitude came from Dr. Edward T. Devine,[3] in his presidential address at the Thirty-third Annual Session of the National Conference of Charities and Correction in Philadelphia, in 1906:

> If I have rightly conceived the dominant idea of the modern philanthropy it is embodied in a determination to *seek out and to strike effectively at those organized forces of evil, at those particular causes of dependence and intolerable living conditions which are beyond the control of the individuals whom they injure and whom they too often destroy.*
>
> Other tasks for other ages. This be the glory of ours, that the social causes of dependence shall be destroyed.

Although I had not read the foregoing sentences when I delivered a short address before the National Conference at its meeting in Minneapolis the following year, I had adopted substantially the same view. My subject was "The Standard of Living and the Problem of Dependency." The following ex-

[3] Devine, one of the leading pioneers of social work, was then director of the New York School of Philanthropy which soon became the famed New York School of Social Work [ED.].

tract from the first paragraph expresses the main thought of the address:

> Intelligent students and workers in the field of charitable effort no longer impute all pauperism and poverty to deficiencies in the individual. They realize that a considerable proportion of dependency occurs despite the utmost efforts of the individual, despite the absence of unusual sickness, accidents or other misfortunes, despite the presence of individual capacities that are fully up to the average. The true cause of such dependency is to be sought in insufficient incomes and insufficient standards of living.

In the succeeding paragraphs, I described the minimum normal standard of living for a family, in terms of both goods and money, and noted the very large proportion of American families who were unable to maintain this standard owing to insufficient incomes, which in the case of wage earners meant insufficient wages—less than living wages. Finally, I urged the members of the Conference to ascertain what is a minimum normal standard of living and how many families are below this standard because of inadequate wages. Continuing, I said:

> Possessing this knowledge, the members of charity organizations, and all who speak or write on the problem of dependency, can accomplish a splendid work of education. They can bring home to well-meaning but thoughtless employers some idea of the amount of poverty that is due to their failure to pay living wages; they can help very materially to bring upon employers who are not well-meaning the condemnation of public opinion; they can contribute to the enactment of laws which directly or indirectly will enforce an adequate standard of compensation and of living; they can educate the whole public into a more accurate conception of the proportion of poverty that is due to social causes, and out of the complacent notion, which is still all too common, that the poverty stricken have only themselves to blame.

The foregoing extract sets forth two distinct but closely related propositions: first, a very large proportion of destitution is caused by economic factors; second, these factors cannot be removed without a large measure of intervention by the state. The latter proposition I had already defended in *A Living Wage*. In the succeeding years, my conviction on this point has grown stronger rather than weaker. I have never ceased to regard the economic causes of social distress as providing a pertinent application of the profound principle laid down by Pope Leo XIII in the encyclical *Rerum Novarum:*

> Whenever the general interest, *or any particular class* [italics mine] suffers or is threatened with mischief which can in no other way be met or averted, it is the duty of public authority to intervene.

Early in the year 1908, I wrote an article of some fifteen thousand words on "Charity and Charities" for the *Catholic Encyclopedia*. The introductory section described the nature and obligations of the virtue of charity as taught by the Catholic Church and gave brief accounts of the charitable achievements of the non-Catholic religions, particularly Judaism. The concluding paragraphs discussed the place of Catholic charity in present society. Fully four-fifths of the article was devoted to the history of charity in the Catholic Church from the Apostolic age to our own time. The historical section concludes with the following sentences:

> . . . Surveying the whole historical field of Catholic charity, we are justified in saying that, in proportion to her resources, the Church met the various forms of distress of every age more adequately than any other agency or system; that her shortcomings in charitable activity were due to the nature of the peoples and civilizations, and to the political, social, economic, and religious conditions in which she worked; that the instances of heroic charity which stand to her credit surpass by an immeasurable distance all instances of that class outside her fold; that the individual gifts to charity which she has inspired are likewise supereminent; and that, had she been permitted to reorganize and develop her char-

ities without the interference of the Reformation, the amount of social distress, and of social injustice as well, would be much smaller than it is today.

In March, 1910, I addressed the annual meeting of the National Consumers League[4] at Milwaukee on "A Minimum Wage by Legislation." This paper, with some amplification, I presented again in May of the same year before the Division on Occupational Standards at the Thirty-seventh Annual Session of the National Conference of Charities and Correction in St. Louis. In this address, I stated that considerably more than one-half of the male, adult wage earners of the country were receiving less than $700 annually. This amount, I said, was the minimum that would suffice for the decent maintenance of a family in the smaller cities. For the larger urban centers I put the required sum at $800 and for New York City at $900. These estimates I based upon the findings of a volume published in 1909 by Professor Robert Coit Chapin and entitled *The Standard of Living Among Workingmen's Families in New York City.* It will be observed that these estimates are some 15 to 20 per cent higher than those which I had embodied in *A Living Wage,* but the difference is readily explained. In the first place, Dr. Chapin had made a much more extensive investigation of the cost of living than was possible for me in 1905; in the second place, his computations were made some four years later than mine, and during that period there had occurred a not inconsiderable rise in prices and in the cost of living. In passing, I note that Dr. Chapin's book was the first of a long series of carefully prepared and well-balanced studies on the minimum cost of living of the working class in the United States.

Returning to the address under consideration, I observe that after reciting at some length the manifold evil results, so-

---

[4] The National Consumers' League, established in 1898, sought to influence factory conditions by directing women's purchases [ED.].

cial, industrial, moral, intellectual, and physical of the low-wage situation, I declared that the only measure holding out any hope as a remedy was "the establishment by law of minimum rates of wages that will equal or approximate the normal standards of living for the different groups of workers." Finally, I endeavored to meet and refute the principal objections confronting this proposal: it was novel; it would restrict freedom of contract; it was contrary to the "due process" clause of the Constitution; it was not enforceable; the resulting increase in wages would bring about higher prices, lessened demand for goods, and greater unemployment. In this year of 1941, the first of these objections has become antiquated; the second has lost most of its appeal, whether popular or technical; the third has been effectively refuted by a decision of the United States Supreme Court;[5] the fourth and fifth have been in large measure discredited respectively by the administration of the Federal Fair Labor Standards Act and by general experience. No additional objection possessing any great degree of cogency has been brought forward in the thirty-one years that have gone by since I delivered that address.

These two addresses were probably the first important public utterances made in the United States in advocacy of minimum-wage legislation. They hastened and promoted the introduction of bills for this purpose in more than one state legislature.

Later on, in the same year of 1910, I took part in the discussion of a paper on "The Problem of Dependency" read by Robert Biggs at the first annual meeting of the National Conference of Catholic Charities held in Washington. My contribution was very short and dealt with only one aspect of the subject, namely, "Insufficient Housing." Several other pa-

---

[5] *West Coast Hotel Company versus Parrish*, 1937. (The Court upheld a minimum wage law enacted in the state of Washington [ED.].)

pers and discussions at this meeting showed that the new Catholic organization was quite as much concerned with the social causes of poverty as was the older and larger association.

As already noted, my address at the St. Louis Conference of Charities and Correction was given before the Division on Occupational Standards. This division of the Conference had been set up one year previously for the specific purpose of formulating a set of employment and living standards which would describe the minimum conditions sufficient to place the worker beyond the need of charitable assistance. In other words, the members of the Conference wanted to ascertain as accurately as possible the quantity of goods and the quality of living which would enable wage earners to do without the ministrations of the social worker. Since the committee for this division was not ready to make a final report in 1910, its existence was continued, but under a new title, "Standards of Living and Labor." I was a member of the committee from its inception in 1909 and was elected chairman for the year 1913.

At the Thirty-ninth Annual Conference held in Cleveland in 1912, the committee presented its report on "Standards of Living and Labor." Although the chairman of the committee, Mr. Owen R. Lovejoy, discussed and explained at considerable length the standards adopted by the committee, the formal statement of "Social Standards for Industry" was relatively brief. The first paragraph of the statement is as follows:

> The welfare of society and the prosperity of the state require for each individual such food, clothing, housing conditions, and other necessaries and comforts of life as will secure and maintain physical, mental and moral health. These are essential elements in a normal standard of living, below which society cannot allow any of its members to live without injuring the public welfare. An increasing percentage of our population derives the means to maintain this normal standard through industry. Industry, therefore, must submit to such public regulation as will make it a means of life and health, not of death or inefficiency.

The minimum standards were arranged under six heads: Wages, Hours, Safety and Health, Housing, Term of Working Life, and Compensation or Insurance. Under the first head, the most important paragraph demanded a living wage which should be sufficiently large to provide the worker and his family with insurance against sickness and old age. Under the second head, a demand was voiced for the eight-hour day and the six-day week. Safety and health were held to include the provision of safety appliances and sanitary conditions, the prohibition of poisons, standardized inspection and regulation of occupation according to the degree of hazard. Under housing, the committee demanded for every family a safe and sanitary home and laid down in considerable detail the specifications implied in the concept. The term of working life was described as the period between "a minimum age to protect against premature labor and a maximum age beyond which the laborer should find himself economically independent of daily labor." Translating this generality into specific requirements, the committee called for prohibition of all wage-earning occupations for children under sixteen years of age and also prohibition of employment of women in occupations where work compels standing constantly. Finally, the committee demanded compensation for industrial workers on account of accidents, trade diseases, permanent disability, old age, and unemployment.

Such were the principal but by no means all the items in the "Platform of Minimums," as this collection of standards came to be called. While a considerable number of them have been adopted through legislation or otherwise, some of the most important and most necessary still await establishment; for example, living wages and adequate housing. The task assigned to the committee by the National Conference was brilliantly and comprehensively executed. For various reasons it will be a long time before the National Conference will be required to formulate another group of "Standards of Living and Labor." . . .

For some half-dozen years before I left for Washington in September, 1915, I had served as vice-president of the Associated Charities of St. Paul. While my contribution to the effectiveness of that organization was neither great nor conspicuous, I took considerable interest in its activities, first, because they were directed to the welfare of human beings and, second, because of the discussions and differences at the meetings concerning methods and policies.

In 1912, I was chosen president of the Minnesota State Conference of Charities and Correction. At the annual meeting that year I took as the subject of the presidential address "The State and Social Distress." At some length, I endeavored to define the principles and policies which separate the proper sphere of the state from that which properly belongs to the individual. Concerning the former, I said:

> The State, and only the State, can prevent a large part, probably the larger part, of the social distress which is due primarily to environment. In the physical order it can and ought to provide suitable economic conditions, by enforcing reasonable minimum standards of labor and livelihood. Specifically, it should prohibit the employment of any worker of average capacity at less than living wages, or for a longer day than is consistent with the material and moral health of the individual and the race, or in unsafe and unsanitary work places. It should also forbid child labor, and interdict the employment of women and young persons at tasks that are harmful to health or morals. Insofar as the wage earners are unable to protect themselves against the unfavorable contingencies of life and employment by adequate savings or insurance, the State should supply the deficiency. Hence the need in many communities of workmen's compensation laws, labor exchanges, insurance against sickness, accidents, unemployment, and disability, and a system of old age pensions. In a word, the State ought to provide and enforce all those economic and in-

dustrial conditions which are necessary and sufficient for normal and reasonable human life. This will not injure individual initiative, or individual freedom, or the individual desire to excel. It will merely lift the plane of competition, and confine these qualities within reasonable and healthy limits. . . .

By way of conclusion, then, we observe that the sphere of the State in dealing with social distress is by no means small. Neither is it indefinitely large. It is confined within fairly definite limits by certain clear and fundamental principles. Neither in the field of prevention nor in that of relief is it wise or right for the State to do anything that can be done as well by voluntary agencies; and wherever practicable it should subsidize, cooperate with and supplement private effort.

In order to complete in this chapter the record of my activities in the domain of charity or social work, I shall include a brief account of my connection with the *Catholic Charities Review*,[6] and several paragraphs from two addresses before groups of social workers. The first issue of the *Catholic Charities Review* appeared in January, 1917. For the first four years, I was the editor and manager, writing all the editorials and finding "copy" to fill each issue. After I gave up that responsibility, I acted for several years as contributing editor. Most of my editorials and practically all my contributed articles dealt with industrial questions rather than with topics in the field of social work; nevertheless, most of my productions had some fairly obvious relevancy to the problems of social workers. I never permitted myself to forget the relation between poverty, charitable relief, and low wages.

The first of the two addresses mentioned above was delivered at the commencement exercises of the New York School of Social Work in 1920. The subject was "A Practical Philosophy of Social Work." It dealt almost entirely with the differences between the two philosophies of social work held

---

[6] The publication of the National Conference of Catholic Charities, an organization of trained and professional social workers [ED.].

respectively by the members of secular agencies and those in Catholic organizations. I grouped the principal differences between these two theories or philosophies under these heads: Motives; Attitude Toward Religious Principles; Methods; Attitude Toward State Administration. What I said on these points in the address I still hold to be substantially correct. The following paragraphs present the interpretation that I then gave of the Catholic philosophy on these four subjects:

> The Catholic philosophy regards love of God as the highest and most fundamental motive of social service. That is to say, it holds that the needy neighbor should be assisted because of his relation to God, because he is made in the image and likeness of God, because he is the adopted child of God and the adopted brother of Christ; and also because Christ has commanded us to relieve the neighbor who is in distress, particularly as seen in the twenty-fifth chapter of St. Matthew. Catholics maintain that this is a much more effective motive than love of the neighbor for his own sake or for the sake of society; for the human being in distress assumes a much greater value when he is thought of in relation to God, and there is grave danger that assistance to the neighbor for his own sake alone will be converted into the service of society as a whole, and the ignoring of the intrinsic worth of the individual. . . .
>
> According to the Catholic philosophy, religious principles are of supreme importance in social service. We believe that religion and religious morality should control every department of human life; and we maintain that religion and religious morality are a most important element in the life of the person to whom social service is extended. Young dependents, all delinquents and defectives, and a very large proportion of adults who are in distress require the aid of religion in order to enable them to lead normal lives. . . .
>
> All intelligent Catholics admit that all the modern scientific methods of social service are essentially sound. Indeed, we are predisposed to this conclusion, inasmuch as these methods, in their main outlines at least, were stated and defended nearly four hundred years ago by the Spanish philosopher, Juan Luis Vives, and repeated at greater length more than three-quarters of

a century ago by Frederic Ozanam, the founder of the Society of St. Vincent de Paul. The views of Vives on this subject have been so well appreciated in this institution that a translation of them into English was published by the school some three years ago. Scientific methods of social service are sometimes misused and made odious by injudicious exponents of the secular philosophy, just as they are sometimes mistrusted and condemned by incompetent Catholics. But there is no difference of principle between the two philosophies on the subject of scientific methods; the only difference that occurs is in their application. . . .

According to the Catholic view, the question whether State funds devoted to the relief of the distressed and to the care of dependents should be administered by the State, or by private agencies, is entirely one of expediency. There is no question here of principle. If a private agency can administer State funds, always under adequate State supervision, in such a way as to produce a greater amount of more beneficial service, that is the better arrangement. Moreover, there are special reasons for desiring that dependents, especially young dependents, should be cared for in Catholic, rather than in State institutions; namely, the necessity of giving them adequate training in religion and religious morality. If this can be done with the aid of State money in Catholic institutions so as to produce better social and civic results than would be obtained through the same expenditure of State money in State institutions, there can be no possible doubt that this arrangement is preferable.

The second discourse was spoken before the National Conference of Social Work, in Cleveland, May 30, 1926. The subject was "The Spiritual Element in Social Work." Here are the most significant paragraphs:

. . . The spiritual element in social work is the recognition of the soul as the supreme good in a human being. It is the soul which gives to man his intrinsic worth as a person, instead of a mere means to the welfare of society. Because of his soul, his personality, his intrinsic worth, the human individual is endowed with certain rights which may not be disregarded even in the interest of social progress. After all, social progress means the progress of human beings. Apart from human beings, social progress and society itself are empty abstractions. To use any class of human beings as mere instruments to social advantage is in reality to subordinate one group of persons to another, albeit a larger, group of persons. For such a policy there can be no moral justification. The only defense available is that which may be based upon considerations of brute force.

If this conception of the human individual as having intrinsic worth seem intangible or metaphysical, the answer is that every ultimate standard of values is intangible and metaphysical. To the person who believes that weak and socially useless individuals ought to be sacrificed to social welfare, society appears as good in itself, as metaphysically good. To the question, why should we further the interests of society, the answer must be in terms of metaphysics. At least the assumption must be made that society is its own justification, that there is no further end to which society might be made an instrument. . . .

Disregard the spiritual element in man and his essential sacredness, and you can set no logical or certain limit to the process of subjecting the supposedly less desirable individuals to the assumed welfare of society. If the abstraction which we call society is worth more than certain individuals, then it may be worth more than any number of individuals, however large, whom the social experts or the politicians may regard as a social liability.

Etymologically, social reform means the reform of any condition or institution which affects a social group. Divorce, the liquor traffic, public health, and methods of poor relief, may be objects of social reform, as well as the distribution of wealth, the hours of labor, and the incomes of the laboring classes. All the six standards formulated by the National Conference of Charities and Correction as described in the immediately preceding chapter, exemplify proposals of social reform. However, there is a widespread practice of confining the term to reform of industrial or economic conditions and institutions. Apparently, the underlying idea is that these comprise the most important province of social reform. It is chiefly in this sense that the phrase will be used in the present chapter. The reform movements, activities, and writings to be described and discussed herein are mainly economic.

In November, 1907, I published an article in the *Catholic World*,[7] under the title, "The Fallacy of Bettering One's Position." The general thesis was that the indefinite improvement of one's economic condition and the unlimited elevation of one's standard of living, are detrimental to right and reasonable life. After describing in some detail the ways in which increased income can be and usually is expended for "better" housing, food, clothing, amusement and recreation, and "social" activities, I concluded that the theory underlying this expenditure implies that "more abundant life means the multiplication of sensations, possessions and pleasurable experiences." This theory, I continued, is false, for the important thing is not the number but the kind of wants that a man satisfies. When the needs of health and moderate comfort have been supplied, "additional sense-satisfactions contribute little or nothing to the development of body, heart, or mind. . . . They exert a damaging influence upon morals, mind, health and happiness."

The foregoing propositions I endeavored to establish by specific descriptions of the evil effects of excessive expenditures upon health, morals, character, religion, altruism, the control of the animal appetites, the capacity for hard work, the birth rate, and genuine happiness. In relation to happiness, I quoted a passage from Friedrich Paulsen's well-known work, *A System of Ethics:*

> When we compare the self-confidence of the dying eighteenth century, with the opinion which the dying nineteenth century has of itself, we note a strong contrast. Instead of the proud con-

---

[7] A publication of the Missionary Priests of St. Paul the Apostle, commonly known as the Paulist Fathers [ED.].

> sciousness of having reached a pinnacle, a feeling that we are on the decline; instead of joyful pride in the successes achieved and joyful hope of new and greater things, a feeling of disappointment and weariness, and a premonition of a coming catastrophe.

In the awful events and conditions that now afflict the world, this premonition seems to be finding complete and devastating fulfillment.

In the February, 1908, issue of the *Catholic World* I discussed, in a complementary article, "The Cost of Christian Living," under each of the five most important needs: housing, food, clothing, amusement and recreation, and "social activities," and concluded that "the annual expenditure for material goods in the case of the overwhelming majority of moderately sized families, ought not to exceed $6,500. Probably the range of expenditure which would afford the best conditions of Christian life for a considerable majority of all American families lies between $2,000 and $5,000 per annum."

Eight years later, I returned to this subject in my book *Distributive Justice*.[8] There I discussed it in connection with the "Duty of Distributing Superfluous Wealth." Having defended the proposition that in our society men are morally obliged to distribute *all* their superfluous goods in some form of charity, philanthropy, civic or social betterment, I said that the chief obstacle in the way of this highly desirable practice was an exaggerated conception of "reasonable" needs, and an inadequate conception of superfluous goods, both arising out of a false theory of welfare. "It is commonly assumed that to be worthwhile life must include the continuous and indefinite increase of the number and variety of wants, and a corresponding growth and variation in the means of satisfying them."

My estimate of the maximum reasonable annual expenditure

---

[8] *Distributive Justice,* by John A. Ryan (New York: The Macmillan Company, 1927).

by a family at that time is stated in the following sentences:

> Somewhere between ten and twenty thousand dollars a year lies the maximum expenditure that any family can reasonably devote to its material wants. This is independent of the outlay for education, religion, and charity, and the things of the mind generally. In the overwhelming majority of cases in which more than ten to twenty thousand dollars are expended for the satisfaction of material needs, some injury is done to the higher life. The interests of health, intellect, spirit and morals would be better promoted if the outlay for material things were kept below the specified limit.

The increase which the above estimate indicates over that which I made in 1907 is mainly accounted for by the intervening rise in prices, but partly by a more comprehensive acquaintance with actual living needs and standards. About ten years later, in an address before the Canadian Conference of Social Work, I cited the estimate given by Paul H. Douglas and Mrs. Douglas in their little book entitled *What Can a Man Afford?* They held that an expenditure of $20,000 per year was sufficient to cover all items of family expenses except charity, religion, and education. This figure they arrived at, not in the endeavor to find a reasonable maximum, but as incidental to their attempt to ascertain the proportion of income which should be given by the various classes of families in the United States in order to meet the required national budget of philanthropy. To the objection of the man with an income of one-half a million dollars that he should not be required to give 50 per cent of it in charity and that he ought not to be asked to live like the man with an income of $50,000, Mr. and Mrs. Douglas replied:

> Our scale is indeed somewhat of a counsel of perfection if one is going to take all our present standards as normal. But the fact plain to our view is that the luxury side of current standards is not and need not be normal. . . . The social climbers of all ranks, especially the great middle groups of incomes, will be more

quickly affected to sane living and reasonable generosity by the concrete example of their financial superiors than by any amount of preaching.

The analysis and evaluation of the items of family expenditure which I made in 1907 and the conceptions of welfare and reasonable standards of living which I then defended, I still hold to be sound. The estimate which I made in 1916 of the maximum expenditure which any family can reasonably devote to its material wants, is likewise still adequate and valid. If all our rich and well-to-do families adopted this standard they would do more to allay class antagonism than is attainable by any quantity of reactionary criticism or platitudinous exhortation.

Someone might object that the recommendations made in the immediately preceding paragraphs are out of harmony with the economic theory of underconsumption which I have for a long time defended.[9] If the full operation of our industrial plant and full employment requires that our people spend more and save less, should we not welcome large expenditures by any group of persons, regardless of the income class to which they belong? The answer is that such spending is desirable as a lesser evil than an equal amount of saving, but it is not normal nor ideal. Although the total expenditures of those families that exceed $10,000 to $20,000 a year is large, it is much smaller than would be the additional spending by the lower income groups if the rich and the well-to-do dispensed all their surplus in the form of wages, charitable giving, and philanthropy. To be sure, if these classes should reduce their living standards and expenditures for consumption goods without distributing the amount thus saved to the lower income classes, the net effect would be harmful to industrial welfare.

---

[9] The theory that unemployment is caused by an imbalance between consumption and investment came to Ryan's attention while he was a student at Catholic University [ED.].

The situation is simply this: our economy demands a great increase in spending for consumers' goods; the bulk of this will have to come from the lower economic classes; therefore, anything which enables them to increase their total amount and proportion of consumption, whether through higher wages, lower interest rates, or wider distribution of the superfluous goods of the rich and the well-to-do, will directly make for larger employment and greater business activity. In a word, reasonable standards of living maintained by the rich and the well-to-do, combined with a better distribution of their superfluous income, would be in accord with both the Christian teaching on wealth and our national economic welfare.

In 1908, I addressed the National Catholic Educational Association on "The Study of Social Problems in the Seminary." After describing briefly the importance of the economic factor in political, civil, social, and international life, I said that the priest who does not realize this situation will accomplish considerably less than would otherwise be within his power. The priest needs to know the following facts and the reasons therefor: that the attitudes of many governments toward the Church are largely determined by economic factors; that many popular movements which seem to be political are at bottom industrial; and that the economic status of men greatly influences their notions about the morality of some of the most important activities and institutions of our time. The priest who does not discern the economic causes of the differing ethical judgments which men pass, for example, upon the trust, the trade union, profits and wages, will not command adequate authority as a teacher of morality. I quoted the following saying of Archbishop Von Ketteler, the first and probably the greatest of modern Catholic social reformers:

> If we wish to know our age, we must endeavor to fathom the social question. The man who understands that knows his age. The man who does not understand it finds the present and the future an enigma.

Continuing, I said that the priest "must give special attention to the condition and aspirations of the wage earners," and I pointed out that in some of the countries of Europe a large proportion of the workers had become alienated from the Church because the clergy lacked knowledge of and interest in their specific problems. While there is little danger that the Catholic clergy of America will lose sympathy with the desire of the masses for industrial freedom and industrial opportunity, there is a real danger that their sympathy will not be equaled by their knowledge. . . .

In July and August, 1909, I published in the *Catholic World* two articles under the head, "Program of Social Reform by Legislation." The first dealt with legislative measures in favor of wage earners, while the second proposed legislation in the interest of the consumers. Under the former head, I advocated minimum-wage legislation, the eight-hour day, minimum working age of sixteen years for children, the creation of boards to provide for conciliation and arbitration in labor disputes, state employment agencies, municipal housing, and state insurance against unemployment, accidents, sickness, and old age.

In the second group of proposed legislative measures, I placed national and state ownership of railroads, express companies, telegraphs and telephones, and municipal ownership of gas and electric lighting, waterworks, and street railways; also state and national retention of the ownership of all mineral and forest lands that have not been alienated. As regards monopolies which are outside the field of public utilities, I recommended government control of the prices of things produced by those concerns whose exceptional efficiency suggested that they should continue to exist as monopolies. In the field of taxation, I advocated progressive imposts upon incomes and inheritances, and also partial appropriation of future increases in the value of land. Finally, I declared that the government should regulate the stock and produce exchanges in order to prevent the manifold evils of speculation. . . .

Some of the proposals advocated in the foregoing paragraphs have already been enacted into law; all of the others I still hold to be valid, with a few modifications which are suggested by changes in economic conditions that have occurred in the last three decades. Government ownership of railroads is no longer required in order to prevent excessive charges for carrying freight and passengers and the receipt of excessive returns on railroad investments. For the great majority of the railroads, these socially undesirable advantages no longer exist. When government ownership comes, its principal cause will probably be the inability of the railroads to pay dividends and to perform their public functions adequately. The last three sentences apply likewise to street railways.

Since public regulation of most of the other utilities has shown more or less improvement in the last thirty years, the necessity for public ownership is not so acute as it was at the beginning of that period. While I still believe that the latter would be preferable to private ownership, I realize that it can come about only gradually and in piecemeal fashion.

The proposal to curb the exactions of private monopolies through government determination of prices, is less valid now than it seemed to be in 1909. When the National Emergency Economic Committee has completed its long investigation and made its recommendations for legislative policies concerning monopolies, the American people will be in a better position than ever before to find the proper solution of this baffling problem.[10] In the meantime, one proposal which I offered in 1912 remains sound and helpful, namely, government competition with the most intractable of the monopolistic concerns. This method has proved very effective in electric power production: witness the T.V.A. So far as feasible, it should be extended throughout that industry.

---

[10] The reference is to the Temporary National Economic Committee authorized by Congress in 1938 to investigate the effects of monopoly on the American economy.

The principal modification which I would now make of the proposals which I offered in 1909 and 1912 has to do with the taxation of land. While I still believe that the transfer to land of taxes on improvements and the taxation of future increases in land value are reasonable, I realize that their scope has been greatly diminished. As a matter of fact, the general increase in land values, both urban and rural, has practically ceased. More than one factor accounts for this change but the principal one is the decline in the birth rate. The recommendations which I made in 1912 concerning land taxation have practical application now to only a few cities and a small amount of other lands which are exceptionally situated.

In 1910, I wrote an article for the *Catholic Encyclopedia* on "Moral Aspects of the Labor Union." Premising that the moral aspects of an institution are ascertained by examining its constitution, its end, its results and the means employed in pursuit of the end, I declared that no evidence exists to show that the constitution of the typical labor union in the United States today is immoral. With regard to the aims and results of the union, I said that the former were generally good, and that the evil results were morally outweighed by the good results, admitting, however, that there are and have been some exceptions to both these generalizations. . . .

My discussions of the social question differed from those carried on by some Catholic journals and speakers in two main respects. The latter sometimes explained and denounced Socialism without offering any constructive proposals; hence, they created the impression that existing industrial conditions stood in no need of reformation. While they based their criticism of Socialism upon Pope Leo's encyclical, *Rerum Novarum,* they not infrequently ignored the positive and reformist doctrines of that great document. Persons who listened to these men or read their productions sometimes drew the inference that Pope Leo had said nothing favorable to labor unions, and that his only reference to private property was in his denunciation of Socialism. As a matter of fact, the great "Pontiff of the Workingmen" made some of the strongest statements ever uttered on the necessity and justice of labor organization, and his proposal for the reform of the property system is one of the most fundamental and far-reaching that has been offered in modern times:

> Speaking summarily, we may lay it down as a general and perpetual law, that Workmen's Associations should be so organized and governed as to furnish the best and most suitable means for attaining what is aimed at, that is to say, for helping each individual member to better his condition to the utmost, in body, mind and property.
>
> . . . The law, therefore, should favor ownership, and its policy should be to induce as many people as possible to become owners.
>
> Many excellent results will follow from this; and first of all, property will certainly become more equitably divided. For the effect of civil change and revolution has been to divide society into two widely different castes. On the one side there is the party which holds the power because it holds the wealth; which has in its grasp all labor and all trade; which manipulates for its own benefit and its own purposes all the sources of supply, and which is powerfully represented in the councils of the State itself. On the other side there is the needy and powerless multitude, sore and suffering, always ready for disturbance.

The second difference between my speeches on economic questions and the pronouncements of some Catholic speakers and journals, was that mine were sometimes criticized as too "radical." When I advocated forthrightly the organization of labor and defended most of the principal methods of labor unions, I was occasionally put down as a "dangerous agitator" (the epithet "subversive" had not yet been invented). When I advocated public ownership of public utilities, or a legal minimum wage, I was sometimes stigmatized as a Socialist, or at least as "socialistic." Did not the professional labor leaders, the labor organizers, and all the other disturbers of peaceful relations between capital and labor, use much the same arguments as mine? And did not Socialism propose government ownership of public utilities and government fixing of labor compensation?

Of course, I appealed to the authoritative declarations of Pope Leo XIII; but this defense did not always silence critics whose study of Leo's great encyclical was neither extensive nor profound. Many years later, when Leo's teaching had become much better and much more widely understood, an able non-Catholic clergyman, who was also a high official of the Federal Council of Churches said to me: "You have a very great advantage over men in my position. We have to guard against offending the members of many different denominations, while you can hang your 'radical' utterances upon a Papal encyclical."

In the years of which I am now writing, however, the procedure thus humorously characterized by my good Methodist friend was not always effective. While my knowledge of the traditional social teaching of the Church (I have already referred to my extensive reading of economic history at the turn of the century) as well as my intimate acquaintance with *Rerum Novarum,* assured me that I was on solid ground, I occasionally felt anxiety over the reflection that some of my prominent fellow Catholics regarded my teaching as unorthodox. However, I never permitted myself to become discouraged, nor was I ever seriously tempted to lessen my activities or to compromise or soften the principles in which I believed. At the banquet which was given in my honor on the occasion of my investiture as Domestic Prelate to His Holiness, Pope Pius XI, December 6, 1933, I said:

> Many times men, both within and without the Church, have expressed admiration at what they were pleased to term my courage in enunciating and defending my opinions on industrial questions. At the risk of losing that particular halo, I will confess

that whatever courage I may seem to have displayed was quite unconscious or at least inadvertent. What was there to fear? Ecclesiastical censure? But I knew that I was not departing from the teaching of the Church. Suspicions of my orthodoxy by prominent persons within the Church? Denunciations by industrialists and newspapers? The knowledge that my name was sometimes spoken without affection in the highest social circles? No normal person could be indifferent to this sort of disapproval. I do not pretend that I enjoyed it, but to withstand it did not require courage. All that was necessary was a right sense of comparative values. To have been deterred by such opposition from teaching the sound doctrine would have been to turn my back upon my plain duty, to apostatize from the truth. It would have meant not merely burying, but dishonoring what talents I had received from God.

PART THREE

In the Path of Big Business

8.

The Reverend Washington Gladden Shuns Tainted Money

Of all the problems confronting progressives, the most difficult was their relationship to the business community: How to regulate the corporations, how to control their influence over the political process, and how to avoid the seductions of wealth in their own lives. All these questions concerned Washington Gladden, but when he died in 1918 he was perhaps best remembered for his refusal, thirteen years earlier, of a gift by John D. Rockefeller to the Protestant Board of Missions. Few other reformers refused endowments in so total a fashion as Gladden describes, in the following selection.

The son of a country schoolmaster in Pottsgrove, Pennsylvania, Gladden was born in 1836, educated at Williams College, and ordained in 1860. He was called to parishes in several eastern cities and for a time held a job on a newspaper in New York City. He grew acquainted with urban problems and wrote several books on the subject, including *Working People and Their Employers*, published in 1876. But not until 1882, when he became pastor of the First Congregationalist Church of Columbus, Ohio, did he achieve a reputation as the chief spokesman of the Social Gospel. When he discovered that several businessmen in his congregation were instrumental in breaking a strike of coal miners, he was moved to write *Applied Christianity*, the greatest of his many books. Published in 1886, it had an influence among reformers second only to George's *Progress and Poverty.*

In the early spring of 1905 our churches were surprised by the announcement that a gift of one hundred thousand dollars had been made to our Foreign Mission Board by the president of the Standard Oil Company. The donor was not a member of our communion. The first statements respecting the gift conveyed the impression that it had not been solicited, that the only agency of the Board in the matter had been that of a passive recipient of a gift brought to its doors. The explanations of the authorities, and all the earlier newspaper comments, assumed that this was so. It was admitted by some of these apologists that it would not have been right for the Board to seek contributions from such a source; but that when they were freely offered, they could not be rationally refused. These representations and admissions clearly indicated some uneasiness of mind on the part of the recipients, and made it plain that the nature of the alliance into which they had entered was not altogether satisfactory to them.

For there had come, very promptly, an emphatic declaration against the acceptance of money from this source. As soon as the gift was announced, I wrote a letter to the *Congregationalist,* protesting against the action by which the Mission Board was drawing our churches into a dishonorable alliance; declaring that the money thus bestowed had been iniquitously gained, and that we could not accept it without being partakers of the iniquity. Similar protests came from a considerable number of the best men in our denomination. A strong group of ministers in the vicinity of Boston took up the matter with vigor and united in a dignified and temperate memorial to the Board against the reception of the gift. Presently,

---

From Washington Gladden, *Recollections* (New York and Boston: Houghton Mifflin Co., 1909), pp. 401–409.

however, it transpired that the money had been paid over and most of it expended before any announcement was made; the protest against the acceptance was therefore futile. That the money should be returned was the clear dictate of sound morality, but of that there seemed little hope. The practical question concerned the future action of this Board, and of our other missionary organizations. That a great wrong had been done and a serious injury inflicted upon the churches represented in this society seemed to some of us very clear; that wrong must be confessed with shame; the question was whether it should be repeated. On that question there arose a debate in which the whole country was enlisted. It must be said that the debate revealed a widespread need of elementary instruction in the first principles of ethics. It exhibited, in a startling manner, the extent to which the moral perceptions even of leaders in the church have been blunted and confused by the worship of money. So much have we all become accustomed to think and say, in our religious, educational, and philanthropic enterprises,—"The one thing that we need is more money,"—that it has become quite too easy to subordinate many of the higher considerations for the sake of getting money.

The prompt answer of many amateur moralists to our protest was that money has no moral character; that one man's dollar is as good as another man's—will buy as many Bibles, pay as many missionary salaries, do as much good. When we replied to this by asking whether money contributed by highwaymen and pirates—booty which they were known to have taken from their victims—should be received with thanks by churches and missionary societies, it was generally admitted that that would be inadvisable. Even the law would discourage this kind of benevolence.

The plea was then made that money to which the owner had a clear legal title must be taken without questioning. But there is much to which there is a clear legal title which differs but little, when weighed in the scales of a sound morality, from stolen money; and the proposal to stand on a bare legality did not commend itself to sensitive consciences.

It was then asserted that a good share of the money contributed for religious and charitable purposes has been obtained by doubtful means, and that it is impossible for us to make discriminations. To this, the answer was that we proposed no quixotic inquisition into the character of the offerings which are thrown upon the contribution plate; we would assume that all these are honest dollars unless we knew the contrary. Moreover, when any man makes an offering in a wholly impersonal way, without calling attention to his gift or seeking recognition for it, we have no call to investigate his motives or his character. The case in which the moral difficulty arises is that of a man who is known to have accumulated his wealth by unsocial or flagitious methods, and who, in bestowing it, wishes the grateful recognition of those who receive it.

The real question which emerged from all this haze is simply this: What is the right relation between moral teachers and the possessors of predatory wealth? It is impossible to deny the existence of a considerable class of persons who have obtained great wealth by predatory methods, by evasion and defiance of law, by the practice of vast extortions, by getting unfair and generally unlawful advantages over their neighbors, by secret agreements, and the manipulation of railway and government officials; by such violations of law as have been brought to light in thousands of indictments in the rebate cases; by the use of trust funds for private gain; by manifold acts that tend to corrupt the character and destroy the foundations of the social order. The national government has been expending much of its strength, during the past three years, in the detection and punishment of crimes of this character. And it is a notorious fact that some of those who have gained great wealth by such methods have been diligently and in many cases successfully seeking to establish close relations between themselves and the moral teachers of the country. The question is what these moral teachers ought to do about it. What attitude should they maintain toward such men as those whom our government has, for the last three years, been persistently endeavoring to convict and punish? Ought they to go into partnership with them in the business of religion or of education or of philanthropy?

To the suggestion of partnership those thus challenged are apt to demur. "We have proposed no such thing as partnership," they protest. But what else shall it be called? If you persuade a man to invest one hundred thousand dollars of his capital in your business, is he not, to all intents and purposes, a partner in your business? Will he not be, in his own eyes, and in yours, and in the eyes of the whole community, associated with you in your business? And can the moral teachers of the community afford thus to associate themselves with men who are setting the laws at defiance, and trampling on all the principles of justice and humanity in their ruthless pursuit of gain?

It would seem that if the churches and the colleges of the land have any clear calling, it is that of making abhorrent and detestable, in the sight of the youth, the conduct of men who are amassing great wealth by methods which tend to the overthrow of free government and the destruction of the social order. They will not fulfill this calling by building churches or endowing mission boards with money contributed by such men, or by erecting college halls that bear their names. No amount of money that such givers can contribute can compensate for the lowering of ideals and the blurring of consciences which this kind of partnership involves. Is it really very wonderful that such a moral cataclysm as that which appeared in the insurance investigation should have taken place in our American society?

Such were the convictions which led to the protest against the acceptance by our Mission Board of Mr. Rockefeller's gift.

The question was debated, at the beginning, as I have said, on the understanding that it was a voluntary gift; but it afterward transpired that such was not its character. Mr. Rockefeller had not thrust his offering upon the Board, and he naturally declined to have the case so represented; it was at his demand that an explicit and extended statement was finally made, showing that the officers of the Board had been engaged for more than two years in soliciting this gift. This exhibit disclosed some lack of ingenuousness in the previous conduct of the discussion. If this fact had been clearly stated at the outset, the attitude of many minds toward the transaction would have been different. The question now before the churches was whether this policy should be commended and continued. In answer to this question I gave early notice that a resolution would be offered, at the annual meeting of the Board at Seattle, in October, to this effect: "Resolved, that the officers of this Board should neither invite nor solicit donations to its funds from persons whose gains have been made by methods morally reprehensible or socially injurious."

At the meeting in Seattle this resolution, and the "Statement of Principles" made by the officers of the Board in defending its action, were submitted together. The address which I made in support of my resolution, upon the question, "Shall Ill-Gotten Gains be sought for Christian Purposes?" is published in the volume entitled *The New Idolatry*.[1] The debate was not a protracted one. The "Principles" submitted were not, apparently, such as the corporate members present cared to defend. Yet they were not ready to adopt my resolution, with its practical reproof of the conduct of their officers. To vote it down, and thus officially consent that ill-gotten gains should be solicited by their officers was more than they thought it prudent to do, and therefore the knot was cut by laying the resolution and the "Principles" on the table together. The issue was

[1] New York: Doubleday, Page & Co., 1905 [ED.].

dodged. The officers of the Board were not reproved for what they had done, and they were not authorized to continue their practice. So far as the action of the corporate members was concerned, it was a drawn battle. But there was no question about the verdict of the people. The great audience that listened to the discussion spoke its mind most emphatically. The newspapers of the region, some of which had sneered at the protest before the meeting, were united and enthusiastic in their testimony that it was a righteous protest and ought to be heeded.

I had no expectation, when I went to Seattle, that I could get my resolution adopted; I knew that the majority of the corporate members who would be present were committed against it, and the last words of my speech were these: "Some of you have been kind enough to assure me that I am in a very insignificant minority. That may be; I do not know about that; I leave that to be decided by you. It will not be the first time that I have been in a very small minority, even in this Board; but I have seen such small minorities, in a very few years, grow to overwhelming majorities. 'The safe appeal of truth to time' is one on which I have learned to rest with hope, and I therefore commit with confidence what I have said to you, and to the people of the Congregational churches, and to the kindly judgment of all honorable men." Within three months after the meeting, the officers of the Board, though taking no public action in the matter, were ready to give assurances that the spirit of my resolution would govern their future conduct. The protest was justified and the battle was won.

There can be no doubt that this discussion has cleared the air. Even the man in the street is able see that the alliance of churches and colleges with public enemies is not a good thing; that one man's money is decidedly not as good as another man's—when the acceptance of the money involves partnership with evildoers or condonation of nefarious conduct. Even the politicians are able to see the point. A society was formed in Cincinnati, not long ago, for the protection of the ballot; and George B. Cox,[2] of that city, sent the managers his check for five hundred dollars. They sent it back. Why? Was not George Cox's money as good as any other man's money? The treasurer of the National Republican Committee, in the campaign of 1908, announced that contributions from corporations would not be received, and that those which had been sent in would be returned. Why? Is not a corporation's money as good as the money of a private person? Is there any justification for these scruples? Probably there is. Probably there are compromising relations here that had better be avoided. The politicians are becoming sensitive about such matters. I have no doubt the churches and the colleges will be more so, one of these days.

The response of the people to this protest was one that touched me deeply. Letters from all parts of the Union literally poured in upon me, for months. One could never have guessed that such an issue would stir the people so profoundly. Among these hundreds of strangers who wrote to express their approval were men and women of all ranks and classes, but the testimony that was most grateful came from those outside the church, who had been repelled from it by its seeming subserviency to Mammon, and who were glad to welcome any signs of the breaking of that yoke. I could not reply to all those friendly letters, but I have kept them all; and I trust that some of those who then stretched forth to me a kind hand may read these words and find in them some sense of my gratitude for their words of comfort and good cheer.

---

[2] A saloon proprietor and a leader in the Republican political machine of Ohio, Cox had been indicted for procuring graft. Though not convicted, he remained a vivid symbol of boss rule [ED.].

9.

Ray Stannard Baker Holds on to His Muckrake

"The frontal attack on the strongholds of the new plutocracy," as Vernon Parrington wrote, was led by that group of journalists that Theodore Roosevelt dubbed "muckrakers." But as Ray Stannard Baker explains, these writers not only shaped but also followed public opinion. Their copy sold, and was itself the origin of some fortunes, including that of the publisher S. S. McClure. Some journalists like Baker became so expert in their special fields of exposure that they gave aid in the making of legislation. Baker's assistance to Theodore Roosevelt in railroad regulation was an example of the influence open to newspapermen in the progressive era.

In 1875, when Ray Baker was five, his family moved from Lansing, Michigan, to northwestern Wisconsin, where he attended a one-room schoolhouse. But his real education, he recalled later, was from "the self-sufficient life of the frontier, in which every boy and girl played a part." Baker made his way into Michigan State College, from which he graduated in 1889. He settled in a rooming house in Chicago and found a job on a newspaper. As a reporter he began to "lift a flap of the gorgeous tent, where the music was, and the warmth and the feasting, and to look into the cold wet streets and the littered alleys outside."

His coverage of the army of unemployed veterans who marched

on Washington behind Jacob Coxey won Baker a national reputation. Eventually he came to the attention of McClure, for whose magazine Baker wrote some leading exposés.

Following the break with Roosevelt which he describes in the following selection, Baker became one of Woodrow Wilson's closest associates. He served Wilson in England during the war, accompanied him to Versailles, and wrote his authorized biography in many volumes.

What I remember best about the earlier "exposure" articles—my own as well as those of Ida Tarbell, Lincoln Steffens and others—was the extraordinary reception they had in every part of the country. Reading them again after forty years, the disclosures they make, so sensational then, seem now more or less commonplace; for the facts they contain are no longer *news*. They impress me as being swift-moving, hard-hitting narratives, but some of them seem now to be far too long. I have a feeling that they ought to have been "reader digested"—but don't see quite how that could have been done, since facts, facts piled up to the point of dry certitude, was what the American people then needed and wanted.

The articles do give an impression of sincerity and authenticity. They have much in them of what Ida Tarbell used to call "righteous indignation"—and I realize now, even more keenly than I did then, how much of that they had; for we were ourselves personally astonished, personally ashamed, personally indignant at what we found, and we wrote earnestly, even hotly. My own articles are marked here and there with a kind of hortatory fervor that I should now omit; nevertheless they express what I felt, strongly, at the time. One other point impresses

---

From Ray Stannard Baker, *American Chronicle* (New York: Charles Scribner's Sons, 1945), chaps. 20, 21, 22, pp. 183–204. Copyright 1945 by Charles Scribner's Sons. Reprinted by permission of Charles Scribner's Sons.

me sadly, that while there have been superficial improvements in forty years in the conditions we reported, the deeper-seated injustices remain, still unpurged. We are still far from the democracy of our vision.

I think I can understand now why these exposure articles took such a hold upon the American people. It was because the country, for years, had been swept by the agitation of soap-box orators, prophets crying in the wilderness, and political campaigns based upon charges of corruption and privilege which everyone believed or suspected had some basis of truth, but which were largely unsubstantiated.

Coxey's Army had been a flaming example of unrest. It was only more concretely sensational than the earlier campaigns of the Greenbackers, the Populists, the early Socialists and even the sober Single Taxers. Bryan's campaign in 1896 and those that followed were vigorous, if blind, expressions of the same unrest.

There had also been a confusing "scapegoat era," when the uncertain and ill-informed public felt that if only they could fasten their sins upon some scalawag leader and drive him into the wilderness, all would be well again. Even Theodore Roosevelt, in the earlier days, was looking for "the devil in the mess." So it was that Coxey and Browne[1] had been punished for walking on the grass of the Capitol lawn, and Debs locked up in prison where he became an even more intense revolutionary radical. But the punishment of individuals never accomplished anything; the conditions remained unchanged: the agitators only became more and more vocal. One or two able writers—Henry Demarest Lloyd, for example—and at least one earnest magazine of small circulation, the *Arena,* were appealing to thoughtful people, but had awakened no widespread popular interest. Certain sensational newspapers, Hearst's and others, only added to the confusion and unrest by the more or less ex-

---

[1] Carl Browne, long an agitator among the poor, served as Jacob Coxey's lieutenant and named this army of unemployed "The Commonweal of Christ" [ED.].

travagant reporting of the various disorders, with declamatory editorials, usually proposing political changes that led nowhere. They increased the unrest and indignation of the public without providing the soundly based and truthful information necessary for effective action under a democratic system.

What the early "exposers" did was to look at their world, *really* look at it. They reported honestly, fully, and above all interestingly what they found. And the public, now anxious and indignant, eagerly read the long and sometimes complicated and serious articles we wrote. Month after month they would swallow dissertations of ten or twelve thousand words without even blinking—and ask for more.

We at *McClure's* immediately felt the response—hundreds of editorials and quotations in the newspapers, a deluge of letters, commendations or attacks in political speeches, even references in sermons. We published pages of them in the magazine and in our announcements.

We were often sold out at the newsstands, and our subscription list, as the business manager used to say, was "gaining fast on the up-grade."

Each of us had his own group or groups that were especially interested—Miss Tarbell the business men, Steffens the politicians, and I labor leaders and employers—and the letters we received, the brick-bats as well as the bouquets, seemed highly encouraging to anyone who believed in the democratic method. They showed that ordinary men were not only willing but eager to know the truth.

We also began to receive enthusiastic responses from leaders in American public life, especially students of social, economic or political conditions—to say nothing of argumentative letters from agitators and reformers who criticized us unmercifully for not accepting their particular brands of reform, at the same time that they eagerly appropriated the ammunition we were supplying to belabor other agitators and reformers with whom they did not agree. Occasionally a correspondent would ask indignantly why we ourselves remained so unmoved. I remember one letter from an angry reader, who asked how I could make such exposures without saying in plain terms that these men were thieves and traitors who ought to be in jail. What he wanted was "red-hot invective." I remember thinking considerably about this letter, finally suggesting to my critic that if I became angry, or showed it, he wouldn't. If I "blew off," wouldn't he feel relieved, even satisfied; wouldn't he be tempted to do nothing more about it? But with the ugly facts, the complete picture, the truth, vividly and dispassionately set forth, wouldn't he and other honest men be stirred to the point of doing something about it themselves?

As our campaign advanced it became clearer and clearer that we were by no means alone; that a large number of thoughtful Americans were growing increasingly anxious or indignant about the lawless conditions existing in so many walks of our life. We had strong responses from stimulating and thoughtful leaders in the country. I recall a delightful letter from Carl Schurz, whom I had long admired at a distance, inviting me to come to see him. He had been a notable figure in the state of Wisconsin where I grew up. He was one of the many able Germans who had fled their native land after the revolution of 1848, and had thrown themselves eagerly, even passionately, into the democratic life of America. Schurz had been a general in the Northern army during the Civil War, American minister to Spain, United States Senator from Missouri, Secretary of the Interior in the Cabinet of President Hayes. In his earlier days in Germany he had known Mazzini and Kossuth, and naturally became a warm friend and supporter of Lincoln and a veritable bulwark of strength in the antislavery movement. His whole life had been a struggle against corruption and inefficiency in public life.

I found him in his book-walled study uptown in New York; a tall, gaunt, gray man, then about seventy-five years old. He wore a long dressing gown and looked at me eagerly, smilingly, through his thick glasses. I wish I had made complete notes of the enlightening conversation we had, since it went to the very heart of the fundamental problems in which we were both interested: how men could better learn to govern themselves in a restless, crowded, and more-or-less lawless world. His experience had been so varied and his knowledge of both America and Europe so comprehensive, that I sat willingly at his feet, and came away with a sense of humility and of gratitude, inspired to go forward with the work I had been doing.

There was a quality of the prophet—the philosopher in action—in Carl Schurz that I was not to discover again in any such measure until I came, some years later, to know Louis D. Brandeis. Both of these men had an incorruptable objectivity of mind combined with a sound common sense in public affairs rare in this country or in any other, at any time. I had quite a different attitude toward Theodore Roosevelt with whom, beginning in 1903, I was to have a voluminous correspondence and many lively meetings and conversations.

President Roosevelt was greatly interested in my early labor articles. He wrote me as follows regarding my account of the New York situation and Sam Parks, the labor boss:

> I am immensely impressed by your article. While I had known in rather a vague way that there was such a condition as you describe, I had not known its extent, and as far as I am aware the facts have never before been brought before the public in such striking fashion. How emphatically this revelation emphasizes the need of drawing the line on *conduct*, among labor unions, among corporations, among politicians, and among private individuals, alike! The organs of the Wall Street men of a certain type are bitter in their denunciations of the labor unions, and have not a word to say against the corporations. The labor leaders of a certain type howl against the corporations but do not admit that there is any wrong ever perpetrated by labor men. . . .
>
> I believe in corporations; I believe in trade unions. Both have come to stay, and are necessities in our present industrial system.

But where, in either the one or the other, there develops corruption or mere brutal indifference to the rights of others, and short-sighted refusal to look beyond the moment's gain, then the offender, whether union or corporation, must be fought, and if the public sentiment is calloused to the iniquity of either, by just so much the whole public is damaged.

Can you not come on here and see me some time at your convenience?

I was naturally greatly pleased that he should be impressed by my articles and that I had been able to contribute to his own knowledge of conditions, for he occupied the place of pre-eminent power in the United States, with a field of action and publicity far exceeding that of men like Carl Schurz. What he said echoed across the country, reaching people in every little hamlet and crossroad. What a thing it was, I thought, to have a President who was genuinely interested in these ugly aspects of our common life, and who was not afraid to attack them wherever they might be found. I became for a time his ardent and more or less uncritical follower.

But as the years passed Roosevelt's typical reaction, that of balancing the blame, without going to the root of the matter, and of seeking the "devil in the mess," satisfied me less and less. His actions often seemed to me to be based not upon principles well thought out, but upon moral judgments which were, or seemed to me to be, too hasty. His notion of a square deal was to cuff the radical on one ear and the conservative on the other, without enlightening either. He had no "single track mind"! He ran full-speed on all the tracks at once. Too often he rode down opposition without understanding what it meant, or talked it down with a torrent of phrases. But what energy and gusto he had, what wholesome enthusiasms, what common human goodnesses and courtesies!

I recall my astonishment at receiving an invitation to lecture at Harvard University. Next to the President's invitation to luncheon at Oyster Bay nothing could have awed me more. It had begun with appreciative letters from John Graham Brooks, Professor W. Z. Ripley, Professor F. W. Taussig and others—whom I had thought of as living in a rarefied academic atmosphere far removed from the rough and tough, sweaty, ill-smelling quarrels of coal heavers, rivet drivers, and sweatshop workers. I recall with keen pleasure the dinner with Professor Taussig and a number of other Harvard teachers, the penetrating questions they asked, and the lively discussion that followed. It seemed to me I had never met a group of men more genuinely alive than they, more deeply interested in the real problems that confronted America. I was not only vastly encouraged then, I think of it still as a fine and generous gesture made by those distinguished scholars to an inquirer venturing in a field, their field, where angels might well fear to tread. With one of them I made a friendship of casual meetings and intermittent correspondence that lasted for forty years.

What had worried me most regarding that Harvard lecture was the knowledge that I was not an easy or fluent speaker, and I feared I might not meet the expectations of the fine men who had invited me. I remember trying to reassure myself by quoting from Mr. Dooley that "when a man has something to say an' don't know how to say it, he says it pretty well."

I was full of my subject. As I wrote my father regarding the lecture, I believed that we were on the "verge of a new political struggle in which monopoly of capital, on the one hand, and of labor on the other, will be the chief issues. I am not theorizing: I am dealing with concrete facts. Theories never get under a man's skin: facts do. I shouldn't wonder if some of the things I say tomorrow night may shock the academic mind—which is always about ten years behind the living age."

As a matter of fact I did not shock these men at all: they were not ten years behind the living age—not more than five anyway!—and, after I got started and forgot myself, I think I really interested them and the audience of students who came to hear me.

The early response to the exposure articles was thus encouraging in every way. It seemed for a time that the walls of corrupt Jericho, shaken by the blasts of our trumpets, were already trembling toward complete demolition. I had much still to learn about Jericho.

It was not long before the invitations to speak here and there, to join organizations, to reply to innumerable letters and meet men, some of them really worth while, became a burden and an interruption. I was often glad that I lived seven hundred miles away in Michigan, even though it did involve commuting to New York once or twice every month.

It became clearer every day that we must go on with our "exposure" articles. The popular response had been unmistakable. They were not only profoundly interesting to write—like explorations in an unknown land—but they were plainly helpful. And I was eager for more dragons to slay!

Next after the struggle between capital and labor upon which I had been working, I wanted most of all to understand the railroad problem. It was then one of the leading subjects of discussion in Congress, with proposals to regulate railroad rates and increase public control through the Interstate Commerce Commission, and it was being bitterly agitated by able young political leaders, like LaFollette, in the West.

I began to read everything on the subject that I could get hold of. There really wasn't much to be had in those early days, the dry reports of Congressional committees, a few pamphlets, and a book or two by early agitators like Governor Larrabee of Iowa. There were two or three studies by scholars: *Railroad Transportation; Its History and Its Laws,* by Arthur T. Hadley, afterward president of Yale University; *State Railroad Control,* by Professor Frank H. Dixon; and the book I found best of them all, *The Railroad Problem,* by A. B. Stickney, who had himself been a western railroad president. I studied the discoveries that LaFollette was making in Wisconsin and got the advice of some of the foremost experts in the country, such as Professor W. Z. Ripley of Harvard, Dr. Carroll D. Wright, who had been United States Commissioner of Labor, and John Graham Brooks, then President of the American Social Science Association. I talked with members of Congress who were interested in the pending bills.

More encouraging than anything else was the enthusiasm expressed by Theodore Roosevelt. He was attacking the problem, then as dangerous as any in the entire political field, with what seemed to me to be real sincerity, real determination. Could there be a finer thing to do than to help him by building up popular understanding behind him?

I may say that up to this time I had little or no interest in Roosevelt as a political leader—or, indeed, in political issues generally. My only concern was to learn about the railroad problem—and if it led into the White House I intended, if possible, to follow it there.

In my earliest personal acquaintance with the "redoubtable Teddy," as he himself liked to be called, he was a soldier, not a political leader. This was in 1898, upon his return from the Spanish War in Cuba. I went down with him to Montauk Point where the Rough Riders were in camp, and wrote one of the first, if not the first, extended biographical articles about him, published in *McClure's Magazine,* November, 1898.

It was the personality of the man that chiefly attracted me. I remember how deeply I had been impressed by a call I made upon him when he was Commissioner of Police in New York City. When I entered the huge room that was his office he was dismissing his last visitor and I saw him turn quickly in his swivel chair to an open book on the draw-shelf. In the few seconds that I took to reach his desk he was absorbed in that book—a book, he told me later, on Sioux Indian culture.

"It is surprising," he said, "how much reading a man can do in time usually wasted."

I thought I had never before come across such concentration of purpose. He seemed never to waste a moment of time. In later years, as I came to know him better, I had further illustrations of this characteristic. I was sometimes asked to meet him while he was being shaved in the little anteroom that adjoined his office. This process had its anxieties and alarms, for the President could not talk without gesticulating. I was usually unable to get in a word of what I wanted to say until the barber reached his chin. I often wished he had a double one!

His energy, his ubiquity, his versatility were astonishing. I recall cutting out a bit of verse from the British *St. James Gazette,* thus characterizing him:

> Smack of Lord Cromer, Jeff Davis a touch of him,
> Little of Lincoln, but not very much of him,
> Kitchener, Bismarck, and Germany's Will,
> Jupiter, Chamberlain, Buffalo Bill.

During 1904 I recollect having had one or two talks with the President on the railroad problem which was then rising ominously on the political horizon. In one very long letter to me in August, 1904, he had set forth his attitude regarding this and other dangerous issues. It seemed to me to be too vague and general, not firmly nailed down with documented facts.

On January 2, 1905, I received this letter:

> MY DEAR MR. BAKER:
>
> When are you coming down again? I think your last article in *McClure's* is far and away the best discussion of lynching that I have seen anywhere. You know how much I admire your treatment of labor matters; but upon my word I think this is even superior. I am anxious to see you. Come down some time when you can take lunch with me.
>
> Sincerely yours,
>
> (Signed) THEODORE ROOSEVELT.

I was in Washington on January 28 and lunched with the President at the White House. It was a charmingly informal meal, the only guest besides myself being Mrs. Henry Cabot Lodge. I find this account in my notebook:

"The President is fond of laughing out in a big, hearty way

and of joking with his boys. He chaffed Archie upon spilling his gravy, setting the table to laughing by inquiring, 'Am I the father of swine?' and planned, with all the zest of a boy, an afternoon horseback ride with Ted. After the meal the President drew me aside where we continued to talk, chiefly on the subject of railroad legislation.

"His chief trouble was with the Senate.

" 'The reformers complain because I will not go to the absurdity of refusing to deal with machine Senators, but I must work with the material that the states send me. Senator Platt[2] came in this morning and asked me to do six things. Five of them I granted because they were reasonable and just: the sixth I refused because it was not just. Senator Platt went away satisfied and will help me.' "

The President was especially impatient with the radical reformers:

"One must proceed in this railroad legislation by evolutionary methods, not by revolution."

Speaking of his own difficulties, he said he thought no President save Washington and Lincoln were confronted by more difficult questions.

"I am no genius," he said, "but I am working hard to do the right thing all the time."

The President said he had sent my article on labor conditions in the mines of Colorado to Colonel Carroll D. Wright, Commissioner of Labor, who had made an independent investigation and reported that my report was "accurate and fair." At the same time he criticized an article I had written on "Lawless Finance," on the ground that it laid all the blame on the business interests of the country, and declared that bribery was due quite as much to the blackmailing demands of legislators.

"But Mr. President," I tried to argue, "my job is not to assess

---

[2] Senator Thomas C. Platt of New York, the former Republican boss of the state [ED.].

blame on anyone: I am trying to get at the facts and report them as truthfully as I can."

A few days later, at a formal luncheon given to honor Carroll D. Wright, where there were many distinguished guests, the President inveighed with characteristic vigor against the "pinhead opposition in the Senate" and then came out roundly: "I want to be specific—such pinheads as [Senators] Morgan and Bacon."[3]

In the October (1905) number of *McClure's* appeared the announcement of my new series, called "The Railroads on Trial," and I well remember the editorial perspiration it caused in the making. We said in part:

> Charges of the utmost seriousness have been, for a long time, and are now being preferred against the men who control and operate the railroads of the country. They are at this moment upon trial, not merely because President Roosevelt has called a special session of Congress to decide whether these men have properly conducted the large interests intrusted to their care, but they are on trial before the higher court of public opinion. . . .
>
> The chief purpose of Mr. Baker, in the present work, is to make just such an investigation as every citizen himself would make if he could command the time. And he has brought to the investigation exactly the interest of any reader of *McClure's Magazine*—that of the American voter, who is deeply concerned in the welfare of his country.

The warm approval of my first articles by the editors of *McClure's*, both S. S. McClure and John S. Phillips, encouraged me to ask President Roosevelt if he would like to see the proofs of it. He responded on September 8 as follows:

> My dear Mr. Baker:
>
> Yes, I should greatly like to see the proof of your November article, and that not because of any good I can do you, but because I have learned to look to your articles for real help. You

---

[3] Senator Augustus O. Bacon of Georgia and Senator John T. Morgan of Alabama were leaders in Roosevelt's opposition [ED.].

have impressed me with your earnest desire to be fair, with your freedom from hysteria, and with your anxiety to tell the truth rather than to write something that will be sensational, that will appeal to shallow and ignorant people, and that will make your articles widely read and admired for the moment by crude theorists. I shall look forward to seeing the proof.

With regard,
Sincerely yours,
(Signed) THEODORE ROOSEVELT.

So I sent him the proof, I need not say with what fear and trembling, for his approval might be the measure of the usefulness of the entire series I had planned. He could command the incomparable sounding board of the White House. I was greatly relieved to have his letter of September 13:

MY DEAR MR. BAKER:

I haven't a criticism to suggest about the article. You have given me two or three thoughts for my own message. It seems to me that one of the lessons you teach is that these railroad men are not to be treated as exceptional villains but merely as ordinary Americans, who under given conditions are by the mere force of events forced into doing much of which we complain. I want so far as I can, to free the movement for their control from all rancor and hatred.

Sincerely yours,
(Signed) THEODORE ROOSEVELT.

I began to hear from people all over the country, including some of the ablest experts in that field. A member of the Interstate Commerce Commission wrote that the article on rebates was "certain to influence public sentiment deeply. You are doing splendid work: go ahead." Professor Ripley of Harvard wrote me that the "last article" was "extremely good and promises everything for the future." While such letters as these gave me assurances that I was on the firm ground of fact and could defend myself there, the messages that came to the magazine from the little men of the West—cattle growers and fruit growers and small business men—and there were a great many of them—pleased me far more.

I endeavored in all these articles, even more than I had in writing on the labor problem, to bring out the facts, the truth, with no "final solution" to present, no pet remedy to recommend. As I wrote my father from Wichita, Kansas, where I had found the problems unusually complex:

"The further I get the less sure I become as to remedies, the further I am from recommending any fine-spun theory which is to cure all the evils. I have lots of letters from socialists and other extremists scolding me because I do not draw the conclusions they think I should and recommending their particular brands of salvation."

I had, for example, a good-humored letter from Upton Sinclair, who was an enthusiastic socialist, in which he said that he had read my last instalment, and remarked that "you can beat even the rest of the folks on *McClure's* for getting together facts minus conclusions."

This ironical comment I regarded as high praise.

For I doubted then, and I have doubted ever since, short-cuts and wholesale solutions. Changes in institutions are indeed necessary, but as John Stuart Mill said long ago in his autobiography, they are attended with "less benefit" than ardent spirits expect. It seems to be a failing peculiarly American to begin dosing before the diagnosis is complete; we dislike to be quiet and slow; we hate to think things through. We believe in formulas and slogans, we like "drives." We have a pathetic faith in legal enactments such as the 18th Amendment, and changes in the "system" such as the initiative and referendum. There may be considerable education of individual minds in the process of campaigning for such reforms, but it is astonishing how little, how very little, they change actual conditions.

I am not even sure of democracy as a universal cure—that is, if it means what it seems to mean to many people. But I am strong for democracy as a way of life—if it means what I think it ought to mean.

Ignorance is the real enemy.

The fireworks following the publication of my articles were not slow in beginning. My articles were not to be left unanswered. The railroads had a powerful and well-financed organization to reach, and influence, the public opinion to which I was appealing so hopefully. I had found nothing like it in my studies of the labor problem, or indeed, in the investigations for my earlier articles on certain aspects of "lawless finance." Here, I saw at once, I was getting down into and coming to understand the heart of the matter—*where the truth really hurt.*

The President, who was at work on his address to Congress, was also making the same discovery, considerably, I think, to his surprise. He wrote asking if I knew anything about a man named Rathom, and what he was doing. It was a great satisfaction to be able to inform him immediately that I knew Mr. John R. Rathom and his pamphlet "The Farmer and His Friends," and that he was employed by a powerful publicity agency which represented the railroads. No money was spared in putting the railroad's interests before the people, in such a way as not to seem to come from the railroads. I said in part:

"As for John Rathom, I believe what he tells me, that he spends no corrupt money; and I am fair enough to wish that the railroad side may be fully and honestly presented to the people—as I told him. But they do *not* present their case frankly as the railroad case: they conceal their identity, issue cunningly prepared statistics and plausible pamphlets which *assume* to present the problem fairly. In John Rathom's address—the foundation of the pamphlet you send me—Rathom appears as the farmer's friend, not the hired railroad agent which he really is. His letterheads declare him to be a lecturer. Thus by deceit these publicity agents not only seek to influence public opinion, but they employ all the *great leverage of the power of the railroads, their advertising, their passes, their political influence.*

And when worse comes to worse, as it did last year in Wisconsin, they will buy newspapers outright. It is anything to muffle the truth!

"To meet such conditions, the quality of truth-telling must be peculiarly bold and vigorous, else it does not strike home. It warms a man's soul to see the facts about the railroads and life insurance coming out. If once the truth can be got out and spread abroad, there is something fine in the way the people act upon it."

Just about this time I began to see innocent looking little articles in various newspapers, some of which I cut out and pasted in my notebooks. Here is one:

"An influential senator, one of the leaders of the upper branch, says President Roosevelt is already tired of his venture into the railway regulation field and wishes he had kept out of it. 'He is in a hole in this matter,' said the senator in question, 'and he is now looking to us to help him out. If we adopt his recommendation and pass the legislation he asks for we shall throw the country into a panic and he will have to take the responsibility for it—he and the Republican party together. We shall do no such thing. We will save the President from that blunder.' Mr. Roosevelt took up this agitation without having given the subject proper study. . . . Now he is weary of the whole thing and his active mind is turning to new toys. He is a man who must have a new plaything in the line of national policies about once in so many days. He springs a scheme and because he can't get it through in five minutes he grows tired of it and takes up a new hobby. That is the way it has been with this railway rate business . . ."

There were many variations in this insidious form of attack. I was suspicious to the point of certainty as to where it came from.

On October 16, I was surprised to receive from the President the galley proofs of his proposed message to Congress, accompanied by the following notation:

"Now I send you herewith the first proof of my message, dealing with corporations—that is, the first seven galleys. Of course I must ask you to keep it strictly confidential; but will you give me any comments which your experiences teach you ought to be made thereon?"

I need scarcely comment upon the deep joy and satisfaction I felt at being thus consulted by the President—or the seriousness of the responsibility I felt. I knew perfectly well how little I really knew about the complicated problems involved in the new legislation, but then, who was there at that time who did? I also knew that my chances to help would be greatly enhanced by keeping the confidence and co-operation of the man in the White House, who could so wonderfully reach all the people of the country.

I confess that I was much disappointed with the message upon the first reading of it. It was too general, there was too much of the President's favorite balancing of good and evil—the good corporation against the bad corporation—and what seemed to me the lack of sureness in striking at the "guts" of the evil, as he himself had called it. I was terribly afraid that he was plumping for a solution that, while it might help a little, and look good politically, would fail to reach the heart of the matter.

I knew that my only course, so far as the President's message was concerned, was to tell him the truth as I saw it. Why shouldn't I? I had no party allegiances, and I wanted no office. So I centered specifically and directly upon what seemed to me the most important defect in his recommendations—writing him on November 11, 1905:

> The chief recommendation in the message is that the Commission be given power to fix a *maximum* rate. I have just been in the West studying the relations of the Beef Trust and the railroads. The tap-root of Armour's power, as you know, is railroad favoritism, and I have asked myself over and over, trying to see the question on every side, whether the power to fix a maximum

rate, which you suggest, will touch this specific case of injustice. Armour's evil power arises in part from his ability to force the railroads to give him a lower rate on dressed beef than they give the unorganized cattle-growers on their cattle.

The danger in this case lies not in the fact that any rate is too high, indeed both cattle and beef rates are probably too low. The danger is thus *not* a maximum rate but a minimum rate. Armour does not care what the rate is, high or low, so long as he gets his differential, so long as he can force the railroad to make a lower rate on meat than it does on cattle.

Similar conditions prevail in most cases of competition between commodities and between localities. Therefore, Mr. President, it seems inevitable, if we are really to control the rate and to prevent further fattening of trusts upon railroad favoritism, that an impartial governmental tribunal must fix a *definite* rate. . . .

In making this comment I seemed to have touched the sore spot in the message. The President responded immediately:

MY DEAR MR. BAKER:

Many thanks for your letter of the 11th instant. I am inclined to think that it would be better if the Commission had the power to fix a definite instead of a maximum rate; but the Attorney General in his opinion, which of course you have seen, expresses the opinion that the maximum rate is certainly constitutional, whereas it is not certain by any means that the definite rate would be constitutional. The Supreme Court's attitude is more than doubtful on it. Now, the one thing I do not want is to have a law passed and then declared unconstitutional. The maximum rate might not reach cases like you quote . . . but it will do a good deal. . . .

Sincerely yours,

(Signed) THEODORE ROOSEVELT.

Senator Knox is inclined to the exact view Moody[4] takes.

There followed a long and rather heated correspondence on the point. In a letter on November 17th I suggested a remedy that had taken shape after several conferences I had had with

---

[4] Attorney General William Henry Moody.

able students of the question—that is, to "empower the commission, not to fix a rate, but to *condemn* a rate, whether too high or too low, leaving to the railroad itself the power of making the changes. . . . Administered by a commission of high-class intelligence, such power could be exercised to the utmost advantage of abused shippers, and it would also enable the railroads themselves to cast off such an old man of the sea as the Beef Trust. . . ."

I also said in my letter:

> I do not think this power to condemn would reach the seat of the difficulty with such certainty as the power to fix a definite rate, but it would, in my opinion, be far more efficacious than the power to fix a maximum rate. . . .

The President responded with a four-page typewritten letter beginning with the statement, "I think you are entirely mistaken in your depreciation of what is accomplished by fixing a maximum rate" and defending the original remedy he had proposed. His attitude in the correspondence which followed was so characteristically emphatic that I believed my suggestion would come to nothing. What was my surprise, when I read the message in its final form as delivered to Congress, to find that the President had inserted a paragraph, almost in my own words, regarding the regulation of minimum rates. While it was what I had hoped, it was so hedged about and weakened with limitations that its usefulness seemed doubtful. But it was *something:* and there are the best of evidences that it helped in the passage of the Hepburn Act.

I developed my relationships with Theodore Roosevelt somewhat more fully in the last chapter than was perhaps necessary, in order to explain what soon followed—the attack made by the President on the magazines and magazine writers for their campaigns of exposure of corruption in the business and political life of the United States. I remembered one day that spring (1906) meeting a friend on the street.

"Hello, Muckraker," he bantered me.

I did not at first know what my friend meant, but I speedily found out. At a meeting of the famous Gridiron Club in Washington, an organization for encouraging candor in the relationships of public officials and newspaper correspondents, the President had charged the writers of the "exposure articles" with extravagance and untruthfulness, likening them to the "Man with the muckrake" in Bunyan's *Pilgrim's Progress.* He had attached a name of odium to all the writers engaged in exposing corruption regardless of whether they deserved it or not.

The news of the attack spread like wildfire over the country. The President, always intoxicated by the discovery of a new catch-phrase, was apparently delighted with the response he had received, and since the speeches at the Gridiron Club were never reported, he announced that he would make the same address a few weeks later at the laying of the cornerstone of the office building of the House of Representatives, April 14, 1906.

It was difficult for me to understand this attack, considering all that had recently happened, all that the President owed to the investigations and reports of at least some of the magazine writers, the more than friendly relationships that had existed in my own case, the many letters of approval he had written regarding the work I had been doing.

I believed then, and have believed still more firmly since—it seems now to be the opinion of historians generally—that the work of the magazines in setting forth the evil conditions then existing had been of great service in arousing the public to support the President's efforts. John Chamberlain, in his excellent book, *Farewell to Reform,* remarks that the muckrakers did "an incalculable amount of good," and goes on to quote

William Archer, who wrote (in the British *Fortnightly Review* for May, 1910) that "the influence of the *McClure* type of magazine; . . . paved the way for President Roosevelt and potently furthered the movement with which his name will always be identified."

In this article Archer spoke of the *McClure* type of article as a "richly documented, soberly worded study in contemporary history." " 'Thorough' and 'understatement,' " he said, "were the two pre-eminent *McClure* words. And if *McClure's* turned up plenty of corruption, why, corruption was the dominant fact of American life at the time."

"Muckraking," he goes on to say, "provided the basis for the entire movement toward Social Democracy that came to its head in the first Wilson Administration."

The more I heard of the President's proposed address, the more anxious and indignant I became, the more fearful that such an attack might greatly injure the work which we were trying honestly to do. I finally decided to write him the following letter (April 7, 1906):

My dear Mr President:

I have been much disturbed at the report of your proposed address to the Army and Navy Union; and I am writing you now because you have so often expressed your willingness to hear from me at any time.

Admitting the criticism may in certain instances have gone too far and that at this moment too little emphasis may be laid upon the "good in the world," which I quite agree with you is predominant—or what would be the use of trying to arouse it to action?—it seems to me of the utmost importance that we maintain the right in this country of speaking the truth upon any subject whatsoever. As Lowell said: "Democracy in its best sense is merely the letting in of light and air." Now, the letting in of light and air in the matter of current business conditions, toward which you yourself have contributed more than any other man, and for which your administration will, I sincerely believe, be chiefly remembered, is neither pleasant nor profitable for the rascals upon whom the light is turned. Even admitting that some of the so-called "exposures" have been extreme, have they not, as a whole, been honest and useful? and would not a speech, backed by all of your great authority, attacking the magazines, tend to give aid and comfort to these very rascals, besides making it more difficult in the future not only to get the truth told but to have it listened to? And the first to stop the work of letting in the light and air will be those who have been trying honestly to tell the whole truth, good and bad, and leave the field to the outright ranters and inciters. Already there exists an indiscriminating attack upon the so-called exposures which may prevent the careful study of modern conditions and the presentation of the facts in a popular form.

Very sincerely yours,
(Signed) RAY STANNARD BAKER.

I had an immediate response from the President as follows:

April 9, 1906.

MY DEAR MR BAKER:

I am in receipt of your letter of the 7th instant. One reason I want to make that address is because people so persistently misunderstand what I said, that I want to have it reported in full. For instance, you misunderstand it. I want to "let in light and air," but I do not want to let in sewer gas. If a room is fetid and the windows are bolted I am perfectly contented to knock out the windows; but I would not knock a hole into the drain pipe. In other words, I feel that the man who in a yellow newspaper or in a yellow magazine (I do not think it worth while to say publicly what I will say to you privately, that Hearst's papers and magazines are those I have in mind at the moment, as well as, say the New York *Herald* and similar publications, daily and monthly) makes a ferocious attack on good men or even attacks bad men with exaggeration or for things they have not done, is a potent enemy of those of us who are really striving in good faith to expose bad men and drive them from power. I disapprove of the whitewash brush quite as much as of mud slinging, and it seems to me that the disapproval of one in no shape or way implies approval of the other. This I shall try to make clear.

I shall carefully read what you say about the railroads.

Sincerely yours,
(Signed) THEODORE ROOSEVELT.

When I read his speech, which he delivered on April 14, I found that he had made no such distinctions in it as he had made in his letter to me. There was indeed the familiar balance of approval and disapproval, whitewashing against mudslinging, but he did not "think it worth while" to acknowledge the service of those men who had been striving to tell the truth, honestly and completely, whose work he had repeatedly approved, and for whose help he had again and again expressed his appreciation. There had recently, indeed, been an outbreak of highly sensational publications—like Lawson's *Frenzied Finance,* and Phillips' *Treason of the Senate,* although even these contained much truth that the public was entitled to have. But the President, unmindful of his own motto, "the square deal," classed all of us together. He certainly knew, even before he received my letter, the interpretation that would be placed upon his attack. The Chicago *Tribune,* on the next day, listed the names of the writers, whether sensational or not, all together, as being cast into outer darkness.

I met the President many times afterward and there were numerous exchanges of letters, but while I could wonder at his remarkable versatility of mind, and admire his many robust human qualities, I could never again give him my full confidence, nor follow his leadership.

10.

Theodore Roosevelt Holds to the Rule of Reason

Theodore Roosevelt admired "the self-sufficient life of the frontier, in which every boy and girl played a part" as much as Ray Stannard Baker did. But to Roosevelt, brought up in a dignified brownstone residence on East Twentieth Street in Manhattan, the frontier meant something else than it did to reformers with a rural upbringing. Roosevelt, who invested and soon lost a part of his inheritance in a Dakota ranch, spent time with cowboys, and wrote a four-volume history of the West, saw the frontier not as symbol of equality and opportunity, but as an environment that fostered strength of character.

Roosevelt valued character. He despised the vulgarity of some of his wealthy friends, who seemed to take all of life as an investment. And he feared what he often regarded as the whining demands of the underprivileged classes. He was not alarmed by monopoly, and he viewed social inequality as a reflection of the natural order of the universe. His battles, as he once explained, took place along the line of conflict that divided law-abiding citizens from outlaws. That distinction, familiar on the frontier, guided Roosevelt's attitude toward businessmen and the trusts. There were "good trusts" and "bad trusts," and he would prosecute the latter. In the chapter of his autobiography presented here, he explains his use of this doctrine.

One of the vital questions with which as President I had to deal was the attitude of the Nation toward the great corporations. Men who understand and practice the deep underlying philosophy of the Lincoln school of American political thought are necessarily Hamiltonian in their belief in a strong and efficient National Government and Jeffersonian in their belief in the people as the ultimate authority, and in the welfare of the people as the end of Government. The men who first applied the extreme Democratic theory in American life were, like Jefferson, ultra individualists, for at that time what was demanded by our people was the largest liberty for the individual. During the century that had elapsed since Jefferson became President the need had been exactly reversed. There had been in our country a riot of individualistic materialism, under which complete freedom for the individual—that ancient license which President Wilson a century after the term was excusable has called the "New" Freedom—turned out in practice to mean perfect freedom for the strong to wrong the weak. The total absence of governmental control had led to a portentous growth in the financial and industrial world both of natural individuals and of artificial individuals—that is, corporations. In no other country in the world had such enormous fortunes been gained. In no other country in the world was such power held by the men who had gained these fortunes; and these men almost always worked through, and by means of, the giant corporations which they controlled. The power of the mighty industrial overlords of the country had increased with giant strides, while the methods of controlling them, or checking abuses by them, on the part of the people, through the Government, remained archaic and therefore practically impotent. The courts, not un-

---

From Theodore Roosevelt, *Autobiography* (New York: Charles Scribner's Sons, 1913), chap. 12, "The Big Stick and the Square Deal," pp. 423–450. Copyright 1913 by Charles Scribner's Sons; renewal copyright 1941 by Edith K. Carow Roosevelt. Reprinted by permission of the publishers.

naturally, but most regrettably, and to the grave detriment of the people and of their own standing, had for a quarter of a century been on the whole the agents of reaction, and by conflicting decisions which, however, in their sum were hostile to the interests of the people, had left both the nation and the several States well-nigh impotent to deal with the great business combinations. Sometimes they forbade the Nation to interfere, because such interference trespassed on the rights of the States; sometimes they forbade the States to interfere (and often they were wise in this), because to do so would trespass on the rights of the Nation; but always, or well-nigh always, their action was negative action against the interests of the people, ingeniously devised to limit their power against wrong, instead of affirmative action giving to the people power to right wrong. They had rendered these decisions sometimes as upholders of property rights against human rights, being especially zealous in securing the rights of the very men who were most competent to take care of themselves; and sometimes in the name of liberty, in the name of the so-called "new freedom," in reality the old, old "freedom," which secured to the powerful the freedom to prey on the poor and the helpless.

One of the main troubles was the fact that the men who saw the evils and who tried to remedy them attempted to work in two wholly different ways, and the great majority of them in a way that offered little promise of real betterment. They tried (by the Sherman law method) to bolster up an individualism already proved to be both futile and mischievous; to remedy by more individualism the concentration that was the inevitable result of the already existing individualism. They saw the evil done by the big combinations, and sought to remedy it by destroying them and restoring the country to the economic conditions of the middle of the nineteenth century. This was a hopeless effort, and those who went into it, although they regarded themselves as radical progressives, really represented a form of sincere rural toryism. They confounded monopolies with big business combinations, and in the effort to prohibit both alike, instead of where possible prohibiting one and drastically controlling the other, they succeeded merely in preventing any effective control of either.

On the other hand, a few men recognized that corporations and combinations had become indispensable in the business world, that it was folly to try to prohibit them, but that it was also folly to leave them without thoroughgoing control. These men realized that the doctrines of the old *laissez faire* economists, of the believers in unlimited competition, unlimited individualism, were in the actual state of affairs false and mischievous. They realized that the Government must now interfere to protect labor, to subordinate the big corporation to the public welfare, and to shackle cunning and fraud exactly as centuries before it had interfered to shackle the physical force which does wrong by violence.

The big reactionaries of the business world and their allies and instruments among politicians and newspaper editors took advantage of this division of opinion, and especially of the fact that most of their opponents were on the wrong path; and fought to keep matters absolutely unchanged. These men demanded for themselves an immunity from governmental control which, if granted, would have been as wicked and as foolish as immunity to the barons of the twelfth century. Many of them were evil men. Many others were just as good men as were some of these same barons; but they were as utterly unable as any medieval castle-owner to understand what the public interest really was. There have been aristocracies which have played a great and beneficent part at stages in the growth of mankind; but we had come to the stage where for our people what was needed was a real democracy; and of all forms of tyranny the least attractive and the most vulgar is the tyranny of mere wealth, the tyranny of a plutocracy.

When I became President, the question as to the *method* by which the United States Government was to control the corporations was not yet important. The absolutely vital question was whether the Government had power to control them at all. This question had not yet been decided in favor of the United States Government. It was useless to discuss methods of controlling big business by the National Government until it was definitely settled that the National Government had the power to control it. A decision of the Supreme Court had, with seeming definiteness, settled that the National Government had not the power.

This decision I caused to be annulled by the court that had rendered it; and the present power of the National Government to deal effectively with the trusts is due solely to the success of the Administration in securing this reversal of its former decision by the Supreme Court.

The Constitution was formed very largely because it had become imperative to give to some central authority the power to regulate and control interstate commerce. At that time when corporations were in their infancy and big combinations unknown, there was no difficulty in exercising the power granted. In theory, the right of the Nation to exercise this power continued unquestioned. But changing conditions obscured the matter in the sight of the people as a whole; and the conscious and the unconscious advocates of an unlimited and uncontrollable capitalism gradually secured the whittling away of the National power to exercise this theoretical right of control until it practically vanished. After the Civil War, with the portentous growth of industrial combinations in this country, came a period of reactionary decisions by the courts which, as regards corporations, culminated in what is known as the Knight case.

The Sherman Anti-Trust Law was enacted in 1890 because the formation of the Tobacco Trust and the Sugar Trust, the only two great trusts then in the country (aside from the Standard Oil Trust, which was a gradual growth), had awakened a popular demand for legislation to destroy monopoly and curb industrial combinations. This demand the Anti-Trust Law was intended to satisfy. The Administrations of Mr. Harrison and

Mr. Cleveland evidently construed this law as prohibiting such combinations in the future, not as condemning those which had been formed prior to its enactment. In 1895, however, the Sugar Trust, whose output originally was about fifty-five per cent of all sugar produced in the United States, obtained control of three other companies in Philadelphia by exchanging its stock for theirs, and thus increased its business until it controlled ninety-eight per cent of the entire product. Under Cleveland, the Government brought proceedings against the Sugar Trust, invoking the Anti-Trust Law, to set aside the acquisition of these corporations. The test case was on the absorption of the Knight Company.[1] The Supreme Court of the United States, with but one dissenting vote, held adversely to the Government. They took the ground that the power conferred by the Constitution to regulate and control interstate commerce did not extend to the production or manufacture of commodities within a State, and that nothing in the Sherman Anti-Trust Law prohibited a corporation from acquiring all the stock of other corporations through exchange of its stock for theirs, such exchange not being "commerce" in the opinion of the Court, even though by such acquisition the corporation was enabled to control the entire production of a commodity that was a necessary of life. The effect of this decision was not merely the absolute nullification of the Anti-Trust Law, so far as industrial corporations were concerned, but was also in effect a declaration that, under the Constitution, the National Government could pass no law really effective for the destruction or control of such combinations.

This decision left the National Government, that is, the people of the Nation, practically helpless to deal with the large combinations of modern business. The courts in other cases asserted the power of the Federal Government to enforce the Anti-Trust

---

1 The case is known in the law books as *U. S.* v. *E. C. Knight,* 156 U. S., Sept., p. 1.

Law so far as transportation rates by railways engaged in interstate commerce were concerned. But so long as the trusts were free to control the production of commodities without interference from the General Government, they were well content to let the transportation of commodities take care of itself—especially as the law against rebates was at that time a dead letter; and the Court by its decision in the Knight case had interdicted any interference by the President or by Congress with the production of commodities. It was on the authority of this case that practically all the big trusts in the United States, excepting those already mentioned, were formed. Usually they were organized as "holding" companies, each one acquiring control of its constituent corporations by exchanging its stock for theirs, an operation which the Supreme Court had thus decided could not be prohibited, controlled, regulated, or even questioned by the Federal Government.

Such was the condition of our laws when I acceded to the Presidency. Just before my accession, a small group of financiers desiring to profit by the governmental impotence to which we had been reduced by the Knight decision, had arranged to take control of practically the entire railway system in the Northwest—possibly as the first step toward controlling the entire railway system of the country. This control of the Northwestern railway systems was to be effected by organizing a new "holding" company, and exchanging its stock against the stock of the various corporations engaged in railway transportation throughout that vast territory, exactly as the Sugar Trust had acquired control of the Knight company and other concerns. This company was called the Northern Securities Company. Not long after I became President, on the advice of the Attorney-General, Mr. [Philander C.] Knox, and through him, I ordered proceedings to be instituted for the dissolution of the company. As far as could be told by their utterances at the time, among all the great lawyers in the United States Mr. Knox was the only one who believed that this action could be sustained. The defense was based expressly on the ground that the Supreme Court in the Knight case had explicitly sanctioned the formation of such a company as the Northern Securities Company. The representatives of privilege intimated, and sometimes asserted outright, that in directing the action to be brought I had shown a lack of respect for the Supreme Court, which had already decided the question at issue by a vote of eight to one. Mr. Justice White, then on the Court and now Chief Justice, set forth the position that the two cases were in principle identical with incontrovertible logic. In giving the views of the dissenting minority on the action I had brought, he said:

"The parallel between the two cases [the Knight case and the Northern Securities case] is complete. The one corporation acquired the stock of other and competing corporations in exchange for its own. It was conceded for the purposes of the case, that in doing so monopoly had been brought about in the refining of sugar, that the sugar to be produced was likely to become the subject of interstate commerce, and indeed that part of it would certainly become so. But the power of Congress was decided not to extend to the subject, because the ownership of the stock in the corporations was not itself commerce."[2]

Mr. Justice White was entirely correct in this statement. The cases were parallel. It was necessary to reverse the Knight case in the interests of the people against monopoly and privilege just as it had been necessary to reverse the Dred Scott case in the interest of the people against slavery and privilege; just as later it became necessary to reverse the New York Bakeshop[3] case in the interest of the people against that form of monopolistic privilege which put human rights below property rights where wage workers were concerned.

---

[2] *Northern Securities Company et al.* v. *U. S.*, 156 U. S., Sept., pp. 391–392.

[3] In *Lochner* v. *New York* (1905) the Court declared unconstitutional a statute limiting the hours of labor in bakeries. The decision was reversed in *Bunting* v. *Oregon* (1917) [ED.].

By a vote of five to four the Supreme Court reversed its decision in the Knight case, and in the Northern Securities case sustained the Government. The power to deal with industrial monopoly and suppress it and to control and regulate combinations, of which the Knight case had deprived the Federal Government, was thus restored to it by the Northern Securities case. After this later decision was rendered, suits were brought by my direction against the American Tobacco Company and the Standard Oil Company. Both were adjudged criminal conspiracies, and their dissolution ordered. The Knight case was finally overthrown. The vicious doctrine it embodied no longer remains as an obstacle to obstruct the pathway of justice when it assails monopoly. Messrs. Knox, [William H.] Moody, and [Charles J.] Bonaparte, who successively occupied the position of Attorney-General under me, were profound lawyers and fearless and able men; and they completely established the newer and more wholesome doctrine under which the Federal Government may now deal with monopolistic combinations and conspiracies.

The decisions rendered in these various cases brought under my direction constitute the entire authority upon which any action must rest that seeks through the exercise of national power to curb monopolistic control. The men who organized and directed the Northern Securities Company were also the controlling forces in the Steel Corporation, which has since been prosecuted under the act. The proceedings against the Sugar Trust for corruption in connection with the New York Custom House are sufficiently interesting to be considered separately.

From the standpoint of giving complete control to the National Government over big corporations engaged in inter-State business, it would be impossible to over-estimate the importance of the Northern Securities decision and of the decisions afterwards rendered in line with it in connection with the other trusts whose dissolution was ordered. The success of the Northern Securities case definitely established the power of the Government to deal with all great corporations. Without this success the

National Government must have remained in the impotence to which it had been reduced by the Knight decision as regards the most important of its internal functions. But our success in establishing the power of the National Government to curb monopolies did not establish the right method of exercising that power. We had gained the power. We had not devised the proper method of exercising it.

Monopolies can, although in rather cumbrous fashion, be broken up by law suits. Great business combinations, however, cannot possibly be made useful instead of noxious industrial agencies merely by law suits, and especially by law suits supposed to be carried on for their destruction and not for their control and regulation. I at once began to urge upon Congress the need of laws supplementing the Anti-Trust Law—for this law struck at all big business, good and bad, alike, and as the event proved was very inefficient in checking bad big business, and yet was a constant threat against decent business men. I strongly urged the inauguration of a system of thoroughgoing and drastic Governmental regulation and control over all big business combinations engaged in inter-State industry.

Here I was able to accomplish only a small part of what I desired to accomplish. I was opposed both by the foolish radicals who desired to break up all big business, with the impossible ideal of returning to mid-nineteenth century industrial conditions; and also by the great privileged interests themselves, who used these ordinarily—but sometimes not entirely—well-meaning "stool pigeon progressives" to further their own cause. The worst representatives of big business encouraged the outcry for the total abolition of big business, because they knew that they could not be hurt in this way, and that such an outcry distracted the attention of the public from the really efficient method of controlling and supervising them, in just but masterly fashion, which was advocated by the sane representatives of reform. However, we succeeded in making a good beginning by securing the passage of a law creating the Department of

Commerce and Labor, and with it the erection of the Bureau of Corporations. . . .

The Standard Oil Company took the lead in opposing all this legislation. This was natural, for it had been the worst offender in the amassing of enormous fortunes by improper methods of all kinds, at the expense of business rivals and of the public, including the corruption of public servants. If any man thinks this condemnation extreme, I refer him to the language officially used by the Supreme Court of the nation in its decision against the Standard Oil Company. Through their counsel, and by direct telegrams and letters to Senators and Congressmen from various heads of the Standard Oil organization, they did their best to kill the bill providing for the Bureau of Corporations. I got hold of one or two of these telegrams and letters, however, and promptly published them; and, as generally happens in such a case, the men who were all-powerful as long as they could work in secret and behind closed doors became powerless as soon as they were forced into the open. The bill went through without further difficulty.

The true way of dealing with monopoly is to prevent it by administrative action before it grows so powerful that even when courts condemn it they shrink from destroying it. The Supreme Court in the Tobacco and Standard Oil cases, for instance, used very vigorous language in condemning these trusts; but the net result of the decision was of positive advantage to the wrongdoers, and this has tended to bring the whole body of our law into disrepute in quarters where it is of the very highest importance that the law be held in respect and even in reverence. My effort was to secure the creation of a Federal Commission which should neither excuse nor tolerate monopoly, but prevent it when possible and uproot it when discovered; and which should in addition effectively control and regulate all big combinations, and should give honest business certainty as to what the law was and security as long as the law was obeyed. Such a Commission would furnish a steady expert control, a control adapted to the problem; and dissolution is neither control nor regulation, but is purely negative; and negative remedies are of little permanent avail. Such a Commission would have complete power to examine into every big corporation engaged or proposing to engage in business between the States. It would have the power to discriminate sharply between corporations that are doing well and those that are doing ill; and the distinction between those who do well and those who do ill would be defined in terms so clear and unmistakable that no one could misapprehend them. Where a company is found seeking its profits through serving the community by stimulating production, lowering prices or improving service, while scrupulously respecting the rights of others (including its rivals, its employees, its customers, and the general public), and strictly obeying the law, then no matter how large its capital, or how great the volume of its business it would be encouraged to still more abundant production, or better service, by the fullest protection that the Government could afford it. On the other hand, if a corporation were found seeking profit through injury or oppression of the community, by restricting production through trick or device, by plot or conspiracy against competitors, or by oppression of wage-workers, and then extorting high prices for the commodity it had made artificially scarce, it would be prevented from organizing if its nefarious purpose could be discovered in time, or pursued and suppressed by all the power of Government whenever found in actual operation. Such a commission, with the power I advocate, would put a stop to abuses of big corporations and small corporations alike; it would draw the line on conduct and not on size; it would destroy monopoly, and make the biggest business man in the country conform squarely to the principles laid down by the American people, while at the same time giving fair play to the little man and certainty of knowledge as to what was wrong and what was right both to big man and little man.

Although under the decision of the courts the National Government had power over the railways, I found, when I became President, that this power was either not exercised at all or exercised with utter inefficiency. The law against rebates was a dead letter. All the unscrupulous railway men had been allowed to violate it with impunity; and because of this, as was inevitable, the scrupulous and decent railway men had been forced to violate it themselves, under penalty of being beaten by their less scrupulous rivals. It was not the fault of these decent railway men. It was the fault of the Government.

Thanks to a first-class railway man, Paul Morton of the Santa Fé, son of Mr. Cleveland's Secretary of Agriculture, I was able completely to stop the practice. Mr. Morton volunteered to aid the Government in abolishing rebates. He frankly stated that he, like every one else, had been guilty in the matter; but he insisted that he uttered the sentiments of the decent railway men of the country when he said that he hoped the practice would be stopped, and that if I would really stop it, and not merely make believe to stop it, he would give the testimony which would put into the hands of the Government the power to put a complete check to the practice. Accordingly he testified, and on the information which he gave us we were able to take such action through the Inter-State Commerce Commission and the Department of Justice, supplemented by the necessary additional legislation, that the evil was absolutely eradicated. He thus rendered, of his own accord, at his own personal risk, and from purely disinterested motives, an invaluable service to the people, a service which no other man who was able to render was willing to render. As an immediate sequel, the world-old alliance between Blifil and Black George was immediately revived against Paul Morton. In giving rebates he had done only what every honest railway man in the country had been obliged to do because of the failure of the Government to enforce the prohibition as regards dishonest railway men. But unlike his fellows he had then shown the courage and sense of obligation to the public which made him come forward and without evasion or concealment state what he had done, in order that we might successfully put an end to the practice; and put an end to the practice we did, and we did it because of the courage and patriotism he had shown. The unscrupulous railway men, whose dishonest practices were thereby put a stop to, and the unscrupulous demagogues who were either under the influence of these men or desirous of gaining credit with thoughtless and ignorant people no matter who was hurt, joined in vindictive clamor against Mr. Morton. They actually wished me to prosecute him, although such prosecution would have been a piece of unpardonable ingratitude and treachery on the part of the public toward him—for I was merely acting as the steward of the public in this matter. I need hardly say that I stood by him; and later he served under me as Secretary of the Navy, and a capital Secretary he made too.[4]

We not only secured the stopping of rebates, but in the Hepburn Rate Bill we were able to put through a measure which gave the Inter-State Commerce Commission for the first time real control over the railways. There were two or three amusing features in the contest over this bill. All of the great business interests which objected to Governmental control banded to fight it, and they were helped by the honest men of ultra-conservative type who always dread change, whether good or bad. We finally forced it through the House. In the Senate it was referred to a committee in which the Republican majority was under the control of Senator Aldrich, who took the lead in opposing the bill. There was one Republican on the committee, however whom Senator Aldrich could not control—Senator Dolliver, of Iowa. The leading Democrat on the committee was Senator Tillman, of South Carolina, with whom I was not on good terms, because I had been obliged to cancel an invitation to him to dine at the White House on account of

---

[4] Appointed in 1904, Morton resigned, under public pressure, in 1905 [ED.].

his having made a personal assault in the Senate Chamber on his colleague from South Carolina; and later I had to take action against him on account of his conduct in connection with certain land matters. Senator Tillman favored the bill. The Republican majority in the committee under Senator Aldrich, when they acted adversely on the bill, turned it over to Senator Tillman, thereby making him its sponsor. The object was to create what it was hoped would be an impossible situation in view of the relations between Senator Tillman and myself. I regarded the action as simply childish. It was a curious instance of how able and astute men sometimes commit blunders because of sheer inability to understand intensity of disinterested motive in others. I did not care a rap about Mr. Tillman's getting credit for the bill, or having charge of it. I was delighted to go with him or with any one else just so long as he was traveling my way—and no longer.[5]

There was another amusing incident in connection with the passage of the bill. All the wise friends of the effort to secure Governmental control of corporations know that this Government control must be exercised through administrative and not judicial officers if it is to be effective. Everything possible should be done to minimize the chance of appealing from the decisions of the administrative officer to the courts. But it is not possible Constitutionally, and probably would not be desirable anyhow, completely to abolish the appeal. Unwise zealots wished to make the effort totally to abolish the appeal in connection with the Hepburn Bill. Representatives of the special interests wished to extend the appeal to include what it ought not to include. Between stood a number of men whose votes would mean the passage of, or the failure to pass, the bill, and who were not inclined towards either side. Three or four sub-

---

[5] The split between Roosevelt and Tillman had been more serious than this account suggests. On at least one occasion Tillman had insulted the President. Their momentary reconciliation was a dramatic event [ED.].

stantially identical amendments were proposed, and we then suddenly found ourselves face to face with an absurd situation. The good men who were willing to go with us but had conservative misgivings about the ultra-radicals would not accept a good amendment if one of the latter proposed it; and the radicals would not accept their own amendment if one of the conservatives proposed it. Each side got so wrought up as to be utterly unable to get matters into proper perspective; each prepared to stand on unimportant trifles; each announced with hysterical emphasis—the reformers just as hysterically as the reactionaries—that the decision as regards each unimportant trifle determined the worth or worthlessness of the measure. Gradually we secured a measurable return to sane appreciation of the essentials. Finally both sides reluctantly agreed to accept the so-called Allison amendment which did not, as a matter of fact, work any change in the bill at all. . . .

Thanks to this law and to the way in which the Inter-State Commerce Commission was backed by the Administration, the Commission, under men like Prouty, Lane, and Clark, became a most powerful force for good. Some of the good that we had accomplished was undone after the close of my Administration by the unfortunate law creating a Commerce Court[6]; but the major part of the immense advance we had made remained. There was one point on which I insisted, and upon which it is necessary always to insist. The Commission cannot do permanent good unless it does justice to the corporations precisely as it exacts justice from them. The public, the shippers, the stock and bondholders, and the employees, all have their rights, and none should be allowed unfair privileges at the expense of the others. Stock watering, and swindling of any kind should of course not only be stopped but punished. When, however, a road is managed fairly and honestly, and when it renders a

[6] The Mann-Elkins Act of 1910 created a Federal Court of Commerce with power to hear appeals from the decisions of the Commission. Roosevelt does not mention that the Court was abolished in 1913 [ED.].

real and needed service, then the Government must see that it is not so burdened as to make it impossible to run it at a profit. There is much wise legislation necessary for the safety of the public, or—like workmen's compensation—necessary to the well-being of the employee, which nevertheless imposes such a burden on the road that the burden must be distributed between the general public and the corporation, or there will be no dividends. In such a case it may be the highest duty of the commission to raise rates; and the commission, when satisfied that the necessity exists, in order to do justice to the owners of the road, should no more hesitate to raise rates, than under other circumstances to lower them.

So much for the "big stick" in dealing with the corporations when they went wrong. Now for a sample of the square deal.

In the fall of 1907 there were severe business disturbances and financial stringency, culminating in a panic which arose in New York and spread over the country. The damage actually done was great, and the damage threatened was incalculable. Thanks largely to the action of the Government, the panic was stopped before, instead of being merely a serious business check, it became a frightful and Nation-wide calamity, a disaster fraught with untold misery and woe to all our people. For several days the Nation trembled on the brink of such a calamity, of such a disaster.

During these days both the Secretary of the Treasury and I personally were in hourly communication with New York, following every change in the situation, and trying to anticipate every development. It was the obvious duty of the Administration to take every step possible to prevent appalling disaster by checking the spread of the panic before it grew so that nothing could check it. And events moved with such speed that it was necessary to decide and to act on the instant, as each successive crisis arose, if the decision and action were to accomplish anything. The Secretary of the Treasury took various actions, some on his own initiative, some by my direction.

Late one evening I was informed that two representatives of the Steel Corporation wished to see me early the following morning, the precise object not being named. Next morning, while at breakfast, I was informed that Messrs. [Henry C.] Frick and [Elbert H.] Gary were waiting at the office. I at once went over, and, as the Attorney-General, Mr. Bonaparte, had not yet arrived from Baltimore, where he had been passing the night, I sent a message asking the Secretary of State, Mr. Root, who was also a lawyer, to join us, which he did. Before the close of the interview and in the presence of the three gentlemen named, I dictated a note to Mr. Bonaparte, setting forth exactly what Messrs. Frick and Gary had proposed, and exactly what I had answered—so that there might be no possibility of misunderstanding. This note was published in a Senate Document while I was still President. It runs as follows:

THE WHITE HOUSE, WASHINGTON,
November 4, 1907.

My dear Mr. Attorney-General:

Judge E. H. Gary and Mr. H. C. Frick, on behalf of the Steel Corporation, have just called upon me. They state that there is a certain business firm (the name of which I have not been told, but which is of real importance in New York business circles), which will undoubtedly fail this week if help is not given. Among its assets are a majority of the securities of the Tennessee Coal Company. Application has been urgently made to the Steel Corporation to purchase this stock as the only means of avoiding a failure. Judge Gary and Mr. Frick informed me that as a mere business transaction they do not care to purchase the stock; that under ordinary circumstances they would not consider purchasing the stock, because but little benefit will come to the Steel Corporation from the purchase; that they are aware that the purchase will be used as a handle for attack upon them on the ground that they are striving to secure a monopoly of the business and prevent competition—not that this would represent what could honestly be said, but what might recklessly and untruthfully be said.

They further informed me that, as a matter of fact, the policy of the company has been to decline to acquire more than sixty per cent of the steel properties, and that this purpose has been persevered in for several years past, with the object of preventing these accusations, and, as a matter of fact, their proportion of steel properties has slightly decreased, so that it is below this sixty per cent, and the acquisition of the property in question will not raise it above sixty per cent. But they feel that it is immensely to their interest, as to the interest of every responsible business man, to try to prevent a panic and general industrial smash-up at this time, and that they are willing to go into this transaction, which they would not otherwise go into, because it seems the opinion of those best fitted to express judgment in New York that it will be an important factor in preventing a break that might be ruinous; and that this has been urged upon them by the combination of the most responsible bankers in New York who are now thus engaged in endeavoring to save the situation. But they asserted that they did not wish to do this if I stated that it ought not to be done. I answered that, while of course I could not advise them to take the action proposed, I felt it no public duty of mine to interpose any objections.

Sincerely yours,

(Signed) THEODORE ROOSEVELT.

HON. CHARLES J. BONAPARTE,
Attorney-General.

Mr. Bonaparte received this note in about an hour, and that same morning he came over, acknowledged its receipt, and said that my answer was the only proper answer that could have been made, having regard both to the law and to the needs of the situation. He stated that the legal situation had been in no way changed, and that no sufficient ground existed for prosecution of the Steel Corporation. But I acted purely on my own initiative, and the responsibility for the act was solely mine.

I was intimately acquainted with the situation in New York. The word "panic" means fear, unreasoning fear; to stop a panic it is necessary to restore confidence; and at the moment the so-called Morgan interests were the only interests which retained a full hold on the confidence of the people of New York —not only the business people, but the immense mass of men and women who owned small investments or had small savings in the banks and trust companies. Mr. Morgan and his associates were of course fighting hard to prevent the loss of confidence and the panic distrust from increasing to such a degree as to bring any other big financial institutions down; for this would probably have been followed by a general, and very likely a worldwide, crash. The Knickerbocker Trust Company had already failed, and runs had begun on, or were threatened as regards, two other big trust companies. These companies were now on the fighting line, and it was to the interest of everybody to strengthen them, in order that the situation might be saved. It was a matter of general knowledge and belief that they, or the individuals prominent in them, held the securities of the Tennessee Coal and Iron Company, which securities had no market value, and were useless as a source of strength in the emergency. The Steel Corporation securities, on the contrary, were immediately marketable, their great value being known and admitted all over the world—as the event showed. The proposal of Messrs. Frick and Gary was that the Steel Corporation should at once acquire the Tennessee Coal and Iron Company, and thereby substitute, among the assets of the threatened institutions (which, by the way, they did not name to me), securities of great and immediate value for securities which at the moment were of no value. It was necessary for me to decide on the instant, before the Stock Exchange opened, for the situation in New York was such that any hour might be vital, and failure to act for even an hour might make all subsequent effort to act utterly useless. From the best information at my disposal, I believed (what was actually the fact) that the addition of the Tennessee Coal and Iron property would only increase the proportion of the Steel Company's holdings by about four per cent, making them about sixty-two per cent instead of about fifty-eight per cent of the total value in the country; an addition, which, by itself, in my judgment (concurred in, not only by the Attorney-General but by every competent lawyer), worked no change in the legal status of the Steel corporation. The diminution in the percentage of holdings, and production, has gone on steadily, and the percentage is now about ten per cent less than it was ten years ago.

The action was emphatically for the general good. It offered the only chance for arresting the panic, and it did arrest the panic. I answered Messrs. Frick and Gary, as set forth in the letter quoted above, to the effect that I did not deem it my duty to interfere, that is, to forbid the action which more than anything else in actual fact saved the situation. The result justified my judgment. The panic was stopped, public confidence in the solvency of the threatened institution being at once restored.

Business was vitally helped by what I did. The benefit was not only for the moment. It was permanent. Particularly was this the case in the South. Three or four years afterwards I visited Birmingham. Every man I met, without exception, who was competent to testify, informed me voluntarily that the results of the action taken had been of the utmost benefit to Birmingham, and therefore to Alabama, the industry having profited to an extraordinary degree, not only from the standpoint of the business, but from the standpoint of the community at large and of the wage-workers, by the change in ownership. The results of the action I took were beneficial from every standpoint, and the action itself, at the time when it was taken, was vitally necessary to the welfare of the people of the United States.

I would have been derelict in my duty, I would have shown myself a timid and unworthy public servant, if in that extraordinary crisis I had not acted precisely as I did act. In every such crisis the temptation to indecision, to nonaction, is great, for excuses can always be found for nonaction, and action means risk and the certainty of blame to the man who acts. But if the man is worth his salt he will do his duty, he will give the people the benefit of the doubt, and act in any way which their interests demand and which is not affirmatively prohibited by law, unheeding the likelihood that he himself, when the crisis is over and the danger past, will be assailed for what he has done.

Every step I took in this matter was open as the day, and was known in detail at the moment to all people. The press contained full accounts of the visit to me of Messrs. Frick and Gary, and heralded widely and with acclamation the results of that visit. At the time the relief and rejoicing over what had been done were well-high universal. The danger was too imminent and too appalling for men to be willing to condemn those who were successful in saving them from it. But I fully understood and expected that when there was no longer danger, when the fear had been forgotten, attack would be made upon me; and as a matter of fact after a year had elapsed the attack was begun, and has continued at intervals ever since; my ordinary assailant being some politician of rather cheap type.

If I were on a sail-boat, I should not ordinarily meddle with any of the gear; but if a sudden squall struck us, and the main sheet jammed, so that the boat threatened to capsize, I would unhesitatingly cut the main sheet, even though I were sure that the owner, no matter how grateful to me at the moment for having saved his life, would a few weeks later, when he had forgotten his danger and his fear, decide to sue me for the value of the cut rope. But I would feel a hearty contempt for the owner who so acted.

There were many other things that we did in connection with corporations. One of the most important was the passage of the meat inspection law because of scandalous abuses shown to exist in the great packing-houses in Chicago and elsewhere. There was a curious result of this law, similar to what occurred in connection with the law providing for effective railway regulation. The big beef men bitterly opposed the law; just as the big railway men opposed the Hepburn Act. Yet three or four years after these laws had been put on the statute books every honest man both in the beef business and the railway business came to the conclusion that they worked good and not harm to the decent business concerns. They hurt only those who were not acting as they should have acted. The law providing for the inspection of packing-houses, and the Pure Food and Drugs Act, were also extremely important; and the way in which they were administered was even more important. It would be hard to overstate the value of the service rendered in all these cases by such cabinet officers as Moody and Bonaparte, and their outside assistants of the stamp of Frank Kellogg.

It would be useless to enumerate all the suits we brought. Some of them I have already touched upon. Others, such as the suits against the Harriman railway corporations, which were successful, and which had been rendered absolutely necessary by the grossly improper action of the corporations concerned, offered no special points of interest. The Sugar Trust proceedings, however, may be mentioned as showing just the kind of thing that was done and the kind of obstacle encountered and overcome in prosecutions of this character.

It was on the advice of my secretary, William Loeb, Jr., afterward head of the New York Custom-House, that the action was taken which started the uncovering of the frauds perpetrated by the Sugar Trust and other companies in connection with the importing of sugar. Loeb had from time to time told me that he was sure that there was fraud in connection with the importations by the Sugar Trust through the New York Custom-House. Finally, some time toward the end of 1904, he informed me that Richard Parr, a sampler at the New

York Appraisers' Stores (whose duties took him almost continually on the docks in connection with the sampling of merchandise), had called on him, and had stated that in his belief the sugar companies were defrauding the Government in the matter of weights, and had stated that if he could be made an investigating officer of the Treasury Department, he was confident that he could show there was wrongdoing. Parr had been a former school fellow of Loeb in Albany, and Loeb believed him to be loyal, honest, and efficient. He thereupon laid the matter before me, and advised the appointment of Parr as a special employee of the Treasury Department, for the specific purpose of investigating the alleged sugar frauds. I instructed the Treasury Department accordingly, and was informed that there was no vacancy in the force of special employees, but that Parr would be given the first place that opened up. Early in the spring of 1905 Parr came to Loeb again, and said that he had received additional information about the sugar frauds, and was anxious to begin the investigation. Loeb again discussed the matter with me; and I notified the Treasury Department to appoint Parr immediately. On June 1, 1905, he received his appointment, and was assigned to the port of Boston for the purpose of gaining some experience as an investigating officer. During the month he was transferred to the Maine District, with headquarters at Portland, where he remained until March, 1907. During his service in Maine he uncovered extensive wool smuggling frauds. At the conclusion of the wool case, he appealed to Loeb to have him transferred to New York, so that he might undertake the investigation of the sugar underweighing frauds. I now called the attention of Secretary [of the Treasury George B.] Cortelyou personally to the matter, so that he would be able to keep a check over any subordinates who might try to interfere with Parr, for the conspiracy was evidently widespread, the wealth of the offenders great, and the corruption in the service far-reaching—while moreover as always happens with "respectable" offenders, there were many good men who sincerely disbelieved in the possibility of corruption on the part of men of such high financial standing. Parr was assigned to New York early in March, 1907, and at once began an active investigation of the conditions existing on the sugar docks. This terminated in the discovery of a steel spring in one of the scales of the Havemeyer & Elder docks in Brooklyn, November 20, 1907, which enabled us to uncover what were probably the most colossal frauds ever perpetrated in the Customs Service. From the beginning of his active work in the investigation of the sugar frauds in March, 1907, to March 4, 1909, Parr, from time to time, personally reported to Loeb, at the White House, the progress of his investigations, and Loeb in his turn kept me personally advised. On one occasion there was an attempt made to shunt Parr off the investigation and substitute another agent of the Treasury, who was suspected of having some relations with the sugar companies under investigation; but Parr reported the facts to Loeb, I sent for Secretary Cortelyou, and Secretary Cortelyou promptly took charge of the matter himself, putting Parr back on the investigation.

During the investigation Parr was subjected to all sorts of harassments, including an attempt to bribe him by Spitzer, the dock superintendent of the Havemeyer & Elder Refinery, for which Spitzer was convicted and served a term in prison. Brzezinski, a special agent, who was assisting Parr, was convicted of perjury and also served a term in prison, he having changed his testimony, in the trial of Spitzer for the attempted bribery of Parr, from that which he gave before the Grand Jury. For his extraordinary services in connection with this investigation Parr was granted an award of $100,000 by the Treasury Department.

District-Attorney [Henry L.] Stimson, of New York, assisted by Denison, [Felix] Frankfurter, Wise, and other employees of the Department of Justice, took charge of the case, and carried on both civil and criminal proceedings. The trial in the action against the Sugar Trust, for the recovery of duties on the cargo of sugar, which was being sent over the scales at the time of the discovery of the steel spring by Parr, was begun in 1908; judgment was rendered against the defendants on March 5, 1909, the day after I left office. Over four million dollars were recovered and paid back into the United States Treasury by the sugar companies which had perpetrated the various forms of fraud. These frauds were unearthed by Parr, Loeb, Stimson, Frankfurter, and the other men mentioned and their associates, and it was to them that the people owed the refunding of the huge sum of money mentioned. We had already secured heavy fines from the Sugar Trust, and from various big railways, and private individuals, such as Edwin Earle, for unlawful rebates. In the case of the chief offender, the American Sugar Refining Company (the Sugar Trust), criminal prosecutions were carried on against every living man whose position was such that he would naturally know about the fraud. All of them were indicted, and the biggest and most responsible ones were convicted. The evidence showed that the president of the company, Henry O. Havemeyer, virtually ran the entire company, and was responsible for all the details of the management. He died two weeks after the fraud was discovered, just as proceedings were being begun. Next to him in importance was the secretary and treasurer, Charles R. Heike, who was convicted. Various other officials and employees of the Trust, and various Government employees, were indicted, and most of them convicted. Ernest W. Gerbracht, the superintendent of one of the refineries, was convicted, but his sentence was commuted to a short jail imprisonment, because he became a Government witness and greatly assisted the Government in the suits.

Heike's sentence was commuted so as to excuse him from going to the penitentiary; just as the penitentiary sentence of [Charles W.] Morse, the big New York banker, who was convicted of gross fraud and misapplication of funds, was commuted. Both commutations were granted long after I left office. In each case the commutation was granted because, as was stated, of the prisoner's age and state of health. In Morse's case the President originally refused the request, saying that Morse had exhibited "fraudulent and criminal disregard of the trust imposed upon him," that "he was entirely unscrupulous as to the methods he adopted," and "that he seemed at times to be absolutely heartless with regard to the consequences to others, and he showed great shrewdness in obtaining large sums of money from the bank without adequate security and without making himself personally liable therefor." The two cases may be considered in connection with the announcement in the public press that on May 17, 1913, the President commuted the sentence of Lewis A. Banks, who was serving a very long term penitentiary sentence for an attack on a girl in the Indian Territory; "the reason for the commutation which is set forth in the press being that 'Banks is in poor health.' "

It is no easy matter to balance the claims of justice and mercy in such cases. In these three cases, of all which I had personal cognizance, I disagreed radically with the views my successors took, and with the views which many respectable men took who in these and similar cases, both while I was in office and afterward, urged me to show, or to ask others to show, clemency. It then seemed to me, and it now seems to me, that such clemency is from the larger standpoint a gross wrong to the men and women of the country.

One of the former special assistants of the district-attorney, Mr. W. Cleveland Runyon, in commenting bitterly on the release of Heike and Morse on account of their health, pointed out that their health apparently became good when once they themselves became free men, and added:

"The commutation of these sentences amounts to a direct interference with the administration of justice by the courts. Heike got a $25,000 salary and has escaped his imprisonment, but what about the six $18 a week checkers, who were sent to jail, one of them a man of more than sixty? It is cases like this that create discontent and anarchy. They make it seem plain that there is one law for the rich and another for the poor man, and I for one will protest."

In dealing with Heike the individual (or Morse or any other individual), it is necessary to emphasize the social aspects of his case. The moral of the Heike case, as has been well said, is "how easy it is for a man in modern corporate organization to drift into wrongdoing." The moral restraints are loosened in the case of a man like Heike by the insulation of himself from the sordid details of crime, through industrially coerced intervening agents. Professor [Edward A.] Ross has made the penetrating observation that "distance disinfects dividends"; it also weakens individual responsibility, particularly on the part of the very managers of large business, who should feel it most acutely. One of the officers of the Department of Justice who conducted the suit, and who inclined to the side of mercy in the matter, nevertheless writes: "Heike is a beautiful illustration of mental and moral obscuration in the business life of an otherwise valuable member of society. Heike had an ample share in the guidance of the affairs of the American Sugar Company, and we are apt to have a foreshortened picture of his responsibility, because he operated from the easy coign of vantage of executive remoteness. It is difficult to say to what extent he did, directly or indirectly, profit by the sordid practices of his company. But the social damage of an individual in his position may be just as deep, whether merely the zest of the game or hard cash be his dominant motive."

I have coupled the cases of the big banker and the Sugar Trust official and the case of the man convicted of a criminal assault on a woman. All of the criminals were released from penitentiary sentences on grounds of ill health. The offenses were typical of the worst crimes committed at the two ends of the social scale. One offense was a crime of brutal violence; the other offenses were crimes of astute corruption. All of them were offenses which in my judgment were of such a character that clemency towards the offender worked grave injustice to the community as a whole, injustice so grave that its effects might be far-reaching in their damage.

Every time that rape or criminal assault on a woman is pardoned, and anything less than the full penalty of the law exacted, a premium is put on the practice of lynching such offenders. Every time a big monied offender, who naturally excites interest and sympathy, and who has many friends, is excused from serving a sentence which a man of less prominence and fewer friends would have to serve, justice is discredited in the eyes of plain people—and to undermine faith in justice is to strike at the foundation of the Republic. As for ill health, it must be remembered that few people are as healthy in prison as they would be outside; and there should be no discrimination among criminals on this score; either all criminals who grow unhealthy should be let out, or none. Pardons must sometimes be given in order that the cause of justice may be served; but in cases such as these I am considering, while I know that many amiable people differ from me, I am obliged to say that in my judgment the pardons work far-reaching harm to the cause of justice.

Among the big corporations themselves, even where they did wrong, there was a wide difference in the moral obliquity indicated by the wrongdoer. There was a wide distinction between the offenses committed in the case of the Northern Securities Company, and the offenses because of which the Sugar Trust, the Tobacco Trust, and the Standard Oil Trust were successfully prosecuted under my Administration. It was vital to destroy the Northern Securities Company; but the men creating it had done so in open and above-board fashion, acting under what they, and most of the members of the bar, thought to be the law established by the Supreme Court in the Knight sugar case. But the Supreme Court in its decree dissolving the Standard Oil and Tobacco Trusts, condemned them in the severest language for moral turpitude; and an even severer meed of condemnation should be visited on the Sugar Trust.

However, all the trusts and big corporations against which we proceeded—which included in their directorates practically all the biggest financiers in the country—joined in making the bitterest assaults on me and on my Administration. . . .

11.

Ida Tarbell Discovers "The Golden Rule in Industry"

The "rule of reason" that defined and helped to curb illicit business practices led Ida Tarbell and others to discover "the golden rule in industry." The attack on bad monopoly implied appreciation of good monopoly. Miss Tarbell, known nationally as "the terror of the trusts" following her exposé of the Standard Oil corporation in 1904, recalls in the following chapter from her autobiography the decline of her career as muckraker. Her appreciation of rational industrial techniques led her to a fresh start as biographer of business leaders like Judge Elbert H. Gary and Owen D. Young.

Ida Tarbell was born on a farm in Erie County, Pennsylvania, in 1857. When oil was discovered in Titusville two years later, her father moved to the oil region and became the first manufacturer there of wooden oil tanks. Miss Tarbell grew up to know the oil region and many of its prominent men. The crucial experience of her youth, the assassination of Lincoln, led her in later life to write numerous books about him. Graduating from Allegheny College in Meadville in 1880, she taught school for a time and then became editor of the *Chautauquan*. In 1891 she went to Paris to study and earned a living contributing stories to American newspapers. On a tour of Europe, S. S. McClure discovered her. She wrote a series on Napoleon, another on Lincoln, and then entered on her muckraking career. In 1908 she became associate editor, under John Phillips, of the *American Magazine.*

I was done with the tariff, but it was out of the tariff that my next serial came—born partly of a guilty conscience! In attempting to prove that in certain highly protected industries only a small part of a duty laid in the interest of labor went to labor I had taken satisfaction in picturing the worst conditions I could find, badly ventilated and dangerous factories, unsanitary homes, underfed children. But in looking for this material I found, in both protected and unprotected industries, substantial and important efforts making to improve conditions, raise wages, shorten hours, humanize relations.

My conscience began to trouble me. Was it not as much my business as a reporter to present this side of the picture as to present the other? If there were leaders in practically every industry who regarded it not only as sound ethics but as sound economics to improve the lot of the worker, ought not the public to be familiarized with this belief?

At that moment, and indeed for a good many years, the public had heard little except of the atrocities of industrial life. By emphasizing, the reformers had hoped to hasten changes they sought. The public was coming to believe that the inevitable result of corporate industrial management was exploitation, neglect, bullying, crushing of labor, that the only hope was in destroying the system.

But if the practices were not universal, if there was a steady, though slow, progress, ought not the public to recognize it? Was it not the duty of those who were called muckrakers to rake up the good earth as well as the noxious? Was there not as much driving force in a good example as in an evil one?

From Ida Tarbell, *All in the Day's Work* (New York: The Macmillan Company, 1939), chap. 14, "The Golden Rule in Industry," pp. 280–300.

The office was not unfriendly to the idea. As a matter of fact *The American Magazine* had little genuine muckracking spirit. It did have a large and fighting interest in fair play; it sought to present things as they were, not as somebody thought they ought to be. We were journalists, not propagandists; and as journalists we sought new angles on old subjects. The idea that there was something fundamentally sound and good in industrial relations, that in many spots had gone far beyond what either labor or reformers were demanding, came to the office as a new attack on the old problem. Mr. Phillips, always keenly aware of the new and significant, had his eye on the movement, I found, and was willing to commission me to go out and see what I could find.

This was in 1912, and for the next four years I spent the bulk of my time in factories and industrial towns. The work took me from Maine to Alabama, from New York to Kansas. I found my material in all sorts of industries: iron and steel in and around Pittsburgh, Chicago, Duluth; mines in West Virginia, Illinois, and Wisconsin; paper boxes and books and newspapers everywhere; candy in Philadelphia; beer and tanneries and woodwork in Wisconsin; shirts and collars and shoes in New York and Massachusetts. I watched numberless things in the making: turbines and optical lenses, jewelry and mesh bags, kodaks and pocketknives, plated cutlery and solid silver tea services, Minton tableware and American Belleek, cans and ironware, linen tablecloths and sails for a cup defender, furniture I suspected was to be sold in Europe for antiques, and bric-a-brac I knew was to be sold in America as Chinese importations, railroad rails and wire for a thousand purposes, hookless fasteners and mechanical toys. I seemed never to tire of seeing things made. But do not ask me now how they were made!

I never counted the number of factories I visited. Looking at the volume in which I finally gathered my findings, I find there are some fifty-five major concerns mentioned; but these were those which in my judgment best illustrated the particular point I was trying to make. There were many more.

My visits had to be arranged beforehand. I took pains to make sure of my credentials, but I soon discovered that my past work served me well. The heads of the industries and many workmen were magazine readers, liked to talk about writers and asked all sorts of curious questions about men and women they had become acquainted with in *McClure's* and the *American:* Kipling, Baker, Steffens, Will White, Edna Ferber, just coming on at that time. There was often considerable asperity at the top when I presented my letters of introduction. They set me down as an enemy of business; but again and again this asperity was softened by a man's love of Abraham Lincoln. He had a habit of reading everything about Lincoln that he could put his hands on, collected books, brought out my "Life" to be autographed. That is, while I was *persona non grata* for one piece of work, another piece softened suspicion and opened doors to me.

My first move in a factory was to study the processes of the particular industry. Machines were not devils to me as they were to some of my reforming friends, particularly that splendid old warrior Florence Kelley, then in the thick of her fight for "ethical gains through legislation." To me machines freed from heavy labor, created abundance. That is, I started out free of the inhibition that hate of a machine puts on many observers. I think because of this I was better able to judge the character of a factory, to see its weak as well as its good points. I was able to understand what the enemy of the machine rarely admits: that men and women who have arrived at the dignity of steady workers not only respect, but frequently take pride in, their machines.

Again, I gave myself time around these factories. The observer who once in his life goes down for a half a day into a mine or spends two or three hours walking through a steel mill, naturally revolts against the darkness, the clatter, the smoke, the danger. As a rule he misses the points of real hardship; he also misses the satisfactions. As my pilgrimage lengthened, I became more and more convinced that there is no trade which has not its devotee.

"Once a miner, always a miner." "Once a sailor, always a sailor." One might go through the whole category.

"Why," I now and then asked miners, "do you stay by the mine?"

"I was brought up to it." "I like it." "Nobody bothers you when you are working with a pick." "Nice and quiet in the mines."

"But the danger!"

"No worse than railroading." "My brother got killed by a horse last week."

In the end I came to the conclusion that there was probably no larger percentage of those who did not like the work they were doing than there is in the white-collar occupations. In the heavy industries particularly, I found something like the farmer's conviction that they were doing a man's job. It made them contemptuous of white-collar workers.

I spent quite as much time looking at homes as at plants. The test I made of the industrial villages and of company houses was whether or no, if I set myself to it, I could make a decent home in them. I found even in the most barren and unattractive company districts women who had made attractive homes. There was the greatest difference in home-making ability, in the training of women for it. The pride of the man who had a good housekeeper as a wife, a good cook, was great. I do not remember that a man ever asked me to come to his house unless he considered his wife a good housekeeper. I remember one so proud of his home that he took me all over it, showing with delight how his Sunday clothes, his winter overcoat, the Sunday dress of his little girl, were hung on hangers with a calico curtain in front to keep them clean. His housekeeper, in this case a mother-in-law, confided to me in talking things over that night that in her judgment the reason so many men drank was that the women did not know how to keep house.

Visiting with the family after the supper dishes were cleared away, I managed to get at what was most important in their lives. After steady work it was the church. After minister or priest, the public-school teacher was the most trusted friend of the household. In many places, however, I found her authority beginning to be divided with the company nurse, for the company nurse was just being added to industrial staffs. Many of my reforming friends felt that in going into a factory and taking a salary a nurse was aligning herself with the evil intentions of the corporation, but the average man did not feel that way. She helped him out in too many tight places.

As to the relation of workmen to their union—for often they belonged to a union—I concluded that in the average industrial community it was not unlike that of the average citizen to his political party and political boss.

Both the union and the employer seemed to me to be missing opportunities to help men to understand the structure of industry, perhaps because they did not themselves understand it too well, or sank their understanding in politics. Both union and employer depended upon one or another form of force when there was unrest, rather than education and arbitration. In doing this they weakened, perhaps in the end destroyed, that by which they all lived.

The most distressing thing in mills and factories seemed to me to be the atmosphere of suspicion which had accumulated from years of appeal to force. I felt it as soon as I went into certain plants—everybody watching me, the guide, the boss, the men at the machines.

But to conclude that because of this suspicion, this lack of understanding, which keeps so many industries always on the verge of destruction, there were no natural friendly contacts between the management and the men is not to know the world. I found that practically always the foreman or the boss, sometimes the big boss, in an industry had come up from the ranks. In various industrial towns I found the foreman's family or the superintendent's family living just around the corner, and his brother, perhaps his father, working in the mine or the mill. He was one in the family who had been able to lift himself. Nor did it follow that there was bad blood between a "big boss" and the head of a warlike union. I had been led to believe they did not speak in passing. I had supposed that, if Samuel Gompers and Judge Gary [of U. S. Steel] met, they would probably fly at each other's throat; but at the Washington Industrial Conference in 1919, standing in a corridor of the Pan-American Building, I saw the two approaching from different directions. They were going to pass close to me. I had a cold chill about what might happen. But what happened was that Mr. Gompers said, "Hello, Judge," in the friendliest tone and Judge Gary called cheerfully, "Hello, Sam." And that was all there was to it. Later, when I was to see much of Judge Gary, trying to make out what the famous Gary code meant, and how it was being applied, we talked more than once of Samuel Gompers and his technique. The Judge had great respect for him as a political opponent, as well he might.

It is hard to stop talking when I recall these four years, drifting up and down the country into factories and homes. The contrast between old ways and new ways was always before me. Many a sad thing I saw—nothing more disturbing than the strikes, for I managed to get on the outskirts of several and follow up the aftermath, which was usually tragic.

There was the ghastly strike in certain fertilizer plants at Roosevelt on the Jersey coast. I followed it through to its unsatisfactory end. Rival labor and political bodies fought each other for days while the men with drawn and hopeless faces loafed in groups in saloons or on doorsteps.

"All going to the devil while their unions fight," said the woman who gave me my meals in the only boarding house in the desolate place. "I am for the union, but the union does not know when they go into a strike which they can avoid what they are doing to men. It turns them into tramps. They leave their families and take to the road. It is better that they leave. I think the women often think that, so they won't have any more babies. No, the union does not see what it does to men. But what are the men going to do when things were like they were in this place? You know what their wages were. You know what a hellish sort of place this is. What are they going to do?"

It was the men who saw industry as a cooperative undertaking who gave me heart. I do not mean political cooperation, but practical cooperation, worked out on the ground by the persons concerned. The problems and needs of no two industrial undertakings are ever alike. For results each must be treated according to the situation. The greatest contributions I found to industrial peace and stability came when a man recognized that a condition was wrong and set out to correct it.

There was Thomas Lynch, president of the Frick Coke Company of Westmoreland County, Pennsylvania. Tommy Lynch had swung a pick before John Lewis did and, like Lewis, had risen by virtue of hard work and real ability, from one position to another—one to become the head of a group of mines, the other to become the head of a group of miners. But no union could keep up with Tommy Lynch in the improvements he demanded for his mines and miners. It was he who originated the famous slogan "Safety First." When I talked with him about rescue crews he swore heartily, "Damn rescue work—prevent accidents."

Tommy Lynch's work did not end in the mine. He had a theory that you could not be a good worker unless you had a good home. He literally lifted some seven thousand company houses, which he had inherited from an old management, out of their locations between high mountains of lifeless slag and put them onto tillable land, gave every woman water in her kitchen and a plot of land for a garden.

In 1914, when I was first there, out of 7,000 homes 6,923 had gardens. And such gardens! It took three days for Mr. Lynch and two or three other distinguished gentlemen to decide on the winners of the nine prizes given for the finest displays. They were estimating that the vegetable gardens yielded $143,000 worth of vegetables that year. I went back to see what they were doing with those gardens in the middle of the late depression. There were even more of them, and they were even more productive. Knowing what the garden meant, the miners had turned to the cultivation with immense energy. The company had plowed and fertilized tracts of untilled land near each settlement, and the men were raising extra food for the winter. Many of these miners were selling vegetables in the near-by town markets.

Believing as I do that the connection of men and women with the soil is not only most healthy for the body but essential for the mind and the soul, these gardens aroused almost as much thankfulness in my heart as the safety work.

But Tommy Lynch could not have worked out his notions of safety and gardening without the cooperation of the miners, even if it was sometimes begrudging.

Then there was Henry Ford attacking the problem which most concerned his plant, labor turnover—in his case something like 1200 per cent. He had come into the industrial picture with his minimum wage of five dollars a day just before I began my work. In May of 1915 I set up shop for ten days in a Detroit hotel in order to study what he was doing. The days I spent in and around the Ford factory; nights, tired out with observations and emotions, I came back to a hot bath and dinner in bed, talking my findings into a dictaphone until I fell off to sleep.

Connections had not been hard to make. There was then at the head of Ford publicity an experienced and able gentleman who realized that articles in *The American Magazine* on the Ford plant, whether favorable or not, were good for the concern, and who saw to it that I had every chance. Mr. Ford himself was my first important objective. He saw me in his big office looking down on the plant, a plant then employing eighteen thousand men. At the first glimpse of his smiling face I was startled by the resemblance to the picture of the young Lincoln which had played such a part in the launching of the Lincoln articles in *McClure's*. It was the face of a poet and a philosopher, as in the young Lincoln there was a young Emerson.

Like a poet and a philosopher, Henry Ford was unhurried. He was no slave to his desk. I saw it practically abandoned when he was wrestling with the successor to Model T. "Mr. Ford does not often come in," my conductor told me. "He is wandering through the factories these days. We never touch his desk."

He was boyish and natural in off hours. Coming into the private lunchroom for officers at the plant, where I judged a place was always left for him, I saw him throw his long right leg over the back of the chair before he slid leisurely into the seat.

"I have got an idea," he said. "People complain about the doors of the car—not convenient. I am going to put a can opener into every car from now on and let them cut their own."

He delighted in the flow of Ford jokes, wanted to hear the latest, to see it in the house organ.

When he saw me, it was he who did the talking, and he seemed to be straightening out his thoughts rather than replying to my questions. When I asked him his reasons for mass production he had a straight-away answer.

"It is to give people everything they want and then some," he said. And then he went on to enlarge in a way I have never forgotten.

"There's no reason why everybody shouldn't have everything he needs if we managed it right, weren't afraid of making too much. Our business is to make things so cheap that everybody can buy 'em. Take these shears." He picked up a handsome pair of large shears on his desk. "They sell for three or four dollars, I guess. No reason you couldn't get them down to fifty cents. Yes, fifty cents," he repeated as I gasped. "No reason at all. Best in the world—so every little girl in the world could have a pair. There's more money in giving everybody things than in keeping them dear so only a few can have them. I want our car so cheap that every workman in our shop can have one if he wants it. Make things everybody can have—that's what we want to do. And give 'em money enough. The trouble's been we didn't pay men enough. High wages pay. People do more work. We never thought we'd get back our five dollars a day; didn't think of it; just thought that something was wrong that so many people were out of work and hadn't anything saved up, and thought we ought to divide. But we got it all back right away. That means we can make the car cheaper, and give more men work. Of course when you're building and trying new things all the time you've got to have money; but you get it if you make men. I don't know that our scheme is best. It will take five years to try it out, but we are doing the best we can and changing when we strike a snag."

What it simmered down to was that if you wanted to make a business you must make men, and you must make men by seeing that they had a chance for what we are pleased to call these days a good life. And if they are going to have a good life they must not only have money but have low prices.

There was much more, I soon found, than five dollars a day and upwards that was behind the making of men at Ford's. There was the most scientific system for handling mass production processes that I had ever seen. Tasks were graded. A workman was given every incentive to get into higher classes. But I was not long at Ford's before I discovered that it was not this system, already established, it was not the five dollars, it was not the flourishing business, it was not advertising—deeply and efficiently and aggressively as all these things were handled —which at the moment was absorbing the leaders of the business. It was what Mr. Ford was calling "the making of men." It was a thoroughly worth-while and deeply human method. Mr. Ford knew that, do all you can for a man in the factory—a short day, higher wages, good conditions, training, advancement—if things are not right for him at home he will not in the long run be a good workman. So he set out to reorganize the home life of the men.

It was done by a sociological department made up at that time of some eighty men all taken out of the factory itself, for Mr. Ford's theory was then that, no matter what you wanted done, you could always find somebody among the eighteen thousand "down there," as he called it, that was qualified. So they had selected eighty for social service work and these men were doing it with a thoroughness and a frankness which was almost as important as the five dollars a day had been.

"Paternal" was the adjective generally applied to the Ford method; but one of the interesting things about Mr. Ford is the little effect a word has on him. Call a thing what you like, it is the idea, the method, that he is after. If that seems to him to make sense, you may have your word—it doesn't trouble him.

So they went energetically about their determination to add to what they were doing for the making of men inside of the factory a thorough overhauling of the men's lives outside. There were certain things that were laid down as essential. You had to be clean—cleanliness had played no part in the lives of hundreds of these men. But when they did not get their "big envelope" and asked why, they were told it was because their hands were dirty, they didn't wash their necks, didn't wear clean clothes. Ford's men must be clean. Already it had made an astonishing difference in the general look of the factory. And this cleanliness was carried by the sociological department into the home. The men must be kept clean, and the women must do their part. Many of the women as well as the men were discovering for the first time the satisfaction of cleanliness. "Feels good," said a working woman to me, reluctant but thorough convert according to my conductor. "Feels good to be clean."

They were enemies of liquor, and no man who drank could keep his place. But he was not thrown out: he must reform. And some of the most surprising cures of habitual drunkenness that I have ever come across I found in the Ford factory in 1915.

There was a strong sympathy throughout the factory for derelicts. There were four hundred men in Ford's when I was there who had served prison terms. Nobody knew them, but each had his special guardian; and no mother ever looked after a child more carefully than these guardians looked after their charges.

In this social work Mr. Ford was constantly and deeply interested. As nearly as I could make out, there was nothing of which they all talked more.

I dined one night with four or five of the officers, including Mr. Ford, and while I had expected to hear much about mass production and wage problems the only thing I heard was, "How are you getting on with Mary?" "How about John?" "Do you think we can make this housing scheme work?" That is, what I was discovering at Ford's was that they were not thinking in terms of labor and capital, but in terms of Tom, Dick, and Harry. They were taking men and women, individuals, families, and with patience and sense and humor and determination were putting them on their feet, giving them interest and direction in managing their lives. This was the Henry Ford of 1916.

But work like that of Tommy Lynch and Henry Ford depended upon individual qualities of a rare and exceptional kind, also upon the opportunity to test ideas. Neither Lynch nor Ford was willing to let bad situations, a stiff problem alone. It challenged their wits, particularly when it concerned men in mine and factory. They were not hampered by dogmas or politics. They did things in their own way, and if one method did not work tried another; and both had a rare power to persuade men to follow them. They were self-made, unhampered products of old-fashioned democracy, and both were thorns in the flesh of those who worked according to blue prints, mechanized organizations or the status quo. But the success of both with the particular labor problems they tackled was the answer to critics.

Only how could men of lesser personality, lesser freedom of action, and lesser boldness in trying out things follow? They could not. They had to have a more scientific practice if they were to achieve genuine cooperation in working out their problems. And what I was seeing in certain plants, as I went up and down the country, convinced me it had come in the Frederick Taylor science of management.

I had first heard of Taylor in the *American Magazine* office. John Phillips had sensed something important on foot when he read that Louis Brandeis, acting as counsel for certain shippers in a suit they had brought against the railroads, had told the defendants that they could afford lower rates if they would reorganize their business on the lines of scientific management which Frederick Taylor had developed. They could lower rates and raise wages.

"And who is Frederick Taylor?" asked Mr. Phillips. "Baker, you better find out."

And so Frederick Taylor had come to know the *American* group, and he had given to the *American*, much to our pride, his first popular article explaining what he meant by scientific management. In the following letter Mr. Taylor tells a protesting friend why he gave it to us:

> I have no doubt that the Atlantic Monthly would give us a better audience from a literary point of view than we could get from the American Magazine. But the readers of the Atlantic Monthly consist probably very largely of professors and literary men, who would be interested more in the abstract theory than

in the actual good which would come from the introduction of scientific management.

On the other hand, I feel that the readers of the American Magazine consist largely of those who are actually doing the practical work of the world. The people whom I want to reach with the article are principally those men who are doing the manufacturing and construction work of our country, both employers and employees, and I have an idea that many more persons of that kind would be reached through the American Magazine than through the Atlantic Monthly.

In considering the best magazine to publish the paper in, I am very considerably influenced by the opinion I have formed of the editors who have been here to talk over the subject; and of these Ray Stannard Baker was by far the most thorough and enthusiastic in his analysis of the whole subject. He looked at all sides in a way which no other editor dreamed of doing. He even got next to the workingmen and talked to them at great length on the subject. I cannot but feel, also, that the audience which reads the work of men of his type must be an intelligent and earnest audience.

Mr. ———, who has just been here, suggested that among a certain class of people the American Magazine is looked upon as a muckraking magazine. I think that any magazine which opposed the "stand-patters" and was not under the control of the moneyed powers of the United States would now be classed among the muckrakers. This, therefore, has no very great weight with me.

Taylor believed like Henry Ford that the world could take all we could make, that the power of consumption was limitless. "To give the world all it needs is the omission of industry," he shouted at me one day I spent with him at Boxley (his home near Philadelphia)—shouted it with many picturesque oaths. I have never known a man who could swear so beautifully and so unconsciously.

Mr. Taylor's system in part or whole had been applied in many factories which I visited in my four years. You knew its outward sign as soon as you entered the yard. Order, routing, were first laws, and the old cluttered shops where you fell over scattered material and picked your way around dump heaps were now models of classified order. A man knew where to find the thing he needed, and things were placed where it took the fewest steps to reach them.

Quite as conspicuous as the physical changes in the shop was the change in what may be called its human atmosphere. Under the Taylor System the business of management was not only planning but controlling what it planned. Management laid out ahead the day's work for each man at his machine; to him they went with their instructions, to them he went for explanations and suggestions. Office and shop intermingled. They realized their mutual dependence as never before, learned to respect each other for what they were worth. Watching the functioning, one realized men had come to feel more or less as Taylor himself felt: that nothing of moment was ever accomplished save by cooperation, which must be "intimate and friendly." Praised once for his work on the art of cutting metal he said a thing all leaders would do well to heed:

"I feel strongly that work of any account in order to be done rightly should be done through true cooperation, rather than through the individual effort of any one man; and, in fact, I should feel rather ashamed of any achievement in which I attempted to do the whole thing myself."

Nothing was more exciting to me than the principles by which Taylor had developed his science. They were the principles he had applied to revolutionary discoveries and inventions in engineering. I made a brief table of them. They make the best code I know for progress in human undertakings:

1) Find out what others have done before you and begin where they left off.

2) Question everything—prove everything.

3) Tackle only one variable at a time. Shun the temptation to try more than one in order to get quick results.

him as an illumination, and for some years he held tight to i
preaching it to political bosses, to the tycoons of Wall Stree
the Brahmins of Boston, confronting them with amazing frank
ness and no little satisfaction with their open disregard of it
meanings. He became greatly disillusioned finally by discovering that men were quite willing to let their opponents act
upon the Golden Rule but much less so to be governed by it
themselves.

My first realization that Steffens was struggling with the problem which confronted us all—that is, whether we should stick to our profession or become propagandists—was one day when I looked up suddenly to find him standing by my desk more sober, less certain of himself than I had ever seen him.

"Charles Edward Russell has gone over to the Socialist party," he said. "Is that not what we should all be doing? Should we not make *The American Magazine* a Socialist organ?"

I flared. Our only hope for usefulness was in keeping our freedom, avoiding dogma, I argued. And that the *American* continued to do.

In the years that were to come, wars and revolutions largely occupied Steffens. Wherever there was a revolution you found him. He wrote many brilliant comments on what was going on in the world. When he came back from Russia after the Kerensky revolution he was like a man who had seen a long hoped-for vision.

"I have looked at the millennium and it works," he told me.

It was to be the practical application of that Golden Rule he had so long preached. But to my mind the Russian Revolution had only just begun. The event in which he saw the coming of the Lord I looked on as only the first of probably many convulsions forced by successive generations of unsatisfied radicals, irreconcilable counterrevolutionists. When I voiced these pessimistic notions to Steffens he called me heartless and blind.

4) Hold surrounding conditions as constant and uniform as possible while experimenting with your variable.

5) Work with all men against no one. Make them want to go along.

There is enduring vitality in these principles and there is universality. They are as good for battered commonwealths as for backward disorganized industries. Think what it would mean in Washington today if all the experimenters began where others had left off, if no demonstrated failure was repeated, if theory was held to be but 25 per cent of an achievement, practice 75, if one variable at a time was experimented with, if time were taken for solutions and above all if everybody concerned accepted "intimate and friendly" cooperation as the most essential of all factors in our restoration.

This hunt for practical application of the Golden Rule in industry left me in much better spirits than my studies of transportation and tariff privileges. The longer I looked into the latter the deeper had been my conviction that in the long run they would ruin the hope of peaceful unity of life in America. They seemed to me inconsistent with democracy as I understood it and certainly inconsistent with my simple notions of what made men and women of character. Were we not getting a larger and larger class interested only in what money would buy? Particularly did I dislike the spreading belief that wealth piled up by a combination of ability, illegality, and bludgeoning could be so used as to justify itself—that the good to be done would cancel the evil done. What it amounted to was the promotion of humanitarianism at the expense of Christian ethics; and that, I believe, made for moral softness instead of stoutness.

But there was nothing soft about the experiments I had been following. Where they succeeded, it was by following unconsciously in general Taylor's stiff principles. Patient training, stern discipline, active cooperation alone produced safety, health, efficient workmen, abundance of cheap honest output. I had faith in these things. They were the foundation of genuine social service. All desired goods followed them as they became part of the nation's habit of life, reaching down to its lowest depths.

Many of my reforming friends were shocked because the one and only reason most industrial leaders gave for their experiments was that it paid. Generally speaking, the leaders were the kind who would have cut their tongues out before acknowledging that any other motive than profit influenced them. Certainly they sought dividends; but they believed stability, order, peace, progress, cooperation were back of dividends. That industry which paid must, as Mr. Ford said, "make men." That the right thing paid, was one of their most far-reaching demonstrations. Men had not believed it. They were proving the contrary; so in spite of the charge of many of my friends that I was going over to the enemy, joining the corporation lawyer and the company nurse, I clung to the new ideals. What I never could make some of these friends see was that I had no quarrel with corporate business so long as it played fair. It was the unfairness I feared and despised. I had no quarrel with men of wealth if they could show performance back of it untainted by privilege.

Sometimes I suspected that the gains I set forth as practical results of this experimenting inside industry were resented by those who had been working for them for years through legislation, organization, agitation, because they had come about by other methods than theirs and generally in a more complete form than they had ventured to demand. But that the idealists had been a driving force behind the new movement inside industry was certain. Their method could not do the thing, but it could and did drive men to prove it could be done.

My critics who charged me with giving comfort to the enemy did not see that often this enemy disliked what I was trying to do even more deeply than my so-called muckraking. Indeed, he took those pictures of new industrial methods and principles

as a kind of backhanded muckraking—indirect and so unf
It threw all established methods of force into a relief as dam
ing as anything I ever had said about high duties and ma
ulations of railroad rates.

Whatever challenges my new interest aroused, however
fused my own defense of it was, I knew only that I sh
keep my eye on it and report any development which see
to me a step ahead. That, of course, was counting on conti
editorial sympathy in the *American*. But hardly had I fini
my book before that sympathy was cut off by a chan
ownership.

The change was inevitable, things being as they were i
magazine world after 1914. The crew who had manne
little ship so gallantly in 1906 when we left *McClure's* ha
only one of its numbers. A few months after we starte
coln Steffens withdrew. He objected to the editing
articles, demanded that they go in as he wrote them. Th
editorial principles were being applied to his productio
were applied to those of other contributors. They w
principles which he himself had been accustomed to a
and to submitting to on *McClure's*. The editorial bo
cided the policy could not be changed and accepted
resignation.

Back of his withdrawal, as I saw it, was Steffens'
dissatisfaction with the restrictions of journalism. He
wider field, one in which he could more directly influ
litical and social leaders, preach more directly his n
the Golden Rule, which certainly at that time was h
guide.

Certainly it was the creed of the *American*. It ha
been John Phillips' answer to our fervent efforts
things, "The only way to improve the world is to pers
follow the Golden Rule."

I suppose Steffens had heard of the Golden Rule
certain he had never thought about it as a practical
improving society. It seemed to me, at the time, that

But there were other forces working against the type of journalism in which we believed. We were classed as muckrakers, and the school had been so commercialized that the public was beginning to suspect it. The public is not as stupid as it sometimes seems. The truth of the matter was that the muckraking school was stupid. It had lost the passion for facts in a passion for subscriptions.

The coming of the War in 1914 forced a new program. It became a grave question whether, under the changed conditions, the increased confusion of mind, the intellectual and financial uncertainties, an independent magazine backed with little money could live. In undertaking the *American* we had all of us put in all the money we could lay our hands on. We had cut the salaries of *McClure's* in two, reduced our scale of living accordingly, and done it gaily as an adventure. And it had been a fine fruitful adventure in professional comradeship. We had made a good magazine, and we were all for making a better one and convinced we could do it. "I don't think," Ray Baker wrote me not long ago, "that I look back to any period of my life with greater interest than I do to that—the eager enthusiasm, the earnestness, and the gaiety!" But we had come to a time when under the new conditions the magazine required fresh money, and we had no more to put in.

The upshot was that in 1915 the *American* was sold to the Crowell Publishing Company. The new owners wanted a different type of magazine, and John Siddall, who had been steadily with us since I had unearthed him in Cleveland as a help in investigating the Standard Oil Company, was made active editor. Siddall was admirably cut out to make the type of periodical the new controlling interests wanted. I have never known any one in or out of the profession with his omnivorous curiosity about human beings and their ways. He had enormous admiration for achievement of any sort, the thing done whatever its nature or trend. His interest in humankind was not diluted by any desire to save the world. It included all men.

He had a shrewd conviction that putting things down as they are did more to save the world than any crusade. His instincts were entirely healthy and decent. The magazine was bound to be what we call wholesome. Very quickly he put his impress on the new journal, made it a fine commercial success.

Gradually the old staff disintegrated. Peter Dunne went over to the editorial page of *Collier's*—Bert Boyden went to France with the Y.M.C.A.—Mr. Phillips remained as a director and a consultant—Siddall would hear of nothing else. "He is the greatest teacher I have ever known. I could learn from him if I were making shoes," he declared. And years later when, facing his tragic death, he was preparing a new man to take his place he told him solemnly, "Never fail to spend an hour a day with J. S. P. just talking things over."

As for me it was soon obvious there was no place for my type of work on the new *American*. If I were to be free I must again give up security. Hardly, however, had I acted on my resolution before along came Mr. Louis Alber of the Coit Alber Lecture Bureau, one of the best known concerns at that time in the business. Mr. Alber had frequently invited me to join his troupe, and always I had laughed at the invitation: I was too busy; moreover I had no experience, did not know how to lecture. Now, however, it was a different matter. I was free, and I might forget the situation in which I found myself by undertaking a new type of work. Was not lecturing a natural adjunct to my profession? Moreover, Mr. Alber wanted me to speak on these New Ideals in Business which I had been discussing in the magazine, and he wanted me to speak on what was known as a Chautauqua circuit, a kind of peripatetic Chautauqua. Perhaps my willingness to go had an element of curiosity in it, a desire to find out what this husky child of my old friend Chautauqua was like.

At all events I signed up for a seven weeks' circuit, forty-nine days in forty-nine different places.

PART FOUR

In Battles for Democracy

12.

Frederic Howe Befriends the Irish

For several generations reformers had worried about control of the democratic process by special interests. Here a railroad bought a legislature. There a manufacturer bought a judge, or a duty on competing imports. Political machines, riding herd over the immigrant quarters of cities, were among the worst offenders. The poor sold their votes for small favors, and the only solutions to this problem appeared in the guise of civil service reforms and campaigns for honest government.

The immigrant poor had a different view of the matter, as Frederic Howe discovered. In an Irish ward in New York City, Howe learned what progressives had to learn over the country: the alternative to distrusting the poor in politics was to serve them.

Howe was born in 1867 in Meadville, Pennsylvania, where, as a child, he sat in Sunday school across the aisle from Ida Tarbell. He followed her at Allegheny College, and in 1892 he received a doctorate from the Johns Hopkins University, where he studied under Richard Ely and Woodrow Wilson. Subsequently, while attending the New York Law School, he joined Dr. Charles Parkhurst's Vigilance League. When "Jerry," an Irish barkeeper, convinced him that saloons stayed open on the Sabbath in order to meet exorbitant city taxes, Howe left the League and took further instruction in politics at Jerry's bar-rail. After receiving a law degree, Howe settled in Cleveland, where he was associated closely with mayor Tom Johnson's reforms, served on the city council and eventually in the state senate. In 1914 Woodrow Wilson appointed his former student Commissioner of Immigration. In that capacity Howe established the first federal employment office, in New York City.

Out of the Vigilance League, through with regulating my poor man's club, I continued to take refuge in the friendly saloon across the street. When the future looked dark and I had a sense of failure, Jerry's greetings were heartening. He too was insecure and unhappy underneath his blithe Irish manner, and we understood each other. I was often in need of encouragement, for my work at the law meant little to me and interested me not at all. I was trying to do two years' work in one and earn a living at the same time. The secretary of the law school had found me a job in a lawyer's office. There I worked from nine until three. Then I took lectures from three to six, and studied listlessly until midnight. I earned five dollars a week running errands, serving legal notices, making collections, and, with a second-hand typewriter, copying pleadings and briefs which I did not understand. The chief business of my employers seemed to be the collection of electric-light bills from saloon-keepers. This was intrusted to me. In making collections I had to sit around saloons with officers of the law carrying out writs of execution. I spent most of my time on the Bowery and the lower East Side.

My fall from dignity was complete. I felt mentally soiled by the work I was doing. I was compromising my university degree and I wondered if I could ever crawl back to a place among the men I revered. I had come to New York to do

---

From Frederic C. Howe, *The Confessions of a Reformer* (New York: Charles Scribner's Sons, 1925), chap. 7, "My Friends the Irish," pp. 56–61.

editorial work on a magazine or to rise rapidly on a metropolitan newspaper. Yet here I was, living in a cheap boarding-house, spending my days making collections in saloons, or pounding a typewriter in the office of a lawyer who knew nothing about jurisprudence, mediaeval texts, or Roman law. And for some reason which I did not approve of I liked the work on the East Side better than the empty formulas I learned in the law school. I liked the Tammany officials better than the old English worthies whose opinions were quoted with so much veneration in the textbooks.

And during that winter some of my political ideals suffered a collapse as complete as my dignity. I did not know they were going until they were gone. Politics I had believed was the business of a gentleman. It should be in the hands of good men—men who had succeeded in business, who observed the conventions of life, who had graduated from universities. Goodness would cure political ills. The scholar in politics was the ultimate ideal, the ideal of Plato, of James Bryce, of Woodrow Wilson. By disinterested service, by not wanting anything for ourselves, the state could be redeemed.

Equipped with this philosophy, I sat about saloons with officers of the law, and came across a view of life that I had not known before. Here was a world of political reality. Here politics was part of everyday life, part of the family, of religion, of race. Politics was daily work. My state was an abstraction. On the Bowery it was a real thing—a city block, a voting precinct, or a ward. To me politics meant disinterested service. To the people of the East Side it meant getting something for themselves and their friends. To me duty to the state was the important thing; to them the duty was to themselves. Government meant the district leader, the policeman, the local boss. They and the police court magistrates were the only officials the people had any interest in. The district leader had to be placated like a heathen idol, by service at primaries and elections and in other ways. He was good to those who served him and dangerous to those who did not. Faithfulness to him brought coal and food, outdoor relief, an annual outing to Coney Island at somebody's expense. It brought security in a strange land under strange laws which might get one into trouble. Faithfulness to the boss was the only civic idea. To the poor, politics meant bread and a circus. The idea of service was there but it was very different from my idealized abstraction. The God the priest talked about was nearer the people than the God I would have had them worship.

Politics was a hierarchy. The ward boss had precinct bosses under him. They were almost always saloon-keepers or contractors, and they had vassals who hoped to become petty bosses if they were faithful. There were jobs to be had as policemen or firemen, and at the start there was street-cleaning and work under city contractors. The East Side had an ethical code of rewards and punishments. Fealty was the first obligation. Betrayal of the boss or the clan was an unforgivable offense. Everybody understood it. The judge sympathized with it. The policeman was the creature of it. To be loyal to one's friends, to stand by the gang, to do as you were told, until you were in turn selected to tell others what to do, was all that the Constitution, the Bill of Rights, and the government of the United States meant to the average man in lower New York twenty-five years ago.

These practical East Side politicians, whose every act my code condemned, were Irish. They were kindly, tolerant; good companions. Their system was human and simple, something any one could understand. It took graft and gave graft. It took graft from the saloon-keepers, prostitutes, contractors, and big business interests as naturally as its members took help and gave help to neighbors when sick or in need.

It was the Irish clan transplanted to New York. As I watched its workings and remembered the praise lavished in the university on the English conception of government, I saw an age-long conflict between the Anglo-Saxon and the Celt. The Irish have wanted a state that did things for them; the Anglo-Saxons have wanted a state that did nothing. The English had no need of such a state. They were interested in making money, in getting on in the world. Business should do as it pleased; the state should own nothing and be nothing beyond a big policeman. Politics in England was a negative thing, aristocratic, distrustful of the people. My conception of politics as the business of gentlemen seemed now to have a shadow cast alongside it. It occurred to me that the British state, ruled by men of wealth and leisure, was ruled for them, not for the people; they unwillingly allowed others a share in it. I found myself leaning unaccountably to the Irish view of things. They warmed the state into a human thing, made frank demands on it for things they could not get for themselves. They provided an amalgam to extreme Anglo-Saxon individualism, which had an aversion to the state and a resentment of any extension of its activities beyond routine things. I began to think that perhaps politics had a human side, perhaps the state should do things for the happiness of its people instead of being merely a policeman. And perhaps things had to be gotten by the people who needed them most, not for them by some scholar or leader. I began to lose my distrust for the uneducated and the poor, who I had thought should hardly wield so sacred a thing as the ballot. I learned to take an interest in people. They had hardly existed for me before. Some priggishness I think went out of me, unwillingly, through my schooling on the streets of lower New York.

The Tammany politician was also a realist, a realist like Jerry the bartender. He was as ignorant as a child about my state, he knew nothing of the Constitution; his politics were quite unmoral. His instructor was the man above him. From top to bottom the state was something that served you, not something that you served. The sermons of Doctor Parkhurst, the Bulletins of the Reform Club and Civil Service Reform League never penetrated below Twenty-third Street. To these political realists the reformer was a queer bird; he talked bunk. He wanted something for himself as did they.

In the decades that have passed since that illuminating winter I have never ceased to like the Irish. I should not like to think of America with them left out. Because of their wanting things in New York we have playgrounds, public baths, Central Park, Riverside Drive. Their instinct for collectivity made the docks and the ferries public property. They have given us our water-supply and fire department, a wonderful library service, and as good a school system as is probably to be found in any large city. And under Tammany Hall a system of local taxation was created that is unsurpassed for honesty and efficiency in this country or abroad. Unconsciously aiming to shape the state to human ends, the Irish have made New York what it is.

I was unlearning again as I had unlearned at the university. There I had escaped from the opinions of neighbors, from the unquestioned authority of the Sunday-school and the church, the undoubted purity and respectability of the Republican Party. I had acquired new sanctions, the sanctions of educated men, teachers, scholars. The state should be governed by men trained as Plato would have them trained; by disinterested men, by men not moved by personal gains or identified with machine politics. These university dogmas were intellectual. Leaders were men who had achieved success in the realm of thought or in business. Their ideals of statesmanship were taken from England, from men who dedicated their lives without remuneration to the service of the state. I clung to these new sanctions of conduct. My confidence in my own kind was not impaired. I still believed that America would be aroused only through disinterested service. But this faith was strangely confused by new human equations, by the warmer point of view of the Tammany leader and his followers in the tenements of the lower East Side.

13.

Josephus Daniels Defends the Color Line

In the Southern states the antitrust and political reforms of progressivism were often in advance of the North. The direct primary, for example, existed in most Southern states by the time it was adopted in Wisconsin in 1903. In North Carolina, as Josephus Daniels recalls, attacks on the tobacco trust bordered on civil war.

In the South, however, the color line determined the limits of progressivism. In North Carolina, for example, a fusion of Negro Republicans and white populists had ruled the state from 1894 to 1897. Thereafter, Negro disfranchisement laws and terror established white supremacy. Progressives like Josephus Daniels defended white rule at the same time that they attacked the politics of the saloon and the domination of the trusts.

Daniels was born in 1862 in Washington, North Carolina. He studied law, working his way through school as a newspaper reporter, and by the age of twenty-two he managed three newspapers. In 1894 he became editor and publisher of the Raleigh *News and Observer*, and he remained in one or the other of those posts for fifty-three years. A close friend of William Jennings Bryan, Daniels supported him in three elections. In 1912 he backed Wilson, who appointed him Secretary of the Navy. From 1933 to 1942 Daniels served as Ambassador to Mexico.

In 1902, as in every year, there were strong editorials in *The News and Observer* and other papers, in the effort to prevent lynchings in North Carolina. The early part of the year was marked by a horrible one at Salisbury. Two boys were lynched for killing Miss Cornelia Benson. Governor [Charles B.] Aycock offered a reward for each person in the lynching party, a sum aggregating $30,000, and *The News and Observer* said it was not lynching, but was premeditated murder. Governor Aycock directed Solicitor Hammer to proceed to Salisbury and make a thorough investigation, and to leave no stone unturned to apprehend the culprits and bring them to justice. In March, a Negro, charged with poisoning the family of Dr. David Tayloe, of Washington, was taken from the jail at Williamston and lynched, and in August a Negro who was being taken to jail in Edenton for assault, was shot down as he was being carried from the jail. In August also Tom Jones, a Negro alleged rapist, was lynched near Kinston, and a Lenoir County jury formally made its findings as to the lynchers by saying the man was lynched "by parties unknown to the jury, obviously by an outraged public acting in defense of their homes, wives, daughters and children. In view of the enormity of the crime by said Tom Jones, alias Frank Hill, we think they would have been recreant to their duty as good citizens had they done otherwise." *The News and Observer* said the mob should have placed the criminal in jail, applied to the Governor for a special term, which would have been ordered at once, and lawfully hung him on the gallows. It also said that Governor Aycock had done more to prevent lynchings than any other Governor in the country and nothing distressed him so much as that lynching should disgrace his administration.

Early in 1902 was organized what later came to exert power-

From Josephus Daniels, *Editor in Politics* (Chapel Hill: The University of North Carolina Press, 1941), chaps. 34, 39, pp. 401–438. Copyright 1941 by The University of North Carolina Press. Reprinted by permission of the publishers.

ful influence, the Anti-Saloon League, of which N. B. Broughton was president. This organization embraced in its membership many of the strongest men in the State. It held meetings in Raleigh during sessions of the Legislature and promoted State prohibition. Upon its organization, *The News and Observer* said, "With the education of the people, the temperance spirit will spread and the day will come when the saloon will no longer be open in North Carolina. It will come step by step, as public sentiment demands it and is ready for it." This proved to be a good prophecy. It did not come until over one third of the counties of the State went dry and many of the towns had voted out the saloons, and in a dozen or more towns the saloons had been displaced by the dispensary.

I was surprised, seeing that I generally lived up to a policy of refusing to accept liquor advertisements, to find in going over some old files that *The News and Observer,* in July, 1895, carried an advertisement of the Salisbury Liquor Company, whose copy read: "Fine Old Corn Whiskey A Specialty," and also an advertisement of "Old Nick" which had been manufactured in Yadkin County for a century. I was all the more surprised, seeing that later when I was a strong advocate of State prohibition there was a sharp clash with the distiller who had inherited the Old Nick distilleries, which were put out of business by the State prohibition law. He sought to have his distillery exempted by trying to incorporate it as a town, . . .

Before the session of the Legislature of 1903 opened I began an agitation for an act forbidding the sale or manufacture of liquor except in incorporated towns and revoking the incorporation of certain cross-roads controlled by distillers. I also advocated legislation providing for referendum as to whether a town wished prohibition, dispensaries, or saloons. It was pointed out that it was more difficult to deal with the distilling curse, but one thing was evident: the people demanded the abolition of the distilleries and would not much longer tolerate their demoralizing and debauching influence. . . .

When the legislation was pending in the Senate in 1903, there was a hearing which brought to Raleigh hundreds and maybe thousands of people. I do not recall ever before seeing great multitudes of women in the legislative halls wearing their badges and telling legislators that prayer meetings were being held all over the State. . . .

In the latter part of October, 1903, Booker T. Washington came to Raleigh. He spoke at the Negro State Fair to a great audience of white and colored people and made a profound impression. *The News and Observer* declared he was the greatest man of his race in the achievement of leading them in the right lines. I went out to hear him speak. He was very unlike the old-time eloquent Negro orator such as Fred Douglass or Joseph C. Price. They were old-fashioned orators who made people weep and cry. Booker was modern and more like a professor or business man than an orator. He had humor too, but of a sort all its own. He left no bitterness. He greatly pleased men of both races. The substance of his address was to urge upon his race the necessity of efficiency in whatever they undertook. He deplored the fact that too many of them were willing just to get through with a job so that it would pass. He illustrated it in this way: "A few years ago you would travel from Richmond to New Orleans and you would not find any white barbers or whitewashers anywhere, but now in the cities of the South, these two trades, which had been monopolized by the Negroes, are being invaded by the white people." He told the Negroes they could retain these trades and hold their places as brick masons and in other trades by doing their work so well that the Southern people would not feel compelled to patronize newcomers. He urged industrial education. He said that the future of the Negro race depended upon the relations of the Negroes and the white people in the South. With wisdom, he counselled each to trust the other, to be mutually helpful and to understand that the destiny of the

Negroes in the South was to be worked out through understanding between the races who were to live in the South. He counselled the white people to help the Negroes, pointing out instances of white men who had shown great interest in improvement of the Negro race in education and trades. It was a refreshing and wholesome speech, and ever afterwards all who heard him felt that he was indeed, not only a practical apostle to his race, but also a friendly adviser to the white people.

I met Washington first in 1894 when I was chief clerk in the Interior Department. He called with reference to Tuskegee's getting part of the appropriation under the Morrill act. All educational matters were under the direction of the Interior Department. Hoke Smith[1] had known Washington before and received him cordially. He highly approved of the work Tuskegee was accomplishing. I had liked Booker Washington then because he early showed himself the ablest leader of his race. We were friends ever after, and I accepted an invitation to make an address when his statue was unveiled at Tuskegee after his death.

In the same issue of *The News and Observer* that commented on Booker T. Washington in 1903, was an editorial on "The Evolution of Abe Middleton." In the Fusion days Abe had been the leader of the Negro Republicans of Eastern North Carolina. In the Legislature and elsewhere he had taken a prominent part in Fusion politics.[2] There was a strong feeling against him among the white people of his county because he had organized the Negroes for fusion. In its editorial *The News and Observer* said that he was no longer Abe, but

---

[1] Hoke Smith, future governor of Georgia and senator from that state, had been Grover Cleveland's Secretary of the Interior [ED.].

[2] Though Middleton had been a leader in the fusion of Republicans and Populists that ruled North Carolina from 1894 to 1897, his "prominent" part in the legislature had been as assistant doorkeeper. In a final session of the lower house, acting under the direction of the speaker, he barred a white member from leaving. The incident fanned racial hatred for many months [ED.].

Abraham, the father of the new Negro agricultural progress in North Carolina; that, since he had retired from politics and had given his time to farming, he had become a successful farmer and as president of the Negro Fair was leading his race along the lines which alone could bring it prosperity and usefulness.

The day after Booker T. Washington was in Raleigh and *The News and Observer* had an editorial headed "Can Do Nothing But Good," and praised Washington's speech, a storm broke, the echoes of which resounded for many months in North Carolina and created long controversy. In its issue of November 1, 1903, in great headlines *The News and Observer* had the following:

> "PROFESSOR BASSETT SAYS NEGRO WILL WIN EQUALITY."
>
> "HE ALSO SAYS BOOKER WASHINGTON IS THE GREATEST MAN SAVE GENERAL LEE BORN IN THE SOUTH IN ONE HUNDRED YEARS."
>
> "SOUTHERN LEADERS SLANDERED."
>
> "DIRE PREDICTIONS OF COMING CONFLICT BETWEEN THE RACES."
>
> "STRUGGLE WILL GO ON AS LONG AS ONE RACE CONTENDS FOR ABSOLUTE INFERIORITY OF THE OTHER."
>
> "DARE NOT NAME END."

Under these headlines my paper printed an article by Dr. John Spencer Bassett, a professor in Trinity College, which had appeared in the *South Atlantic Quarterly*, October, 1903, issued at Trinity College, in which the writer said Booker Washington, "take him all in all, is the greatest man, save General Lee, born in the South in a hundred years." He suggested the equality of the races and predicted there would be a conflict between the two races, saying that "the struggle of the negro will not be so unequal as now," adding "I do not know just what form the conflict will take. It may be merely a political conflict; it may be more than that."

In printing this article *The News and Observer* printed all the sensational sentences in caps. It had an editorial headed, "Stir Up the Fires of Race Antipathy." It had three columns about the matter, called Bassett (bASSett) a freak, quoting, as fitting Bassett, what Senator Joe Brown, of Georgia, had said of Ingalls, he was "a right smart fellow, but he hain't got no sense." The paper named all the great Southerners of the past hundred years and asked, "Will Trinity College applaud the statement that Booker T. Washington is greater than Craven, its founder, or Duke or Kilgo?"[3] and asked, "Does he [Bassett] pray with his face turned toward Tuskegee?" It admitted that Booker T. was, as it had said only two days previously, the wisest and greatest leader of the Negro race, but it denied him the position which Professor Bassett had given him. On the next day, it had another long article with the following headlines:

"KINDLED FLAME OF INDIGNATION."

"THE PEOPLE FEEL THAT PROFESSOR BASSETT'S UTTERANCES ARE AN OUTRAGE."

"EAST AND WEST AROUSED."

"AN IMPASSIONED EDITORIAL IN THE ARGUS."

"CAPTAIN J. B. EDGERTON, LEADING CITIZEN AND METHODIST OF GOLDSBORO, WRITES 'IF I HAD A SON UNDER PROFESSOR BASSETT, I WOULD WIRE HIM TO PACK HIS TRUNK AND LEAVE ON THE FIRST TRAIN'."

"DENUNCIATION AT DURHAM."

In the continuing days, *The News and Observer* printed,

---

[3] Braxton Craven, first president of Trinity College; Washington Duke, founder of the tobacco fortune, and Trinity's benefactor; and John C. Kilgo, then Trinity's president [ED.].

under "The Spirit of the Press," editorials from most of the newspapers denouncing Bassett's appraisement of the great men of the South. They were practically unanimous in their disapproval. Communications poured into *The News and Observer* by the score and the storm increased in violence. On November 10, Professor Bassett printed an article in the Durham *Herald* in which he undertook to explain:

> "Between the races is a wide gulf and I should be the last man to try to bridge it. I had no thought of social equality in my mind. I was thinking only of the industrial and civic outlook of the negro race. . . .
>
> "The word 'greatest' as used by me has been given a meaning which I did not have in my mind. I had only reference to one's capacity to break over fearful impediments and achieve success."

The News and Observer said his explanation was sorely in need of crutches and added, "Professor bASSett doesn't make it any worse. We feared, when he came to explain, that he would regret excepting General Robert E. Lee, but he lets it stand that Lee is greater than Booker. Small favors thankfully received."

Outside of Durham, every paper in North Carolina, except the Charlotte *Observer,* the *Biblical Recorder,* the *Caucasian,* and the *Progressive Farmer,* vigorously condemned the Bassett article, and many of them demanded that he should retire. Even the North Carolina *Christian Advocate,* organ of the Methodist Church (Western Conference) said, "We think, however, that duty demands that we express most emphatically our disapproval of some utterances of Professor John Bassett." The Raleigh *Christian Advocate,* edited by Rev. Dr. Ivey, said, "For the life of us we cannot see the remotest connection between the affair and the question of free speech." It called for the earliest attention of the Board. Later Dr. Ivey criticized those who were using the Bassett utterance "to injure Dr. Kilgo."

Some churches passed resolutions condemning Bassett's utterances and the papers were full of denunciatory comments by many citizens. *The News and Observer,* on November 13, printed interviews with the county superintendents of the State, who were holding a meeting in Raleigh condemning Bassett, and in its issue of November 15 had an article with the following headlines:

> "Kilgo Will Stand by Bassett—Three Preachers Fail in Efforts to Secure Meeting of the Trustees of Trinity College. What Trinity Now Needs. The Great Majority of the Methodist Laymen Think the Time Has Come for Dr. Kilgo To Retire with Dr. Bassett for the Good of the College."

A day or two afterward, in its news columns, *The News and Observer* said that Dr. Bassett would offer to resign and that his "letter of resignation is written for special meeting of the trustees called for Tuesday to consider Bassett's article." On the 20th it said, "Bassett Resigns." On December 2 the headlines of *The News and Observer's* news story were:

> "Rejects Bassett's Offer to Resign. The Trustees of Trinity College Were in Session from Seven-thirty Last Night to Two-Forty this Morning. Little Was Given Out and It Was Known the Meeting Was of Deepest Interest and Filled with Discussion, but Beyond What Is Quoted Above, Nothing Can Be Said Except That the Trustees Will Give Out a Statement Today."

On December 3, the headlines of *The News and Observer* were as follows:

> "Eighteen—Seven—Thus They Voted. Senator F. M. Simmons and Dr. T. N. Ivey Led the Fight against the Retention of Professor Bassett. A Burst of Applause. Dr. Kilgo Loosed Vitriolic Floods upon the Press of the State and upon *The News and Observer* in particular. Begun Reading Headlines from the Latter and These Aroused the Only Unanimous Applause of the Trustees."

President Kilgo and the members of the faculty sent a communication to the trustees, the concluding paragraph being as follows:

> "The undersigned, therefore, members of the faculty of Trinity College, in all sincerity, with all the emphasis they can command, urge upon your honorable body to decline to accept the resignation of Professor Bassett. We urge you to say of Trinity College what Thomas Jefferson, the founder of American democracy, said of the institution which he established: 'This institution will be based upon the illimitable freedom of the human mind. For here we are not afraid to follow the truth wherever it may lead nor to tolerate error so long as reason is left free to combat it.' "

Each member of the faculty presented a sealed envelope containing his resignation if Bassett was asked to resign. The trustees, in a statement, made the following declaration: "It clearly appears the faculty and the students disagree with certain of Professor Bassett's opinions so far as we can ascertain, unanimously. Neither do we agree with them."

They declined to accept Bassett's resignation on the ground, as set forth at length, of devotion to "academic liberty" and at the same time passed a resolution of "absolute confidence in Dr. Kilgo."

For years Kilgo had gone about the State, in many sermons, addresses, and statements denouncing Jefferson and all his teachings in most vicious language. For example, in a sermon in Raleigh in 1900 he called Jefferson "a religious monster."[4] Colonel Webster (Methodist), former Speaker of the House, in his paper said, "It is Jefferson's political principles that are an offense to Dr. Kilgo and the Dukes, whose mouthpiece he is, and not the great man's doubts and fears upon religious matters." Kilgo followed up his denunciation of Jefferson in Raleigh by publishing a pamphlet dealing with Jefferson's re-

---

[4] Kilgo, a former evangelistic preacher, had denounced Jefferson's views on religion [ED.].

ligion, and Colonel Webster wrote, "The Dukes (who are dyed-in-the-wool Republicans) are probably furnishing the money for this attack on Democracy, and the dead Jefferson cannot sue them for libel."

And in a crisis, Kilgo had no argument or plea except to invoke the doctrine of the much denounced Jefferson! Shades of Monticello!

The day after the meeting of the trustees, some students of Trinity College, imbibing the idea that *The News and Observer* had attacked the college and inspired by the criticism of the paper by President Kilgo, lynched, on the campus, a stuffed figure labelled "Josephus Daniels." *The News and Observer* said that was "an evidence of the liberal spirit prevailing at Trinity College under Dr. Kilgo."

The next day *The News and Observer* had an editorial saying that Bassett had committed the unpardonable sin and that Dr. Kilgo, in his speech, had read an editorial in *The News and Observer* on the expulsion of President Andrews from Brown University because he stood for bi-metalism, an editorial in which *The News and Observer* had denounced Brown University because of this proscriptive policy.[5] My paper said that the complaint of thousands of Trinity College people was that the President and Dr. Bassett permitted their opinions to be shaped by rich trust magnates either to defend or apologize or overlook the illegal or wrong methods of the cigarette trust company, that they spoke to please the trust, and free speech was not involved. "The rich men give large sums to the college," it said, and "That differentiates them from Brown." The paper asked further if anybody ever heard of Dr. Kilgo or Dr. Bassett having an opinion that clashed with the opinion of the head of the tobacco trust. Two days later the North Carolina Press Association held a meeting and denounced the

---

[5] In 1897 President E. Benjamin Andrews of Brown University resigned in the wake of attacks on his support of free silver [ED.].

action of the students of Trinity College in hanging the editor of *The News and Observer* in effigy. The next day *The News and Observer* had an editorial, "Completely Boxed The Compass," in which it said that for months Dr. Kilgo had gone through the state denouncing Jefferson as "a monster," and now his whole defense is based upon declarations quoted from this "monster." Dr. Kilgo and his associates had tried to make the people believe, particularly the Methodist people, that *The News and Observer* was the enemy of Trinity College and I wrote an editorial headed, "The Enemies of Trinity College," in which I said:

> "As the president of Trinity College, Dr. Kilgo has made blunder after blunder, denounced good man after good man, exhibited a spirit of venom and proscription to this and that leader, spit upon this tradition and shown contempt for that sentiment dear to the hearts of old-fashioned Methodists. Those who are determined to stand by him at all hazards, finding that his course could not be successfully defended, have fallen back whenever he was criticized to the untrue and stereotyped reply, 'Oh, he is an enemy of Trinity College.'
>
> "Who are the enemies of Trinity College? They are the men in the faculty who write and speak things that are false, absurd, fantastic, egotistical, malicious—give utterance to the sentiments that shock the best sentiments of the state; students at the college who sing of hanging an infirm Methodist preacher on a sour apple tree and are guilty of lynching; trustees who, shutting their eyes to the demand of a great church that has entrusted them with the management of a great college, use their positions to keep at its head and in its faculty men who will destroy the usefulness of the institution by making it alien to North Carolina Methodism and North Carolina policies; patrons and preachers who, from a false conception of loyalty and caring more for upholding Dr. Kilgo and Dr. Bassett in a wrong cause than to broaden the usefulness of a great institution and to bring men in touch with the heart of the great Master of the Church which established it. . . .
>
> "The friend of Trinity College is he who would apply the remedy necessary, not failing to use the knife. A surgical oper-

ation separating Dr. Kilgo and Dr. Bassett from all connection with the institution will save it to the state and to the Church. This paper has always been the friend of Trinity College."

The echoes from the Bassett letter and resignation went over into the new year. On January 7, 1904, the quarterly convention of the Hertford Methodist Church passed resolutions endorsing the minority of the trustees of Trinity College in demanding Bassett's resignation and condemning an article in the Boston Evening *Transcript* which, they said, insulted the preachers. Presiding Elder Underwood, who was present, tried to prevent the passage of the resolution but could not do so. It was referred to in *The News and Observer* next day as follows:

"So far as known, Mr. Underwood is the only presiding elder who has sought to aid in the attempt to 'destroy the *News and Observer.*' He hastily stopped his own subscription and is understood to have advised other preachers to do likewise. He also wrote a long article published in the organ of the cigarette trust and Southern Railroad, formerly called the Raleigh *Tribune*, and now called the *Morning Post*, attacking *The News and Observer*. It is in his district that his policy is first repudiated, a healthy sign."

Shortly after the Hertford resolution, the Raleigh *Christian Advocate*, which had been greatly offended by the article in the Boston Evening *Transcript*, said its editor was one of the trustees who voted that Bassett ought to retire from the professorship at Trinity College. The pro-Bassett article infuriated him and had the effect of greatly strengthening the position of *The News and Observer* in the Bassett-Kilgo controversy.

After the storm blew over, Dr. Bassett actually resigned and the resignation was given and accepted with a feeling of relief. He went to Smith College, where he won high position both as a teacher and as an author. Away from the pro-trust environment and anti-Jefferson policy then permeating Trinity and approved by the Dukes, Dr. Bassett was never heard afterward to give expression to antagonism to State universities and to other ideas which, in the atmosphere in Durham in the early nineties, caused him to win criticism. Instead, he developed into an able teacher of history and sound economics, such as Jefferson and Jackson and Wilson incarnated. His *Life of Andrew Jackson* is his great work and is by many regarded as an authoritative life. During the Wilson administration in his new environment he was one of the ardent supporters of Wilson's progressive policies and one of the ablest advocates of the League of Nations. He took such strong and able leadership in the fight for the League that he was proposed by many Democrats as candidate for United States Senator from Massachusetts on that issue. I did not see him after he resigned from Trinity College, except in Washington on one occasion, until he came to Raleigh some years later. I called on him at his hotel and went with him to the Governor's mansion to call regarding some matter relating to historical research in which he was engaged. There was no stiffness in the meeting and no reference to his article which had created such an uproar or to my being hung in effigy by his students. I asked Dr. [Edwin A.] Alderman, who was a teacher of Bassett at the University, about him, and he said that at Chapel Hill he had observed Bassett's abilities but that Bassett had eccentricities and sometimes felt, in his young manhood, that he must be against the prevailing sentiment. So when he was opposing the majority opinion in North Carolina he felt that he must be right.

It would be impossible to appraise truly what happened in those days without understanding the atmosphere of the period. Only a few years previously North Carolina had been governed by a political combination in which Negroes furnished the largest part of the vote. Under the Russell[6] administration such things happened as infuriated the white people

---

[6] Governor Daniel L. Russell was elected as a Fusionist in 1896 [ED.].

of the State and caused them to organize Red Shirt brigades to drive out Fusion. When they had attained victory, they had disfranchised the illiterate Negroes and the question of whether this disfranchisement would stand made anything that touched upon it a matter of great importance politically. The people who had won this victory at such great price felt that Dr. Bassett's article would have the effect of reopening the race question, and all of us were more intemperate in denunciation of it, because of the surrounding conditions, than we would have been at any other time. The vigorous denunciation by Dr. Kilgo of Jefferson, his tirades against Bryan and the organization of the farmers who believed that the Duke tobacco trust was impoverishing them—all these things contributed to make a state of mind into which Bassett's article threw the match that lighted the fires of indignation, which stirred the State.

As usual in those times, whenever any matter came up for discussion, Josiah William Bailey, editor of the *Biblical Recorder,* got into the controversy. Bailey, taking up the cudgels for Bassett and Kilgo, made a statement that *The News and Observer* was "trying to take captive the Bride of Christ" and "hectoring the religious denominations"; that "it would invade the Church and dictate to them"; that "it has coolly assumed that neither officials, boards nor churches have rights which it must respect"; and that "*The News and Observer* had put forth a terrible and desperate effort to lord it over God's heritage." Bailey called *The News and Observer* a "paper red-handed with personal and political persecution, reeking with the smell of personal ambition to rule," and added, "The people must destroy this attempt to take captive the Bride of Christ or they themselves will be destroyed." *The News and Observer,* replying to Bailey's criticisms, quoted from his praise of the paper in the temperance fight, showing that he was an echo of Dr. Kilgo in the fight on the paper, and said:

"Nine-tenths of the Methodist laymen are tired of Kilgo and Bassett and will not be quiet while their fantastic, vicious and incendiary sensationalism is injuring the college that is dear to them. The contest that is going on in the Methodist Church is to decide whether Trinity College shall be a Methodist and Southern Institution or an annex to the cigarette trust, alien to North Carolina Methodism. The *Biblical Recorder* joins the Southern Railway, Cigarette Trust, whiskey ring and the Kilgo-Bassett crowd to destroy *The News and Observer* because it will not wear any yoke, corporate or ecclesiastical. . . .

"Bailey's animosity toward *The News and Observer* is political and is based on nothing but politics. It goes back to several years ago when this paper exposed his truculency to the cigarette trust, the Southern Railway's attempt to dominate North Carolina politics and his insidious attempt to advance the interests of the Republican Party in North Carolina.

"Through manipulations, this would-be-dictator of his Church and this political boss actually got a Baptist association somewhere in western North Carolina to pass a resolution that *The News and Observer* was 'an enemy of the Baptist Church.' For what? Solely because I exposed his political duplicity.

"I defied his assumption then to destroy *The News and Observer*. I defy him now in his second attempt to have it boycotted and annihilated.

"Bailey was office-holder on Russell's manure pile, took his per diem, but although he lived here, actually drew three dollars a day for subsistence, but offered to pay it back in the face of investigation.

"Everybody in North Carolina knows that editor Bailey in politics runs with the Charlotte *Observer*, the *Morning Post* and other anti-Democratic journals."

The circulation managers of my vociferous competitor, the *Post*, about that time were boasting that its circulation was piling up. *The News and Observer* countered by showing that, while there were twenty newspapers printed in Raleigh going out as second class mail, *The News and Observer* paid more postage than all others combined, and this statement was given officially from the Postmaster. . . .

In the period of the Clark-Kilgo controversy, with the Tobacco Trust always in the background, the tobacco growers were indignant because of the low price the trust was paying for their crops. "It is not Duke's money that is making Trinity College rich," the growers of the weed said, "but our money. The Dukes withhold fair payment for our crops and get the glory of benevolence to an educational institution. We are the real donors."

In February, *The News and Observer* printed an article by Andrew Joyner, who had made a careful study of the amount of money paid for tobacco on the various tobacco markets in North Carolina. This showed that the Tobacco Trust had cut tobacco prices in half and the article pointed out that $5,000,000 had been lost by the farmers through the Tobacco Trust, the exact shortage being $5,178,395.00. Editorially the paper said that the law of supply had nothing to do with the reduction of the price; that the trust fixed the price at its own sweet will.

That summer, the farmers held a great meeting in Rocky Mount, with three thousand present. They passed resolutions against the tobacco trust, which were called by *The News and Observer* "a new declaration of freedom." The plan of the campaign was outlined by Colonel J. Bryan Grimes and the farmers were determined, if necessary, to organize to buy their own tobacco on the markets. The whole State was agitated by the starvation tobacco prices. Jesse Brake, the leading farmer of Edgecombe County, said, "Four hundred and fifty pounds of tobacco bring $14.65 and the American Tobacco Company is confiscating the farmers' tobacco. It has put up the cost of the manufactured articles three cents. It has had a six-cents tax taken off, yet it puts the farmers' tobacco down one third." Chief Justice Walter Clark compared the trust to war and famine. *The News and Observer* said, of the meeting at Rocky Mount, "But the sleeping lion will be aroused and the American people will yet be delivered from their present slavery to the men whose dishonest dollars now dominate."

14.

Robert La Follette Curbs the Interests

When Robert La Follette was elected governor of Wisconsin in 1900, progressivism began to reach high tide. Wisconsin served as the movement's laboratory in which reform legislation and legislative strategy were refined into doctrine. No part of his program originated with La Follette. His unique role was to weave a variety of reforms, including the direct primary, regulation of railroads, equalization of corporate taxes, a civil service, and social security, into an over-all program that would shift the fulcrum of government away from business and toward popular control.

La Follette was born in 1855 in a pioneer home in Wisconsin's Dane County. He attended the state university and its law school. His public career began in 1880, when he decided to run for the office of county prosecutor. Instead of consulting the local Republican leadership, he rode around the county on an old work-horse and spoke directly to farmers in the fields. Though usually answered with an "Ain't you over-young?" La Follette was elected by a margin of 93 votes. Thus, in characteristic fashion, he began a career that led through the U.S. House of Representatives to the governor's mansion, to the Senate, and at last, in 1924, to a campaign for the Presidency at the head of the Progressive Party ticket.

In the following passage from his autobiography, written as a campaign document in 1911, when he hoped for a Republican nomination for the Presidency, La Follette recalls his first trials and early victories in the Wisconsin statehouse.

Success, for a new movement, often presents quite as serious problems as defeat. Not only had we to deal with that part of the old machine element which now offered to support us with protestations of confidence, but we had also to hold back and keep together the enthusiasts in our own ranks.

As soon as my nomination in 1900 was a foregone conclusion and I began to think of what our convention platform should be and what we should try to do in our first legislature these problems within our own ranks began to concern me. For example, one of the strongest and ablest men among us was A. R. Hall,[1] who had been so persistent in his efforts to obtain anti-pass legislation. He was now making a dogged fight for a railroad commission to regulate rates. Each session he would introduce a bill, make a speech upon it if possible, and see it go down to defeat. He did not expect to pass a bill, indeed his bill was not such a measure as I should have been willing to make a fight for as a law covering that subject. But it served a good purpose in keeping the matter before the legislature.

Now, I was as keen for railway regulation in Wisconsin as any one could well be. I had been deeply interested in the problem as a boy when it was the leading state issue in the Granger period, and had become a real student of the subject as a member of the House of Representatives in 1886 and 1887.

From Robert La Follette, *La Follette's Autobiography: A Personal Narrative of Political Experiences* (first edition, 1911; Madison: The University of Wisconsin Press, 1960), chaps. 6, 7, pp. 103–128. Reprinted by permission of the copyright owners, The Regents of the University of Wisconsin.

---

[1] Assemblyman Albert R. Hall was among La Follette's earliest supporters and closest associates [ED.].

It had an important place in my plans for a comprehensive state program. But as a matter of tactics, I did not consider it wise to bring it forward for immediate and serious consideration. In our campaigns we had emphasized two issues chiefly: direct primaries and railroad taxation. We had found it important to keep the field of discussion narrowed to the subjects which could be adequately treated in a single address. We had tried to make the people masters of these two issues, and, as events proved, we had succeeded. If we now attacked the larger problem of railroad regulation, as Hall urged us to do, we should have too many issues to present clearly and thoroughly to the people in one campaign and would arouse the doubly bitter opposition of the railroads. The railroads had begun to see that some reform in taxation was inevitable, and while they would certainly resist to the end, they believed, secretly, that they could pass on any increase in their taxes to the public by increasing their rates. We might, therefore, get a taxation law, but if we proposed also to push railroad regulation at that time and assert the power of the state to fix rates, the railroads would call to their support all the throng of shippers who were then receiving rebates, and would probably defeat all our railroad measures. If we centred on railroad taxation alone, of course we should have with us, quietly if not openly, all the big shippers and manufacturers who knew perfectly well that railroad taxes should be increased and that such increases would tend to reduce the proportion which they had to pay.

I therefore took time from the campaign and arranged a meeting with Hall at Haugen's home in River Falls. I presented the case strongly to him, urging him not to offer his resolution calling for railroad regulation at the convention. I did not want the convention to go on record against a thing we were all in favor of. We were the best of friends, Hall and I. He was a constant visitor in our home and every member of the family loved him. But he was very insistent about pushing his measure in season and out; he wanted to make a record, and he thought that the fight should be unremitting. Finally, however, he promised to withhold his resolution, and I believe we made better progress in the long run by building our structure of reform step by step. I have always felt that the political reformer, like the engineer or the architect, must know that his foundations are right. To build the superstructure in advance of that is likely to be disastrous to the whole thing. He must not put the roof on before he gets the underpinning in. And the underpinning is education of the people.

In the convention which followed, in August, 1900, I was unanimously nominated for governor, and in November the state gave me the largest majority ever given up to that time to a gubernatorial candidate. On January 7, 1901, I took the oath of office.

Up to the time that the legislature met on January 9th, I felt that we should be able to go forward steadily with the reforms for which the people of the state had declared. I even felt that the machine politicians who came to me offering their support were really convinced that the reforms we demanded were inevitable and that they would no longer oppose them. I was yet to learn the length to which the corporations and the machine politicians who represented them would go in their efforts to defeat our measures. They now carried out openly their plans for stealing the legislature.

When the legislature met there was a general gathering of the machine leaders at the capital. They attended my inauguration and there was no manifestation of hostile purposes. But forty-eight hours afterward the mask was off. The newspapers on the morning of January 9th contained the startling announcement that the "Stalwart" Republicans (as the machine element of the party now for the first time called themselves) were in control of the senate and that they proposed to fight the administration measures. This was the first intimation we had that the old leaders were secretly planning to defeat the legislation pledged in the platform. It was a great shock to us. I found it hard to believe that men elected upon issues so clearly presented would have the hardihood to turn about so quickly.

Our friends were in undisputed control of the lower house of the legislature, the assembly, and after a hasty conference we decided to pay no attention to the sinister reports regarding the senate, hoping that they might not be true.

All the governors before me, so far as I know, had sent in their messages to the legislature to be mumbled over by a reading clerk. I knew that I could make a very much stronger impression with my recommendations if I could present my message in person to the legislature in joint session. I felt that it would invest the whole matter with a new seriousness and dignity that would not only affect the legislators themselves, but react upon the public mind. This I did: and in consequence awakened a wide interest in my recommendations throughout the state.

The predominant notes in the message were direct primaries and railroad taxation—one political and one economic reform.

The railroads at that time paid taxes in the form of a license fee upon their gross earnings. The report of the Tax Commission showed that while real property in Wisconsin paid 1.19 per cent. of its market value in taxes, the railroads paid only .53 per cent. of their market value (based on the average value of stocks and bonds) or less than one half the rate paid by farmers, manufacturers, home owners and others. Upon this showing we contended that the railroads were not bearing their fair share of the burdens of the state. The Tax Commission suggested two measures of reform. One of their bills provided for a simple increase in the license tax, the other provided for a physical valuation of the railroads and a wholly new system of taxation upon an ad valorem basis, measures which I had earnestly advocated in my campaign speeches, and recommended in my message. I regarded this latter as the more scientific method of taxation. The Commission stated that while they had so framed the bills as to err on the side of injustice to the people rather than to the railroads, the passage of either of them would mean an increase of taxes paid by railroads and other public service corporations of more than three quarters of a million dollars annually.

No sooner had the taxation and direct primary bills been introduced than the lobby gathered in Madison in full force. Lobbyists had been there before, but never in such numbers or with such an organization. I never saw anything like it. The railroads, threatened with the taxation bills, and the bosses, threatened by the direct primary, evidently regarded it as the death struggle. Not only were the regular lobbyists in attendance but they made a practice during the entire winter of bringing in delegations of more or less influential men from all parts of the state, some of whom often remained two or three weeks and brought every sort of pressure to bear on the members of the legislature. The whole fight was centred upon me personally. They thought that if they could crush me, that would stop the movement. How little they understood! Even if they had succeeded in eliminating me, the movement, which is fundamental, would still have swept on! They sought to build up in the minds of the people the fear that the executive was controlling the legislative branch of the government. They deliberately organized a campaign of abuse and misrepresentation. Their stories were minutely detailed and spread about among the hotels and on railroad trains. They said that I had completely lost my head. They endeavored to give me a reputation for discourtesy and browbeating; stories were told of my shameless treatment of members, of my backing them up against the wall of the executive office, shaking my fist in their faces and warning them if they did not pass our bills I would use all my power to crush them. In so far as anything was said in disparagement of the administration members of the legislature it was that they were sycophants who took their orders every morning from the executive office. The newspapers, controlled by the machine interests, began to print these abusive statements and sent them broadcast. At first we took no notice of their campaign of misrepresentation, but it grew and grew until it got on the nerves of all of us. It came to be a common thing to have one after another of my friends drop in and say: "Governor, is it true that you have had a row with———? Is it true that you ordered———out of the executive office?"

It seems incredible, as I look back upon it now, that it could be humanly possible to create such an atmosphere of distrust. We felt that we were fighting something in the dark all the while; there was nothing we could get hold of.

In spite of it all, however, we drove straight ahead. After the bills prepared by the Tax Commission were in, the primary election bill was drafted and redrafted and introduced by E. Ray Stevens of Madison, one of the ablest men ever in public life in Wisconsin, and now a judge of the circuit court of the state. The committee having it in charge at once began a series of open meetings, and the lobby brought to Madison people from every part of the state to attend the hearings and to protest. Extended speeches were made against it, and these were promptly printed and sent broadcast. The most preposterous arguments were advanced. They argued that the proposed law was unconstitutional because it interfered with the "right of the people to assemble!" They tried to rouse the country people by arguing that it favored the cities; they said that city people could get out more readily to primaries than country people. It did not seem to occur to them that practically every argument they made against the direct primary applied far more strongly to the old caucus and convention system.

But we fought as vigorously as they, and presently it began to appear that we might get some of our measures through. It evidently made an impression on the lobby. One night, after the legislature had been in session about two months, Emanuel

Phillipp[2] came to my office. He moved his chair up close to mine.

"Now, look here," he said, "you want to pass the primary election bill, don't you? I will help you put it through."

"Phillipp," I said, "there is no use in you and me trying to mislead each other. I understand and you understand that the senate is organized against both the direct primary and the taxation bills. You know that better than I do."

"Well," he said, "now look here. This railroad taxation matter—wouldn't you be willing to let that go if you could get your primary bill through? What good will it do you, anyhow, to increase railroad taxation? We can meet that all right just by raising rates or by changing a classification here and there. No one will know it and we can take back every cent of increased taxes in rates from the people."

"Phillipp," I said, "you have just driven in and clinched the argument for regulating your rates. And that is the next thing we are going to do. No," I said, "these pledges are straight promises."

"But," he argued, "if you can get this primary election bill through you will have done a great thing. And I will pass it for you, if you will let up on railroad taxation."

"Just how will you pass it?" I asked.

"How will I pass it?" he repeated. "How will I pass it? Why, I'll take those fellows over to a room in the Park Hotel, close the door and stand them up against the wall. And I'll say to them, 'You vote for the primary election bill!' And they'll vote for it, because I own them, they're mine!" And this was Phillipp's last interview with me.

Still other and even more desperate measures were resorted to as the fight advanced. I have already spoken of the manner in which the machine had secured control of most of the

---

[2] Phillipp, leader of the regular Republicans in the state, was returned to power in 1915 when he was elected governor [ED.].

newspapers of the state, but there was still one great independent newspaper in Milwaukee—the *Sentinel.* It had been controlled and edited by Horace Rublee, one of that older group of independent journalists which included such men as Joseph Medill, Charles A. Dana, Horace Greeley and Henry J. Raymond. Rublee was temperamentally cold and dispassionate, but endowed with a keen intellect and the highest sense of honor. He treated everything from the heights. He never hesitated to assail corruption wherever it existed, even in the Republican party. After Horace Rublee's death, the *Sentinel* continued to be a thorn in the flesh of the bosses. It attacked [Henry C.] Payne and [Charles] Pfister so sharply for the way in which they were running the politics of Milwaukee, that they finally brought libel suits against it for hundreds of thousands of dollars. The managers of the paper stood their ground and served notice that they would answer and prove their charges. Then suddenly the people of Milwaukee learned that the *Sentinel* had been sold for an immense sum to Pfister.

Thus the bosses gained control of the chief organ of public opinion in our greatest city: the people were left with no large English-speaking Republican daily to fight for their cause. The long series of abuses that arose under a city government controlled by political rings in both parties for the benefit of ringsters—that, in my view, has led to the Socialist uprising in Milwaukee.

Hardly had the news of the transfer of the *Sentinel* been made public than I was afforded strong evidence of its intentions for the future. Mr. [Lansing] Warren, who had been editor of the Chicago *Inter-Ocean* when it was the organ of Charles T. Yerkes of franchise fame, was appointed editor of the *Sentinel.* And one of the first things he did was to come to Madison and call on me at the executive office.

"Governor La Follette," he said, "I suppose you are aware of the fact that Mr. Pfister is now the owner of the Milwaukee *Sentinel.*"

I told him I had heard such a report.

"I suppose you know," he said, "the power of the *Sentinel* in state politics. I have come to see you by Mr. Pfister's direction, to say to you that the paper prefers to support your administration and will do so provided you change your attitude on the subject of primary elections and railroad taxation. If the *Sentinel* opposes your administration, you will be defeated and retired to private life. You are a young man. You are popular with the people. With the support of the *Sentinel* you can have a successful career."

He then went on to argue that the people were not fit to make their own nominations, which led to a considerable discussion of the direct primary. "If you will let up," he said finally, "the legislature will be taken care of."

"Mr. Warren," I said, "I have campaigned this state for direct nominations and equal taxation for several years. The convention which nominated me adopted a platform specifically promising that these measures should be enacted into law. These were the two main issues upon which I was elected governor, and I propose to go on fighting for them."

"Well," he said, "if that is your answer, the *Sentinel* will begin skinning you to-morrow."

I replied, "You may be able to prevent the passage of this legislation, and you may defeat me, but I will use all the power that the people have given me to fulfill every pledge in the platform. And you may carry that to Mr. Pfister as my answer."

Mr. Warren bowed himself out of the office, and the war on us began from that moment.

The Milwaukee *Sentinel* had been a sort of political bible in the state. It went into every corner of Wisconsin. The character which Rublee had given to it made it the final authority with thousands of readers.

From that moment it became the organ of the opposition. It supported every form of privilege. The result has been that the party which it championed has lost control of Milwaukee, the boss who owned it and the bosses it so ardently supported have been wholly retired from power in Wisconsin, and the corporations back of those bosses have been reined in by the laws of the state.

But for the time being the change in the *Sentinel* made our fight bitterly hard. It strengthened the opposition. For a long time I paid no attention to its misrepresentations and personal attacks. But finally, about 1904, I began holding a copy of it up to my audiences, telling them just what it stood for and appealing to the people of Wisconsin to drive it out of their homes; saying that the people ought only to support those papers that served the public; that the papers that were organs of corporations should depend upon the corporations for their support. And that is what the people of the country ought to do to-day. They ought to support the newspapers and magazines that are serving their interests. There must always be muckrakers as long as there are muckmakers, and the public owes it to itself to support those publications that stand for the public interest. It does not make any difference what good news service the organs of the corporations offer, turn them out; teach them that they can't prey upon the public and at the same time appeal to the public for support.

Following the change of front in the *Sentinel,* the lobby became more active. Clubs were formed in Madison where members of the legislature could be drawn together in a social way and cleverly led into intimate associations with the corporation men who swarmed the capital. In one of the principal hotels a regular poker game was maintained where members who could not be reached in any other way, could win, very easily, quite large sums of money. In that way bribes were disguised. It was, at that time, against the law to use free transportation in Wisconsin; it was against the law to furnish it; it was against the law to procure it for anybody else. And yet, all through that session of the legislature, members were receiving transportation in the form of mileage books on the state roads for themselves and for their friends. It was notorious that lewd women were an accessory to the lobby organization. Members who could not be reached in any other way were advised that they could receive good positions with railroad corporations after the legislative session was over. Even Congressman [Irvine] Lenroot, then fast rising to the leadership of the assembly, was offered one, which, of course, he did not take.

When we continued to make progress in spite of all this opposition the lobby made another move against us. It brought to bear all the great influence of the federal office-holders who were especially disturbed over the possible effect of a direct primary upon their control of the state. . . .

Finally, before the vote on the direct primary was taken in the senate, Senator Spooner, who rarely came to Wisconsin while Congress was in session, appeared in Madison. He was there only a few days, but he was visited by members of the senate, and we felt his influence strongly against us.

All the efforts of the lobby, combined with the opposition of the newspapers and the federal office-holders, was not without its effect upon our forces. Every moment from the time the senate convened down to the final vote on the railroad taxation bills they were weakening us, wearing us down, getting some men one way, some another, until finally before the close of the session they had not only the senate but a majority of the Republicans in the assembly. It was a pathetic and tragic thing to see honest men falling before these insidious forces. For many of them it meant plain ruin from which they never afterward recovered.

In order to make very clear the methods employed I shall here relate in detail the stories of several of the cases which came directly under my own observation. I shall withhold the real names of the Senators and Assemblymen concerned, because many of them were the victims of forces and temptations far greater than they could resist. If I could also give the names of the men really responsible for the corruption, bribery and debauchery—the men higher up, the men behind the lobbyists—I would do it without hesitation.

How did the lobby get them? Various ways. There was Senator A. He was a poor fellow from a northern district; a lawyer without much practice—rather a weak fellow. I can't remember just on what bill it was, but they got him. When he returned to his district after the session he built an expensive home, to the amazement of all his friends, and then came down to Washington to a federal position.

We depended on Senator B. He made a statement that he could be relied upon to support the direct primary bill. We figured him on our list until about the time that Spooner visited Madison and *he* got away. Senator C. was another man we had counted upon as one of the old reliables in the movement. He was an Irishman and a good talker and debater. They finally got him, too. I remember he came to me one night and said:

"Well, I don't know but what I'm going to disappoint you in my vote on the direct primary bill."

I could not at first think of a word to say—it was a staggering blow.

"Why, C.," I said finally, "if you were to go over to the other side on these measures, it would seem to me like the end of everything. You couldn't do a thing like that. You have been one of the pillars of the movement."

I don't believe I tried to reason with him. It simply was not a case for argument. There was only one side to it, for he himself had been one of our ablest speakers on the stump in favor of the direct primary.

Well, he voted against us, and it is significant that a few months after the legislature adjourned he was appointed to a federal office and is, I believe, still in the service.

Another instance was that of Assemblyman D., who had been for some time quite an active supporter of the reform movement. He was a small business man and came to the legislature from a county in which I was personally very strong. When the committees were being formed, he was counted so much the friend of our measures that he was placed upon one of the most important committees.

He stood with us in the vote on direct primaries, but some little time after that Assemblyman E., who was one of our leaders in the assembly, came into my office one morning. E. was a fine young fellow, and regarded as thoroughly reliable. He was often in the executive office and I trusted him absolutely. Upon the occasion to which I refer he said:

"Governor, I have changed my boarding place"—he had been boarding with some private family, I think—"I have moved over to the Park Hotel."

The Park Hotel was the principal hotel in Madison, and the headquarters of all the lobbyists. I was somewhat surprised and asked him why he had moved.

"Well," he said, "I propose to be where I can watch the game that these lobbyists are playing. I am satisfied that they are working on some of our weak members, and I am going right into their camp to see what they are doing."

Not long after that he came to me and said:

"How much do you know about D.? I notice him about the Park Hotel a great deal talking with lobbyists. There's something about it that I don't like."

Finally in one of his talks about D. he said: "You want to look out for D., they've got him; you will find him going back on railroad taxation."

I was disturbed about it. We were up pretty close, as I remember it, to final committee action on the bill. I therefore telephoned to one of the leading bankers in the town in which D. lived and asked him to come to Madison. This banker had been a university chum of mine—a man of the highest standing, and a constant and loyal supporter of the Progressive movement. He came to Madison and brought with him a prominent merchant of the town, but before they could reach D. the vote had been taken, and the result was so close that it was found that D. had cast the decisive vote against the bill. The banker and his friends took D. into a room in the capitol, and had a very earnest talk with him. They told him he would never be able to make the people believe that he didn't have the money of the railroads in his pocket for his betrayal of our cause. He never got back to the legislature.

A few days later—when this same bill was before the assembly—we were to have another and a still worse shock. I have said that we trusted E. implicitly. He was one of the most enthusiastic men we had, and being a high-spirited, energetic young fellow, he was of great assistance in our fights. Whenever we gathered a little group of the members in the executive office to talk over any critical situation in the legislature, E. was always with us. He was an active young manufacturer. He often talked with us about his business. I think he had some special machine which enabled him to make his product more cheaply than other manufacturers.

One day E. Ray Stevens came into my office and said, "Governor, I wish you would send up and ask E. to come down here. I don't just like the way he talks."

"Why," I said, "Ray, there can't be anything wrong with E."

Then I began to think that he had not been in to see me for three or four days. "Well," I said, "I will send up."

When he came through the door he did not meet me with his characteristic frankness. But I greeted him exactly as usual and said, "E., I want to have a little talk with you."

I moved my chair right up to his, placed my hands on his knees and looked him in the eye a moment before I spoke. Then I asked, "E., what's the matter?"

The tears started in his eyes and the response came at once. "Governor, I can't help it. I've got to vote against the railroad taxation bill." After a moment he added, "I haven't slept any for two or three nights. I have walked the floor. I have thought of resigning and going home."

"Tell me all about it, E.," I said.

"Well," he replied, "you know that all I have in the world I have put into that factory of mine. I have told you about how proud I was of the thing. Now," he said, "this railroad lobby tells me that if I vote for that railroad taxation bill they will ruin me in business. They can take everything I've got. They have threatened to give my competitors advantages over me in railroad rates that will offset any advantages I have with my new machinery. Now, I can't beggar my family. I have a wife and babies."

I said, "E., you can't do this wrong. You can't violate your conscience." I talked to him quite a bit. He got up and walked the floor. He said he would always be for our measures, but he could not risk being driven to the wall. And then he left the office.

A few minutes before the roll call on the bill, E., who sat next to Lenroot, turned to him and said, "Lenroot, in five minutes I am going to violate my oath of office." Lenroot was shocked and said, "What do you mean?" He replied: "It is a question between my honor and my bread and butter, and I propose to vote for my bread and butter." And he voted against the bill.

Assemblyman F. was nominated by a convention that was overwhelmingly for the direct primary. It adopted a platform specifically pledging the nominee to support the direct primary bill, and F., the candidate, formally accepted and agreed faithfully to carry out the instructions of the convention.

During the all-night session in the assembly on the primary bill, F. was called from the floor into the clerk's room by a member of the senate who offered him five hundred dollars to vote against the bill. F. told the lobbyist that he would not dare to go back to his constituents if he voted against that bill, as he had solemnly promised them when nominated to vote for it. F. said he would like to do anything the Senator wanted him to and he would like the five hundred, but he did not dare to violate his pledge. After more of this talk they left the clerk's room. The room was not lighted.

At the time there was lying on a lounge in that room Assemblyman G., who was ill and had been brought from a sick room to attend upon this important session. He recognized F.'s voice and also the name of the Senator, which F. repeatedly used during the negotiations. Assemblyman G. reported the whole matter to Lenroot, who informed me. We agreed that here was a case that we could take into the court if G. would swear to the facts as reported to Lenroot. It was hoped that a successful prosecution might check the bribers in their raid on our legislation.

I sent for G. In Lenroot's presence he repeated the conversation between F. and the senator, just as he had given it to Lenroot. I then called F. to the executive chamber. He admitted the conversation as detailed by G., but was slow about confirming G. as to the name of the Senator which he had used again and again in discussing the five-hundred-dollar proposal while in the clerk's room.

Another interview was arranged, at which time he promised to tell everything. Before that interview the lobby did such effective work with both F. and G. that their memories utterly failed them as to every important detail of the whole event, and without these two witnesses there was no case.

Such was the opposition we had to meet on all of our measures, the lobby standing together as one man against both the taxation and the direct primary bills.

It was about the middle of March, after inconceivable delays, before the Direct Primary bill could be finally gotten up in the assembly for consideration, and it was then bitterly opposed.

When the debate was finally exhausted there was an all-night session so managed in a parliamentary way as to prevent a vote being taken. In the meantime lobbyists were calling members of the assembly outside of the chamber, liquor was brought into the capitol, and into the committee rooms. Members were made drunk and brought back in such a condition of intoxication that they had to be supported to their seats. And yet, in spite of all this, we retained the support of enough members to pass the bill.

When it reached the senate, though the members were hostile to it, they dared not kill it outright. The sentiment in the state, they knew, was too strong. Accordingly, they pursued the usual indirect means of accomplishing the same end—by passing a substitute measure called the Hagemeister bill, which defeated the real purpose of the reform.

This substitute was indeed supported by some of our friends who were affected by the argument that it was a good thing to make a start, that "half a loaf is better than no bread"; that it was necessary at any hazard to "get something on the statute books."

But in legislation *no bread* is often better than *half a loaf*. I believe it is usually better to be beaten and come right back at the next session and make a fight for a thoroughgoing law than to have written on the books a weak and indefinite statute. The gentlemen who opposed us were ingenious. Under the Hagemeister substitute they proposed to try out the direct primary principle with respect to county offices alone. Now, they knew well enough that county elections scarcely touch the real problem of party caucuses, conventions and legislation; that they involve little besides personal strife for small local offices. They expected by the application of such a law to discredit the direct primary by bringing out a miserably small vote with a big expense charged up against it. They knew that it would take several years to try out the experiment and that by that time the Progressive group, unable to prove the excellence of their policies, would have merited the distrust of the people.

I had thought all this out years before. All through our earlier contests we could have obtained some mild or harmless compromises and concessions. But I was clear that we should not stand for anything that did not strike at the root of the whole boss system. So I promptly vetoed the Hagemeister bill and took the severe lashing of the same newspapers which had all along been fighting the direct primary.

My attitude in this case, and in several other similar matters, has given me the reputation of being radical and extreme. And if this is radicalism then indeed I am a radical; but I call it common sense. It is simply the clear comprehension of the principle involved, and the clear conception of the utter destruction of that principle if only a part of it is applied. I have always believed that anything that was worth fighting for involved a principle, and I insist on *going far enough to establish that principle* and to give it a fair trial. I believe in going forward a step at a time, but it must be a *full step.* When I went into the primary fight, and afterward into the railroad fight—and it has been my settled policy ever since—I marked off a certain area in which I would not compromise, within which compromise would have done more harm to progress than waiting and fighting would have done.

The Socialists, for example, assert that the regulation of railroads, for which I have always stood firmly, will not work—that it is a compromise, and that we cannot escape governmental ownership. But I say that regulation is in itself a complete step, involving a definite and clear policy or principle. I *think* it will work, and I know it *ought to be thoroughly tested.* If it proves the correct solution of the problem, we have no farther to go; if it does not, we can take the next full step with confidence that we have behind us that great body of the people who can only be convinced by events. Difficulties leading to social explosions are caused not by too lengthy or hasty strides of progress but by holding back and preventing the people from taking the *next full step forward* when they are ready for it.

So I vetoed the Hagemeister bill, and decided to go again

before the people with the whole issue. I knew the people of Wisconsin thoroughly. I knew from close contact with them what they were thinking, what they believed. I knew also that I was advocating a sound principle which no amount of abuse or misrepresentation could finally defeat. I felt sure they would support me—as indeed they did when the time came, and most loyally.

After the direct primary matter was disposed of, the railroad taxation bills took foremost place in the legislature. By this time the lobbyists had reached a good many of our men and we began to fear that we could not even control the assembly. They held back the taxation bills and were evidently trying to smother them. I waited patiently and hopefully for the legislature to act. Weeks went by. Hearings were strung out. It was perfectly plain that it was their plan to beat the bills by delay. Every hour, in the meantime, the corroding influence of the lobby was at work. Business connections, social diversions, the poker room, entertainments of every kind, decent and otherwise, were employed, and all I could do, as I sat there day by day watching the precious time go by, was to communicate with the legislature in one of two ways—by message, or by personal appeal to the members to redeem the promises that we had made to the people as a basis for our election. The one way was provided for in the constitution, the other was not. But I could not be stopped from making appeals to those members; I could not. It was very well known that I was the only man in the capitol who could crowd that legislature to do its duty. That is why they attacked me chiefly. As the editor of the *Sentinel* said to me: "If only you will take your hands off, we can take care of the legislature." They argued thus to me: "You have sent in a strong message, you have made good so far as you are concerned, and the people will understand. Now quit, quit, and you can have anything you want."

But I could not see the corruption going on all around me,

I could not see honest measures promised to the people beaten by wholesale bribery without doing the utmost I could to prevent it. About that time the legislature passed and sent up to me a bill taxing the dogs owned in the state. The humorous absurdity of such a measure at once struck me—the attempt to raise a few hundred dollars in taxes upon dogs owned by a class of people already overburdened with taxes, while the corporations of the state were paying hundreds of thousands of dollars less than their just share! I therefore made it the occasion of a message to the legislature in which I vetoed the dog tax bill and in the course of which I endeavored to outline the true principles of taxation. I also held up to view, as I had done in my veto of the Hagemeister bill, the exact conditions in the senate, showing how the lobby had corrupted the representatives of the people. Both of these messages struck home and stung, as I intended they should, and both attracted so much attention throughout the state that the legislature was forced to a consideration of the bills. After a brief fight, however, both of the railroad taxation bills were defeated.

Thus the session of 1901 closed without our having accomplished any of the important things that we had set out to do. More than this, it had enabled the lobby and the bosses, now more strongly organized than ever, to win over some of our leaders. They even secured a manifesto signed by more than half of the Republican members of both branches of the legislature criticising me sharply for what they claimed to be my encroachment upon the constitutional rights of the legislative branch of the state government, and organized themselves into a league to fight the Progressive movement.

I freely admit that as governor I used all the power and prestige of the office to secure the legislation that had been promised to the people. I arraigned the legislature as derelict of duty. No normal condition would warrant any executive, state or federal, in calling the legislative department so sharply to account as I did in the veto of the Hagemeister bill and in the veto of the dog tax bill, but in this case the situation was not normal; after a series of campaigns the Republican party, the party in control of the government of Wisconsin, had pledged in the platform of 1898 a reform of the nominating system, and of the unequal and unjust tax laws, and the legislature elected on that platform had defeated the will of the people and denied them the legislation for which a majority of them had declared.

Again in 1900 the same pledges had been made. The people in the election had by more than one hundred thousand majority voted that such legislation be enacted, and again the legislature had defied the will of the electorate. It was plainly the end of representative government in Wisconsin. It was the rule of a minority through trickery, bribery and corruption. It was a state of revolt. The situation called for extraordinary, aggressive and strong action on the part not only of the executive but of every man who cared to see democracy maintained. The abuse of power was not on the part of the executive. It was on the part of the legislature. The legislators were the ones who were abusing their power. The executive was obeying the mandate of the people.

I understood perfectly well not only that the position which I was taking would raise an issue with the legislature, but that it would be made the basis of a bitter attack upon me. But I was content to go to the people with my messages, and place my record side by side with the record of the legislature, and let it be fully discussed and talked out with plenty of time for the people to consider whether I had taken a course menacing to a republican form of government, or whether this legislature was undermining and destroying every semblance of representative government. So, when this manifesto was promulgated, I accepted the issue. I caused many thousands of copies of the messages which were criticised to be printed and sent broadcast over the state.

If this had been all, therefore, I might have looked upon

the situation more hopefully. But the strain under which I had worked for six months, the high pressure, the long hours, the anxiety—I suppose I worked more than eighteen hours a day steadily—had so impaired my health that as soon as the legislature adjourned, I broke down completely, and for practically a year afterward I was ill, part of the time dangerously. This also was made the occasion for unremitting attack. They published stories that I was losing my mind, that I had softening of the brain—anything to discredit me with the people of the state. But there was never a moment that I was not determined that if I lived I would fight it out with them again.

At the opening of the legislature of 1903, I felt that the time had arrived to advance vigorously with the railroad regulation issue. There were good reasons for doing this. We had the support of the public. We had discussed the subject pretty thoroughly in the preceding campaign, so that the people were prepared to back us up strongly in our plans. It had been a difficult campaign, but it was indeed illuminating. And that was fortunate, for it was tremendously important at that particular time to have the issue clearly understood and the voters united upon it. As I have already related, the Progressives had suffered defeat in the legislature of 1901. All the important measures they had urged at that session failed of passage. Besides that, I was seriously broken in health for many months. Even a year later, when it became necessary for me to make a campaign for renomination as governor, I was so ill that I could not make a single speech. The old machine seized upon this situation to conduct a campaign of unexampled vigor. Organized in what was called the Eleventh Story League, because they occupied the entire eleventh story of a Milwaukee office building, they spent money without stint. They canvassed the entire state, they purchased the editorial opinions of upward of two hundred Republican newspapers, they issued many pamphlets attacking our movement, their speakers were untiring. But in spite of the furious campaign made against me, I was renominated. This result was brought about chiefly, I think, by the publication of a "Voter's Handbook" of one hundred and forty-four pages in which we set forth the truth about our work, about our plans for railroad taxation and direct primaries, and told specifically by what corrupt methods the Progressives had been defeated in the legislature of 1901. We printed 125,000 copies of this book and placed it in the hands of influential men in every part of the state.

I had not yet regained my strength when I began my speaking campaign in Milwaukee, September 30, 1902, but I improved steadily and spoke every day to the end of the campaign.

Mayor [David] Rose of Milwaukee, the Democrat who ran against me, had the support of the Republican machine; nevertheless I was easily reelected by some 50,000 plurality.

In the course of our campaign we had not only advocated our railroad taxation bills but we had also endeavored to show the people conclusively how futile it was to stop short with laws increasing railroad taxes when the railroads could easily turn around and take back every cent of that increase by raising their rates. But the chief reason for advancing strongly with this issue was a tactical one. I hoped to make such a hot fight for regulation that before the session was over the railroad lobby would be most happy to let our taxation bills go through, if thereby they could prevent the enactment of a law creating a commission to regulate them.

When the legislature of 1903 met we were overjoyed to find that the Progressives were strong enough to organize both houses, though our majority in the senate was very slight. Irvine L. Lenroot, now a member of Congress from Wisconsin, was elected Speaker of the Assembly. Although Lenroot, who is of Swedish parentage, born in Wisconsin, was only thirty years old, and had served but one term previously in the legislature, he made an enviable record. A ready debater, with a special gift as a lawmaker, he forged rapidly ahead to leadership in the legislature, and impressed his strong personality upon the most important statutes of Wisconsin enacted from 1901 to 1905. He is now winning added distinction as a constructive legislator in the House of Representatives.

For years the railroads had been under serious attack in political campaigns. A. R. Hall had long been diligently hammering away on the subject, and had produced a general impression that conditions were wrong, without any concrete proof of his contentions. Hence it had been possible for the railroads by the production of a few made-to-order statistics to confuse and unsettle the public mind.

I aimed, therefore, in my message, not to make a general attack upon the railroads, but rather to set forth the exact conditions regarding railroad rates and services. I presented fifteen different statistical tables, carefully prepared, demonstrating the excessive transportation charges imposed by the railroads upon the people of the state. I compared our railroad-made rates with the state-made rates of the neighboring commonwealths of Illinois and Iowa, applying the comparisons to 151 well-known railroad towns in Wisconsin, Illinois and Iowa, the names of which I gave, together with the specific rates. I showed that these 151 towns were paying on an average 39.9 per cent. more for their transportation charges than towns located at similar distances from markets in Illinois and Iowa. In this way I got down to the vitals of the subject and laid it all before the people so clearly that no one could get away from it. It went straight home to every farmer and shipper in the state. Here was a farmer making shipments, for example, from Baraboo to Milwaukee. I showed that he was paying 59.77 per cent. more freight upon certain products than the farmer of Iowa paid for shipping the same products exactly the same distance to market.

Abusing an individual, calling him a hare-brained theorist, a visionary, a demagogue, an unsafe radical, would not answer these tables and the deductions which I made from them. It was for this reason that the message made such a strong impression throughout the state. However bitterly a newspaper might oppose me, yet my proof of the discrimination in freight rates against the very locality in which it was published simply could not be answered or disregarded.

Immediately the railroads sent their leading lawyers to Madison to meet my charges. One of them published a brief in which he took up table by table the figures I had presented and tried to make some explanation or defense. But he could not budge them; they were unanswerable. Nor could my message be assailed as intemperate; it was as dispassionate as a census report.

One of their statements gave me a further opening. It was charged that in making my comparisons I had unfairly selected stations where exceptional conditions existed, and that I had done this to prove my case, the implication being that elsewhere in the state the rates were not discriminatory.

I decided, therefore, to get out a special message that should once and for all set the whole matter at rest. With the help of Halford Erickson, chief of our bureau of statistics, whom I later appointed a member of the railroad commission, and a corps of clerks, we listed every station on the Northwestern and the St. Paul railroads, the two principal roads of the state, and secured the rates for shipping every sort of merchandise and commodity between those stations and the markets. Then we got corresponding rates and distances in Iowa and Illinois and printed them, with the names of the stations, side by side with those of Wisconsin.

Having in hand this voluminous material, I worked night after night at the executive residence until I wrote a message of 178 printed pages, to which was added many supporting supplementary tables. I sent in this message to the legislature on April 28, 1903, and it furnished a final and unanswerable demonstration that we were paying from 20 per cent. to 69 per cent. higher freight rates in Wisconsin than they were paying for exactly the same service in Iowa or Illinois. I presented it on the day before the hearings on the bill were to open, for I was certain that on that day there would be assembled in Madison, at the behest of the railroads, all the big shippers of Wisconsin. And they actually came by the carload, filled all the hotels, thronged the capitol and surrounded the members of the legislature. They argued, protested, threatened, but they could not controvert my facts.

On the receipt of the message the railroad lobby engineered a plan to break the effect of it by organizing an indignation movement among these big shippers. The meeting, which was held in the state senate, was a cut-and-dried affair at which resolutions were adopted denouncing my message, particularly and especially denying the statements in it that some of the shippers who appeared to oppose the legislation were in receipt of special favors or rebates from the railroads. The greatest excitement prevailed in and about the capitol and all over the state. In fact, I was content to bide my time regarding the action of the shippers. I could not at that moment produce the legal evidence that they were receiving rebates, but I was absolutely sure it existed, and I shall tell later how we secured it.

I knew also that the statement in my message that some of these shippers had been coerced by the railroad companies into appearing before the legislature was perfectly true. I had received calls from some of the smaller manufacturers and merchants who told me confidentially that they were ostensibly to fight the legislation, but wanted me to know, privately, that they were in favor of it, that they were afraid if they did not come when they were summoned by the railroads they would be punished by increases in their rates, delays in furnishing cars, and in many other ways.

The regulation bill did not pass at that session, nor did we expect it to pass. But the contest accomplished the purposes we had chiefly in mind. It stirred the people of the state as they had never been stirred before, and laid the foundations for an irresistible campaign in 1904. It also gave the lobby so much to do—as we had anticipated—that it could not spend any time in resisting our measures for railroad taxation. It also forced some members of the legislature who were really opposed to us, and who intended to vote against the regulation bill, to vote with us on the taxation bill as a bid for the favor of the people of their districts.

So, at last, after all these years of struggle, we wrote our railroad tax legislation into the statutes of Wisconsin. As an immediate result, railroad taxes were increased more than $600,000 annually. When I came into the governor's office, on January 1, 1901, the state was in debt $330,000 and had only $4,125 in the general fund. But so great were the receipts from our new corporation taxes, and from certain other sources, that in four years' time, on January 1, 1905, we had paid off all our indebtedness and had in the general fund of the treasury $407,506. We had so much on hand, indeed, that we found it unnecessary to raise any taxes for the succeeding two years.

Indeed, we so reorganized and equalized our whole system of taxation that the state to-day is on a sounder, more business-like foundation than ever before. We brought in so much property hitherto not taxed or unequally taxed that, while the expenses of the state have greatly increased, still the burden of taxation on the people has actually decreased. While corporations in 1900 paid taxes of $2,059,139 a year, in 1910 they paid $4,221,504 a year, or more than double. Wisconsin to-day leads all the states of the union in the proportion of its taxes collected from corporations. It derives 70 per cent. of its total state taxes from that source, while the next nearest state, Ohio, derives 52 per cent.

In 1903 we passed an inheritance tax law which yielded us $26,403 in the following year and has increased steadily since.

In 1905 I recommended a graduated income tax which has

since been adopted by the state. It is the most comprehensive income tax system yet adopted in this country. Those who receive incomes of over $500 must make a return to the tax assessor. The tax at 1 per cent. begins on incomes above $800 in the case of unmarried people and above $1,200 in the case of married persons, increasing one half of 1 per cent. or thereabout for each additional $1,000, until $12,000 is reached, when the tax becomes 5.5 per cent. On incomes above $12,000 a year the tax is 6 per cent.

All of these new sources of income have enabled us to increase greatly the service of the state to the people without noticeably increasing the burden upon the people. Especially have we built up our educational system. In 1900 the state was expending $550,000 a year on its university; in 1910 it appropriated over $1,700,000, and there has been a similar increase for our normal and graded schools and charitable institutions. Under the constitution the state debt is limited to $100,000, so that we must practically pay as we go. Recently we have been building a state capitol to cost $6,000,000, at the rate of $700,000 to $1,000,000 a year from current funds.

After the railroad taxation bills were out of the way in the legislature of 1903 a law was passed, upon my recommendation, providing for the appointment of a corps of expert accountants to investigate the books of the railroad companies doing business in Wisconsin with a view to ascertaining whether they were honestly and fully reporting their gross earnings upon Wisconsin business. The railroads had always been left practically free to assess themselves; that is, they transmitted annually to the state treasurer the reports of gross earnings on which they paid a license fee of 4 per cent. in lieu of all taxes, and no one connected with the state knew whether these reports were accurate or not. I was confident, also, and so stated, that such an examination of the companies' books would finally settle the facts as to whether the railroads of Wisconsin were or were not paying rebates to the big shippers. And, as I have said, I wanted the legal evidence. As no one could make an argument against such an investigation, we got the law.

Expert accountants were immediately employed and presented themselves at the main offices of the railroads in Chicago. The railroad officials did not exactly refuse them admittance, but asked them to come again. In this way they succeeded in securing some weeks of delay; for what purpose or for what preparation we were never able to learn. But in course of time the Wisconsin accountants were admitted to their offices, and made a thorough investigation, resulting in the discovery that rebates had been given to the amount of something like $1,100,000 during the preceding period of six years. In short, we found that in reporting gross earnings the railroads had left out all account of these secret rebates and we therefore demanded the payment of taxes upon them. The railroads carried the cases to the supreme court, but the state was finally victorious and we recovered over $400,000 in back taxes from the railroads in this one case.

The investigation also showed clearly that many of the big manufacturers and shippers of Wisconsin had long been receiving very large sums in rebates in violation of the Interstate Commerce act. I recall that one firm received as much as $40,000 in rebates in one year, and this firm had been particularly active among the lobbyists. Another firm received $60,000 a year; others, various sums, large and small. The violence, indeed, of the opposition on the part of the shippers and the fury of their denunciation of the governor for intimating that rebating was practised in Wisconsin could be pretty well gauged by the amounts they were proven to have received.

We had now passed one of the two great measures so long struggled for—the railroad taxation bill. The other, that providing for direct primaries, seemed almost within reach.

I prepared that part of my message which dealt with direct nominations of candidates for office as though on trial for my life. I felt that the legislature simply *must* be made to see its duty and that we *must* pass the direct primary at that session.

I feared that if it failed again, after six years of agitation, we might begin to lose ground with the public. There comes a time when public interest cannot be sustained in further discussion of a subject no matter how important. The people will give an administration their support two or three times and then they begin to expect results.

The primary bill as introduced easily passed the assembly, and after a long and hard fight we finally got it through the senate by accepting a provision submitting the act on a referendum to the voters of the state in the election of 1904. The machine senators let it go through with this provision because, first, it left the caucus and convention system in force for nearly two years longer. They felt that they would thus have another chance to secure our defeat and get control of the state. It also gave them a chance to defeat the measure, if they could, at the polls. They believed, I am confident, that the people themselves would fail to adopt it; they still thought that it had back of it only "agitators" and "demagogues." It was necessarily a lengthy measure, with some forty or more sections, and they figured that to present the details of a complex bill was a task too great for us in a campaign involving other important issues. Under the referendum as now adopted in many states publication of such measures is provided for at public expense, months in advance of the election, and there is wide distribution of literature on the subject. But there was no such provision in Wisconsin at that time and they relied on the difficulties and expense we would have in reaching all the voters, and on their own ability to checkmate us.

But, as usual, the bosses were mistaken in their estimate of the intelligence of the people. When the time came the Democratic party as well as the Republican party declared for it, and although a desperate fight was made upon the measure at the polls, nevertheless it carried in the election of 1904 by a majority of over 50,000.

Except for one omission I think it is the most perfect law for the nomination of candidates by direct vote ever enacted. It failed to make provision for the second choice, which permits voters to indicate on the ballot not only their first choice of candidates for each office, but a second choice as well, thereby positively assuring a nomination by the group of the party which is actually in the vast majority.

We struggled for a second choice amendment to our Wisconsin primary law for nearly seven years, and finally obtained it in the session of the legislature of last year (1911). I can trace most of the political misfortunes we have in Wisconsin since the adoption of the primary law to this omission. The machine system of politics requires no second choice, because the boss determines who shall be candidates and prevents rivals from dividing up the machine vote. But it is an essential part of the Progressive belief that there shall be no boss system; no one to give and no one required to take orders; the field is open to everybody, and so there are always men to divide up the Progressive vote, while the machine vote is solid. Thus the machine can win out even when the Progressives are in the vast majority.

This happened in the primary election for United States Senator in Wisconsin in 1908. There were two Progressives in the field against Stephenson, both very strong men—McGovern, now governor, and State Senator Hatton—and they split the Progressive vote between them. Stephenson thus slipped in between and received a plurality of the votes.

It was this omission of the second choice provision, with the opening it gave for a man like Stephenson to spend a large sum of money to secure his nomination (his recorded expenditure was $107,000), that has furnished the chief cause of complaint against the Wisconsin primary system. People do not stop to think that under the old caucus and convention system the amounts spent in an election were often many times as great and no account was made of them. A second choice provision, such as we now have in Wisconsin, ought to be the law of every state which has a direct primary.

We needed one thing more in connection with the primary

law, and that was a stringent Corrupt Practices Act to prevent the corrupt use of money in primaries and in elections. We tried hard to get such a law in 1903. We failed at that time, but Wisconsin now has an admirable measure which will make it impossible for any candidate to spend money as Mr. Stephenson did in 1908.

One other measure of great importance also came up strongly in the session of 1903. It grew directly out of our miserable experience with the lobby, and was designed to abolish these corrupt influences which had for decades controlled legislation in Wisconsin. We began fighting for such legislation as early as 1897, and I urged it in messages to three different legislatures, but it was not until 1905 that our anti-lobby law was finally enacted. The Wisconsin statute requires all lobbyists or representatives, employed and paid for their services, to register themselves in the office of the secretary of state, specifying the character of their employment, and by whom employed. The statute prohibits such lobby agents or counsel from having any private communication with members of the legislature upon any subject of legislation. The lobby is given the widest opportunity to present publicly to legislative committees, or to either branch of the legislature, any oral argument; or to present to legislative committees or to individual members of the legislature written or printed arguments in favor of or opposed to any proposed legislation; provided, however, that copies of such written or printed arguments shall be first filed in the office of the secretary of state. This law rests upon the principle that legislation is public business and that the public has a right to know what arguments are presented to members of the legislature to induce them to enact or defeat legislation, so that any citizen or body of citizens shall have opportunity, if they desire, to answer such arguments. . . .

15.

George Norris Unhorses an Old Guard

In 1936, after five terms in the U.S. House of Representatives and four in the Senate, George Norris, then seventy-six years old, planned to retire. But the President of the United States said, "if I were a citizen of Nebraska, regardless of what party I belonged to, I would not allow George Norris to retire from the Senate, whether he wanted to or not." Forty thousand citizens of Nebraska agreed and signed a petition urging Norris to run again. He did, and won his fifth term as senator.

Norris' momentous legislative career, which included the authorship of TVA, of the twentieth or "lame-duck" amendment to the Constitution, and of some of the key labor laws of the thirties, began in 1903, two years before La Follette came to Washington. Unlike La Follette, Norris arrived as a staunch McKinley Republican, "conservative and proud of it." He had been a district judge in Nebraska, twice defeating the Populist candidate for the post. In later years he concluded, in retrospect, that he had probably been unjust to the Populist Party. "It represented human misery and poverty. It came into existence as naturally as the seasons."

The central theme of Norris' career was refusal to abide party rule when it ran counter to his principles. His life gives testimony against the common assumption that party allegiance is the prerequisite of political success. Norris' ascendancy began as a part of the insurgent revolt against Taft Republicanism. In 1912 he supported Roosevelt's Bull Moose candidacy, and in 1917 he broke party ranks to be one of six senators to vote against the declaration of war. Throughout the 1920's he stood against his own party to fight the electric-power trust. In 1928 he supported Al Smith. In 1936 he was finally read out of the Republican Party. Through all these years he was not once defeated.

In the following selection he recalls the beginning of the insurgent revolt and perhaps its most dramatic moment, the unhorsing of Speaker of the House, Joe Cannon, in 1910.

Great power tends to make men contemptuous of opposition.

In the early hours of the struggle to strip Speaker Joe Cannon of those official prerogatives which enabled him to bend the House of Representatives to his will, Mr. Cannon probably failed to sense any grave danger in the challenge which the insurgent group tossed to him.

He and the loyal regular Republican organization were taken by surprise in that St. Patrick's Day uprising of 1910. Arrogance—born of a firm belief that the long-standing rules of the House would continue in force without substantial change—blinded them.

The factor of surprise contributed generously to the success of the fight I led against Cannonism, while millions of Americans looked on.

Now, more than thirty-four years later, I think the country gave us credit for more than actually was accomplished in reform, probably because, for the first time, there had been a challenge to the autocratic power of the Speaker of the House.

From George Norris, *Fighting Liberal: The Autobiography of George Norris* (New York: The Macmillan Company, 1945), chap. 13, "The Unhorsing of Speaker Joe Cannon," pp. 121–132.

Even then the nation did not understand the technicalities and the parliamentary peculiarities of that struggle. It knew that Boss Cannon had been beaten, and that was enough for it. Since then, other millions of men and women have come to voting age; and to them that battle of March, 1910, is but a fleeting memory of an event long past.

In its essence, though in different form, that same fight goes on constantly in this country. The individuals participating are of only passing importance; the fact of the struggle is all that really counts. The unceasing effort to make democratic government really and truly responsive to popular will, and to human welfare, may present itself as it did in the Cannon fight, or under entirely different aspects.

Under the rules, the channels of legislative expression were not free and open. Speaker Cannon could shut them off at his desire. He was literally a czar, with power to be used for good or evil.

Mr. Cannon was not better and no worse than many men in Congress. He was capable in machine politics. He was, perhaps, the most efficient and the most articulate representative of that blighting philosophy in America which places loyalty to party at the top of the list of duties and responsibilities of citizenship. In personal appearance and in habits, he was fitted ideally for the part he played in that particular period of American history. He was disarming in his attitude toward newcomers in the House. Frequently he was brusque and curt, and when aroused he pulled no punches; but in customary contact he had a mellowness that attracted men.

I came under his displeasure early, because I would not stay hitched to his cart; and I never really knew Joe Cannon until after he was licked.

Hedged in as he was in the powerful post of Speaker, he lost contact with the members of the House in the months preceding that insurgent uprising, and did not sense the full measure of the revolt that was in progress.

From the day that I was sworn into office, I noted the rising resentment against his autocratic rule. The natural result was the organizing of members known as insurgents. I know it to be a fact that the single objective which brought these men together was the taking from the Speaker of the vast, brutal power which the rules of the House gave him to control the action of individual members.

Speaker Cannon should not have been caught off guard: there was abundant evidence of growing discontent, in the atmosphere of the chamber when the House was in session, and the cloakroom gossip. It was Mr. Cannon's genuine confidence in party discipline that made him so fearless; and this confidence was his undoing.

Yet, only a short time before, there was a development which clearly foretold what would happen if the right opportunity arose.

There had been many rumors in Washington about the leasing of coal and timber lands in Alaska by President Taft's Secretary of the Interior, Richard A. Ballinger. The President's dismissal of Chief Forester Gifford Pinchot had not terminated a controversy over the policy of conservation of natural resources. It had in fact fed the flames. It became common knowledge that a congressional investigation of the Department of the Interior and the Bureau of Forestry would accomplish what executive action had failed to bring about; Secretary Ballinger was to be vindicated; the investigators were to apply a copious coat of whitewash. The press openly speculated upon the men who might be selected to make the investigation.

A concurrent resolution was introduced in both branches of Congress calling for the appointment of a joint committee. It passed the Senate, and the Vice President was authorized to name the five members from that body.

When the resolution came up in the House, I had made up my mind to take the appointment of its investigators from the

Speaker, if possible, and to permit them to be named from the floor.

While the resolution was under consideration, Representative John Dalzell of Pennsylvania was serving in the chair (Mr. Dalzell performed the chores regularly for Speaker Cannon). He was a staunch Republican regular, and I could not expect to get recognition from him to offer my substitute for the concurrent resolution.

Representative Dalzell was a precise man, and I had observed his luncheon habits:

Regularly at one o'clock, he would leave the chamber for a sandwich, a cup of coffee, and a piece of pie at the House restaurant. That practice was as fixed as the clock itself.

When Representative Dalzell vacated the chair, Walter Smith followed him as the presiding officer. Representative Smith, who also was a regular, was a close personal friend and had been thoughtful and considerate on many occasions. While the discussion continued, I eyed the clock anxiously: as the hour hand moved towards one, Representative Dalzell started down the aisle. When he neared the door, I walked over to Smith and asked him if I might have a little time.

"How much do you want?" he asked me.

"Not over two minutes," I answered.

"I'll give you five minutes," he replied. "Just as soon as the present speaker finishes, I will call on you."

It was exactly what I desired. I had hardly gotten back to my seat before Congressman Smith recognized me. I had hastily written out the substitute proposal, and without any delay presented an amendment to the resolution, by which the House as a body would make its own appointments to the investigating committee, instead of authorizing the Speaker to make the appointments.

My substitute carried by the narrow margin of 149 to 146, with insurgents and Democrats supporting it; and an investigation launched as a gesture to political expediency turned into a thoroughgoing overhauling which had considerable influence in the next presidential election.

That victory gave the insurgents new heart in their weary fight: they had scored against the Speaker, and his power, after attaining a cancerous growth, had suffered a setback.

Those who have received the ballot since the struggle against Speaker Cannon should observe the practical effects of the rules under which the House was functioning until Speaker Cannon's overthrow. Those rules, as applied by Mr. Cannon, disfranchised the minority. This had been true for a long time. Under both Republican and Democrat majorities the Speaker, when the need arose, had the power to hold the House under rigid control.

Every special rule first has to be agreed to by the House, and frequently the question was asked: "Why did the members of the House vote for these tyrannical special rules?"

Often I asked myself the same question. The rules seemed so obnoxious no fair-minded man could support them. But in a parliament as large as the House of Representatives, it is necessary to expedite business by the adoption of special rules governing the consideration of much of the legislation which comes before it. The unwieldiness of the membership of the House meant that unless there was some curtailment of debate, and some limitation of the freedom to offer amendments, it would be unable to proceed in an orderly manner or to advance legislation, and would be beset and weighted down by interminable delay.

Failure to limit debate and amendment of a tariff bill, for example—containing thousands of items affecting all regions of the country—would have meant months, or even years, of delay in the passage of the bill.

It was the abuse of the rules, and not the purposes for which they had been drafted, which was at fault. They left so many tempting loopholes. Every two years the members knew they were confronted with the appointment of the various standing committees; and one man, the Speaker, possessed absolute authority to do what he pleased in these selections. He held in his hands the political life of virtually every member. He could reward the faithful, and he could punish the "guilty."

I doubt if any Speaker in the history of Congress was as ruthless as Joe Cannon sometimes was.

Through his domination and control of the Committee on Rules, he likewise had a formidable lever to dictate the action of the House itself. Speakers chosen from the ranks of both political parties had had the same power, but no one could have made more effective use of it.

Inevitably members knew they would be pleading on bended knee before the Speaker for favors to perpetuate themselves in office.

Specifically, these obstacles made the path of reform difficult:

An ordinary procedure to amend the rules was blocked because there was no way at that time to discharge the committee.

There was no procedure under which a committee could be compelled to report upon either a resolution or any bill referred to it.

So when resolutions to change the rules were introduced—and there were thousands of them—all that the Committee on Rules had to do was to pigeonhole them and permit them to die a slow, lingering death: it became the graveyard of resolutions.

Quite by accident, in the unguarded moment I knew would come, the opening for a reformation of those rules presented itself. The Constitution provided, "Each House may determine the rules of its proceedings."

In this usage I thought there could be no doubt that the word "may" was to be construed as meaning "shall." Otherwise, there was no method provided by the Constitution to establish the rules for the United States Senate or for the House of Representatives. The two legislative branches created by the wise framers of government would have been powerless to accomplish anything without rules to govern their deliberations. It seemed so plain, so clear, so logical to me that the constitutional provision was in effect compulsory upon each House to adopt proper rules.

The Constitution likewise stipulated: "The actual enumeration [to determine the membership of Congress] shall be made within three years after the first meeting of the Congress of the United States, and within every subsequent term of ten years, in such manner as they shall by law direct." This is in Section 2, Article I, of the Constitution.

Representative Edgar Crumpacker of Indiana, chairman of the Committee on Census, reported a bill which provided for the taking of a new census.

Apparently it had been overlooked until the session was well advanced. It was placed on the House calendar, but under the rules it could not have been reached in the regular order of business prior to adjournment. The general House rules decreed bills should be taken up in the same order they were reported to the House by the committee. Always after Congress was in session, many bills were reported out and placed on the calendar without any chance of consideration.

Representative Crumpacker's census bill was far down on the list.

Nevertheless, he undertook to call it up for consideration, out of the regular calendar order. A point of order was made promptly against his motion to advance the census bill; but Speaker Cannon ruled Mr. Crumpacker's motion was in order because the constitutional provision, which gave it preference, superseded the general House rules.

An appeal from the Speaker's decision resulted in Mr. Cannon being overruled. The House itself decided it was not in order to take up the census bill, notwithstanding the Constitution. I thought the Speaker's decision was wrong and the House action in overruling him correct, and I voted to support the appeal from the Speaker's ruling. The next day the Cannon forces had arranged to have all faithful followers present, and Representative Crumpacker offered the same motion which had been rejected the day before.

The machine had been oiled properly this time. When the appeal was taken from the Speaker's decision ruling the Crumpacker motion in order, Mr. Cannon was sustained by the votes of the Republican regulars. They therefore decided, on that fateful day, that the constitutional provision conferred a constitutional privilege supreme over the general rules of the House.

It was the hour for which I had been waiting patiently.

I had in my pocket a resolution to change the rules of the House. Unknown to anyone, even to my closest insurgent colleagues, I had carried it for a long time, certain that in the flush of its power the Cannon machine would overreach itself. The paper upon which I had written my resolution had become so tattered it scarcely hung together. That was the best evidence of long waiting for the minute that had come, and the frequency with which I had studied it alone in my own office.

I had become convinced that, if a constitutional provision for taking the census was entitled to precedence over the general House rule, then the constitutional provision giving to both branches of Congress the right to make their own rules must receive the same recognition.

What was sauce for the goose had to be sauce for the gander.

In the debate that followed, and in widespread public discussion, it was charged I was illogical because each time I had voted against the Speaker on the appeal taken from his decision, and by so voting had established that I did not believe the constitutional provision applied.

Even now, as I see it, there was no inconsistency in the course that I followed. My resolution to change the rules of the House was entitled to the same consideration—no more and no less—than Speaker Cannon and the Republican majority accorded to Representative Crumpacker's census bill. It was the House that decided the issue; and it was my duty as a member to accept that judgment, and follow it, even if I believed the construction which had been adopted was erroneous.

The smoke of battle over Mr. Crumpacker's census bill still hung in the House chamber when I sent my resolution forward to be read, and arose to claim for it constitutional privilege.

I remember a feeling of curious detachment from the ripple of surprise, and the new tenseness that set in, as the resolution was read. I had formulated no definite battle lines although I had weighed the possibilities with great care. So in that moment it seemed to me triumph was near. I felt I knew the temper of the House, growing resentment against the ironclad orders Mr. Cannon had imposed. I had waited so long, watchful day after day during weeks of weary frustration, for the opportunity I felt would present itself in good season.

Here it was.

Every member of the House knew full well the stakes of this battle.

The resolution I introduced provided that the Committee on Rules in the House of Representatives should be constituted as follows:

> That the country be divided into eight separate districts, that each district shall contain as near as possible the same number of representatives of the majority party represented in the house. Then in each one of these districts, the members of the majority party shall meet and select one of their own party, who would become a member of the committee on rules, and that they should certify their action to the clerk of the house.
>
> That the country should be divided into seven districts, each district containing as near as practicable the same number representing the minority members of the house, and that such districts

should meet and select one of their party, and should immediately report action to the clerk. That members thus reported should become the committee on rules of the house of representatives.

That the committee should select its own chairman from its own members.

That the speaker should not be a member of the committee on rules.

This resolution provided a Committee on Rules of fifteen members, eight representing the majority party, and seven the minority party, distributed throughout the entire country so that each member was representative of the entire country.

It took from the Speaker the right to appoint anybody on the Committee on Rules, and the committee thus constituted was to have the power and duty of appointing the members of all the other standing committees of the House.

It stripped the Speaker of his power, thoroughly and effectively.

I felt these provisions likewise would distribute the committee appointments over the country, making it impossible to pack any committee with members from any section, representing any special interests. It would be a thoroughly democratic organization of all the committees of the House. It would free any member of the House from obligation to the Speaker.

I think it was the most democratic plan ever proposed in Congress in the selecting of committees. It would necessarily have placed the power to select committees in the hands of a representative House group from all sections of the country, and while it would have given majority control to the party in power it, nevertheless, would have divided responsibility much more closely between the two parties.

The words of the resolution hardly had died on the air when the Republican floor leader, Representative James Mann of Illinois, raised the point that my resolution was out of order.

Decision, of course, rested with the Speaker.

The entire membership knew with equal sureness that Mr. Cannon would sustain that point of order, and that I would appeal at once. It was then up to the House to decide whether my resolution was in order, and whether the House desired to consider it.

If Speaker Cannon's emotions rose he held them well in check. Under parliamentary law, he had the right to ask for debate when it became his duty to rule on a point of order. If he desired, he could call upon individual members to express their opinion and to offer arguments either for or against sustaining the order. If he ruled immediately upon the appeal a vote would follow; and if the Democratic and insurgent members stood solidly in support of my resolution I should be sustained. In that event, the resolution would come to an immediate vote.

In the uncertainty of the attitude of Democratic members, and the absence of some of his supporters, he decided to play for time in the hope of reorganizing his lines. It seemed to me I could read his thoughts as he looked over the chamber. My resolution had come up so unexpectedly that among the absentees were members who had gone out of the city. Mr. Cannon's hope rested solely upon bringing them in or recruiting some support from Democratic members. He decided to keep the House in session and the point of order under debate while he reserved his decision.

I did not believe any parliamentarian, giving proper consideration to the decision which the House had reached, upon Representative Crumpacker's bill, could exclude my resolution.

All of us knew that the debate, however long and extended, would have no influence upon the Speaker's decision. It continued through the late afternoon and throughout the night, supposedly for the enlightenment of Mr. Cannon in ruling properly on the question of order. He was not in the chair during those dragging hours of discussion, or for a share of the following day. The debate which he had set in motion progressed without the guest of honor. He was at his hotel. The shadows gathered, darkness closed in, crowds thronged the gallery. On the floor groups of members gathered. The clock moved past the midnight hour, then into the early morn and gray dawn.

While the debate was in progress, the Republican insurgents held several meetings, and Democratic members of the House caucused, recognizing that unless they stood by in support the struggle to change the rules must fail. The Democrats knew their votes meant victory, and a split in their ranks would result in defeat.

As the spokesman for the insurgent bloc, I conferred on a number of occasions during the night with Representative Champ Clark, the Democratic floor leader, and his close parliamentary officer, Representative Oscar Underwood of Alabama, deservedly recognized as one of the best parliamentarians of the House.

To my surprise Mr. Clark and Mr. Underwood told me the Democrats would not support us. They said that they did not like my method of selecting the Committee on Rules, and did not believe the authority which my resolution gave the committee should prevail. In order to get the Democrats solidly behind it, they told me, I should have to agree to an amendment to my resolution providing simply that the power to select committees should be taken from the Speaker.

I was stunned.

For a moment I saw victory, which I had felt was so near, slipping away. My spirit was chilled although afterward I was told I was the calmest man in the chamber and seemed to incarnate confidence.

The House itself, they insisted, should elect members of the Committee on Rules.

It seemed to me we could not win in this fight without agreeing to the Democratic proposal, which would make a definite improvement over existing conditions but contained many serious faults.

Yet, in the heat of battle, I hated to give it my approval.

I reported the facts to my insurgent colleagues, and they expressed dissatisfaction. Many of them were opposed to making the concession to the Democrats; but after full discussion they reached a conclusion to which I agreed, that bitter as the dose was, we must take it in order to be sure of obtaining some improvement such action would bring about.

I reported to Clark and to Underwood that we would agree to their proposal, and offered to substitute for my resolution the simple proposal that the Committee on Rules should be elected by the House itself.

I have always been deeply regretful that the Democratic members of the House took this position at that time. Many of the Democratic members were sympathetic with the position the Speaker had taken. They were expecting confidently to control the House in the next election, and they wanted to acquire the great power for a Speaker of their own choice which we were endeavoring to take away from Joe Cannon.

Late in the afternoon of the next day Speaker Cannon announced he was ready to rule, and the debate came abruptly to an end.

The Speaker began to talk in matter-of-fact tones of the rights of the majority. In the deep silence of the floor and the galleries, men listened intently. At the end of ten minutes, he announced his ruling, sustaining the point of order against the proposal I had presented.

Promptly an appeal was taken, this time by the Democrats, and a vote ordered, which resulted in Mr. Cannon being overruled, 182 to 160.

Thus, my amended proposal for the selection of the Committee on Rules by the House came to a vote, was accepted 191 to 156, and the long dynasty of the all-powerful Speaker came to an end.

I never thought it was personal pique which prompted Speaker Cannon to submit his resignation immediately as soon as the tumult of the decision had been brought under control.

I regretted the motion which was made to accept it, voted against it, and was pleased when it was defeated. I was criticized severely at the time for my opposition to accepting Mr. Cannon's resignation. Some of my insurgent colleagues condemned me sharply because of my failure to vote with them. I was in an embarrassing position as a result of the fight that I had led. But I had no personal feeling against the Speaker. My opposition was solely to his frightful abuse of power. I saw no logic in his resignation, and that feeling was shared by some of the other insurgents, including Representative Gardner of Massachusetts, one of the best parliamentarians of the House. I had not prepared that resolution to punish an individual. I was shooting at the system. I wanted simply to take from Mr. Cannon the autocratic powers which his office and the old rules of the House had conferred upon him.

I have never ceased to regret that the original resolution had to be sacrificed in order to terminate an unbearable condition in American government. I felt and still feel the original resolution would have strengthened the institution of Congress.

While the overthrow of Joe Cannon awakened rejoicing, and represented a great victory for democratic control of the House, it did not place the power where it would be exercised in the most practical and democratic way.

It left appointment of the standing committees largely to the partisan machines.

It left the deliberations largely to powerful monopolies.

That night I returned home triumphant in a decent fight, and disappointed that its fruits could not have been even greater. That is the struggle which the people of a democracy face. Frequently they must compromise in order to achieve partial reform. If victory were full and complete, there would be no new political battlefields in due time. Progress and change are constant and eternal.

16.

William Prendergast Goes Bull Moose

By 1912 Republican insurgents were ready to take control of their party. Robert La Follette seemed the likeliest candidate, but in February Theodore Roosevelt, in response to a pre-arranged appeal from several Republican governors, announced that his "hat is in the ring."

One of Roosevelt's most loyal supporters, William Prendergast, Controller of the City of New York, here recalls the campaign for Roosevelt's nomination, which reached its climax in the convention of the Progressive Party, in Chicago on August 5. One of the few experienced politicians to support Roosevelt through this final phase of his career, Prendergast gives his appraisal of the mixed company in which he found himself.

William Prendergast was born in 1867 in New York City. At fourteen he went to work in a Manhattan millinery establishment. He became a credit investigator and eventually succeeded in a variety of enterprises including real estate, banking, and railroads. In 1910 he was elected controller and remained in that office until 1917. Soon after the war he was appointed chairman of the New York State Public Service Commission, a post from which he resigned in 1930 because of disagreements with Governor Franklin Roosevelt.

It had never occurred to me during 1911, a year very much occupied with official and political matters, that the following year would prove to be the most absorbing political year of my life. From its beginning until its very end it was a season of active politics. I wonder now how I managed to give adequate attention to my work in the comptroller's office, but a review of what was done shows that public work was not neglected.

From the very beginning of 1912 it was evident that Colonel Roosevelt would contest the Republican Presidential nomination of President Taft. Some will say that his efforts in this respect were motivated solely by personal ambition, and a craving for the power vested in the Presidency, which he had already exercised so vigorously and effectively for practically eight years. I felt confident then, and still hold to the opinion, that he recognized new and imposing responsibilities attaching to the Presidency, and did not consider that President Taft was mindful of them. My association with him after his return from Europe in June 1910 convinced me of his sincerity. For myself, I believed he was on the right track, especially as I was one of those who for a long time felt that the more advanced interests and fulfillment of the democratic ideal were not appreciated by the men in control of the old parties. I was sure of this, as far as the Republicans were concerned.

I might be asked if the Democratic Party was not alert to new ideas, as shown by its support of Mr. Bryan. My answer is that the men in control of the great city machines, and the business interests in the Democratic Party, had to support Mr. Bryan with the certainty that he was not acceptable to a majority of the people, and could not be elected. Perhaps the best explanation of my own attitude at this time, is to quote

---

From *The Reminiscences of William A. Prendergast,* in The Oral History Collection of Columbia University, Butler Library. Reprinted by permission of Eleanor Prendergast and William A. Prendergast, Jr.

from an article I wrote for the *Christian Advocate* (Published in October of 1912), as follows:

> We have reached the point in our history when we realize that the nation has tremendous social, economic and industrial problems. The solution of those problems cannot be left to the parties that shrink from accepting full responsibility for the task. If their platforms mean anything this is exactly the position of the Republican and Democratic parties. On the other hand, the Progressive platform is a frank statement of our national needs. It is a brief for humanity. It says that the interests of the individual should be the chief concern of the state. It maintains that the hours of labor, the nature of labor, the vicissitudes of labor, the responsibilities of labor and the risks to health incident to labor, are all proper subjects of governmental interest. It says that child labor must be abolished throughout the nation. It declares that women who must perform physical labor shall not work beyond their strength, and that the hours of such labor shall be limited by law, not for their sake alone, but for the future of America. It regards the natural resources of the country as a national possession and declares that they must be conserved for the benefit of all the people, and protected against private exploitation.
>
> These are among the specific doctrines of the Progressive Party which it stands ready to incorporate into governmental law and procedure. It does not assert that it has discovered a panacea for all the ills of the body politic, but it recognizes the fact that such ills exist and it pledges itself to a determined and continued effort to cure them.

So much for ideas and doctrines, but they are fruitless without active political work. In order to enforce principles it is necessary to control conventions, and this requires having the necessary quota of delegates. In New York we realized that the fight was an uphill one. Among Republicans holding important offices as of that time, I was the only one who declared for Colonel Roosevelt. We realized that we had no chance of carrying the primaries in New York County (Manhattan Borough) against the Republican organization, especially as there was no direct primary law at that time. An earnest canvass was made, accelerated by a great meeting in Carnegie Hall on March 20th. I presided and introduced Colonel Roosevelt, who made what many considered his best speech in the pre-convention campaign. There was an overflow crowd which was accommodated in a lower hall, and I was called from my chairmanship of the main meeting to address it. An interesting incident of the meeting was the presence, in an aisle seat not far from the platform, of Mr. William Barnes, chairman of the Republican state committee, who was naturally a very interested spectator, and also one of the Colonel's most bitter and able opponents. In the primary election we polled 16,000 votes, or one-third of the total vote cast. This was regarded by politicians generally as very significant, as we were without the necessary election district works, a usually fatal disadvantage.

These primaries were for the election of Congressional district delegates to the national convention, and delegates to the state convention, which would elect the delegates at large to the national convention, and adopt a platform which would express the views of the party in the state. I was elected a delegate to the national convention from a Brooklyn district, and also a delegate to the state convention. No effort was made to prevent my elections as a delegate, although I was opposed to the position which the regular party organization had taken in the Presidential contest.

The state convention met at Rochester on April 10th. On my arrival the night before the newspaper men asked me if I intended to oppose the endorsement of President Taft for reelection. I assured them I did, and would speak against the platform that I knew would be presented. They also wanted to know how many delegates I could rely upon for support, and I said probably not more than eighty to one hundred. One of the members of the press party asked me if I had any idea of the nature of the speech that the president of Columbia University, Nicholas Murray Butler, was going to make as presiding officer of the convention. I said no, but I would be glad to see it in advance, and was promptly given a copy of the speech with the request that I return it as quickly as possible. I went to my room at once and read the speech. It could not have been more slurring, or slighting, towards Colonel Roosevelt, or provocative of ill-feeling on the part of those who were supporting him. While I considered the speech a piece of very bad tactics, I was not displeased that it gave me every encouragement to make a vigorous attack, especially as I represented a small minority of the convention. It really was the inspiration, incentive, and justification of the speech I wanted to make.

Later in the evening I met Senator Elihu Root in the hotel lobby. He greeted me almost merrily, asking, "Well, how is the Roosevelt Party?"

I said, "Senator, it is very small, but very determined."

Senator Root laughed heartily, and during our conversation I said, "Senator, have you seen President Butler's speech which he will deliver as temporary chairman?"

The Senator replied, "No, I have not."

I then remarked, "Well, Senator, I have, and if the speech were designed to anger everyone in the state who is friendly to Colonel Roosevelt, it will certainly be a very successful effort."

The Senator became quite grave, and said, "I am sorry to hear you say that." I was told that after the convention was over, Senator Root said, "President Butler's speech left a great deal to be desired."

President Butler was made temporary chairman, and later permanent chairman of the convention. His speech fulfilled all the adverse possibilities I had drawn from it. His references directed at Colonel Roosevelt, though somewhat veiled, were impolite, to interpret them mildly. A comment comparing the colonel to a "political patent medicine man," peddling nostrums, was to say the least, unwise. His lecturing of Republicans on their duty was offensively paternal. President Butler's fine literary style, and splendid delivery, were no compensation for the severity of his speech.

The convention adjourned until the following day, and the newspapermen immediately besieged me for a statement in reply to the chairman's speech. They were not satisfied when I assured them I was going to reply the next day. Naturally loving a battle, they pressed for something on the spot. I was not disinclined to agree with them and prepared a two paragraph statement, almost every word of which was dipped in poison. As publicity, the statement was a success, as the Rochester papers boxed it on their front page for the benefit of the public and the delegates. That President Butler was extremely angry with me was quite reasonable, and he displayed his displeasure at the following session. I must confess I was always sorry for the tone of my criticism, but that particular afternoon I felt that a fight could not be carried on with feathers.

When the convention met the following day, and the permanent organization had been effected, the platform, with a strong endorsement of President Taft, was submitted. The principal speeches made in its behalf were those of Senator Root and Speaker Wadsworth of the New York State Assembly. After the platform had been read, I was one of those who asked the chair for recognition, but President Butler ignored me. On my second attempt, he did the same thing. This aroused some interest, but when he pursued the same course the third time I arose, the delegates and general audience quite understood that he proposed to slight me, and there was some laughter, as well as evidences of disapproval.

However, the machine having exhausted its list of platform defenders, the chair had no recourse but to grant me the privilege of the platform. The general audience and the thronged galleries gave me a hearty welcome. The Illinois primaries had been held the day before and had been swept by Colonel Roosevelt. I had hoped that an opportunity to make use of this result would present itself, and it did in almost the first few minutes of my speech. When I announced that I was not in favor of the renomination of President Taft, a delegate shouted, "Taft's all right." I instantly exclaimed "And Illinois's all right too." The applause that greeted my sally was so pronounced as to show that no matter what the delegates thought the great audience outside the delegates was strongly for Colonel Roosevelt, and they showed this unmistakably throughout my speech. I used only a few notes, but my mind had been saturated with the issues and there was no difficulty in marshalling my thoughts in an orderly way. . . .

Colonel Roosevelt sent me a telegram, dated April 11th, which read as follows:

PLEASE ACCEPT MY MOST SINCERE THANKS FOR YOUR SPLENDID WORK AT ROCHESTER.

Later, he stated to friends, one of whom told me, that my speech was one of two of the ablest addresses that had been made on his behalf during the pre-convention campaign. . . .

In my reference to the pre-convention campaign, I have omitted mention of the candidacy of Senator Robert M. LaFollette of Wisconsin. It was the general opinion that he had ceased to be a factor. It may be advisable, however, to make this general reference to him. Under any reasonable definition of a Progressive, Senator LaFollette was entitled to that designation. He had shown this as the Governor of Wisconsin, and his work in the U.S. Senate had emphasized this reputation. It was natural that he had been one of the most active leaders of the revolt within the Republican party against President Taft. Although unquestionably imbued with the convictions of a forward-looking Republican, and with more of the evangelistic spirit than many of his Progressive associates in the Senate, it seemed to me that, with the exception of the people of his own state, he never seemed to have attracted a devotional following, the characteristic that Colonel Roosevelt possessed to a potent degree.

Some short time after the colonel's return from Africa Senator LaFollette called upon him at Oyster Bay. After the interview it was said that he appeared to be in a satisfied state of mind. He may have felt that if an opposition leader against President Taft was to be named, he was the man. In any event, he started on a determined campaign for the Republican nomination, but while making an address at a dinner in Philadelphia early in 1912 (at which Governor Woodrow Wilson was present in behalf of his own candidacy) he was stricken, and from that time on could not further his campaign.[1] It is certain, however, that he bitterly resented Colonel Roosevelt's entrance in the Presidential race and never ceased to show his animosity. This was expressed in blistering terms by his spokesman when his name was presented to the national convention.

The mention of Governor Wilson reminds me that I entertained quite an interest in his campaign, as I looked upon him as the most formidable candidate the Democratic Party could name. I will also refer to a personal meeting with him in his campaign for the nomination. In the course of the campaign, Mr. Wilson carried on a continuous and impressive speaking program. He sought, and in many cases received, the courtesy of invitations from the Democratic organizations of important states and cities to deliver addresses in behalf of his candidacy. But when it came to New York City, it was evident that he would have to depend for his forum upon associations, or political organizations, outside those of Tammany Hall, or the Brooklyn party organizations. It was well known that he wished to speak in Brooklyn, and the question was finally re-

---

[1] La Follette, under great personal tension, delivered a rambling speech. The view that he had been "stricken" lost him key support and furthered Roosevelt's candidacy [ED.].

solved by his being given a dinner by the Brooklyn League, a prominent civic organization the membership of which was largely Republican.

I had the pleasure of sitting on the right of Governor Wilson, and it was the only time I ever met him. He conversed with me most of the time. I explained to him the general political situation in Brooklyn, and pointed out a number of the important people there and their activities. He made an admirable speech, politic in every way, but never qualifying his political convictions. This was especially true when he discussed the tariff question, at which point he addressed himself in felicitous terms directly to the Republicans present, drawing a good deal of merriment and applause. After the dinner was over, Mr. Timothy L. Woodruff[2] discussed Mr. Wilson with me, and said, "There is a very important man. He will certainly be heard from in a big way." This was a real prophecy.

The primary campaign ended with what seemed to be an advantage to Colonel Roosevelt. While it was evident that neither of the leading candidates was assured of a positive majority, each side accepted the idea that the contest was very close, and that the verdicts of the committee on credentials would be decisive in determining the control of the convention and the Presidential nomination.

The next move was upon the national convention which met at Chicago on Tuesday, June 18, 1912. . . .

The history of this convention proves that it was the work of the Committee on Credentials that decided the nomination for President, and the consequent stirring results. The deliberations of the committee, dominated by the adherents of President Taft, never showed the slightest inclination to depart, no matter what the facts of each case might show, from the set-

---

[2] Woodruff, former lieutenant governor of the state, was leader of Kings County Republicans [ED.].

tled plan to decide the contested cases from the southern states in favor of President Taft. . . .

One of the interesting features of the convention, from Saturday June 15th to Wednesday the 19th, was a series of almost continuous meetings held in the great assembly room of the auditorium annex in the interests of Colonel Roosevelt. It was almost a continuous mass meeting. Men stood up and discussed the issues of the convention, and efforts were made to get important speakers to address the throngs that filled the rooms. The most popular orator was William E. Borah of Idaho, and there were many calls for him. As the first session of the convention ended on Tuesday, it was perfectly evident that the Taft forces were in control and interest in these meetings waned. Senator Borah was not as much in evidence, and the sceptics said he was not going to sacrifice his chance of reelection that year. Many of us attached to Colonel Roosevelt's causes, looked upon Senator Borah's position with a friendly and sympathetic eye.

The first session of the convention on June 18th was probably one of the most turbulent meetings of any national political convention in our history. The great question at issue was whether the roll of delegates as prepared by the national committee should be accepted as the preliminary roll. On this list appeared the names of the delegates who had been approved by the Committee on Credentials, including the many contested seats from the solid South. The debate was long and angry. The speeches were many. Governor Hiram Johnson, recently elected as California's chief executive, spoke strongly for the Roosevelt side but his speech was marred by exhibition of bad temper which helped neither his cause nor himself, although I think there was general regret that he had not made a better showing. Later in the convention he spoke, and his effort met with general satisfaction as far as he was personally concerned. The Taft speakers were hooted and cat-called without mercy, the people in the galleries being the chief castigators. On the other hand, when William Flinn of Pittsburgh, one of the chief props of the none too savory Republican machine in that city, endeavored to make a purist speech for Colonel Roosevelt's side, he aroused derision and scorn of a virile type.

It is needless to rehearse the proceedings which, with the end of the Wednesday session, showed that the national organization, dominated by Taft supporters, had determined to control the convention, irrespective of the rights or wrongs of the men claiming to be the responsible representatives of their districts. The situation had resolved itself into this: Those in control of the party organization were willing to sacrifice the Presidency in order to retain the domination of the party machinery in the interest of what they believed best for the Republican Party and the country. No matter what selfish and narrow views controlled their actions, they must save the party from Theodore Roosevelt and his so-called New Nationalism.

The surface methods employed in the convention were to a certain degree deplorable. The point that aroused the most criticism was Chairman Elihu Root's decision that the delegates who were occupying contested seats had the right to vote on their own credentials. When Senator Root was passing on the points raised in the debate on this vital question, Senator Boies Penrose of Pennsylvania stood beside him, and, many people felt, was guiding him. This incident aroused much criticism and I referred to it in adverse terms in my Orchestra Hall speech on the following Saturday night, at which the Progressive Party was launched. I had always had great confidence in Senator Root and admiration for his abilities. This incident did not destroy either. It may be that he was technically correct, but his action helped the perpetration of what many righteously considered a great wrong. The organization of the convention guaranteed the renomination of President Taft, and paved the way for the most stirring event in the history of the Republican Party.

What could Colonel Roosevelt do? That he would refuse to accept the result was certain, but would he bolt? Most of the seasoned politicians doubted this. How could a former Republican President desert his party? It was evident that the regulars did not understand Theodore Roosevelt out of office any more than they had understood him when in office. This was the great mistake of the men who had engineered and obtained the control of the convention.

Late Wednesday afternoon word came to a number of the colonel's closest friends asking that they attend a meeting at the auditorium annex that night, and no one invited doubted that something of a sensational nature would be discussed. There were between thirty and forty people present. It was a peculiar meeting room, with seats placed in a gallery setting on one side, leaving ample open space for those who wished to speak. There were a number of talks, strongly denunciatory of the conduct of the convention. It was at this meeting that Mr. Frank A. Munsey was said to have announced that if Colonel Roosevelt decided to run for President he would support him to the extent of his entire fortune. Quite some years after a prominent man made that statement to me, but I assured him that as one of those present I knew that Mr. Munsey had said that he would support Colonel Roosevelt with all the facilities and power of his newspapers. . . .

Just after the nominating speeches were over, a man came to me and said, "Colonel Roosevelt would like to have you call on him at his hotel." I left at once, but learned at the annex that the colonel and Mrs. Roosevelt had gone for a drive. I called later and saw the colonel. He betrayed none of the excitement that had been so evident during the week. In fact, I was glad to see that he was quite calm. He thanked me for calling so promptly, and said, "Mr. Prendergast, I am going to ask you if you will support me in case I decide to be a candidate for President." Before I could answer, he went on, "If you prefer to think this over, I want you to do so, and not say anything at this time unless you are well prepared to."

I merely answered, "Colonel, I have considered this very situation, and I have decided to support you."

He expressed his thanks very feelingly and remarked, "I hope you will go to the Orchestra Hall meeting tonight,[3] and if asked to do so, present my name." After a little further talk I left. When I reached my own hotel I found this hand-written letter:

CONGRESS HOTEL
AND ANNEX
N. M. Kaufman, Pres.
CHICAGO . . . June 22/12.

MY DEAR MR. PRENDERGAST:

Col. Roosevelt will be greatly pleased to have you place his name in nomination at the meeting tonight.

Mr. Davis of Pennsylvania is to make the seconding speech.

Very sincerely,
JAMES R. GARFIELD

To anyone who was there, and certainly to any one who had a part in the proceedings, the Orchestra Hall meeting was one never to be forgotten. The beautiful and fairly spacious hall overflowed with people; every box was filled beyond capacity, and it seemed that the entire diplomatic corps that had attended the Republican Convention was on hand. Notably among the latter was Count Johann von Bernstorff, the German Ambassador, and his party. I knew him slightly then, but during the next few years knew him much better, and liked him.

---

[3] Roosevelt's followers, including 344 delegates who had not voted at the regular convention, met that evening in Chicago's Orchestra Hall [ED.].

Governor Hiram Johnson of California presided, and there were many speeches. I presented Colonel Roosevelt's name as a candidate for President. This meant that we were in earnest. I think my speech was more of an evangelistic exhortation than a political effort. A commentator writing in a Philadelphia paper said it was an extreme piece of "rhetorical fustian," or words to that effect, but that for the occasion it was a success. Asserting that the nomination had been stolen from Colonel Roosevelt, I invoked the commandment, "Thou shalt not steal." Mr. Harris M. Crist of the Brooklyn *Eagle*, took great joy in calling attention to the fact that the colonel, who was not present, but spoke later, resorted to the same pronouncement of Moses. But all this was the natural result of what most people believed was a great injustice that should be righted.

Colonel Roosevelt's entrance was impressive, and no one questioned that a war was really on. His speech was very pleasing to his audience. Some newspapermen and others noted that in his speech he did not make an absolute commitment to run for President. His words on this point were somewhat qualified but I attribute this to a reasonable caution justified under the conditions. That my interpretation was correct is, I think, warranted by the following letter three days after the meeting at Orchestra Hall:

THE OUTLOOK
287 Fourth Avenue
New York

Office of
Theodore Roosevelt

June 25th, 1912.

DEAR PRENDERGAST:

If it is entirely convenient to you, and not otherwise, I wish you could come down tomorrow (Wednesday) evening to Oyster Bay, either by the 4.28 or the 5.30 train from Pennsylvania Station, and spend the night with me, when we could talk over the whole situation. Do not come if it is inconvenient, of course, but I should really like to see you. There is much that I wish to talk over with you. Meanwhile, do get into touch with Woodruff and Halpin at once, and issue a call signed only by yourself asking all progressives, of whatever party affiliations, to get immediately in touch with us, and stating that we intend to run a complete ticket from President to School Superintendent in every part of the State, and that all men who believe in the right of the people to rule as against the power of the bosses, and social and industrial justice, should join with us.

Apparently the Democrats have troubles of their own too!

Ever yours,
(signed) THEODORE ROOSEVELT
per S.H.

The Hon. William Prendergast,
Comptroller, New York City.

This letter, however, had other significances and was the first important document that the colonel had issued since the famous Orchestra Hall meeting the preceding Saturday night. It contained a very succinct statement of the Progressive Party's principles, and also indicated that the campaign was to be expedited and to be a vigorous one.

My attention was arrested by the fact that, while I was to cooperate with Woodruff and Halpin, the call for recruits was to be signed by me "only." I did not discuss this point with anyone, and this is the first occasion upon which I have divulged it. It indicated to me that the colonel, while he appreciated and desired the help of the men mentioned, preferred that the "call to action" be signed by one who was not a strict organization man, or in other words desired to subordinate the idea that his fortunes were in the hands of those who were best known as regulars, or machine politicians. . . .

In addition to the call I issued a statement inviting those who were in sympathy with our views to call upon me, and a few days later interviewed some two hundred people at my office.

It was an arduous but interesting task and I felt it was necessary to do it in order to get a close-up impression of the general standing of the men upon whom we would have to rely for help. I must say now what I thought then. I was not stimulated, but somewhat depressed by the experience. Perhaps I expected too much. There were among my callers men who had been relegated from offices or leaderships in the Republican ranks to the realms of obscurity, a few former Tammany leaders who had lost their standing in that organization, many party workers of both parties who had never achieved any prominence, independents who felt that this new party would be the means through which they could realize some importance in a new party organization, and a number of idealists who felt that the opportunity had come, through a new party, to shape their ideas into realities. Most of the latter type were those whom Colonel Roosevelt later described as "the lunatic fringe." But it was no time to betray fears or disappointments, and what I have said above I kept a deep secret even from my associates. . . .

It must not be presumed that we in New York were alone working vigorously in behalf of the new movement. There was great activity in many states and good organizations were being formed. It was a tremendous task and a particularly difficult one to undertake during a campaign. . . .

The time before the Progressive National Convention at Chicago passed quickly and the election of delegates from New York made the days very interesting. Many representative men, in most cases Republicans or former members of the party, agreed to serve as delegates and the delegation was, on the whole, a representative one. It included, however, men and women who had never heretofore taken part in active politics, being recruited largely from the class devoted to social service, and in some cases men and women actively engaged in that work. A novel plan, due I think to Chairman Hotchkiss's initiative, was followed of having the delegates meet at

Rochester, there having an impromptu state convention of a few hours' duration, and proceeding from there in a special train to Chicago. This idea was a decided success. Among others, I spoke at the meeting, but the principal value of the plan was to bring the delegation together and enable them to become better acquainted.

During the trip, however, some developments proved that all was not harmony. It had been suggested, and tacitly understood, that Mr. Timothy L. Woodruff would be elected chairman of the New York delegation. The newer element in the delegation had come to the conclusion that Mr. Woodruff was really too much of a politician to hold that position, and on the train there developed a counter movement. It had no particular candidate, but it would not have Mr. Woodruff. I spent the afternoon in my room and was visited by some of the delegates, but did not discuss the question of Mr. Woodruff and the chairmanship. In the evening, however, tiring of being alone, I went to the observation car, where I understood there was quite a gathering. I found that the argument going on about the chairmanship was both fast and furious, but I took no part in it. The Honorable Oscar Straus, distinguished diplomat and former Cabinet officer, was there, and I observed he was trying to harmonize the situation, but without much success. He apparently realized this and suggested to me that I visit him in his room. He also invited one of the women opponents of the Woodruff candidacy. We discussed the subject, and I took the position that Mr. Woodruff, with his long political experience, was a decided addition to the Progressive Party, that he had made a great sacrifice in leaving the Republican Party, and as there was certainly nothing against his character, he being on the contrary, a man of very high character, I thought he should be elected. Mr. Straus felt that we should try to compose the situation in some way, and work for a solution, which I assured him was very desirable.

No solution was found, and in Chicago on Monday morning

that part of the delegation opposed to Mr. Woodruff called on Colonel Roosevelt and gave him their views. The colonel handled them most diplomatically, but nothing was decided. This element then came forward with the proposition that they would vote for Mr. Woodruff's election, with the understanding that when any announcements were to be made in the convention, some other person would officiate in Mr. Woodruff's place. No comment on this suggestion is necessary. The New York delegates had their organization meeting. Mr. Woodruff was elected chairman, and no one presented the absurd suggestion I have described. However, all this had certain significance. This wholly unpolitical element in the delegation had its dangers, as well as its advantages, and this incident was a precursor to later developments. . . .

The National Progressive Convention held on August 10th was a remarkable gathering. It was only in part a political convention. Otherwise, it was made up of men and women who for many years had been working and preaching for reforms. They had, however, lacked organization or other strong media through which to further their ideas. Consequently, here was their opportunity, and it is needless to say that the colonel's stirring utterance, "We stand at Armageddon, and battle for the Lord" inflamed them with enthusiasm. For this element of the convention, and it was an important one, a medium had at last been found for their crusading spirits, and with them the battle cry was "Onward Christian Soldiers." I had great sympathy for these people and their ideas, but I could not help being doubtful of their usefulness in the work of hardened politics, and the administration of government. The public attendance at the convention was very large, and the delegates, mostly self-appointed, had every evidence of popular interest and approval for their work.

17.

Jane Addams Stands at Armageddon

Among the reformers who came as delegates to the Progressive Party convention, the most famous and best loved was Jane Addams. Hull House had survived two stormy decades to become a model for settlements throughout the nation. The numerous publications, speeches, and reports of its director had brought her to the pinnacle of the new profession of social work. Miss Addams had also become active in the cause of international peace. In 1907 she published her *Newer Ideals of Peace,* in which she argued that relief of hardships at home would eliminate foreign wars.

The social workers in Chicago's Coliseum wrote many of their demands into the party's platform. It included a plank in support of woman suffrage, another prohibiting child labor, and a third that contained substantially the minimum standards for industry drawn up by the National Conference of Charities and Corrections. The platform also contained a program for a big navy and a demand to fortify the Panama Canal. That, as Jane Addams recalled a few weeks later, writing in *McClure's,* was a difficult pill to swallow.

During the convention of the Progressive party in Chicago, one constantly encountered members of the American Economic

---

Jane Addams, "My Experiences as a Progressive Delegate," *McClure's,* XL (1913), 12–14.

Association, the National Conference of Charities and Corrections, the Civil Service Reform League, and similar bodies, until one feared that a few students of social conditions were endeavoring, through the new party, to secure measures which, although worthy, have after all recommended themselves to only a very small group out of all the nation. To an incorrigible democrat this was, naturally, very alarming. I was first reassured when I met a friend, whom I had last seen at the earlier Chicago convention before the Resolutions Committee, where he was presenting a plank which later left a slight residuum in the compressed labor paragraph adopted by the Republican party, and where I was presenting an equal suffrage plank which left no residuum at all. I remarked, in passing, that we were both getting a better hearing than we did in June, and he replied that we were not in the usual position of bringing men around to a new way of thinking, but that we were being met more than half way by men definitely committed to progress along all lines.

I gradually discovered that the situation was, in reality, the very reverse of what I had feared. The dean of a university law school acted as chairman of the Committee on Resolutions, and men conversant with the later developments in social legislation supplied information concerning similar legislation abroad; but these men, with the so-called practical members of the committee, were not representing the opinion of any individual, nor the philosophy of any group. They were trying, as conscientious American citizens, to meet that fundamental obligation of adapting the legal order to the changed conditions of national life—in the words of a Kansas member, "to formulate our own intrinsic, self-vindicating laws." The members of the committee had all experienced the frustration and disappointment of detached and partial effort. They had come to this first national convention of the Progressive party, not only to urge the remedial legislation which seemed to them so essential to the nation's welfare, but to test its validity and vitality by the "inner consent" of their fellow citizens, to throw their measures into the life of the nation itself for corroboration.

The program of social legislation placed before the country by the Progressive party is of great significance to the average voter, irrespective of the party which may finally claim his allegiance. Aristotle is reported to have said that politics is a school wherein questions are studied, not for the sake of knowledge, but for the sake of action. He might have added that politics are most valuable as a school because the average man has an inveterate tendency not to study at all unless he sees the prospect of action ahead of him. During the present campaign, measures of social amelioration will be discussed up and down the land, as only party politics are discussed, in the remotest farm-house to which the rural free delivery brings the weekly newspaper; certain economic principles will become current, and new phrases will enter permanently into popular speech.

The discussion of the Progressive party platform will further surprise many a voter into the consciousness that the industrial situation in America has developed by leaps and bounds, without any of the restraining legislation which has been carefully placed about it in Europe. He will be told, for instance, that although twenty-nine European countries prohibit all night work for women, only three of our States have taken such action. He will learn of the long hours and overstrain to which the working-women of America may be subjected. If he is convinced that a girl who pushes down a lever with her right foot eight or nine thousand times a day is making so poor a preparation for motherhood that her work reacts in an "impaired second generation," he will be quick to see that it is the business of government to protect her, certainly in a republic whose very continuance depends upon the intelligence and vigor of its future citizens.

Such matters, doubtless, have a technical aspect, but they are in essence human, and intimately allied to the experiences of the average voter. But it is only when such needs are discussed in politics that he sees "where he comes in" and begins to be "worried."

The members of the Resolutions Committee were possessed of knowledge which it is, after all, a great responsibility not to submit to the nation. If a man knows, for instance, that fifteen thousand of his fellow citizens are killed in industry every year —as if every adult male in a city of seventy-five thousand were put to death—and that half a million of men are crippled,—as if every adult male in a State the size of Minnesota were annually maimed,—it is not sufficient for his peace of mind to know that a small group of public-spirited citizens are constantly agitating in various State legislatures for a system of industrial insurance, and that a yet smaller group of manufacturers successfully oppose such effort because their interests are threatened. The members of the committee knew that such problems belong to the nation as well as to the State, and that only by federal control, through the Inter-State Commerce Regulations, can great corporations be made to assume the injury of workmen as one of the risks of industry; only when human waste shall automatically involve a reduction in profits will a comprehensive system of safeguards be developed, as Germany has clearly demonstrated. Such facts should be made public to the entire country, for it is no abstract theory which would lead one State after another to act upon this knowledge; it is self-preservation. Legislation forced by actual conditions is like the statutory laws, which in the first instance were reactions to felt needs.

It did not seem strange that women were delegates to this first convention of the Progressive party, and it would have been much more unnatural if they had not been there, when such matters of social welfare were being considered.

When a great political party asks women to participate in its first convention, and when a number of women deliberately accept the responsibility, it may indicate that public-spirited women are ready to give up the short modern role of being good to people and to go back to the long historic rôle of ministration to big human needs. After all, our philanthropies have cared for the orphans whose fathers have been needlessly injured in industry; have supported the families of the convict whose labor is adding to the profits of a prison contractor; have solaced men and women prematurely aged because they could find no work to do; have rescued girls driven to desperation through overwork and overstrain. Remedial legislation for all these human situations is part of the Progressive party platform; and as the old-line politician will be surprised to find during this campaign that politics have to do with such things, so philanthropic women, on their side, will be surprised to find that their long concern for the human wreckage of industry has come to be considered politics. When we develop the courage to commit our principles to reality, we will not only enlarge our concept of truth, but we will give it a chance to become humanized and vital. It is as if we thrust a dry stick of a principle into moist, fruitful earth, and as if it returned to our hands so fresh and blooming that we no longer have an impulse to use it as a chastening rod upon the evildoer, but, wondering, hold it as a new-born pledge of the irresistible power of life to quicken and to heal.

In spite of many reassuring experiences on the part of the women who identified themselves with the Progressive party, during the three days of the convention there were inevitable moments of heart-searching and compunction. But, because one felt curiously at home, there was the utmost freedom of speech and a quick understanding of hidden scruples which one was mysteriously impelled to express.

We were, first and foremost, faced with the necessity of selecting from our many righteous principles those that might be advocated at the moment, and of forcing others to wait for a more propitious season. To illustrate from my own experience: For many years I have advocated international peace;

to that end, I have been a member, sometimes an official, of various international, national, and local peace societies, and have zealously written and spoken upon the stirring theme of international arbitration. But, when I sat as a delegate in the convention of the Progressive party, I voted to adopt a platform, "as a whole," which advocated the building of two battleships a year, pending an international agreement for the limitation of naval forces.

I confess that I found it very difficult to swallow those two battleships. I know only too well the outrageous cost of building and maintaining them—that fatal seventy cents out of every dollar of federal taxes which is spent indirectly for war; and I would fain that the Progressive party had added no more to this preposterous and unnecessary burden, that it had been ready to commit the future to arbitration.

It was a serious matter even to appear to desert the cause and the comrades with which I had been for so many years identified. Believing, however, as I do, that we prepare ourselves for sudden deeds by an infinite series of minor decisions we have previously made, and that our convictions are, after all, determined by our sincerest experiences, I read over the documents of my long advocacy of peace, to find that I had consistently pursued one line of appeal. I contended that peace is no longer an abstract dogma, but that marked manifestations of "a newer dynamic peace" are found in that new internationalism promoted by the men of all nations who are determined upon the abolition of degrading poverty, disease, and intellectual weakness, with their resulting inefficiency and tragedy.

It is therefore not surprising that I should have been attracted to a party which pledged itself to work unceasingly for "effective labor legislation looking to the prevention of industrial accidents, occupational diseases, overwork, involuntary unemployment, and other injurious effects incident to modern industry." The men in every-day contact with the economic conditions of our industrial cities have estimated that the total number of casualties suffered by our industrial army is sufficient to carry on perpetually two such wars, at the same time, as our Civil War and the Russo-Japanese War; that the casualties in the structural iron trade, in the erection of bridges and high buildings, bear the same percentage to the number of men engaged as did the wounded to the total number of troops in the battle of Bull Run. After all, when a choice was presented to me between protesting against the human waste in industry or against the havoc in warfare, the former made the more intimate appeal, and I identified myself with the political party which not only protests against such waste, but advances well considered legislation to prevent it.

Industrial Insurance Acts to protect the thousands of young immigrants who each year take the return journey across the Atlantic, maimed and crippled because the republic to which they have given their young strength failed to protect them as they would have been safeguarded at home, may but precede the successful conclusion of arbitration treaties.

Perhaps that ancient kindliness which "sat beside the cradle of the race" can not assert itself, in our generation, against warfare, so long as we stultify ourselves by our disregard of the shocking destruction in industry. The federal government through its own recent experience is leaning to the new humanitarianism. The wonderful sanitary system and daily regimen which preserved the life and health of the workers who dug the Panama Canal ought to make it very difficult for the same government to build upon the same spot huge fortifications whose very existence threatens with destruction that same human stuff which it has so painstakingly kept alive.

During the three days of the Progressive convention, one felt not only the breakdown of the old issues which had furnished both parties with their election cries for half a century, but the inevitable emergence of a new position.

A new code of political action has been formulated by men who are striving to express a sense of justice, socialized by long effort to secure fair play between contending classes; men who have learned that it can not be done by *a priori* reasoning, but must be established upon carefully ascertained facts.

Through the action of the Progressive party, remedial legislation is destined to be introduced into Congress and into every State legislature, by men whose party is committed to the redress of social wrongs and who have promised their constituents specific measures adapted to the changing and varied conditions of our industrial life.

18.

Theodore Roosevelt Sums It Up

As the Presidential nominee of the Progressive Party, Theodore Roosevelt held together an uneasy alliance of professional politicians, social reformers, and a few business magnates. In a campaign that won him more than four million votes Roosevelt stressed his concept of a "New Nationalism," which he usually described as a combination of big business, big government, and strong diplomacy. With these the nation could reap the benefits available to the strong and could afford much welfare legislation. In the following statement Roosevelt explains how he came to believe in these principles.

The progressives lost the election to Governor Woodrow Wilson of New Jersey, who had regarded most of Roosevelt's platform as state paternalism. Eventually Wilson accepted the Progressive program and pushed some of it through Congress.

I suppose I had a natural tendency to become a Progressive, anyhow. That is, I was naturally a democrat, in believing in fair play for everybody. But I grew toward my present position, not so much as the result of study in the library or the reading of books—although I have been very much helped by such study and by such reading—as by actually living and working

---

Theodore Roosevelt, "How I Became a Progressive," *The Outlook*, October 12, 1912. Here reprinted from *The Works of Theodore Roosevelt* (New York: Charles Scribner's Sons, 1932), XVII, 315–319.

with men under many different conditions and seeing their needs from many different points of view.

The first set of our people with whom I associated so intimately as to get on thoroughly sympathetic terms with them were cow-punchers, then on the ranges in the West. I was so impressed with them that in doing them justice I did injustice to equally good citizens elsewhere whom I did not know; and it was a number of years before I grew to understand, first by associating with railway men, then with farmers, then with mechanics, and so on, that the things that I specially liked about my cow-puncher friends were, after all, to be found fundamentally in railway men, in farmers, in blacksmiths, in carpenters—in fact, generally among my fellow American citizens.

Before I began to go with the cow-punchers, I had already, as the result of experience in the legislature at Albany, begun rather timidly to strive for social and industrial justice. But at that time my attitude was that of giving justice from above. It was the experience on the range that first taught me to try to get justice for all of us by working on the same level with the rest of my fellow citizens.

It was the conviction that there was much social and industrial injustice and the effort to secure social and industrial justice that first led me to taking so keen an interest in popular rule.

For years I accepted the theory, as most of the rest of us then accepted it, that we already had popular government; that this was a government by the people. I believed the power of the boss was due only to the indifference and short-sightedness of the average decent citizen. Gradually it came over me that while this was half the truth, it was only half the truth, and that while the boss owed part of his power to the fact that the average man did not do his duty, yet that there was the further fact to be considered, that for the average man it had already been made very difficult instead of very easy for him to do his duty. I grew to feel a keen interest in the machinery for getting adequate and genuine popular rule, chiefly because I found that we could not get social and industrial justice without popular rule, and that it was immensely easier to get such popular rule by the means of machinery of the type of direct nominations at primaries, the short ballot, the initiative, referendum, and the like.

I usually found that my interest in any given side of a question of justice was aroused by some concrete case. It was the examination I made into the miseries attendant upon the manufacture of cigars in tenement-houses that first opened my eyes to the need of legislation on such subjects. My friends come from many walks of life. The need for a workmen's compensation act was driven home to me by my knowing a brakeman who had lost his legs in an accident, and whose family was thereby at once reduced from self-respecting comfort to conditions that at one time became very dreadful. Of course, after coming across various concrete instances of this kind, I would begin to read up on the subject, and then I would get in touch with social workers and others who were experts and could acquaint me with what was vital in the matter. Looking back, it seems to me that I made my greatest strides forward while I was police commissioner, and this largely through my intimacy with Jacob Riis, for he opened all kinds of windows into the matter for me.

The conservation movement I approached from slightly different lines. I have always been fond of history and of science, and what has occurred to Spain, to Palestine, to China, and to North Africa from the destruction of natural resources is familiar to me. I have always been deeply impressed with [Justus] Liebig's statement that it was the decrease of soil fertility, and not either peace or war, which was fundamental in bringing about the decadence of nations. While unquestionably nations have been destroyed by other causes, I have become convinced that it was the destruction of the soil itself which was perhaps the most fatal of all causes. But when, at the beginning of my term of service as President, under the influence of Mr. Pinchot and Mr. Newell, I took up the cause of conservation, I was already fairly well awake to the need of social and industrial justice; and from the outset we had in view, not only the preservation of natural resources, but the prevention of monopoly in natural resources, so that they should inhere in the people as a whole. There were plenty of newspapers, the New York *Times, Sun,* and *Evening Post,* for instance, which cordially supported our policy of conservation as long as we did not try to combine it with a movement against monopolization of resources, and which promptly abandoned us when it became evident that we wished to conserve the resources not for a part of the people but for all of the people.

The country-life movement was simply another side of this movement for a better and juster life. From Mary E. Wilkins to Sarah O. Jewett, in story after story which I would read for mere enjoyment, I would come upon things that not merely pleased me but gave me instruction—I have always thought that a good novel or a good story could teach quite as much as a more solemnly pretentious work, if it was written in the right way and read in the right way—and then my experience on farms, my knowledge of farmers, the way I followed what happened to the sons and daughters of the farmers I knew, all joined to make me feel the need of arousing the public interest and the public conscience as regards the conditions of life in the country.

Here again I have been fortunate enough to live with my own people, and not to live as an outsider, but as a man doing his share of the work. I know what the work and what the loneliness of a farmer's life too often are. I do not want to help the farmer or to help his wife in ways that will soften either, but I do want to join with both, and try to help them and help myself and help all of us, not by doing away with the need of work, but by trying to create a situation in which work will be more fruitful, and in which the work shall produce and go hand in hand with opportunities for self-development.

Very early I learned through my reading of history, and I found through my association with reformers, that one of the prime difficulties was to get the man who wished reform within a nation also to pay heed to the needs of the nation from the international standpoint. Every little city or republic of antiquity was continually torn between factions which wished to do justice at home but were weak abroad, and other factions which secured justice abroad by the loss of personal liberty at home. So here at home I too often found that men who were ardent for social and industrial reform would be ignorant of the needs of this nation as a nation, would be ignorant of what the navy meant to the nation, of what it meant to the nation to have and to fortify and protect the Panama Canal, of what it meant to the nation to get from the other nations of mankind the respect which comes only to the just, and which is denied to the weaker nation far more quickly than it is denied to the stronger.

It ought not be necessary to insist upon a point like this, with China before our very eyes offering the most woful example of the ruin that comes to a nation which cannot defend itself against aggression—and China, by the way, offers the further proof that centuries of complete absence of militarism may yet result in the development of all the worst vices and all the deepest misery that grow up in nations that suffer from overmuch militarism. Here again I learn from books, I learn from study, and I learn most by dealing with men.

I feel that the Progressive party owes no small part of its strength to the fact that it not only stands for the most far-reaching measures of social and industrial reform, but in sane and temperate fashion stands also for the right and duty of this nation to take a position of self-respecting strength among the nations of the world, to take such a position as will do injustice to no foreign power, strong or weak, and yet will show that it has both the spirit and the strength to repel injustice from abroad.

PART FIVE

In Wartime

19.

Jacob Riis Asserts His Patriotism

Progressives could be found on all sides of debates over foreign policy. About half of those whose memoirs are included in this book opposed either the Spanish American War or World War I. The rest supported both. As a group, progressive reformers acquiesced to the strong sense of nationalism that was sweeping across the land after 1898.

In foreign affairs progressives often felt a strong obligation to right wrongs and to consider American ideals as standards for other nations. As at home, they valued direct action. Theodore Roosevelt commented about Jacob Riis that he "was emphatically a 'doer of the world' and not either a mere hearer or a mere preacher." Roosevelt may well have been directing attention to Riis's lifelong battle against the slums. But Riis, as the following passage from his autobiography illustrates, believed also in "doing" internationally.

Riis was born in 1849, in Denmark, in the town of Ribe, which was under attack by invading German armies. As the Germans broke through, Riis's mother carried him to safety. It was, as he later recalled, an undistinguished beginning, especially since the ancient town had once been the "seat of the fighting kings that had made Denmark a power to be reckoned with." In 1870 Riis emigrated to America. Arriving in New York City, his first act was to buy a holster and a six-shooter, of which he was promptly relieved by a friendly policeman. In the following year he volunteered to fight in the Franco-Prussian War, but missed the ship that took volunteers to Europe. It was the first of the three wars he missed. Eventually Riis settled down as a police reporter on a New York newspaper. His ruthless exposés of tenement conditions brought him to the attention of police commissioner Theodore Roosevelt, whose lifelong friend he remained.

When Roosevelt had gone to Washington to help fit out the navy for the war with Spain, I spent a part of the winter there with him, and Mulberry Street took it for granted that I had at last been "placed" as I should have been long before. There was great amazement when I came back to take my old place. The truth was that I had gone partly to observe what went on at the capital for my paper, and partly to speed on the war, in which I was a hearty believer from the first. It was to me a means, first and last, of ending the murder in Cuba. One of the very earliest things I had to do with as a reporter was the *Virginius*[1] massacre, and ever since it had been bloodshed right along. It was time to stop it, and the only way seemed to wrest the grip of Spain from the throat of the island. I think I never quite got over the contempt I conceived for Spain and Spanish ways when I read as a boy, in Hans Christian Andersen's account of his travels in the country of the Dons, that the shepherds brought butter from the mountains in sheep's intestines and measured them off in lengths demanded by the customers by tying knots upon them. What was to be expected from a

From Jacob Riis, *The Making of an American* (New York: The Macmillan Company, 1901), chap. 14, "War for the Last Time," pp. 243–246.

[1] The *Virginius*, a gun-runner supplying Cuban revolutionaries, was captured by Spanish authorities in 1873. Among the fifty-three of her crew summarily executed were several Americans [ED.].

country that sold butter by the yard? As the event showed, it ran its navies after the same fashion and was justly punished. I made friends that winter with Dr. Leonard Wood,[2] whom we all came to know and admire afterwards as General and Governor Wood; and a fine fellow he was. He was Roosevelt's friend and physician, and we spent many strenuous hours together, being in that mood.

For the third time in my life, and the last, I wanted to go to the war, when they went, and oh! so badly. Not to fight,—I had had all I needed of that at home,—but to tell the truth about what was going on in Cuba. The *Outlook* offered me that post, and the *Sun* agreed heartily; but once more the door was barred against me. Two of my children had scarlet fever, my oldest had gone to Washington trying to enlist with the Rough Riders, and the one next in line was engineering to get into the navy on his own hook. My wife raised no objection to my going, if it was duty; but her tears fell silently—and I stayed. It was "three times and out." I shall never go to the war now unless in defence of my own home, which may God forbid. Within a year I knew that, had I gone then, I should most likely not have returned. I had received notice that to my dreams of campaigning in that way there was an end. Thankful that I had been spared, I yet took leave of them with a sigh; most illogically, for I hate the sight of human suffering and of brutal passions aroused. But deep down in my heart there is the horror of my Viking forefathers of dying in bed, unable to strike back, as it were. I know it is wicked and foolish, but all my life I have so wished to get on a horse with a sword, and slam in just once, like another Sheridan. I, who cannot sit on a horse! Even the one Roosevelt got me at Montauk that was warranted "not to bite or scratch" ran away with me. So it is foolishness, plain to see. Yet, so I might have found

---

[2] Commander of the "Rough Riders," Wood subsequently became the military governor of Cuba [ED.].

out which way I would really have run when the call came. I do hope the right way, but I never have felt quite sure.

The casualties of war are not all on the battlefield. The Cuban campaign wrecked a promising career as a foreign correspondent which I had been building up for some ten or fifteen years with toilsome effort. It was for a Danish newspaper I wrote with much approval, but when the war came, they did not take the same view of things that I did, and fell to suppressing or mutilating my letters, whereupon our connection ceased abruptly. My letters were, explained the editor to me a year or two later when I saw him in Copenhagen, so—er-r—ultra-patriotic, so—er-r—youthful in their enthusiasm, that—huh! I interrupted him with the remark that I was glad we were young enough yet in my country to get up and shout for the flag in a fight, and left him to think it over. They must have aged suddenly over there, for they were not that way when I was a boy. The real fact was that somehow they could not get it into their heads that a European bully could be whipped in one round by "the States." They insisted on printing ridiculous despatches about Spanish victories. I think there was something about codfish, too, something commercial about corks and codfish—Iceland keeping Spain on a fish diet in Lent, in return for which she corked the Danish beer—I have forgotten the particulars. The bottom fact was a distrust of the United States that was based upon a curiously stubborn ignorance, entirely without excuse in a people of high intelligence like the Danes. I tried hard as a correspondent to draw a reasonable, human picture of American affairs, but it seemed to make no impression. They would jump at the Munchausen stories that are always afloat, as if America were some sort of menagerie and not a Christian country. I think nothing ever aggravated me as did an instance of that kind the year Ben Butler ran for the Presidency. I had been trying in my letters to present the political situation and issues fairly, and was beginning to feel that they *must* understand, when I received a copy of my paper from Copenhagen and read there a "life" of General Butler, which condensed ran something like this:—

"Mr. Butler was an ambitious young lawyer, shrewd and full of bold schemes for enriching himself. When the war with the South broke out, he raised all the money he could and fitted out a fleet of privateers. With this he sailed for New Orleans, captured the city, and, collecting all the silver spoons it contained, freighted his vessels with them, and returned to the North. Thus he laid the foundation for his great fortune, but achieved lasting unpopularity in the South, which will prevent his election to the Presidency."

I am not joking. That was how the story of the silver spoons looked in Danish a quarter of a century after the war. Really, now, what would you have done? I laughed and—well! made remarks by turns, and in the end concluded that there was nothing else that could be done except buckle to and try again; which I did.

20.

Mary Simkhovitch Musters a Settlement House

In contrast to Jacob Riis, who helped to establish her settlement house, Mary Kingsbury Simkhovitch had no taste for war. In 1917 she threw herself into the war effort partly to help defend the nation's honor, mostly to help end the war quickly.

She was born in 1867 in Boston's fashionable suburb of Chestnut Hill. Among her neighbors were Lowells and Saltonstalls and also Alice Lee, who, as Mrs. Simkhovitch recalls, in 1880 married "a promising young man of good family," named Theodore Roosevelt.

After graduating from Boston University, she continued her studies at Radcliffe and then at the University of Berlin, where she worked with the same Alfred Wagner who had earlier inspired Richard Ely. There she met a Russian student, Vladimir Simkhovitch, who immigrated to America in 1898 and married her.

Returning to the United States, Mrs. Simkhovitch worked in several settlements and in 1901 opened her own Greenwich House on Jones Street, at the center of the most densely populated block on the west side of Manhattan. There, and later on Barrow Street, "Mrs. Sims," as she was known, ministered to Irish, Italian, and Negro working people for forty-five years.

There were two great evils facing us in 1917. One was to go into the war, and the other was to stay out. Whatever the outcome, war was bound to bring in its train not only the loss of life and the destruction of property, but also new social alignments, a re-evaluating of customs, habits and outlooks, a redistributing of wealth and power. Gradually, step by step, we slipped into war in the presidency of Wilson, who won his second term with the slogan "He kept us out of war."

The settlements throughout the country had no illusions about war. No one was taken in by glory and by all the romantic propaganda afloat. But there was a sharp difference of opinion in regard to our participation in the conflict. Many of the ablest and most distinguished leaders in the settlements were pacifists wholly opposed to war on any grounds.

At the National Federation of Settlements meeting in Valencia, Pennsylvania, in June, 1917, when I was president, this difference of point of view came to an issue. The National Federation went on record as supporting the war, while sending messages of fraternal greetings to all our international associates.

There were many of us, and all of us at Greenwich House were of that number, who believed that we were faced with a choice of evils of which the greater was staying out of the war. Going in meant standing by a code of honor where "scraps of paper" and *Lusitania* sinkings could have no place.

Though we felt bound to do our best in the corner of the world where we were, we had at any rate the grim knowledge that whatever the result would be, it would be bad. We knew enough to know that war would leave inevitable ravages. But we fancied (and who can ever know whether we were wrong?)

From Mary Simkhovitch, *Neighborhood: My Story of Greenwich House* (New York: W. W. Norton & Co., 1938), chap. 9, "The War at Home," pp. 181–196. Copyright 1938 by W. W. Norton & Co. Reprinted by permission of Helena Simkhovitch.

that the ravages of what we conceived to be dishonor would be still more devastating.

The settlements were with very few exceptions opposed to being used as recruiting stations. Their accent was on the civil services for which their experience in dense city neighborhoods had prepared them. As one looks back upon those years and sees so many things to laugh at or cry over, the years from 1917 to Armistice Day seem to have been in someone else's life whose story had been told one.

Of course, many of our associates went across. Our girls' worker, Betty Porter, was with the "Y" in the huts at the front. Beulah Hurley was with the Friends. She was trained in domestic science and had taught household economics at the House and knew a great deal about farming. When she was assigned the task of convoying cattle from one country to another and was in charge of feeding starving children, it was after all her own field on a grand scale. Miss Porter, who had been a leader of social clubs, was naturally good at making life as attractive as might be for people in grave danger. And when Eddie Ranges and Irving Israel and some other of our club boys got leave at Christmas time it seemed on the whole quite natural that, though so far away, Miss Porter should meet them in Paris, where, as they wrote, "they had a Greenwich House Christmas together."

Our president, Herbert Parsons, went from New York to Washington, where from the War Office he, too, departed for France. Dr. Hans Zinsser, also on our Board, had the great responsibility of delousing the army and coping with venereal disease. Elizabeth Witter, a young California resident, left us for the war, where her beautiful voice was greatly loved. But when these and many others had gone, there was a household left who gave their time to the various civil services according to their training and gifts.

Mabel Spinney, my associate, headed the Food Administration for the West Side of lower Manhattan. With her popularity in the neighborhood, and her energy and enthusiasm, she achieved the impossible. For she actually got our Italian neighbors to use brown flour for their macaroni! She held tenement house meetings, getting one woman in each tenement to call in the others in the same house, and there she and her associates, Italian-born or native American, would explain the government's food directions in so persuasive a way as to accomplish the desired end. Also we sold the reconstituted powdered milk to the long lines that formed in front of the House.

It was in the fall of 1916 that we came over to the new House. What a job to move all our belongings! And should we ever get used to the new House? Would it seem homelike? But we were bound it should. Our new appointments were very few. We used the chairs from the old House; the dining room table went down in the foyer; the old desk of the Jones Street house became the information desk; the old serving table resumed its task.

When we had our formal opening in January, 1917, the plaster wasn't very dry and it was a cold night, but we felt ourselves launched that night, and I, for my part, was bound that sentimental longings for the "good old days of Jones Street" should be squelched in the bud.

Barrow Street was as good as Jones Street, and it was interesting to make a fresh start with the old friends and the old ideas finding new expression. There's no doubt about it, just as ideas ought to have each its own habitat or form, so forms react on ideas. No doubt the new House affected the development of activities, but after all the House was built in the light of our past fifteen years of experience and so there was no real break.

A big building seven stories tall, no matter how camouflaged by its colonial façade, which reduces its size to the onlooker from Seventh Avenue, needs a good deal of coal to heat it. Coal was scarce. We gave up using the dining room and drawing room entirely. We had our meals down in the laundry next to the gas-heated kitchen. Perhaps this informality and privation, even though slight, was a help in building up the social life in the new House.

In the residents' and our own apartments oil stoves were placed in the bathrooms, but otherwise we got along with no heat. We expected this would last indefinitely, but one day the Fuel Administration decided it would like to use our House. "Certainly," we said. And we gave them the big room on the fifth floor called the Pastime Room, named for the club that had supplied all its furnishings and whose headquarters the room was. The club generously gave up the room, but its icy temperature was evidently too much for the Fuel Administration, for the very next day tons of coal poured into our basement and the oil stoves retired for good!

Heatless days and nucoa (butter substitute) and brown bread were a healthful discipline. There was of course no hardship in this diet, which saved white flour and fats and sugar for the soldiers. Indeed, fasting suddenly became a virtue again, after having been snobbishly looked down upon by the sophisticated. Lent ceased to look ridiculous. Reflection on this food rationing makes one wonder if perhaps bran muffins were not the only good that came out of the war!

Knitting became the general occupation of women. In the opera (strictly non-German) women knitted as they sat in the boxes. At our House there was a large group of women, mainly of German descent, who knitted steadily an untold number of sweaters and scarfs.

The most fantastic "war service" in New York was perhaps the war gardens. It is true that in the suburbs good potato fields could be made out of lawns, as in the case of Lounsberry, the Parsons' place in Rye. At our farm in Whitehouse, New Jersey, too, my husband grew on his three hundred acres great fields of grain enriched by the hardwood ashes his foresight had secured. But in New York City to use the scraps of land inch-deep on Manhattan's rock foundation was really only a joke. These war gardens were a little symbol of many fantastic happenings in the name of patriotism, while the deadly life of the trenches was tragically going on.

We were proud of our neighborhood boys at Verdun and Château-Thierry. Many of them were privates, but we had second lieutenants and cooks among our club boys. We kept in touch with many of the neighbors who were in the service. We organized a War Service Bureau which helped the neighbors in any way they needed—with assistance about mail, with information about the various kinds of payments, with any friendly help that was wanted.

Our Washington Square neighbor Margaret Norrie was the leader of this enterprise. Every day Mrs. Norrie spent long hours at work. She organized a group of neighborhood women into a corps of assistants who districted the community. Each had her quota for which she was responsible; and as one drive after another took place this group by its familiarity, each member with her own district, was able to bring to the citizens various messages the government desired brought to their attention.

This War Service Bureau was the local popular center which brought together all the elements in the neighborhood—the churches, lodges, political groups or what not—with an understanding and common action which the fusing spirit of the war induced.

Mrs. Norrie, with her conservative background and education, was the loved leader of this group. She had a native simplicity in approach both to people and to problems which was as effective as it was natural. From this firsthand work in wartime she went on in later years to an ever broadening comprehension both of the economic problems at home and of the problems of international relationships which the war brought into the glare of public attention.

The Red Cross also had its local office at the House. And at Christmas time for a month the big auditorium was converted into a special post office to which the neighbors brought their packages for their husbands, sons and brothers across the ocean.

There were meetings, too, of all the young girls in the community addressed by women physicians giving them a better understanding of their own lives and a more adequate way of meeting the problems of young womanhood.

Then there was the state military census, an enumeration of the capacities of the population. Our House had a large district to cover, and the residents and other volunteer workers, as well as the members attached to the War Service Bureau, all went out armed with a long questionnaire to register the occupations and various abilities of the population. In foreign homes this was often a difficult task. I took my assignments with the others; my own district brought me to the Spanish boarding-houses and cafés of the upper west side of our section. It must all have seemed very strange to them.

The part our foreign-born soldiers played was brought to me in all its tragic remoteness when a poor soldier with hands without fingers came before the War Claims Committee sitting at the House. He could speak only Italian. He did not know why he had come upon such a fate; he knew only, indeed, that it was fate, something like a storm or a fire, an "act of God," as the insurance people say.

The Liberty Loan drive was one of the later efforts of the government to secure co-operation from the civilian population. That group occupied the alcove at the right of the foyer, the War Service Bureau the alcove at the left while the Red Cross and the Food and Fuel Administrations had offices on other floors.

The Liberty Loan four-minute-men came in and out from their speechmaking; the amount of money secured was posted, and greater excitement accompanied the sale of bonds than the other smaller types of saving certificates or stamps. A great deal of money was raised from small subscribers; but most of the minor securities were in later years, I believe, cashed or sold.

A wealthy Italian neighbor, Mr. Personeni, kindly loaned us his place on Staten Island for a day camp and garden. There under Max and Irene Nelson's guidance about a hundred boys learned to do garden work. They came down on the ferry every morning, and incidentally most of them learned to swim. This was the summer when our president loaned his place, Lounsberry, for our girls' club. There our club girls helped in canning fruits and vegetables. These canning clubs and food demonstrations given in our hall in the new building were very popular. In 1917, also, the Sutherland Neighborhood Center at Public School 3 was operated by us as an additional opportunity for the neighbors to gather together for recreation. A travel group was popular at this time, perhaps especially because everyone in the neighborhood had a realistic and a very poignant interest in Europe.

During this time I was engaged especially in the work of the Mayor's Committee (Mayor Mitchel) of Women, the Social Welfare Subcommittee of which I was chairman. Dorothy Straight (Mrs. Leonard Elmhurst) was chairman of this committee, and later Miss Ruth Morgan took her place. On this Committee sat for the most part outstanding women in the fields of labor, industry, education, employment and journalism. It was a central group to help in the general work of civilian assistance. If only in times of peace such concentrated efforts in organization could be kept up, we might expect more civic progress. But the speed and pressure were unnatural, and impossible, I suppose, to be sustained over anything but an emergency period, although the United Neighborhood Houses and Welfare Council are good examples of present-day cooperative effort.

Coming home from these meetings, I would find my husband just returning from or going out to the meetings of the Inquiry of which he was a member. This was the group of economists, statisticians, geographers and so forth who, under Colonel House's direction, made analytical reports on various aspects of the problems presented by the war.

If I entered the House late in the afternoon I would meet the mothers coming for their children. For one of the activities at the House that finally turned into the Nursery School in 1920 was the all-day care of the children of working mothers started by the Board of Education as a wartime activity. This was the time when the mothers who formerly were housekeepers and did not work outside the home began to go out to work in factories, in offices or in workshops.

The great exodus of women from the home was, of course, largely accelerated by the absence of men, who were in the war. And industry needed workers. The women anxious for money answered this demand eagerly. The question was what was to become of the little children. The answer was that they should be cared for during school hours either at the school buildings or in some annex which might be a private institution named by public school teachers. This experiment meant that the city was going in for the care of children under the Department of Education. After the war, when things began to settle down into a no longer emergency character, this interesting experiment was left for small groups to continue and develop. The nursery school, begun in England, was studied by groups in America. Both a Montessori class and an informal nursery school were undertaken at the House, but the work began to be promoted in a really satisfactory manner when in co-öperation with Teachers College we opened our Nursery School with Mr. R. J. F. Schwarzenbach's help in 1920.

In 1917 the Greenwich Village Association held a patriotic celebration in Washington Square attended by all local organizations. My father was visiting me at the time, and just as in former years he had always sung *The Star-Spangled Banner* at the Massachusetts Commandery of the Loyal Legion, so that evening in his old age he sang again in Washington Square.

My parents' interest in the House and all that we were doing there was not only a pleasure to us but a source of pride and interest to our neighbors.

The winter of 1918 was desperately cold. The plumbing froze in the neighboring tenements and the gas was turned off. But we found a way to help. We went out in taxis to lumberyards on the water front and brought wood into the neighbors' houses. These were the days of going-away parties for soldiers and sailors, for war wedding parties, when the young husbands were shortly to sail for France.

Very high wages were paid in the war industries, but they did not affect our neighborhood. The working women's forum on Sunday afternoons acquainted many with the rapidly changing industrial status of women. The men's Italian Circle of the district secured two hundred and fifty thousand dollars in subscriptions in the Second Liberty Loan. Winifred Welsh of the Catholic Girls' Club held meetings for the girls of the neighborhood on social standards for girls in wartime. A consumers' group met at the House, selling butter and eggs and reconstituted milk. The War Service Bureau, already referred to, had charge of over fifteen hundred cases, to whom help or advice was given. This Bureau also conducted investigations for the War Risk Insurance Bureau and promoted the sale of War Service Stamps.

The Food Commission sold sugar, onions and potatoes, cooperating with our food demonstrations. We also sold hot dinners to families in which the father was in the service and the mother was working. Work among the Italians in all these fields was carried on by Mrs. Zicarelli, associated with Mrs. Norrie's War Service Group.

By 1919 Greenwich House had representatives in naval aviation, on the Shipping Board, in the Army and Navy Intelligence, in the Committee on Public Investigation and the Labor Adjustment Board. Our members were with the Red Cross also, the Signal Corps and the Friends' Reconstruction Service. Two of our men residents held positions of high responsibility in Russia.

During this period there was a great interest in the "Learn English Campaign." Board of Education classes in the public schools of our neighborhood were crowded, and these classes flowed over into Greenwich House, where there were also additional groups manned by private associations. Our own health center was formally organized at this time.

The Hudson Park branch of the New York Public Library in Leroy Street was as busy as we were with these various civilian activities. They held demonstrations for making war bread and cake, and as part of the United States Food Administration their staff made a house-to-house canvass of surrounding streets. In 1918 they held a milk exhibit. They acted as an information center for the section on Aliens' Counsel of Organization for War Service. They conducted a drive for books for soldiers and sailors. Each branch of the Library had been asked to collect a thousand dollars for this purpose, but our branch raised about two thousand dollars in this far from prosperous neighborhood. They also served as an office for the Legal Advisory Board and held meetings under the auspices of the National War Service Committee.

The days and nights of the war went by in a kind of hypnosis. One was numbed by the constant impact of tragedy. It was both a great excitement and at the same time a dream making the past unreal, as this period in its turn has become unreal in our present. There is something about great shock of either a personal or a social nature that makes a kind of vacuum. One is stunned into nothingness. There is no room for reaction. And so it was, day by day.

These were the days of unjust criticism, when people of German name or origin suffered from open or covert hostility, days when the ships lying at the North River docks were so painted as to camouflage their true height and width, thus making them difficult to attack successfully. These were the days when there were at least some clergy who refused to fly a national flag in a church which was founded by One to whom all men are brothers. These were the days when the good things came out, the capacity for sacrifice, the loyalty to country and to one's sense of values, the spirit of co-operation always latent but induced by stress—and also when the evil things came out, the deep fanaticism, the gullible readiness to be hoodwinked and the ease with which propaganda could be both manufactured and effectively carried on.

During wartime the House not only carried on its many new activities, but it endeavored to continue its own ordinary program. The pottery, the music school, the plays, the club life, all these things kept on. The visiting in the neighborhood went on, of course. The period of at least a certain leisure when studies could be made and published was for the time suspended. My own little book, *The City Worker's World*, was published in 1918. Articles appeared by various members of our group in magazines from time to time, but the war took the last ounce of energy available. The rapid changes involved a continual readjustment of program, and the building up of needed activities in the light of an enlarged experience absorbed the House's attention. The war drank not only the blood of its soldiers, but also the life powers of every thoughtful man and woman of that period. The scars remain.

It was the influenza epidemic in 1918 that seemed the last straw. Suddenly, like a heavy cloud, this pestilence swept over the country. In New York, where it was a great scourge, there had to be rapid organization to bring anything like adequate help to the sufferers. The nurses were gallant and speedy, and the settlements as the old established centers in New York's most crowded neighborhoods took over the burden of both organization and service. Doctors volunteered; neighbors helped one another. But it was all a nightmare. While the death rate as a whole was nearly three per thousand, in our own Ninth Ward it was four and seven-tenths per thousand. This fixed our determination to do whatever we could do to remedy the death and morbidity rates of our district.

As one reflects on all these civilian activities, which existed everywhere throughout the country but which we ran in such concentrated guise in crowded city neighborhoods, one sees there was indeed a rapid mobilization but at the same time no sense of proportion. "War gardens" and brown macaroni didn't get us very far. The state military census as far as I know was never used for anything. The ladies knitting in opera boxes seemed a far cry from the battle of the Marne. But waste is perhaps an inevitable price for emergency organization. On the whole, it was a significant if also partly a childish spectacle. For it meant that the great energy and capacity of the American people can be mobilized by an accepted public opinion with speed and efficiency. It meant that social organization and re-emphasis may be effected when there is a new will and a new goal, even for the renewal of forgotten goals.

One sees the possibilities that the youth of this generation have within their grasp. But "youth" is far from infallible. It faces the future with the advantage of inexperience, but subject to the same passions that have enveloped former generations. The lassitude and disillusion of the war and postwar years is over, however. Politics thought of as the pastime of the second-rate has become once more in newer guise the passion of the young, as indeed it must be if democracy is not to slide down the skids and be supplanted.

21.

Roger Baldwin Defends Civil Liberties and Resists the Draft

A generation of progressives invested government with numerous powers to restrict individual liberties. They had meant to restrict the liberties associated with property; but during and immediately after World War I reformers discovered that the state often does not distinguish between its powers over persons. The war introduced them to a new problem: the right of individual conscience as against the authority of the state. Roger Baldwin's career bridged both these phases in the history of the progressive movement.

Baldwin was born in 1884 in Wellesley, Massachusetts, in the family of a prosperous shoe manufacturer. Descendants of Mayflower immigrants, the Baldwins usually engaged in business or in farming. One exception was William H. Baldwin, Roger's grandfather, who had given up business to establish the Boston Young Men's Christian Union, a center for education and social service. Perhaps with his grandfather in mind, and on the advice of his father's lawyer, Louis Brandeis, Roger Baldwin decided to become a part of the reform movement that stirred over the country.

Finishing at Harvard in 1905, he accepted a position teaching sociology at Washington University in St. Louis. At the same time he became director in a local settlement. In 1907 he became chief probation officer of the St. Louis Juvenile Court. In the following years he was appointed to numerous positions including the city's Children's Commission.

Then, as he relates in the following selection, he accepted a position in New York that led to the founding of the American Civil Liberties Union, whose guiding spirit he has remained until the present day. One of his first cases involved Margaret Sanger's right to make a public speech on birth control.

Convicted for resisting the draft, Baldwin served nine months of his one-year sentence.

My break with the city I had adopted as home came in March, 1917, when I received a telegraphic offer from New York to take the place of the secretary of the Union Against Militarism, Crystal Eastman, then hospitalized with a serious illness. I had been for some months its St. Louis representative. The telegram was signed by friends I respected—Lillian D. Wald, Oswald Garrison Villard, Hollingsworth Wood, John Haynes Holmes and Paul Kellogg—possibly also Owen R. Lovejoy. These were, except for Villard, among my social work colleagues, and Wood, though no social worker, was known to me as a close Quaker friend of my aunt, Ruth Standish Baldwin. It was he who had offered me a year or so before the job of heading up his League to Limit Armaments, a post I refused because of my absorption in St. Louis. But now war was imminent—I was a pacifist by then—and I felt that civic reform would disappear into the background. I accepted the new offer on condition that

---

From *The Reminiscences of Roger Baldwin,* in The Oral History Collection of Columbia University, Butler Library. Reprinted by permission of Roger Baldwin.

I would work for expenses only, and for the duration of the war.

The Union Against Militarism, though organized only for months, was already a strong agency of the forces alarmed by the drift into war with its prospects of conscription and repression. Pacifists, Quakers, Socialists, even non-pacifist liberals, all found in it a common cause. Its directing committee was a roster of the elite in social work and reform. It had opened up offices in Washington and New York, feverishly attacking the more extreme proposals for conducting the war. Already anti-war meetings were being attacked by enraged patriots. So prominent a citizen as Dr. David Starr Jordan, president emeritus of Stanford University, was all but mobbed when he tried to speak. My instincts for protecting freedom of speech and assembly, already cultivated by events in St. Louis, were outraged. I recognized the futility of blocking war measures, but I nourished the hope, proved vain, that effort could check the passionate demands for conscription, for an espionage act to suppress opposition and for summary war powers in the President and the Cabinet.

The Union had access to high places; some of its committee were old associates of Newton Baker, Secretary of War, and even of the President. A dozen Senators and many more Congressmen were of our persuasion. We worked with and through them, but in the end to no avail. We were all swamped by the war fever which increasingly overwhelmed the country. But we were not a little band apart. The anti-war sentiment was reflected in what we recognized was a class opposition to a capitalist war, which we did not share. The Socialist Party came out solidly against the war; so did the IWW and the Farmers Non-partisan League, then strong and radical in the northwest. Our group was motivated by pacifist and civil libertarian principles, and few of us thought in class terms. My personal sympathies lay with this opposition, not on class concepts, but as a force to restrain the excesses of the war fever.

Defeated in the early months of the war in Congress, the Union settled down to a defensive role, preoccupied with the rights of conscientious objectors and with civil liberties for the opponents of the war. Since these activities required the services of many lawyers and specialized attention, the Union formed at my suggestion a Civil Liberties Bureau as a department under my direction. I worked at it from both Washington and New York offices, spending part of each week in each, reporting weekly to the board in New York. . . . The Bureau became independent as the National Civil Liberties Bureau in September, 1917, with the same committee, and with me as director, housed in the same office building, 70 Fifth Avenue, apart from The Union, and indeed several new agencies opposed to the war. . . . Our Civil Liberties Bureau, largely pacifist, professed to be neutral on the war, and solicited support among pro-war liberals concerned with civil liberties—and indeed secured a little. The other agencies were frankly against the war and for a negotiated peace at the earliest practicable—or impracticable—moment. I joined the People's Council and served on its board, but I never felt myself wholly at home among Socialist politicians. . . .

We picked our cases from the press, Quaker and religious journals, the IWW and Socialist organs—and from a growing correspondence as we became known. Our response was to engage counsel for every court case, to publicize the issues, to labor with government officials, and sometimes to raise defense funds. I was in Washington almost every week to present cases and issues to the War, Justice and Post Office departments. I was well enough received, but the action we urged was rarely successful, so great were the pressures against us. I was never discouraged by lack of results; we got enough satisfaction in the effort to keep us going. Newton Baker as Secretary of War was always approachable, and even more, his assistant, Frederick Keppel, former dean of Columbia, whom Hollingsworth Wood knew well enough to call "Fred." The

Attorney General, Gregory, was unapproachable and unsympathetic, but he had two assistants of a different view, John Lord O'Brian of Buffalo, a real friend of civil liberties, and Alfred Bettman of Cincinnati, even more committed. They tried against odds to restrain the fervor of prosecution of district attorneys, and made an impression on the hysteria only toward the end of the war when all prosecutions had to be first cleared in the Department.

The Post Office Department under [Albert S.] Burleson was a graveyard for us. I recollect one interview I attended with Clarence Darrow in behalf of restoring mailing privileges to some barred anti-war publication. Darrow, who supported the war in his cynical way, used all his folksy talents of persuasion on the Postmaster General. Burleson just stared, and finally, when he spoke, dismissed the subject with a terse refusal and turned to telling some story about his native Texas.

We had friends in Congress; they were powerless. Once when I asked Senator LaFollette to help out he led me into his office, shut the door and, putting his hands on my shoulders, said almost with tears that it was hopeless to try for justice, so fanatical had the country and government become. Years later when I met William Ellery Leonard of the University of Wisconsin, himself an opponent of the war like LaFollette, he told me that when he and the Senator met for the first time just after the war they grasped each other's hands in complete silence with the tears streaming down both their faces.

I was not capable of such emotion about the war or the state of the nation. I took the hysteria in my stride, often shocked, often indignant. But I recollect no depression of spirit over it, and I was always ready to fight in my little way for each victim and against every challenge.

Our relations with the War Department, which were the most important to us, since our major concern was with conscientious objectors, continued amicably, and with reasonably satisfactory action at top civilian levels—not the military—until early in 1918 when Newton Baker's office, through Mr. Keppel, wrote us that all cooperation was off. Military intelligence, it appeared, had reported to Baker that the Bureau was encouraging the very conscientious objection we professed to be serving only within the law and regulations. To encourage disobedience to the draft was a crime, and we had of course been scrupulously careful not to give any advice to any man to resist. We had merely advised each man as to the consequences of any course of action he took. But Military Intelligence could hardly be expected to make such distinctions, nor could Secretary Baker be expected to ignore its report.

We resorted then to the device of using Hollingsworth Wood's office and stationery to write our letters to "Dear Fred," and "Fred" was quite willing to work on that basis. That somewhat shaky relation lasted until our office was raided by the FBI in September, 1918, and all cooperation was off.

Our major work with the government to soften the savage treatment of conscientious objectors produced some degree of success. Norman Thomas told the story later in his *Conscientious Objector in America,* based largely on his experience with the Bureau. I found the top civilians responsive enough, but they had to work through the tough military machine, which despised the objectors. Since every objector who did not resist before being drafted and thus went to a civil prison, as I did, became technically a soldier, they were all thrown into military camps. This was the essential evil which Baker and Keppel could not cure, and which resulted in endless brutalities. The courts martial were determined to make examples of all slackers, and handed out sentences of death, life imprisonment and incredibly long terms. They filled the military prison at Fort Leavenworth with objectors. I once visited them at the invitation of Colonel Sedgwick Rice, the commandant—secured at the instance of Mr. Keppel—who was deeply troubled in his very decent heart about keeping such men. He did not suspect my own iniquity and treated me as a VIP house guest. Later, following a prisoners' strike led by the objectors, he urged clemency for the men by cutting the preposterous sentences, a procedure gradually followed, and one which I and the Bureau had constantly put up to the War Department. Colonel Rice was one of the few officers I met with human understanding of objectors, knowing that, whatever he thought of them, their place was not in a military prison or the army. He must have been impressed, as I was, by the sad sight of a whole battalion of members of the House of David, a pacifist religious sect in Michigan, forced to hard labor at the prison, and all looking like prophets out of the Old Testament, bearded, bare-headed, benign, other-worldly.

We tried to modify the law and regulations with indifferent results. The law recognized only members of religious sects historically opposed to war, and even these were obliged to render some service. We and others, after much pressure, finally got furloughs from the army for civilian service, and so relieved them of military contact. But it came late; and while Baker generously ignored the law and included all objectors found by a board to be "genuine," the greatest damage had been done. I followed that board on its final pilgrimage to Fort Leavenworth where the last hundred or so of the doubtful cases had been herded for judgment day. The board was tops—Judge Julian Mack, Harlan F. Stone, then dean of Columbia Law, and an army major, Walter G. Kellogg. Kellogg alone of the three wrote a book later of his experience, and not a good one, as we saw the issues. I thought the hearings fair in the light of the rules as to what constituted "genuine conscience," an impossible test. The fear that slackers would take advantage of conscientious objection was prevalent in the army and in public opinion; but the pressure to conform was so great that few men seeking to escape service took that way out. In all my contacts I do not recollect doubting more than a handful of men who proclaimed their consciences. There *were* slackers; thousands of them, as the records show, men who never could be found after they registered.

The absolutists, men who refused any service whatever, of

course fared worst. All of them went to prison, some four hundred and fifty altogether. I remember one, a Yale graduate, who came before the board and told a simple Christian story of faith in nonresistance, and told it with a quiet smile so eloquently that the board and the few onlookers were stunned into silence. After he was through, nobody spoke until Judge Mack leaned over to him and said "Gray, you are just too good for this world. You'll have to go to prison."

We made no distinctions between men of conscience. They ranged from the fundamentalist Christians, pacifists by inherited and incorporated consciences, to the international-minded Socialists, opposed to all capitalist wars. They included some Irish-Americans who would not "fight on England's side," and some German-Americans who would not fight against their relatives. Whoever they were, if they claimed conscientious refusal, we aided. I did not regard them as men with much of a contribution to make to social progress, and few of them were ever heard from again after the war. Few indeed had the abilities for leadership in any movement, and fewer there were who could articulate their positions in terms of relevant social or political issues. But they all had the courage to stand out, and thus represented a dissenting force, troublesome like all dissenters, hated like all nonconformists in wartime, and yet significant as a symbol of an authority, whatever its expression, superior to the demands of the State. My libertarian heart welcomed them all as that, however diverse.

One Roman Catholic objector, Ben Salmon, stood out. He had interpreted for himself Catholic doctrine to forbid participation in war. He dramatized his refusal by a hunger strike that attracted national attention, and almost died from it. Only the intervention of Father John A. Ryan, whom I sent to interview Salmon, and who found his position consistent with Church doctrine, saved him by a last minute release.

Besides the preoccupation of the Bureau with conscientious objectors, we were involved in court cases under the espionage and draft acts, where the prosecutions rested, as most of them did, on utterances or publications construed as hampering the conduct of the war. Particularly were we involved with the IWW cases, though not in the defense. We formed a committee to raise defense funds and publicize the case. We put our office at the disposal of the General Defense Committee's Eastern agent, Lee Chumley. We were convinced that only anti-war utterances and publications constituted the real evidence, and that the charges of willful obstruction by strikes and sabotage were fabrications. Our view was vindicated later by the courts on the appeals.

Although we enlisted several hundred lawyers throughout the country as volunteer defenders, we actually took part on trial in only a few cases. We had no funds for such expense; we were not prepared for long court trials. But we aided the lawyers engaged by the defense through publicly expressed support, some funds, and by briefs on appeals. That was the beginning of the long record of briefs *amicus* which have marked the ACLU.

All these activities in behalf of "clients" detested by the public, prosecuted by the government and shunned by most liberals inevitably brought attacks on us. Patriotic agencies pointed the finger at us as the source of encouragement of the country's enemies. We were attacked in the press, along with the People's Council, the Socialist Party and IWW. It was remarkable that we escaped action for so long, for no move was made nor inquiry instituted by any government agency until well along in 1918 toward the close of the war.

I had been the object of some concern by the War Department before, but that was apparently cleared up. The Inspector General of the Army had called me to Washington to clear up my record in early 1918. I went, accompanied by John C. Codman of Boston, one of our committee and a Wilsonian liberal who supported the war. I usually took such precautions. The Inspector General had a dossier on me on his desk. He inquired first whether I knew Pancho Villa. The question amazed me. Villa was the Mexican bandit, recently much in the public press. I replied that I had never met the man and was never in Mexico. The General obliged by details; he had a report that I had assisted Villa in one of his raids across the border into Arizona. I hadn't been in Arizona in years and said so. I added that I was a pacifist, as he must know, and that I could not conceivably have had anything to do with a bandit. The General looked puzzled; reports couldn't be that wrong. But the interview cleared me, and no government agency bothered us with an inquiry again.

Then suddenly without forewarning our offices at 170 Fifth Avenue were raided by the FBI in September, 1918, and all our files seized and taken, of all places, to the Union League Club. There was a search warrant, authorizing the seizure of material thought to indicate obstruction of the war. But the agents took everything, my private correspondence with it. My inquiries as to the Union League Club revealed the fact that some wealthy young members of that aristocratic organization were serving as dollar-a-year agents of the Department of Justice. Their patriotic duties, I learned, exempted them from the draft. They were headed by a man I came to know much better later, Archibald E. Stevenson, then a practicing lawyer, later counsel to the "infamous"—Al Smith's word—Lusk investigating committee of the New York legislature, prototype of all those since.

Our board at once acted to ward off a prosecution. We engaged as counsel a New York lawyer with qualifications calculated to get results, George Gordon Battle, counsel to Tammany Hall, Democratic politician who stood in with the federal authorities, and a gentleman of the old Southern school who knew many of our board socially. I never knew what Mr. Battle did, but there was no indictment and the files were ultimately returned. His fee was only $1000.

This was not the only unusual problem for the Bureau at the

time. I presented another: the draft act had caught up with my age group. I was called up for medical examination. Rather than involve the Bureau with my contemplated resistance, I resigned as director. Albert De Silver took over the job. The office was running pretty well crippled with the files at the Union League Club, but we had our furniture, our staff and our list of contributors intact. I helped out unofficially.

Confronted with a date for medical examination I wrote the draft board a polite refusal to appear, and sent a copy to the district attorney, knowing that I was committing a crime. Even before the date set, the authorities acted. I was arrested by an agent at my apartment, taken before the chairman of the draft board, a distinguished lawyer I knew by reputation, Julius Henry Cohen, and given a chance to recant. Mr. Cohen advised me strongly not to be so "contumacious." When I declined to be moved, he ordered me sent to jail to think it over. I spent the first night of my life behind bars, but I thought nothing over. I knew by long experience with the draft act just where I would stand and what the consequences would be.

Next morning, instead of being taken back to the draft board, I was called out of my cell to face a group of hilarious FBI agents whom I had met in the raid on our office and after. They were sent by the district attorney, they said, and were delighted to take me in charge. The head of the group, Rayme Finch, was such a rollicking good fellow that he took all his duties as exciting fun, and nothing could strike his funny bone more keenly than arresting a fellow who had walked himself right into jail. The FBI boys had a big limousine waiting, and I was whisked off amid great merriment to a bang-up breakfast, a shave and then to the FBI office on lower Broadway. My sense of humor was not lacking either, and it all struck me as good clean fun.

At the FBI office, where I was treated as a distinguished visitor, I was interviewed by several assistant United States district attorneys, who with great concern tried to convince me that I would ruin all my future prospects of usefulness by being so cantankerous. One of them, to my surprise, though I took it casually, was an old classmate of mine at Harvard, Leland Duer, quite distressed both over my plight and the reflection on our class. But I knew what course to take, and had all the answers to their arguments. The inescapable indictment followed that morning, and I was offered immediate bail to avoid imprisonment. I refused to consider it, feeling that anyone who had so deliberately violated the law was not entitled to freedom pending trial. I was going to prison anyhow, and the brief time before trial made little difference. As it turned out, jail time counted on my sentence, so I lost nothing.

That night I was lodged in the Tombs Prison in a cell by myself on a tier crowded with federal prisoners—draft dodgers, German aliens, an Indian revolutionist wanted by the British, and violators of the dope laws. Next morning a deputy marshal came for me, and handcuffed to him I was marched down Broadway to the FBI office. It was embarrassing to think I might meet some acquaintance so shackled, and I made it a point to walk ahead of the deputy, dragging him along as if he were my prisoner. When we arrived at the FBI office, Finch was indignant to see me handcuffed. He told the deputy never to do it again; I could be trusted to go wherever I was wanted, since I had locked myself up. After that I was left free to come and go with a deputy or an FBI man.

Finch made me an unexpected proposal which kept me in the company of the FBI for a month. It appeared that the Union League Club boys had mixed up our voluminous files in hopeless confusion and I alone could put them back in order. Would I do it if they brought me daily to the office? Of course I accepted, feeling confident that orderly files would prove our complete innocence, a fact which the district attorney had not yet established to his satisfaction.

So for a month I was lodged nightly in the Tombs, taken mornings to my "office," worked all day, and was returned often late at night. The FBI agents treated me as a guest, and often took me out to dinner and the theater. They even invited my friends to lunch at my request, and once took me to lunch at Norman Thomas' house. I was permitted to visit a dying old aunt, who, flat on her back on her deathbed, tried to understand why I chose such a course, and, giving it up, said, "I do not know whether you are right or not, but I do know you have good blood in you and that will tell." I was lucky in the United States marshal assigned to me, for he confessed that he too was against the war and the draft, and didn't have the guts to resist. He had sought the marshal's job to escape, and he hated himself for it. He atoned a bit by giving me every privilege within his limited power.

Working intimately daily in the FBI office I got to know the insides of some shady operations. Finch with great pride showed me his telephone-tapping equipment, and asked if I wanted to listen in on any conversation; he'd put on anyone I named. I declined. He showed me also a whole setup for forming an IWW local—forms, membership cards, literature. Thus the FBI could catch the "criminals" they made. I was disgusted, and said so, but they laughed me off as just naive. In the course of examining our files I found inserted among the papers by error a report of the FBI on me, headed "Roger Baldwin, IWW agitator." I handed it to Finch without comment. He looked a bit embarrassed for the first time, and said, "We have to make it strong even if it isn't right."

It took a full month working ten hours a day to get that mass of papers in intelligible shape. When it was all done I was ready for trial. Weeks later the files were returned to the Bureau after the district attorney found no cause for action; and they were returned in much better shape than when they left. I had had the time to do what the rush of office work had prevented, and at the United States' expense.

I figured that I better write out what I was to say to the court, knowing how difficult I had found it to explain my position convincingly. I did so sitting on the bunk in my cell early one morning just before trial, and it all came out readily and, to me, persuasively. It was the first attempt to formulate my position, but a lot of thought and experience had gone into it.

I was taken before a United States district judge, Julius Mayer, whose reputation for public service I had long known, on October 30, 1918. The courtroom was crowded with my colleagues and friends. The proceedings were later printed in pamphlet form by a group of them and widely distributed.[1] . . .

[Mr. Baldwin's statement to the court follows (ED.).]

Your Honor, I presume that myself, and not the National Civil Liberties Bureau, is on trial before this court this morning. I do not object to the reading into this record of the letters which the Government's attorney has read. Some of them I did not write. They represent one side of a work which I have been conducting as the Executive Officer of that organization during the past year. Our work is backed up and supported both by those who call themselves Pro-War Liberals, who are supporters of the war, and by those who are so-called Pacifists.

I have not engaged in personal propaganda. I have not made public addresses, except upon the subject matter of this Bureau. I have not written articles, except upon the subject matter of the Bureau, and I have felt throughout that it was a work which could be supported genuinely and honestly by those who opposed the war in principle, and by those who were supporting the war. I believe that the examination of the records of the Bureau now being made by the Department of Justice will conclusively demonstrate that the work has been undertaken with that sole purpose in view, and that it has been in the interest of the solution of certain democratic problems that this country has to face during war time.

---

[1] The proceedings were privately published in November 1918, under the title *The Individual and the State: The Problem as Presented by the Sentencing of Roger Baldwin* [ED.].

I will say, in that connection for instance, that although the Post Office censorship throughout the war has been intolerant, narrow and stupid, but one little pamphlet which we have issued—and we have issued a great many of them—has been excluded from the mails, and that in this Court within the last two weeks an injunction was issued, requiring the Post-Master of New York to accept for mailing all the pamphlets of this Bureau. I think that demonstrates pretty clearly that where the law is narrowly interpreted, rigidly interpreted, arbitrarily interpreted, as it is in the Post-Office Department at Washington, no exception has been taken to the general matter which has been sent out by this organization.

I know that the Government's Attorney is merely attempting to put before this Court my state of mind in taking the position I have about this act—in coming here as its deliberate violator.

I want to read to the Court, if I may, for purposes of record, and for purposes of brevity too, a statement which I have prepared, and which I hope will get across a point of view which the United States Attorney does not consider logical, but which I trust, at least, with the premises I hold, is consistent.

I am before you as a deliberate violator of the draft act. On October 9, when ordered to take a physical examination, I notified my local board that I declined to do so, and instead presented myself to the United States Attorney for prosecution. I submit herewith for the record the letter of explanation which I addressed to him at the time.

I refused to take bail, believing that I was not morally justified in procuring it, and being further opposed to the institution of bail on principle. I have therefore been lodged in the Tombs Prison since my arraignment on October 10. During that period I have been engaged daily at the Department of Justice offices in systematizing the files of the National Civil Liberties Bureau, of which I have been the director. These files had been voluntarily turned over to the Department for examination, and had, through much handling, become seriously disarranged. That work being completed, I am before you for sentence.

And, by the way, may I take this occasion, your honor—this is quite aside from the proceedings—to express my thanks for the courtesy of every officer of this court, and of the Department of Justice, through these trying weeks. It has been exceptional.

The compelling motive for refusing to comply with the draft act is my uncompromising opposition to the principle of conscription of life by the State for any purpose whatever, in time of war or peace. I not only refused to obey the present conscription law, but I would in future refuse to obey any similar statute which attempts to direct my choice of service and ideals. I regard the principle of conscription of life as a flat contradiction of all our cherished ideals of individual freedom, democratic liberty and Christian teaching.

I am the more opposed to the present act, because it is for the purpose of conducting war. I am opposed to this and all other wars. I do not believe in the use of physical force as a method of achieving any end, however good.

The District Attorney calls your attention your Honor, to the inconsistency in my statement to him that I would, under extreme emergencies, as a matter of protecting the life of any person, use physical force. I don't think that is an argument that can be used in support of the wholesale organization of men to achieve political purposes in nationalistic or domestic wars. I see no relationship at all between the two.

My opposition is not only to direct military service but to any service whatever designed to help prosecute the war. I could accept no service, therefore, under the present act, regardless of its character.

Holding such profound convictions, I determined, while the new act was pending, that it would be more honest to make my stand clear at the start and therefore concluded not even to register, but to present myself for prosecution. I therefore resigned my position as director of the National Civil Liberties Bureau so as to be free to follow that personal course of action. But on the day my resignation took effect (August 31) agents of the Department of Justice began an examination of the affairs of that organization, and I was constrained to withdraw my resignation and to register in order to stand by the work at a critical moment. With that obligation discharged, I resigned, and took the next occasion, the physical examination, to make my stand clear.

I realize that to some this refusal may seem a piece of wilful defiance. It might well be argued that any man holding my views might have avoided the issue by obeying the law, either on the chance of being rejected on physical grounds, or on the chance of the war stopping before a call to service. I answer that I am not seeking to evade the draft; that I scorn evasion, compromise and gambling with moral issues. It may further be argued that the War Department's liberal provision for agricultural service on furlough for conscientious objectors would be open to me if I obey the law and go to camp, and that there can be no moral objection to farming, even in time of war. I answer first, that I am opposed to any service under conscription, regardless of whether that service is in itself morally objectionable; and second, that, even if that were not the case, and I were opposed only to war, I can make no moral distinction between the various services which assist in prosecuting the war—whether rendered in the trenches, in the purchase of bonds or thrift stamps at home, or in raising farm products under the lash of the draft act. All serve the same end—war. Of course all of us render involuntary assistance to the war in the processes of our daily living. I refer only to those direct services undertaken by choice.

I am fully aware that my position is extreme, that it is shared by comparatively few, and that in the present temper it is regarded either as unwarranted egotism or as a species of feeble-mindedness. I cannot, therefore, let this occasion pass without attempting to explain the foundations on which so extreme a view rests.

I have had an essentially American upbringing and background. Born in a suburban town of Boston, Massachusetts, of the stock of the first settlers, I was reared in the public schools and at Harvard College. Early my mind was caught by the age-old struggle for freedom; America meant to me a vital new experiment in free political institutions; personal freedom to choose one's way of life and service seemed the essence of the liberties brought by those who fled the mediaeval and modern tyrannies of the old world. But I rebelled at our whole autocratic industrial system—with its wreckage of poverty, disease and crime, and childhood robbed of its right to free growth. So I took up social work upon leaving college, going to St. Louis as director of a settlement and instructor in sociology at Washington University. For ten years I have been professionally engaged in social work and political reform, local and national. That program of studied, directed social progress, step by step, by public agitation and legislation, seemed to me the practical way of effective service to gradually freeing the mass of folks from industrial and political bondage. At the same time I was attracted to the solutions of our social problems put forth by the radicals. I studied the programs of socialism, the I.W.W. European syndicalism and anarchism. I attended their meetings, knew their leaders. Some of them became my close personal friends. Sympathizing with their general ideals of a free society, with much of their program, I yet could see no effective way of practical daily service. Some six years ago, however, I was so discouraged with social work and reform, so challenged by the sacrifices and idealism of some of my I.W.W. friends, that I was on the point of getting out altogether, throwing respectability overboard and joining the I.W.W. as a manual worker.

I thought better of it. My traditions were against it. It was more an emotional reaction than a practical form of service.

But ever since, I have felt myself heart and soul with the world-wide radical movements for industrial and political freedom,—wherever and however expressed—and more and more impatient with reform.

Personally, I share the extreme radical philosophy of the future society. I look forward to a social order without any external restraints upon the individual, save through public opinion and the opinion of friends and neighbors. I am not a member of any radical organization, nor do I wear any tag by which my views may be classified. I believe that all parts of the radical movement serve the common end—freedom of the individual from arbitrary external controls.

When the war came to America, it was an immediate challenge to me to help protect those ideals of liberty which seemed to me not only the basis of the radical economic view, but of the radical political view of the founders of this Republic, and of the whole mediaeval struggle for religious freedom. Before the war was declared I severed all my connections in St. Louis, and offered my services to the American Union Against Militarism to help fight conscription. Later, that work developed into the National Civil Liberties Bureau, organized to help maintain the rights of free speech and free press, and the Anglo-Saxon tradition of liberty of conscience, through liberal provisions for conscientious objectors. This work has been backed both by pro-war liberals and so-called pacifists. It is not anti-war in any sense. It seemed to me the one avenue of service open to me, consistent with my views, with the country's best interest, and with the preservation of the radical minority for the struggle after the war. Even if I were not a believer in radical theories and movements, I would justify the work I have done on the ground of American ideals and traditions alone—as do many of those who have been associated with me. They have stood for those enduring principles which the revolutionary demands of war have temporarily set aside. We have stood against hysteria, mob-violence, unwarranted prosecution, the sinister use of patriotism to cover attacks on radical and labor movements, and for the unabridged right of a fair trial under war statutes. We have tried to keep open those channels of expression which stand for the kind of world order for which the President is battling today against the tories and militarists.

Now comes the Government to take me from that service and to demand of me a service I cannot in conscience undertake. I refuse it simply for my own peace of mind and spirit, for the satisfaction of that inner demand more compelling than any consideration of punishment or the sacrifice of friendships and reputation. I seek no martyrdom, no publicity. I merely meet as squarely as I can the moral issue before me, regardless of consequences.

I realize that your Honor may virtually commit me at once to the military authorities, and that I may have merely taken a quicker and more inconvenient method of arriving at a military camp. I am prepared for that—for the inevitable pressure to take an easy way out by non-combatant service—with guard-house confinement—perhaps brutalities, which hundreds of others (sic) objectors have already suffered and are suffering today in camps. I am prepared for court martial and sentence to military prison, to follow the 200–300 objectors already sentenced to terms of 10–30 years for their loyalty to their ideals. I know that the way is easy for those who accept what to me is compromise, hard for those who refuse, as I must, any service whatever. And I know further, in military prison I shall refuse to conform to the rules for military salutes and the like, and will suffer solitary confinement on bread and water, shackled to the bars of a cell eight hours a day—as are men of like convictions at this moment.

I am not complaining for myself or others. I am merely advising the court that I understand full well the penalty of my heresy, and am prepared to pay it. The conflict with conscription is irreconcilable. Even the liberalism of the President and

Secretary of War in dealing with objectors leads those of us who are "absolutists" to a punishment longer and severer than that of desperate criminals.

But I believe most of us are prepared even to die for our faith, just as our brothers in France are dying for theirs. To them we are comrades in spirit—we understand one another's motives, though our methods are wide apart. We both share deeply the common experience of living up to the truth as we see it, whatever the price.

Though at the moment I am of a tiny minority, I feel myself just one protest in a great revolt surging up from among the people—the struggle of the masses against the rule of the world by the few—profoundly intensified by the war. It is a struggle against the political state itself, against exploitation, militarism, imperialism, authority in all forms. It is a struggle to break in full force only after the war. Russia already stands in the vanguard, beset by her enemies in the camps of both belligerents—the Central Empires break asunder from within—the labor movement gathers revolutionary force in Britain—and in our own country the Nonpartisan League, radical labor and the Socialist Party hold the germs of a new social order. Their protest is my protest. Mine is a personal protest at a particular law, but it is backed by all the aspirations and ideals of the struggle for a world freed of our manifold slaveries and tyrannies.

I ask the Court for no favor. I could do no other than what I have done, whatever the court's decree. I have no bitterness or hate in my heart for any man. Whatever the penalty I shall endure it, firm in the faith, that whatever befalls me, the principles in which I believe will bring forth out of this misery and chaos, a world of brotherhood, harmony and freedom for each to live the truth as he sees it.

I hope your Honor will not think that I have taken this occasion to make a speech for the sake of making a speech. I have read you what I have written in order that the future record for myself and for my friends may be perfectly clear, and in order to clear up some of the matters to which the District Attorney called your attention. I know that it is pretty nigh hopeless in times of war and hysteria to get across to any substantial body of people, the view of an out and out heretic like myself. I know that as far as my principles are concerned, they seem to be utterly impractical—mere moon-shine. They are not the views that work in the world today. I fully realize that. But I fully believe that they are the views which are going to guide in the future.

Having arrived at the state of mind in which those views mean the dearest things in life to me, I cannot consistently, with self-respect, do other than I have, namely, to deliberately violate an act which seems to me to be a denial of everything which ideally and in practice I hold sacred.

[Mr. Baldwin's statement to the Court ends here (ED.).]

As I read over my statement now years later, while I subscribe to its major principles, I am less of a radical in a class-conscious sense, less of an anti-Socialist and more of a moderate. I would, I think, if faced with the issue again, accept the compromise of civilian service provided for objectors in World War II.

The trial got considerable attention in the liberal press and passing notice in the daily papers. I was swamped with messages of congratulations from sympathizers. I was dubious about the reaction of my father and mother, brothers, sisters and relatives for bringing on the family the first mark of a jail-bird in the known heritage. But they all wrote or wired understandingly, and my mother even with approval. It must have hurt; but only one relative, my uncle George Baldwin, a self-made millionaire in the stock market, repudiated me by letter. My brothers, both [in] service, visited me later in jail in their uniforms. My father, disapproving and hostile to my whole record in the war, was tolerant in the tradition of Boston heresy. My aunt, Ruth Baldwin, wholly sharing my views, was in court.

Ten days or so after the trial, during which I cleaned up personal affairs, still lodged in the Tombs and still taken daily to my "office," I was called for by a strange United States marshal to be delivered by subway to the County Prison in Newark which, by contrast with the federal government, housed short-term prisoners—a year and under. It happened to be Armistice Day, November 11th, and I was escorted through the downtown streets, filled with confetti and streamers, to the Hudson Tubes. No handcuffs this time, either. The marshal was a good sort, and we swapped pleasantries over the end of the war when I was just beginning my "war service." We stopped off in a bar for a farewell drink and he then delivered me to the high-walled prison set in the middle of Newark.

There I was just another man in the stream constantly coming and going. But the news of my trial quickly got around and I began to get attentions. The Irish guards were not for "England's war," and they figured any opponent of the war as on their side. The warden himself, a stout Sinn Feiner, had been suspect as a participant in gunrunning. I was quickly among friends who exerted every effort to make me comfortable. My cell door was opened evenings when others were locked in so that I could read and write in the corridor. I was soon made a trustee with duties in the kitchen, where I got the best fare in the house, and the responsibility outside the walls of looking after the greenhouse. That responsibility shortly almost evicted me. Returning from my duties of watering the plants late one evening, I found the usual entrance locked. I searched along the walls until I found a "night bell." I rang. A gruff old guard whom I had not met stuck out his head, inquiring who was there. I replied I was a prisoner, locked out. He said "I don't know you, and I have no orders to let you in. But if you say you belong here, come on in, but don't do it again." I didn't.

Besides my duties as trustee, I could not help putting my

training as reformer to work. It was obvious that all sorts of help were needed for the three hundred or so men always in the jail—some serving sentences, some awaiting trial. Some needed lawyers; some, aid for their families; the library was scant; men were restless without entertainment. So I organized among the prisoners a Prisoners' Welfare League. The warden permitted meetings of all the prisoners; we chose a committee, and I set to work. We collected funds for a lawyer, and got a good one, ready to serve any man with a good case. He later became United States District Attorney—the son of the former Democratic state boss, Jim Smith. We got the public library to set up a branch in the jail. We enlisted the welfare agencies to take up the cases of families in need. We established educational classes and discussion groups. We staged musicals, trained a glee club, and even put on dances among the men. The whole atmosphere of the prison changed. Men were busy with self-appointed chores; each able to do so was helping others. Out of the disorder came order and hope. We attracted the attention of some good ladies interested in prisoners, notably Mrs. Sidney Colgate, a wealthy woman who was unsparing of her time and effort. She and I became close and devoted friends, a friendship which lasted until her death years later, and well described in her book *Off the Straight and Narrow*.

But our reforms hit a snag. The county sheriff, the warden's superior and his opponent, heard that the prisoners were having much too good a time. What he heard correctly was so unusual that he was shocked. He sent for me. In a stormy interview he laid down the law that the League must be disbanded. I refused. I gave the story to the press and alerted the good ladies. A storm broke. The Newark *Daily News*, the most influential paper, was with us; it derided the sheriff. It forced his retreat, especially after Mrs. Colgate got the public support of the county judges. The League went on.

But in the end the sheriff won. I had asked for a transfer to the county penitentiary, where federal prisoners also were sent, because spring was coming on and it was out in the country at Caldwell, with outdoor work. I had had enough of indoors. But the federal authorities had been deaf to my request. The sheriff, however, became my unsolicited sponsor, urging the transfer. Once rid of me he figured the League would fail, and it did. We had had six months of it; a lot of good had been done, but the leadership was too personal to be passed on.

At the county penitentiary, there was already a prisoners' league for a degree of self-government, encouraged by a liberal warden, a member, like myself, of the National Conference of Social Work, and as a German-American less than an enthusiast for the war. I was welcomed by prisoners and guards alike, for the story of our Welfare League was a lift to them all. The guards in that small prison of several hundred men were friendly fellows, with life jobs under civil service, and we were all quickly on first name relations. There was plenty of work outside; there was system; there were entertainments, informality, ball games. I got a job as trustee under the gardener, a German-American socialist, who was so overjoyed at the news of the Spartacus revolt in Munich that he went on a drunk for three days. I couldn't have chosen a better boss for gardening or politics. I worked outdoors with him daily, planting, hoeing, weeding—a healthy life that put me in better shape than in years.

I made close and enduring friendships among the prisoners, for we had a lot of freedom to meet and talk. The warden and I became good friends, too, especially after he had attended a National Conference of Social Work, where my reelection to a standing committee aroused controversy and split the conference. I was defeated, but the warden loyally voted for me and brought back to me the greetings of the many conference leaders who had supported his jailbird. Prejudice among prisoners against conscientious objectors, of which I had heard much in other prisons during the war, did not exist in Caldwell after the war, if indeed it had at all. There were other objectors in the penitentiary—a couple of them personally objectionable characters—but I never heard of their being attacked as slackers. Everyone had his own crime, and while prisoners, like everyone else, formed their own little cliques, no aristocracy of crime was recognized. Money could not classify us; we had none and needed none.

My stay at Caldwell lasted three beautiful spring and summer months, from May to the end of July. I was released ahead of my time by a fluke. My commitment papers instead of reading eleven months and ten days, as ordered by the judge in subtracting my time in jail before the trial, read ten months and eleven days. I wrote the judge to correct it. He wrote back to say he could not—I suspect *would* not—but if it had been the other way around, I have no doubt a correction would have been made. So I profited with a month of unearned freedom in addition to the two for my good behavior—a total of nine months on a year's sentence.

While I wanted to get out of prison, as all prisoners do, I felt an almost inexplicable attachment to the Caldwell prison. It stayed with me in my dreams. I would wake up with a lively sense of having been back there to work or with my friends. It was so strong that I could not resist going back to visit. For two months or more I took every opportunity to go back to chat with the warden and guards, and a few of the prisoners.

The friends I wanted most to see outside were a few I had met either in the jail or the prison. I suppose I was suffering from what in more extreme forms makes some prisoners fearful of facing a world they do not know, and thus cling to the security and routine of what they do. If it was not that, it was at least the hang-over of happy and dramatic days when I had the work that kept me contented, and needed to make no effort to plan the day. I recovered, particularly since I embarked on a new life immediately after my release with my marriage to Madeleine Z. Doty, to whom I had been engaged before my trial, and who had been absent abroad during most of my imprisonment.

My colleagues in the Civil Liberties Bureau welcomed me back with a reception. The newspapers gave me a passing notice. After a honeymoon and respite, I had only one idea in mind: to get an experience I had long wanted and missed, that of an unskilled worker in basic industry. Jim Maurer, president of the Pennsylvania State Federation of Labor, one of my great admirations, had said to me two years before: "You will never understand the labor movement until you have worked with other men with your hands and know that's your only support. And if you go hungry, so much the better." If I was to do anything in civil liberties—and I was not sure of that—labor would be our major client. The unions were stirring; great strikes were in the air; revolutionary movements abroad marked the front pages. I determined to get a little experience anyhow of the life of industrial America as an anonymous worker.

Index

THE AMERICAN HERITAGE SERIES

THE COLONIAL PERIOD

Adams, John *The Political Writings of John Adams: Representative Selections* AHS 8 George A. Peek, Jr.

The English Libertarian Heritage: From the Writings of John Trenchard and Thomas Gordon in The Independent Whig *and* Cato's Letters AHS 32 David L. Jacobson

The Great Awakening AHS 34 Alan Heimert, Perry Miller

Puritan Political Thought AHS 33 Edmund S. Morgan

THE REVOLUTIONARY ERA

The American Revolution as a Democratic Movement AHS 36 Alfred Young

The Antifederalists AHS 38 Cecelia Kenyon

Early American Libertarian Thought: Freedom of the Press from Zenger to Jefferson AHS 41 Leonard W. Levy

Franklin, Benjamin *The Political Thought of Benjamin Franklin* AHS 64 Ralph Ketcham

Paine, Thomas *Common Sense and Other Political Writings* AHS 5 Nelson F. Adkins

THE YOUNG NATION

Calhoun, John C. *Disquisition on Government and Selections from the* Discourse AHS 10 C. Gordon Post

Channing, William Ellery *Unitarian Christianity and Other Essays* AHS 21 Irving H. Bartlett

Democracy, Liberty, and Property: The State Constitutional Conventions of the 1820's AHS 43 Merrill D. Peterson

The Federal Convention and the Formation of the Union of American States AHS 19 Winton U. Solberg

From the Declaration of Independence to the Constitution: The Roots of American Constitutionalism AHS 6 Carl J. Friedrich, Robert G. McCloskey

Gallatin, Albert *Selected Writings* AHS 40 E. James Ferguson

Hamilton, Alexander *Papers on Public Credit, Commerce, and Finance* AHS 18 Samuel McKee, Jr., J. Harvie Williams

Hamilton, Madison, and Jay on the Constitution: Selections from the Federalist Papers AHS 7 Ralph H. Gabriel

Jefferson, Thomas *The Political Writings of Thomas Jefferson: Representative Selections* AHS 9 Edward Dumbauld

Social Theories of Jacksonian Democracy: Representative Writings of the Period 1825–1850 AHS 1 Joseph L. Blau

The Writings of Justice Joseph Story AHS 45 Henry Steele Commager

THE MIDDLE PERIOD

The Antislavery Argument AHS 44 Jane and William Pease

Lincoln, Abraham *The Political Thought of Abraham Lincoln* AHS 46 Richard Current

The Radical Republicans and Reconstruction AHS 47 Harold Hyman

THE LATE NINETEENTH CENTURY

Bryan, William Jennings *The Mind and Thought of William Jennings Bryan* AHS 52 Ray Ginger

The Forging of American Socialism: Origins of the Modern Movement AHS 24 Howard H. Quint

Late Nineteenth-Century American Liberalism AHS 26 Louis Filler

The Populist Mind AHS 50 Norman Pollack

THE TWENTIETH CENTURY

Addams, Jane *The Social Thought of Jane Addams* AHS 69 Christopher Lasch

The American Writer and the Great Depression AHS 63 Harvey Swados

Negro Protest Thought in the Twentieth Century AHS 56 Francis Broderick, August Meier

New Deal Thought AHS 70 Howard Zinn

The Progressives AHS 54 Carl Resek

Roosevelt, Theodore *The Writings of Theodore Roosevelt* AHS 53 William H. Harbaugh

The Supreme Court: Law Versus Discretion AHS 72 Wallace Mendelson

Wilson, Woodrow, *The Political Thought of Woodrow Wilson* AHS 68 E. David Cronon

TOPICAL VOLUMES

The American Economic System: Representative Selections AHS 27 Massimo Salvadori

American Military Thought AHS 75 Walter Millis

The Churches and the City AHS 61 Robert Cross

Freedom of the Press: 1800–1965 AHS 74 Harold L. Nelson

Nonviolence in America: A Documentary History AHS 60 Staughton Lynd

Negro Poetry: Thought in [illegible] AHS 50
[illegible] Brownell, August [illegible]
Negro and [illegible] AHS [illegible]
[illegible] AHS [illegible]
[illegible] Theodore [illegible]
AHS [illegible] Robert [illegible]
[illegible]
Henderson
[illegible] Woodson [illegible]
AHS 65 [illegible] Green

TOPICS [illegible]

The American [illegible]
AHS 58 [illegible]
[illegible]
[illegible]
[illegible]
[illegible] AHS [illegible]
Standard [illegible]

1 P60A

LIBRARY
JUNIOR COLLEGE DISTRICT
ST. LOUIS, MO.